Jazz Makers

VANGUARDS OF SOUND

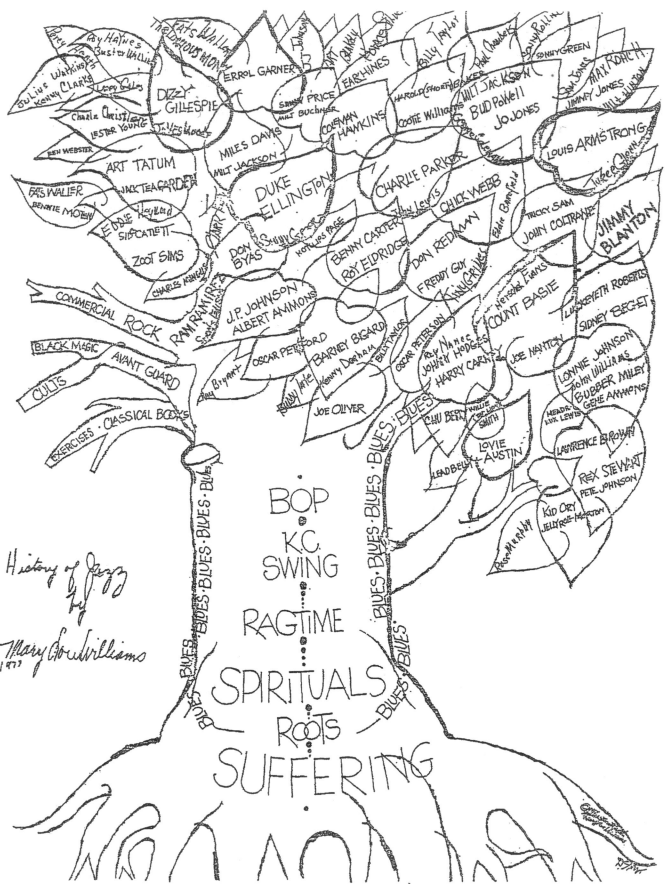

PRINTED AS A PUBLIC SERVICE BY JAZZMOBILE, INC.

Jazz Makers

VANGUARDS OF SOUND

ALYN SHIPTON

OXFORD

UNIVERSITY PRESS

For Angharad

OXFORD
UNIVERSITY PRESS

Oxford New York
Auckland Bangkok Buenos Aires Cape Town Chennai
Dar es Salaam Delhi Hong Kong Istanbul Karachi Kolkata
Kuala Lumpur Madrid Melbourne Mexico City Mumbai Nairobi
São Paulo Shanghai Singapore Taipei Tokyo Toronto
with an associated company in Berlin

Copyright © 2002 by Alyn Shipton
Published by Oxford University Press, Inc.
198 Madison Avenue, New York, New York 10016
www.oup.com

Oxford is a registered trademark of Oxford University Press

Library of Congress Cataloging-in-Publication Data:

Shipton, Alyn.
Jazz Profiles / Alyn Shipton
p.   cm.   —   (Oxford profiles)
Includes discography, bibliographical references, and index.
ISBN 0-19-512689-0
1. Jazz musicians—Biography. 2. Jazz—History and criticism.
I. Title. II. Series.
ML394.S46   2002
784.65'092'2—dc21
[B]   2001053148

9 8 7 6 5 4 3 2 1
Printed in the United States of America
on acid-free paper

On the cover: (insets, clockwise) Count Basie, Miles Davis,
Charles Mingus, and Sarah Vaughan

Frontispiece: The History of Jazz designed by Mary Lou Williams
for a 1973 Jazzmobile poster

Design: Sandy Kaufman
Layout: Loraine Machlin
Picture research: Marty Baldessari
and Meghan Bilton

Contents

Preface

As it moves into its second century, jazz has come a long way. It started with a reputation as "low life" music, associated with bordellos and rent parties. It is now considered an art form on level terms with Western classical music, performed in the great concert halls of the world, but without ever abandoning the visceral excitement and rhythmic drive it had enjoyed from the outset.

This collection of 50 or so biographies, plus a collection of shorter life stories in the "More . . . to Remember" sections at the end of each main part, cannot hope to be a comprehensive narrative history of jazz. For that, you will need to look in the bibliography in the appendix for some suggestions. The select discography in the appendix offers a snapshot history of jazz on CD. It is by no means the whole picture, but sufficient to get a good idea of how the sound of jazz developed. Nevertheless, the lives of the men and women covered in this book are central to the development of jazz; if you read their profiles in sequence, much of the story of jazz itself will unfold. Among them are most of the innovative instrumentalists, bandleaders, and composers who shaped the music as it grew, and who kept its spirit of development alive and well nourished. The discography at the end of each profile will also guide you to CDs to hear how each individual's music progressed.

Not all the musicians here had easy lives. Poverty was seldom far away from the early pioneers, and the specters of alcoholism and drug addiction hang over many of the lives described in the later sections of the book. Yet amid all the hardships, there were individual successes, and above all, a success story for jazz itself, which has continued to develop, and to fight off every challenge that has threatened to kill it off or sideline it from popular awareness. Rhythm and blues, for example, was a threat in the 1940s, but it was absorbed into the playing of many jazz musicians. Likewise, the jazz-rock fusion movement of the 1960s and 1970s, spearheaded by Miles Davis, Herbie Hancock, and Chick Corea, became a new form of jazz in its own right.

In my day-to-day work as a newspaper critic and radio presenter, I constantly hear new discs and new performers. The most heartening thing about jazz as it goes into the 21st century is its resilience, and the number of enthusiastic young musicians who are appearing, ready to take the music forward at a time when many of the founders of jazz are no longer with us. The second century of jazz promises to be just as exciting, exhilarating, and challenging as the first.

Alyn Shipton
Oxford, England

Early jazz met the blues in the Wildcat Jazz Band fronted by the great blues singer Ma Rainey. In a jazz era costume, she was photographed with her band—featuring, from left to right, "Gabriel" on drums, Albert Wynn on trombone, Dave Nelson on trumpet, Ed Pollack on alto saxophone, and "Georgia Tom" Dorsey on piano—in 1924–25.

1 The Pioneers

In New York City's Avery Fisher Hall, the last notes die away. Wynton Marsalis lowers his trumpet and looks at the capacity audience as it breaks into spontaneous applause. Another annual season of Lincoln Center Jazz Concerts gets under way, and there is every sign that jazz music is alive and well, and set to flourish for many years to come.

When ragtime, the blues, military marches, social dances, and the rhythms of African drums came together at the end of the 19th century into what became known as jazz, few of its originators had any idea that they were creating a new and distinctive form of American music that would be filling the world's concert halls well over 100 years later. Throughout that century of development, jazz continued to grow and to absorb new ideas. In the second half of the 20th century, jazz became a truly international music, drawing in musicians from Europe, Africa, Asia, and South America alongside its American originators. It is that very flexibility and adaptability that makes jazz so healthy as it moves into the 21st century.

Individual musicians have always played a very significant role in the development of jazz. Because jazz involves improvisation—the ability to create new melodies and rhythms on the spur of the moment—its direction has been shaped by three distinct groups of people. First are the players, those musicians whose command over their instruments allows them to turn any idea into musical sounds almost at the speed of thought itself. Second are the bandleaders, the organizers who provide a framework in which improvisers can work. Third are the composers and arrangers, who provide the raw material for jazz musicians to play. In practice, these three groups are mixed: many instrumentalists are also bandleaders and composers. Almost all jazz comes from these groups working together, and it is very rarely the product of improvisation alone.

Jazz was not created overnight. The elements that grew together to form the new style of music were present in more than one region of the United States for several years before they coalesced into a recognizable new development. Ragtime, for instance, was a jaunty style of solo piano music with heavily accented or syncopated rhythms. It incorporated the cakewalk (a dance that involves couples strutting, bowing, and kicking, which was popularized by American minstrel shows in the second half of the 19th century and imitated as far away as France by the classical composer Claude Debussy), the jig, and the rhythms imported to the United States from Africa during the period of slavery. In the 1890s ragtime developed particularly in the Midwest, around St. Louis and Sedalia, Missouri, and Indianapolis, although it soon became popular all over North America, from New York to Los Angeles to New Orleans.

The African rhythms that developed in jazz drumming had survived from the Southern plantations. Other African musical traditions that became part of early jazz included field songs known as ring shouts, work songs, and the intensely moving harmonies incorporated into sung hymns or spirituals. In some parts of the South, white owners banned drumming, fearful that the sounds symbolized independence and might be used to signal insurrection. However, before emancipation, in public spaces as far apart as Manhattan and New Orleans, large numbers of slaves gathered on a regular basis to dance, sing, and drum. In many areas, such gatherings were progressively prohibited, even in New Orleans, where they were for many years restricted to the *Place Congo,* as it was called in the Creole French widely spoken in the city, or in English, Congo Square.

Despite efforts to suppress these events, we have some idea of what they sounded like because the folksong collector and musicologist Henry F. Gilbert jotted down many songs and dances, and in 1906 combined them into a thrilling orchestral piece called "The Dance in Place Congo." This was just one of a number of works in which Gilbert recorded the sounds of African-American and Native North American music at a stage when few other musicologists were seriously studying American folk music.

The blues, a fusion of melancholy lyrics with plaintive melodies, developed across the South, although strangely it was not particularly well known in the Southern city where all the elements that went to make up jazz finally combined in the early years of the 20th century: New Orleans.

During the previous half-century, New Orleans had become the most culturally mixed city in North America. There was a predominantly French influence in its opera house and concert halls, with white and Creole (people with mixed African-American, French, and Spanish origins) society enjoying new productions of operas by Giacomo Meyerbeer, Hector Berlioz, and Charles-François Gounod within months of their opening in Paris. The benign climate also stimulated an outdoor life in which all forms of music were developed for parades, picnics, and other social gatherings. Ensembles of various sizes played for these events, and a strong tradition of string bands started up, with mandolins, guitars, and violins performing everything from dances like mazurkas (a Polish folk dance) and polkas to the current ragtime favorites. The city's strongly established Masonic and other fraternal societies all employed bands for their functions, and to a young musician with talent, all kinds of doors were open, regardless of color.

In New Orleans, as in many towns across the United States with large African-American populations, there was a tradition of marching brass bands. It was among the musicians who made up these marching bands that some of the first signs of jazz emerged, as they abandoned the formal written parts and instead improvised their own variations. Soon this developed into a custom that persists to this day for musical funerals, where a brass band plays mournful dirges on the way to the cemetery, then breaks into joyful improvised dances as it returns to the wake. The first legendary figures of New Orleans jazz played in brass bands with exotic names like the Excelsior, the Eureka, and the Imperial.

Trumpeters Buddy Bolden, Manuel Perez, Peter Bocage, and King Oliver were all among the pioneers of this type of music.

Bolden, with trombonist Frank Dusen, also led a band that played for outdoor society events at the city's Lincoln Park. Other groups, like that of John Robichaux , played a form of orchestral ragtime to similar audiences, and this style of gentle, slightly syncopated music was recorded in the 1920s by violinist and bandleader Armand J. Piron. Bolden's spontaneous variations on the popular number "Carnival of Venice" made him famous with local crowds, as did the scatological lyrics to the tunes he played for evening dances in or near the Storyville, the city's red-light district. In the many houses of entertainment in this area where prostitution was legal, there was a constant demand for music. Among the groups that played were children's "spasm" bands that performed with homemade instruments. (One of the best known, the Bouzan Kings, launched the careers of many famous jazz musicians.) The area was also renowned for sophisticated pianists like Tony Jackson, Dink Johnson and Jelly Roll Morton.

As early as 1911, musicians playing what a listener today might recognize as a primitive form of jazz were leaving New Orleans to play as far afield as Chicago and the West Coast. The closing of Storyville in 1917 accelerated the spread of this new music by encouraging many more musicians to leave New Orleans to find work in Chicago and other large cities. However, well before Storyville was shut down, bands like the white groups led by Tom Brown and Johnny Stein had left New Orleans and had become popular in Chicago, where the music they played was called "jass" or "jazz." The word was used to mean "full of pep or excitement," but equally often as a euphemism for sex, consistent with the Storyville dives and dance halls where much of its development occurred.

Stein's band soon became the Original Dixieland Jazz Band, making the first phonograph records of the new music in 1917, and traveling to New York City and then London in the years that followed. The discs contain a cheerful, angular style of music close to ragtime, but incorporating the kind of collective improvisation familiar from the musicians' New Orleans background. They can be said to have launched the Jazz Age.

It is against this background that the first pioneers began to define jazz and the direction it would take in the future. In the 1920s, Chicago became the center for new developments in jazz, and then the spotlight moved to New York. This key period in musical history was also the time when, from the passing of the 18th Amendment in January 1920, the manufacture, consumption, and sale of alcohol became illegal. There is little doubt that the thrill of illegal drinking in "speakeasies"—the forerunners of nightclubs—where jazz was played added to the music's mystique.

In an atmosphere of intense excitement, and a social climate that encouraged the music, there were many innovations. Soloists began to use the jazz group as a jumping-off point for their own flights of creative improvisation. Composers and arrangers produced music to be played by increasingly large groups, giving birth to the first big bands, and in the middle of the decade, the invention of electrical recording made it possible to preserve for posterity a very accurate impression of the sounds these pioneers made.

Scott Joplin

KING OF RAGTIME

S cott Joplin stands just outside the story of jazz itself, as the towering figure in ragtime, a style of music from an earlier era that was just one of the ingredients that went to make up jazz. Yet, without ragtime, early jazz would not have developed in the way that it did. Many early jazz tunes took their structure, a sequence of melodic themes linked together by "bridge" passages, from the way ragtime numbers were written. Throughout the United States, the first jazz pianists, such as Jelly Roll Morton in New Orleans, Eubie Blake in Baltimore, and James P. Johnson in New York City, all wrote and played rags, gradually transforming them as time went by into freer, more improvised pieces, but never losing touch with the strutting rhythms and simple syncopation of ragtime. The first jazz bands played orchestrated versions of ragtime pieces, from adaptations of 12-bar blues, like "The Dirty Dozens," to instrumental arrangements of Joplin's own rags from a famous collection known as the *Red Back Book of Rags*.

In 1907, when this frequently reproduced photograph was first published, Scott Joplin traveled to New York City to raise money for his second opera, *Treemonisha*. Joplin's first opera, *A Guest of Honor*, almost left him in financial ruin when someone in his company ran off with the box office receipts.

None of this would have been possible without the enormous contribution of Joplin, a man who not only composed many of the most influential ragtime pieces, but encouraged many other musicians to play and compose in the style. He was ragtime's most accomplished composer, one of its finest exponents at the piano, and also its most passionate advocate. He took rags into the genres of ballet and opera, and tried to enthuse audiences, promoters, and publishers alike, even when other types of music started to become more popular. He was also one of the last figures in popular music to achieve his fame almost entirely through sales of sheet music rather than recordings. He did make some piano rolls—a forerunner of disc recording that involved a piano being played by a punched paper roll through which compressed air operated the keys. From these it is possible to get an impression of how he might have sounded; but his own public knew him mainly from the string of compositions he issued through his publisher, John Stark.

The life of Scott Joplin is a direct link between the era of slavery and the Jazz Age. He was born just three years after the Civil War ended, as his father, who had been born into slavery, was sharing the experience of thousands of other Southern African Americans of getting used to relative freedom despite the harsh economic conditions of Reconstruction. When Joplin died, the Original Dixieland Jazz Band had already made the first jazz records.

The exact place of Scott Joplin's birth is unknown. The often-cited birth date of November 24, 1868, based on papers filed after his death by his widow, is now thought to be incorrect. Although, his age on various census reports confirms that he was born in 1868. His family traveled around the East Texas area, working in various small towns and villages as tenant farmers, eventually settling in Texarkana, a new town that had been set up as a trade center where two railroads intersected on the Texas–Arkansas border. Giles Joplin, Scott's father, became a railroad worker, and from 1873 until 1880 provided a decent living for his wife and five children until he left home.

All the family were musical, Giles having played in a slave band, and Florence (Scott's mother) being a banjoist and singer. Scott sang and played the banjo as well, but his real talent was for the piano. Although the family did not own one, he was taught to play by several helpful local teachers, including multi-instrumentalist J. C. Johnson and German-born Julius Weiss. During his teenage years, as he continued to develop as a pianist, he composed and sang for his own vocal group, the Texas Medley Quartette, with whom he began to travel throughout the area, performing for local audiences. Living in the African-American community in Texarkana, and playing for the dances and social events of neighboring settlements, Joplin acquired a deep knowledge of folk song and dance traditions that he was later to absorb very effectively into many of his compositions.

Both with his singing group and as a solo pianist, Joplin traveled increasingly farther afield, leaving home close to his 20th birthday and visiting Chicago, St. Louis, and Syracuse, New York, before settling around 1896 in the town of Sedalia, Missouri. During the five years he spent based there, Joplin published his first compositions, including a thrilling depiction of a railroad crash called "Crush Collision March." He both studied music at a local college and taught the subject to others, including his fellow ragtime composers Scott Hayden and Arthur Marshall.

Locally, he became famous playing at a club called the Maple Leaf, and in 1899 he immortalized both the club and himself with the publication of his "Maple Leaf Rag." This piece, which

JAZZ MAKERS

Scott Joplin

BORN

1868
East Texas

DIED

April 1, 1917
New York, New York

EDUCATION

No formal education as a child, but studied with local pianists in Texarkana; attended George R. Smith College for Negroes in Sedalia, Missouri, as a mature music student, the late 1890s

MAJOR INTERESTS

Piano; composing ragtime music

ACCOMPLISHMENTS

Composed the most significant body of piano ragtime, including "Maple Leaf Rag," "Original Rags" (1899); "The Entertainer," "Elite Syncopations" (1902); "Chrysanthemum" (1904); "Ragtime Dance" (1906), "Pleasant Moments" (1909), "Magnetic Rag" (1914). Composed ragtime opera *Treemonisha* (1911). Also was a brilliant pianist who toured the United States as a soloist.

HONORS

Posthumous Pulitzer Prize (1976), commemorative U.S. postage stamp issued in 1983

MUSEUMS AND ARCHIVES

Joplin material in the music collection of the National Museum of American History, Smithsonian Institution, Washington, D.C.

This imaginative illustrated cover is a typical example of those that John Stark used for his publication of Joplin's sheet music. This one dates from 1906.

sold 500,000 copies by 1909, became the best-known ragtime composition, studied by pianists all over the United States. In its wake, Joplin published a number of other pieces, beginning with "Original Rags" (1899) and including his famous "The Entertainer" (1902). His publisher, John Stark, paid Joplin a royalty—an amount for every copy sold—which was an extremely fair and unusual arrangement at a time when most popular tunes were sold for a single cash payment. It cemented an agreement between the men that led Stark to continue to publish much of Joplin's work, and to bring out rags by other promising composers recommended to him by Joplin.

The rags Joplin later wrote include stately, leisurely dances known as slow drags, other dances including waltzes, and novelty pieces that used Hispanic rhythms. He had an extraordinary ability to represent events in music, as in "The Cascades," which depicts an ornamental watercourse constructed for the St. Louis World's Fair in 1904.

The fame brought to him by "Maple Leaf Rag" and his prowess as a pianist could have brought Joplin a comfortable life. However, having mastered writing in the ragtime form, he had greater ambitions. He became a driven man, writing ragtime ballets and operas, and then trying to raise the money and support to present them in public. He traveled widely as a soloist, billed as "The King of Ragtime Composers," and with some of the money he earned he formed a succession of small companies to tour theaters and halls presenting his theatrical works. His ambitions—combined with the fact that many amateur musicians found his new pieces too hard to play, which reduced sales of his music—eventually led to a falling out with John Stark, and what had been a steady stream of income dried up.

One of his published rags, "Ragtime Dance," is a cut-down version of a miniature ballet that he presented in 1899, and still retains the foot-taps (instructions for the pianist to stomp when the dancers would have drummed their feet on the stage) and changes of tempo that were part of that ballet. After moving to St. Louis in 1901, he formed an opera company and toured with his first ragtime opera, *A Guest of Honor*, which unfortunately no longer survives.

Following a move to New York City in 1907, he became obsessed with composing and presenting his second full-length opera, *Treemonisha*. Completed

in 1911, it was performed only once in his lifetime. Devoid of sets, and with no money to pay an orchestra, he put it on in 1915 at the Lincoln Theater in Harlem, New York, directing it from the piano. By then he was already suffering from the terrifying last stages of syphilis, which he had contracted in his youth; he found himself no longer able to play in public as he lost control of his hands. Fellow ragtimer and composer Eubie Blake met him around 1915, and reported that Joplin's legendary skill had already deserted him. Shortly afterward he seemed to be losing the power of speech.

Joplin had been married three times, and his third partner, Lottie Stokes, who was with him throughout the New York period, shared his business interests. Even she could not cope as Joplin slid into syphilis-induced madness. He died in a mental ward of Manhattan State Hospital.

His legacy is remarkable. In addition to Scott Hayden (who was Joplin's brother-in-law from his first marriage) and Arthur Marshall, Joplin helped the careers of many other pianists and composers, black and white, including Louis Chauvin and Joseph Lamb. The skill and range of his compositions inspired other ragtime musicians all over the United States, including one of the first women composers of popular tunes, May Aufderheide, whose "Dusty Rag" of 1908 is a perennial favorite.

Joplin's own music went through a remarkable renaissance from the 1970s onward, completing the process begun in the 1950s when a book called *They All Played Ragtime* was published, drawing attention to what had become

"The greatest ragtime writer who ever lived."

—Jelly Roll Morton

a largely forgotten genre. In 1970, classical scholar and conductor Joshua Rifkin made two albums of Joplin's piano rags that became popular all over the world, and the following year most of Joplin's rags were republished. Soon afterward, the head of the New England Conservatory of Music, Gunther Schuller, made a phonograph record of Joplin's orchestrated rags from the *Red Back Book*, which led to the music being used in the 1973 movie *The Sting*. Pianist Marvin Hamlisch won a Grammy for his playing of Joplin's music on the soundtrack.

Finally, in 1972, after a decade of work by composer William Bolcom and orchestrater T. J. Anderson to reconstruct the complete score, a full production of *Treemonisha* was presented in Atlanta. There, and in a subsequent, revised, version on Broadway, it was hailed as a masterpiece. More than half a century after his death, Joplin's vision and persistence were finally rewarded.

DISCOGRAPHY

The Entertainer. Biograph BCD 101. [Piano roll recordings, some of which are Joplin's own versions.]

Elite Syncopations. Biograph BCD 102. [Piano roll recordings, some of which are Joplin's own versions.]

The Complete Rags of Scott Joplin. Musicmasters 7061-2 C (two-CD set). [All Joplin's rags, played by William Albright.]

Marches, Waltzes, and Rags of Scott Joplin. Musicmasters 01612-67102-2. [Joplin's collaborative rags and most of his waltzes and marches, played by William Albright.]

Treemonisha. Houston Grand Opera Chorus and Orchestra directed by Gunther Schuller. Deutsche Gramophon DG 435 709-2 (two-CD set).

FURTHER READING

Berlin, Edward A. *King of Ragtime: Scott Joplin and His Era*. New York: Oxford University Press, 1994.

Berlin, Edward A. *Ragtime: A Musical and Cultural History*. Berkeley: University of California Press, 1980.

Blesh, Rudi, and Harriet Janis. *They All Played Ragtime*. New York: Knopf, 1950.

Hasse, John Edward, ed. *Ragtime: Its History, Composers and Music*. New York: Schirmer, 1985.

Lawrence, Vera Brodsky. *The Complete Works of Scott Joplin*. New York: New York Public Library, 1981.

Preston, Katherine. *Scott Joplin, Composer*. New York: Chelsea House, 1988.

WEBSITE

http://www.scottjoplin.org

The official site of the Scott Joplin International Ragtime Foundation. Includes biography, news, and plans for a permanent museum to be opened in Sedalia, Missouri.

Jelly Roll Morton

MISTER JELLY LORD

I n the mid-1930s, Jelly Roll Morton would stand on a New York City street corner, near the Rhythm Club in Harlem, and lecture passersby on how he had invented jazz. He was regarded as a colorful loudmouthed character, but few who heard him bragging or saw his flashy clothes and the diamond in his teeth realized that there was more than a little truth in his claims. He may not have invented jazz, but he was its first great composer and one of its finest pianists. When a radio show suggested that W. C. Handy, a blues musician and composer who wrote "St. Louis Blues," was "the originator of jazz, stomps, and blues," the angry Morton fired off an open letter to the newspapers claiming, "I myself happened to be the creator in the year 1902." He signed himself "The World's Greatest Hot Tune Writer."

In reality, Morton was just 12 years old in 1902, too young to have "invented" jazz, but a witness to its beginning. He was born Ferdinand Joseph La Menthe, in a New

This photograph of Morton in his bandleader's clothes was taken in Chicago in 1927, but was used for publicity after he arrived in New York City the following year. In the photograph's legend, Morton advertises himself as "orginator of jazz and stomps."

This 1923 sheet music edition draws together several strands of Morton's life. His old publishers Benjamin and John ("Reb") Spikes jointly composed the piece, and his new publishers Lester and Walter Melrose arranged with Gennett Records to get the piece recorded by the New Orleans Rhythm Kings, with whom Morton himself collaborated on an interracial record session in July of that same year.

Orleans family of French and Spanish origins—the section of society known as Creole. They gave him a picturesque notion of his ancestry, naming him Ferdinand after the King of Spain. His mother, Louise Monette, and stepfather William Mouton (whose surname he adopted) were French-speaking. Jelly later changed his name to Morton "for business reasons . . . I didn't want to be called 'Frenchy'." His godmother practiced voodoo, and Morton held a lifelong belief that she had put a curse on him.

His hometown left an indelible impression on Morton. There were street events, carnivals, parades, and dances. Above all, music was an everyday part of New Orleans life: light classics, dances such as schottisches, a round dance like a slow polka; waltzes; and polkas, ragtime, and the plaintive sounds of blues singers. All these things came together in his piano playing, which combined a brilliant technique on his own test pieces like "Finger-breaker," with a sense of grace, style, and hints of the Spanish rhythms of the Caribbean in Creole-flavored compositions like "Mamanita."

In the red-light district of New Orleans, Storyville, where prostitution was still legal, the young Morton played piano in the "sporting houses," or bordellos. The seamier side of life attracted him, and as a teenager he became a pool shark and a pimp, once using his charm and dexterity to beat the legendary Pensacola Kid, the finest pool-shark in the South. Morton had a large diamond set in his front tooth, the symbol of a man who had made substantial immoral earnings. His nickname "Jelly Roll" is a sexual metaphor similar to the very word "jazz" or "jass" itself.

He took to the road in 1907, playing music for touring shows, in bars or restaurants, and applying his pool-sharking and pimping skills. He was not subservient like many Southern African Americans of the time, and adopted a lifelong practice of referring to everyone, white or black, rich or poor, by their surnames. He never returned home, but treasured sentimental memories of New Orleans. Before settling for a few years on the West Coast in 1917, he spent a short time in several cities: St Louis; Chicago; Memphis, Tennessee; and Mobile, Alabama. In each he outplayed all challengers at the piano.

In Los Angeles, Morton moved in with a woman named Anita Johnson Gonzales, whom he probably met while walking through town. Morton would wear each of his suits in turn over the course of a few hours as he walked

through town to give the impression that he was very wealthy. He briefly managed a dance hall there, and had a share in a gambling club next to a rooming house run by Anita. They made and lost a small fortune, and also briefly ran a club together in San Francisco, which was closed by the authorities because black and white customers were allowed to mix.

Jelly quit California after an argument with his publisher. For years, he had been writing and publishing compositions, but then his publishers, the Spikes Brothers, claimed some of Morton's songs as their own. Morton decided to move to the Melrose Publishing Company in Chicago, whom he trusted, for his future pieces, and so he set off back to the Windy City to find work.

In June 1923, Jelly's recording career began. Over the next couple of years he cut several band and solo discs for a variety of labels until he secured a lucrative contract with Victor in 1926 for his band, the Red Hot Peppers. As each disc appeared, Melrose published the sheet music, helping Morton make as much as possible on the deal. This was necessary, as the powerful Mafia, who took exception to Morton's small-time crimes such as pimping and pool-sharking, prevented him from leading a band in any Chicago dance halls or cabarets, and virtually all his work as a leader was in the recording studio or out of town.

His musicians included several from New Orleans: the Dodds brothers, Johnny St. Cyr, Kid Ory, John Lindsay, and Omer Simeon. "My theory is never to discard the melody," he wrote, and his pieces embellished the many melodies produced by his fertile imagination. His skill in creating miniature

Ferdinand "Jelly Roll" Morton

BORN

October 20, 1890
New Orleans, Louisiana

DIED

July 10, 1941
Los Angeles, California

EDUCATION

Left school between fourth and eighth grades; piano lessons from Professor Nickerson, and an unknown teacher at St. Joseph's University, New Orleans; acquired more expertise in music from fellow musicians in the Storyville district

MAJOR INTERESTS

Piano, composing, bandleading

ACCOMPLISHMENTS

The first significant composer in jazz; produced piano pieces that bridged the gap from ragtime to jazz; wrote and arranged for bands, creating the first recordings in jazz in which the arrangements were tailored expertly to the playing time of 78 rpm discs. Compositions include "Frog-I-More Rag," "Grandpa's Spells," "King Porter Stomp," "London Blues," "Milenburg Joys," "New Orleans Blues," "The Pearls," "Shreveport Stomp" set-pieces for the brief running time of a 78 rpm record (about three minutes) brought him critical acclaim as the first great composer in jazz. These recordings used music to tell a story, such as the funeral march in "Dead Man Blues" or the bustling harborside activity of "Steamboat Stomp."

Jelly moved to New York in 1928, an astute move given the city's growing prominence as the center of the record and publishing business, but a disastrous one for Morton's career as a bandleader. Instead of being able to pick his bands from fellow Louisiana-born musicians as he had done in Chicago, he was forced to put together groups of New York players who were indifferent to his ideas and who lacked his instinctive understanding of the New Orleans style. Morton produced some exciting records with a big band in the late 1920s, and a few genuinely inspired sides, such as "Kansas City Stomps," with a New Orleans lineup, but by the end of the 1920s his career had begun to decline.

This coincided with the Great Depression, and although Morton continued to play occasional well-paid jobs, he could not keep a regular band working and had to return to playing solo or in other people's bands. Gradually Morton slid into the role of a

has-been, berating all who would listen with the many reasons for his woes. Afraid that his godmother's curse was taking effect, he spent much money trying to get the voodoo hex lifted.

When Benny Goodman and Bob Crosby made best-selling discs of his tunes, Jelly failed to restart his career, and Victor let his recording contract lapse. Until his last great burst of recording activity, in 1938–40, Morton spent almost no time in the studio in the 1930s.

Around 1936 he moved to Washington, D.C., to play in a club. It was up two flights of stairs in a none-too-good neighborhood, and visitors recall Morton letting them in with a large bunch of keys, pointing out his home-made "jungle" decor, and demanding a cover charge for entertainment that would be presented.

"What entertainment?" they would ask. "I'm the entertainment," he would say as he pocketed their dollars.

It was from this seedy club in 1938 that researcher Alan Lomax invited him to the Library of Congress to record his life story.

The Library of Congress discs—a rough-and-tumble musical account of his life and times—marked a watershed in Morton's career. His wife, Mabel (née Bertrand), whom he had married

10 years earlier, urged him to give up the club and return to New York City. At the end of 1938 he did so, once more making some records and taking part in radio shows that were fueled by his controversial press attacks on W. C. Handy. This was Morton's final flowering. If he had survived just a few years longer he might have joined in the revival of interest in New Orleans jazz alongside contemporaries like Bunk Johnson and Sidney Bechet. Instead, he failed to make any impression on the jazz tastes of the day, and his return to the spotlight was short-lived.

Discouraged, Morton set off for California in late 1940, partly because he hoped to recapture the magical days of the early 1920s. He even teamed up with Anita again, having left Mabel in New York, where he had been forced to live on welfare. From the West, Morton kept up a stream of letters to Mabel. Things were always just about to look up, even though he could not disguise the fact that he was poor and unwell from her; but in his other letters to friends he was more honest, and told the heartrending story of his final decline. He died in a hospital, with Anita by his bed. She benefited from a suspiciously recent will in which he left her virtually everything, ignoring his wife entirely and leaving only a small royalty income to his sister.

His deathbed poverty was ironic, as Morton's songs have seldom been out of print since then, and hundreds more recordings have been made of his compositions during the last half-century. In his lifetime, the only person consistently sure of his worth was Jelly himself. Now he is recognized by the world at large as the prolific composer, brilliant arranger, and sensational bandleader he always knew himself to be.

DISCOGRAPHY

Blues and Stomps from Rare Piano Rolls. Biograph BCD111. [Modern recording of piano rolls cut by Morton 1924–46.]

The Complete Jelly Roll Morton 1926–1939. RCA Bluebird ND 82361 (five-CD set). [All Morton's sessions for the Victor label, with piano solos, trios, and the Red Hot Peppers, also including his 1939 dates with Sidney Bechet.]

The Library of Congress Recordings. Affinity AFS 1010-3 (three-CD set). [The majority of Morton's autobiographical discs, slightly edited. A differently edited set is issued by Rounder: CD 1091, 1092, 1093, 1094.]

Jelly Roll Morton 1939–1940. Classics 668. [Morton's final discs, made in New York with some old New Orleans colleagues.]

FURTHER READING

Balliett, Whitney. *Jelly Roll, Jabbo, and Fats.* New York: Oxford University Press, 1983.

Dapogny, James. *Ferdinand "Jelly Roll" Morton, The Collected Piano Music.* Washington: Smithsonian Institution; New York: Schirmer, 1982. [Includes biographical essay, list of compositions, and sheet music, plus many illustrations.]

Lomax, Alan. *Mister Jelly Roll: The Fortunes of Jelly Roll Morton, New Orleans Creole and "Inventor of Jazz."* Revised edition. New York: Pantheon, 1993. [Biography constructed from the Library of Congress discs.]

Pastras, Phil. *Dead Man Blues: Jelly Roll Morton Way Out West.* Berkeley: University of California Press, 2001.

Wright, Laurie. *Mister Jelly Lord.* Chigwell, England: Storyville, 1980.

WEBSITE

http://www.duke.edu/~nbp
Site devoted to Morton with biography, discography, and information on his fellow musicians.

King Oliver

THE RAZZIEST, JAZZIEST BAND YOU EVER HEARD

As jazz was emerging in New Orleans as a distinct musical style between 1900 and 1920, its first heroes were the showy trumpeters and cornetists who led the city's bands. The original "king" of the cornet was Buddy Bolden, whose career was cut short by his alarming decline into insanity and hospitalization. The next "king" was Joe Oliver, who eventually took the new sounds of jazz to California, to Chicago, and, through pioneer recordings, to the world.

King Oliver's life is a classic tale of triumph and tragedy. He scaled the heights of popularity, but then fell into hard times as the very musicians he had made famous outstripped him. In early 1920s Chicago, his Creole Jazz Band was the most influential of all black jazz bands, and it launched the career of Louis Armstrong. Later, he formed one of the first big bands in Chicago. His musicians included the most famous names in jazz: clarinetists Barney Bigard, Albert Nicholas, Omer Simeon, and Johnny Dodds; trumpeter Henry Allen; trombonist Kid Ory; banjoists Bud Scott and Johnny St. Cyr; and drummers Paul Barbarin and Baby Dodds. Yet all these men found fame and fortune with leaders other than Oliver, who bravely struggled on into the Great Depression years leading groups of ever more obscure musicians far from the center of musical life.

King Oliver's band visit Comiskey Park, Chicago, in 1919. Clearly visible in the bleachers are (from left to right) drummer "Ram" Hall, Honore Dutrey, trombone; Oliver (in flat cap, holding cornet); and Lawrence Duhé, clarinet.

Joe Oliver's musical development dovetailed exactly with the emergence of jazz. The marching bands of his hometown started to turn their parade music for funerals and civic events into a swinging, partly improvised music that owed less and less to the conventional marches of John Philip Sousa and Arthur Pryor, the leading march composers and bandleaders in the United States at the time. In his teens and early 20s Oliver was a powerful player in these street parades, already able to outblow other players like Manuel Perez and Kid Rena. Oliver had gained experience in a youth band led by Walter Kinchin. He injured his left eye, leaving it protruding and the butt of nicknames for the rest of his life, when Kinchin's band was involved in a fight in Baton Rouge. "Bad Eye" Joe Oliver was a tough customer from early on, and later held his own in rough company by packing a pistol, which he even used to ensure that his band rehearsed diligently.

Oliver played with many of the legends of early jazz, including Sidney Bechet, Frankie Dusen, and Lorenzo Tio, but quickly assumed the honorary title "King" amid stiff competition from other players. Guitarist and raconteur Danny Barker, a child at the time, recalls watching parades go by: "I saw how the crowd gathered closely, listening happily, tingling all over." Oliver and his band were, remembers Barker, "like gods or saints." So, when the red-light district of Storyville closed and work temporarily became scarcer in New Orleans, Oliver was among the first to leave, opening at the Royal Gardens in Chicago early in 1918.

Jazz had been introduced to Chicago by Freddie Keppard, another New Orleans cornetist, as early as 1911, but as World War I drew to a close, the city welcomed the new music in a big way. The Jazz Age had begun. For three years, Oliver worked steadily, often at two venues a night, becoming famous as one of the best cornetists in Chicago. Despite his success, Oliver temporarily left Chicago to venture to California in 1921–22.

After a year in the West, which included work with Jelly Roll Morton in San Francisco, Oliver returned to Chicago. At the Royal Gardens, now renamed the Lincoln Gardens, after the former president, he began his most famous period as a bandleader. In July 1922, he summoned Louis Armstrong to join him on second cornet, a move that created the most influential band in early jazz.

The general public flocked to hear them, with Johnny Dodds on clarinet, Honoré Dutrey on trombone, Baby Dodds on drums, Lil Hardin on piano, and Bill Johnson doubling on banjo and double bass, but their biggest impact was on other musicians. White and black, young and old, players— including those who later gave their names to the style called "Chicago jazz" like Jimmy McPartland, Bud Freeman, Art Hodes, Eddie Condon, and Dave Tough—gathered to hear the sensational interplay between the magisterial Oliver and the young and brilliant Armstrong. The two took unison "breaks" in which the rest of the musicians dropped out, leaving the cornetists playing alone. The breaks were second nature to both men after working in New Orleans parade bands, but they thrilled the Chicago crowds, who had never heard this exciting style before. When the band made its first discs in April 1923, it caused a sensation, and other jazz musicians wore out the recordings learning the parts note for note.

"The razziest, jazziest band you ever heard!" claimed the Chicago *Defender* newspaper. Yet, by the end of the year, the original lineup was separating. Early in 1924 Louis Armstrong and Lil Hardin were married, and soon Louis left for New York City to star with Fletcher Henderson's band. Oliver began his policy of recruiting brilliant

Joseph "King" Oliver

BORN

May 11, 1885
New Orleans, Louisiana

DIED

April 10, 1938
Savannah, Georgia

EDUCATION

Learned music in Walter Kinchin's brass band of young players around 1900; later studied with Bunk Johnson and joined various New Orleans bands in which he perfected his cornet technique: Onward Brass Band, Henry Allen Sr.'s Brass Band, Original Superior Orchestra, Eagle Band, Magnolia Band

MAJOR INTERESTS

Cornet, later trumpet; bandleading; composing

ACCOMPLISHMENTS

Led the most influential band in Chicago for much of the 1920s; launched the careers of many great jazz musicians, including Louis Armstrong; was a key developer of the art of playing muted trumpet solos. Made dozens of influential records, 1923–31. Wrote or co-wrote a number of the most famous tunes in early jazz: "Canal Street Blues," "Chimes Blues," "Dippermouth Blues," "Doctor Jazz," "Snag It," "Snake Rag," "West End Blues"

replacements, and after briefly hiring a trumpeter named Bob Shoffner, Oliver sent to New Orleans for the young Lee Collins. With butterflies in his stomach, Lee took a solo on "Panama Rag." The club's bouncer, Roy Williams, came up to the stand. "Joe," he told Oliver, "that's the first time I've seen you smile since your boy Louis left the band!"

Even Collins's electrifying presence could not recreate the popularity Oliver had enjoyed with Louis Armstrong. So Oliver broke up the band and went to New York City to make some records. On his return, billed as "The World's Greatest Jazz Cornetist" at the Plantation Café, he doubled with his own band at the Lincoln Gardens, but that venue caught fire, and Oliver went into 1925 with no regular band and his library of parts completely burned up.

Like a phoenix from the ashes of the Lincoln Gardens, Oliver changed direction and founded a big band: the Dixie Syncopators. His new group landed the job at the Plantation, and helped to define how jazz could be played by larger ensembles: two trumpets, trombone, and three saxophones, plus rhythm. Local reviewers hailed their "loud, wailing and pulsating" jazz. During this period, Oliver developed his "talking trumpet" technique, using mutes to create a whole range of effects, a piece of showmanship that marked his band out from those of other leaders.

After several successful years, Oliver left Chicago in May 1927. New York City was becoming the new center for jazz, and Oliver moved there along with many other Chicago bandleaders, including Jelly Roll Morton. Until his last record date in 1931, he managed to put together excellent recording bands, even if his day-to-day group was less distinguished. Then Oliver's health degenerated, with the worst possible affliction for a trumpeter: chronic gum disease. Playing cornet for long periods caused havoc to his already-weakened teeth, which wobbled back in his mouth, making it impossible to play, and made blood gush from his gums.

From mid-1931 he was forced to take his band out on the road to survive. They traveled to Wichita, Kansas; Fort Worth, Texas; and Kansas City, Missouri, trading on Oliver's reputation, and often playing for white audiences. As the years went by, the band rode in an ever-less-reliable succession of buses, old cars, and jalopies, and the better musicians quit. Oliver began to miss dates because of his transport, or because he would not accept bookings that he considered beneath his status as "King." On one occasion his band had to burn the tires of their broken-down bus to keep warm as they camped at the roadside through a long, cold night.

By 1936, Oliver settled in Savannah, Georgia, his last veteran bus parked forever in a dusty side street. He did various menial jobs, eventually becoming the janitor of a pool hall.

Sugar Foot Stomp

Music by **JOE OLIVER**
Words by **WALTER MELROSE**

SUCCESSFULLY FEATURED BY
KING OLIVER'S CREOLE JAZZ BAND

MELROSE BROS
MUSIC COMPANY
THE HOUSE THAT BLUES BUILT
177 NO. STATE STREET
CHICAGO, ILL.

The cover for the published edition of Oliver's "Sugar Foot Stomp" (also known as "Dippermouth Blues") features his most famous band. In the group photo are (from left to right) Johnny Dodds, Baby Dodds, Honore Dutrey, Louis Armstrong, Oliver, Lil Hardin Armstrong, and Bill Johnson.

DISCOGRAPHY

King Oliver, Volume One 1923–1929. CDS RPCD 607. [Ten of the best sides by the Creole Jazz Band vividly remastered by Australian engineer Robert Parker and annotated by Bessie Smith's biographer, Edward Brooks.]

King Oliver, Volume Two 1927–1930. CDS RPCD 608. [Sequel to the above, with a mixture of Oliver's later sides.]

The New York Sessions 1929–1930. RCA Bluebird ND 90410. [Highlights from the Victor recordings of Oliver's last years.]

FURTHER READING

Bigard, Barney. *With Louis and the Duke.* Barry Martyn, ed. New York: Oxford University Press, 1985.

Wright, Laurie. *King Oliver.* Chigwell, England: Storyville, 1987.

WEBSITE

http://www.pbs.org/jazz/biography/artist_id_oliver_joe_king.htm

Informative site with pictures and sound files linked to Ken Burns's documentary *Jazz.*

He had always been a more than competent pool player, and in his great New York years had been a regular at the tables, alongside Jelly Roll Morton and Fletcher Henderson. Now he was reduced to sweeping and cleaning, with only the odd game thrown in to recall the great times. His former associates sought him out when they came through on tour. Louis Armstrong is said to have given him a $100 bill— a fortune in the deprived South of the time—and the singer Miss Rhapsody recalls going back to his lodgings where his only souvenir of the great years was a collection of 15 trumpets. He died of a cerebral hemorrhage in his lodgings one night after sweeping out the pool hall.

Louis Armstrong

AMBASSADOR SATCH

Louis Armstrong was the first great genius of jazz. He was born in poverty in New Orleans, yet went on to become the music's most influential soloist and singer. His inspired trumpet playing is instantly recognizable in the hundreds of recordings he made from 1923 until his death in 1971, and his singing voice, which ranged from the high tenor of his youth to the gravelly sounds of his later years, spawned a host of imitators.

Louis was born on the borders of Storyville while it was still an active red-light area, and he was only six years old when its leading pianist, Jelly Roll Morton, left town. Amid the bordellos, the young Louis toured the streets on a cart, selling rags and bones or buckets of coal. On these rounds, he heard through open windows the music that was played for the patrons as it was developing from what we might recognize today as ragtime to something much closer to jazz. In the band of the Home for Colored Waifs, where he was sent after firing a gun in the street on New Year's Day 1913, he learned to play the cornet, and his career began while he was little more than 12 years old.

Like almost all aspiring New Orleans cornetists, Armstrong played in marching bands for parades and funerals. In his late teens he also played in a dance band on the riverboat steamers that went between New Orleans and St. Louis. The leader of the riverboat band was Fate Marable, who had a strong impact on Armstrong's career, helping him begin to learn how to read music. But from the earliest days, Armstrong's mentor was King Oliver, and when Oliver started his new career in Chicago after Storyville was closed down, it was not long before the young Louis traveled north to join Oliver's Creole Jazz Band.

A group of young Chicago musicians, white and black, like saxophonist Bud Freeman, idolized the band and crowded in to hear it at the Lincoln Gardens. "When they played," Freeman wrote, "each chorus seemed to swing more than the previous one until every bit of tension seemed to leave your body."

Soon, Louis was more famous than his boss. His fame grew after he married the band's pianist, Lil Hardin, in 1924, and moved to New York City to join Fletcher Henderson's band, then the best-known black big band in the United States. His time with Henderson was a mixed success, for the suave and sophisticated New Yorkers found him a rough country boy. But his playing won them over, and so did his disarming humor. When he played his very loudest during a passage marked "pp" (for *pianissimo*, meaning "very soft") Armstrong laughed heartily at his mistake, confessing he

thought it meant "pound plenty"! He cut some important discs with Henderson, and also with some of the great blues singers of the time whom Henderson's band accompanied, including Bessie Smith.

A year later Armstrong was back in Chicago, where he began to lead his own small groups, the Hot Five and Hot Seven, in record studios. Lil Hardin was the pianist on many of these sessions, although she and Louis did not remain married for long, and he was subsequently married twice more. His bands made a series of remarkable discs that include many of the best jazz cornet solos he recorded. Through these, in the space of a few years, he altered the whole course of jazz history by abandoning the idea of group or collective improvisation around a theme. He replaced that approach with a single instrumentalist playing extended solos between choruses by the group, to display both inventive musical ideas and technical prowess. His "West End Blues" and other tracks like "Hotter than That" and "Potato Head Blues"

became jazz classics. The wordless vocals he invented when he accidentally dropped the words to "Heebie Jeebies" during a recording session gave the world an early example of a new sound known as "scat" singing. During the years he led these influential recording bands, he changed from playing cornet to the more incisive trumpet.

Louis worked a full schedule, playing with several of Chicago's leading bands like those of Erskine Tate and Carroll Dickerson. Often, as King Oliver had done before him, he appeared at two different venues on the same day, setting up a relentless workload that he kept up for almost the rest of his career.

In 1929, having moved to New York, he made his first discs with a Panamanian pianist named Luis Russell, whose big band backed Louis from 1935 through the mid-1940s, except when Louis made tours to Europe or to the West Coast. This band became known as Louis Armstrong and His Orchestra (although they made many excellent discs without Armstrong under Russell's name, with Henry

"Red" Allen taking the trumpet parts). Throughout the late 1930s, Armstrong and Russell turned out a series of first-rate recordings in which Louis' majestic trumpet glides over the sound of the big band on the popular songs of the day, and with the vocal sections interpreted in Armstrong's characteristic voice. His singing earned him the nickname "Satchelmouth" or "Satch," and later, when he began an impressive round of world travels, he became known as "Ambassador Satch." His near contemporary, guitarist Danny Barker, not only remembers Armstrong playing higher, faster, and better than anyone in New York's many jam sessions, but also how other trumpeters in town even tried to catch colds so that their singing would sound like Louis' throaty voice.

By the late 1940s, very few big band leaders could afford to keep going, as the cost of taking a 14-piece band on the road spiraled rapidly. In a 1946 film called *New Orleans,* in which Billie Holiday also appeared, Louis had played in a seven-piece band with a group of fellow New Orleans veterans. It was so popular that the following year he formed his own small group called the All Stars, which opened at Billy Berg's club in Hollywood in late 1947, and the year after traveled to Europe for the Nice Jazz Festival in France. With such sidemen as pianist Earl Hines, trombonist Jack Teagarden, and clarinetist Barney Bigard, Louis' band lived up to its name; he continued to lead this group until his death.

The All Stars marked a return for Louis to the Dixieland style of jazz he had heard in his youth. In middle age, his trumpet playing was more economical than the rapid flurries of the 1920s, and he sang more. But all over the world new audiences discovered jazz from Louis' golden, burnished tone on the trumpet and his ever-swinging vocals on popular classics like "Hello, Dolly!" "Mack the Knife," and "Wonderful World," with which he was still achieving recording-chart success in his late sixties.

In the late 1960s Armstrong had serious heart problems, but he returned to playing, appearing with his All Stars at the Waldorf Astoria in New York only shortly before his death. He was mourned by millions as the most popular entertainer in jazz. Dizzy Gillespie wrote: "Every trumpeter in the world had to be influenced by him. He changed the modus operandi of music by inventing the solo."

DISCOGRAPHY

The Hot Fives, Vol. 1. Columbia 460821-2. [The earliest Hot Five discs, 1925–26.]

The Hot Fives and Sevens, Vol. II. Columbia 463052-2. [The rest of the 1926–27 Hot Five sessions and the first discs by the augmented group, the Hot Seven.]

The Hot Fives and Hot Sevens, Vol. III. Columbia 465189-2. [Recordings from May–December 1927.]

Louis Armstrong and Earl Hines, Vol. IV. Columbia 466308-2. [The 1928 version of the Hot Five teamed Louis with the brilliant pianist Earl Hines, with whom he was later reunited in the All Stars. Includes "West End Blues."]

Louis in New York, Vol. V. Columbia 466965-2. [Various sides, 1929–30, including the first partnership with Luis Russell's band.]

Laughin' Louis, 1932–33. Bluebird ND 90404. [Early 1930s Armstrong with various big bands, creating definitive versions of tunes like "Basin Street Blues."]

Louis Armstrong: Highlights from His American Decca Years. GRP 26382 (two-CD set). [An excellent cross section of Armstrong's

Louis "Satchmo" Armstrong

Armstrong as millions of fans remember him—both a popular vocalist and entertainer—performing with trombonist and singer Tyree Glenn during a television broadcast by his All Stars in the 1960s.

BORN

August 4, 1901
New Orleans, Louisiana

DIED

July 6, 1971
New York, New York

EDUCATION

Cornet lessons from Professor Peter Davis at the Home for Colored Waifs, New Orleans, Louisiana

MAJOR INTERESTS

Trumpet, singing, bandleading

ACCOMPLISHMENTS

The first great soloist in jazz. Made hundreds of influential records and more than 50 films, including *New Orleans* (1946), *High Society* (1956), *Satchmo the Great* (1957). Topped 1964 recording charts in the United States with "Hello, Dolly!" and 1968 United Kingdom charts with "What a Wonderful World"

HONORS

The Singer Bowl in Queens, New York, was renamed Louis Armstrong Memorial Stadium; a park and statue in his honor were created in New Orleans

MUSEUMS & ARCHIVES

Armstrong collection at the New Orleans Jazz Museum. Queens College plans to open his house in Queens, New York, as a museum; for details see http://independent-musician.com/Louis/

discs from the Luis Russell period to the All Stars, including extracts from his Musical Autobiography, his famous Boston Symphony Hall concert, and collaborations with Ella Fitzgerald and Billie Holiday.]

The California Concerts. MCA GRP 461324. [Two full-length concerts by the All Stars showing how the band's typical live appearances sounded.]

FURTHER READING

Armstrong, Louis. *Swing That Music.* 1936. Reprint, New York: Da Capo, 1993.

——. *Satchmo: My Life in New Orleans.* 1954. Reprint with an introduction by Dan Morgenstern, New York: Da Capo, 1986.

——. *Louis Armstrong in His Own Words.* Thomas Brothers, ed. New York: Oxford University Press, 2000.

Bergreen, Laurence. *Louis Armstrong: An Extravagant Life.* New York: Broadway, 1997.

Collier, James Lincoln. *Louis Armstrong: An American Success Story.* New York: Macmillan, 1985.

Giddins, Gary. *Satchmo.* New York: Dolphin, 1988.

Medearis, Angela Shelf. *Little Louis and the Jazz Band: The Story of Louis "Satchmo" Armstrong.* New York: Lodestar, 1994.

WEBSITES

http://www.nypl.org/research/sc/scl/MULTIMED/JAZZHIST/jazzhist.html
The Louis Armstrong Oral History Project hosted at the Schomberg Center in Harlem, New York.

http://www.satchography.com
A comprehensive on-line discography of Louis Armstrong.

Sidney Bechet

THE WIZARD OF JAZZ

idney Bechet's passionate clarinet and pulsating soprano saxophone combined the profundity of the blues with a dazzling instrumental technique. The Swiss conductor Ernest Ansermet described him in 1919 as "an artist of genius." Alongside Louis Armstrong, he was the most significant soloist in early jazz. However, because he spent many years in Europe, and also because of his famously volatile temperament, Bechet's genius was not properly recognized in the United States until the 1940s, when interest in "traditional" jazz was revived by record collectors and enthusiasts. By then, Bechet was about to move to France, where he spent his final years as a national celebrity.

Like Morton, Oliver, and Armstrong, Bechet belonged to the generation of New Orleans musicians who grew up alongside jazz. Even when Storyville closed in 1917, there were still plenty of opportunities for young players to appear at picnics, rallies, weddings, funerals, and the "ballyhoos" that advertised medicine shows and circuses.

The tubby, pugnacious Sidney Bechet became a celebrity during his teens. "At around twelve years of age, Sidney got himself a cheap tin flute," remembered one contemporary. "He became a virtuoso, a wizard on that tin flute." Bechet's

Sidney Bechet (left) with cornetist Rex Stewart in the RCA Victor studios in Chicago, September 6, 1940. Bechet's forceful playing style often made life difficult for the brass players who accompanied him, but Stewart was a sympathetic and successful frontline partner.

lifelong nickname, the "Wizard of Jazz," stems from those years, with his magical ability on a 10-cent toy. He transferred this mastery to the clarinet, and liked to turn up to hear local bands, concealing his instrument in separate pieces in his pockets. Then, he would assemble the clarinet as he came on stage and blow everyone away with his powerful solos. He also briefly played the cornet in some of New Orleans' many marching bands.

In his entire life, Bechet took only a few lessons. He hated the written exercises given to him by his teacher, "Big Eye" Louis Nelson, and preferred to play truant from school to practice the clarinet alone. By his 20th birthday, Sidney had played with all the best-known bandleaders in New Orleans. However, in common with many of them, he decided to travel north to Chicago to work. One reason was that although there were plentiful opportunities in New Orleans, they paid no better than other occupations, whereas in 1920s Chicago jazz musicians were relatively well paid. For example, trumpeter Doc Cheatham received $85 in one night when he sat in for Louis Armstrong at a Chicago club—the equivalent of several weeks' salary in most bands in New Orleans.

In Chicago, Bechet worked with both King Oliver and Freddie Keppard. His fame spread rapidly, as did his reputation for getting into fights and arguments. There was a notable spat with Oliver, and an even more serious argument that blew up when another member of Keppard's band was paid more than Bechet.

Bechet could have stayed and made his reputation in Chicago. Instead, he accepted Will Marion Cook's invitation to travel to Europe with a large orchestra, along with a wealth of black musicians, dancers, and singers. They set off for London in 1919, and Bechet's decision to travel altered the direction of his life permanently.

In London there was a warm reception for Cook's orchestra when it opened in July 1919. After working with Cook for some time, Bechet moved to a small group, then to a series of other bands until he was deported following a fight in his lodgings. Despite the untimely end of this first European trip, it achieved three things. First, Bechet was singled out for praise by the critics. Second, after buying a soprano saxophone in a London music shop, Bechet increasingly used it in preference to the clarinet. Third, he developed a taste for Europe, where he felt his talents were better appreciated than in the United States.

Back in New York City after his rapid ejection from Britain, Bechet cut a sequence of first-rate discs, some with pianist Clarence Williams and Louis Armstrong. It looked for a while as if, like Armstrong, he would become a star in his own country. Instead, in 1925, he returned to Europe, with singer and dancer Josephine Baker in a show called *La Revue Nègre*. Bechet enjoyed a brief romance with Baker, displaying a penchant for attractive and dynamic women that later led him into other such liaisons, including one with the actress Tallulah Bankhead.

Until late 1930, Bechet was loosely based in Paris but traveled widely in Europe, until a hot-tempered shooting incident landed him in jail in 1928–29, whereupon he moved to Berlin. He wandered all over Europe, as far as Russia. With his Creole background, Bechet loved the European café life and his music brought him plenty of acclaim. Yet his absence from the United States at the time when jazz was developing rapidly meant that the music moved on without him. He was never fully able to capture the ground he lost. In Noble Sissle's big band, with whom he made some recordings, Bechet again traveled to Europe in 1931, and remained in the band when it returned to the United States.

"To tell a story, to grab the listener's attention, to carry him away on a continuously rising curve of excitement . . . was Bechet's musical credo."

—Bob Wilber in *Music Was Not Enough* (1987)

L'INSPECTEUR CONNAIT LA MUSIQUE

Sidney **BECHET**

Claude LUTHER *et son ensemble*

Viviane **ROMANCE** · *Jean* **BRETONNIERE**

BALLETS Catherine DUNHAM

In this poster for Jean Josipovici's 1955 film *L'Inspecteur connait la musique,* Bechet is more prominently featured than the leading actors—illustrating his celebrity status in France at the time. He appears with Claude Luther's band in several scenes of this melodramatic movie.

Great Depression, and the band, which audiences thought old-fashioned, soon folded. The co-leaders went into business running a laundry, where Sidney rekindled a youthful interest in tailoring, and also cooked generously for friends in the back room—no doubt adding an odor of Creole spices to the clothes that he cleaned and pressed! The laundry, like the band, failed, and Bechet rejoined Sissle to make ends meet.

In the late 1930s he was reunited with Ladnier when French critic Hugues Panassié recorded a band playing in the old style. Partly because of Panassié's discs, a revival of interest in New Orleans jazz began, which opened up a new role for Bechet. Already gray and elderly-looking, he now assumed the role of senior statesman of jazz. He made a commercial success of playing the very material that had seemed so unfashionable at the start of the 1930s. From 1938 until mid-1942, when the American Federation of Musicians imposed a ban on recording, Bechet made enough discs to confirm his genius and initiate the New Orleans revival all over the world.

On a disc of "China Boy," made in 1940 with cornetist Muggsy Spanier, Bechet played one of his most elaborate recorded choruses. His pupil, clarinetist Bob Wilber, believes that this exemplifies a routine that Bechet composed and diligently rehearsed. In a jam session, after endless improvisation, Bechet could go into such prearranged material and be sure of outplaying everyone else. There was nobody to compete with, however, when he cut two remarkable sides in which he played all the instruments of the band himself.

Although record collectors and jazz fans began to appreciate Bechet's skill,

Bechet's natural style was to play solo, so he was not really happy in a big band. After leaving Sissle in 1931, he and New Orleans trumpeter Tommy Ladnier formed the New Orleans Feetwarmers to play an energetic brand of Dixieland jazz. For a while they worked in and around New York City. It was still hard to get work during the

for most of the 1940s he worked in relatively obscure circumstances. He was still waiting for his talents to be recognized and rewarded as befitted a player of his experience and stature. This finally happened as a consequence of an invitation from the French critic and discographer Charles Delauney to visit Paris in 1949 for a concert.

In due course, after a triumphal return to Paris and an equally successful flying visit to London, Bechet settled in Europe. He returned a few more times to the United States, but from 1950 his home was in France, and he married an old flame, Elisabeth Zeigler, whom he had gotten to know in his earlier European days.

In the last decade of his life Bechet was finally recognized as the genius he was. With Claude Luter's band he made a series of potent records that defined a new style of traditional jazz, and he became a national hero in France, his legend fueled by the fact that he publicly shared his attentions between his wife and a mistress.

His music blared out from speakers in cafés, and he made appearances on television, notably during a return trip to England, when he appeared on the cult TV show 6.5 Special. His celebrity status was such that it seemed not in the least incongruous that a white-haired jazzman in his 60s should share the stage with young pop groups.

In the very late 1950s, Bechet succumbed to lung cancer and went into a slow but inexorable decline. His talent refused to become dormant, even with the onset of his fatal disease. In a concert in Paris in late 1958, he summoned up all his wizardry to produce one of his very finest shows, even though he was by then desperately ill. Bechet died in Paris on his 62nd birthday.

DISCOGRAPHY

Sidney Bechet 1932–43: The Bluebird Sessions. Bluebird ND 90317 (four-CD set). [84 sides of Bechet's recordings for Victor's Bluebird subsidiary.]

Jazz Classics, Vols. I and II. Blue Note 789384 and 798385. [Cross section of Bechet's work for the Blue Note label, including his famous "Summertime."]

The King Jazz Story Vols. I, II, III, and IV. Storyville 8212, 8213, 8214, 8215. [The output of the sometimes eccentric "King Jazz" label owned by Bechet's long-term colleague, clarinetist Milton "Mezz" Mezzrow, this includes many of Bechet's best small group and duo performances.]

La Nuit Est une Sorcière. Vogue 113414. [Bechet's ballet composed in 1953, with himself as soloist and another extended piece, *La Colline du Delta*, with Claude Luter playing Bechet's solo part.]

FURTHER READING

Bechet, Sidney. *Treat It Gentle.* 1960. Reprint, New York: Da Capo, 1978.

Chilton, John. *Sidney Bechet: The Wizard of Jazz.* 1987. Reprint, New York: Da Capo, 1996.

Wilber, Bob, with Derek Webster. *Music Was Not Enough.* New York: Oxford University Press, 1987.

WEBSITE

http://www.redhotjazz.com/bechet.html
Biography and record details.

Sidney Joseph Bechet

BORN
May 14, 1897
New Orleans, Louisiana

DIED
May 14, 1959
Paris, France

EDUCATION
Brief study with clarinetists Lorenzo Tio, "Big Eye" Louis Nelson, and George Baquet, but mainly self-taught

MAJOR INTERESTS
Clarinet, soprano saxophone, band-leading, composing, teaching

ACCOMPLISHMENTS
Equaled only by Louis Armstrong as a soloist in early jazz; made dozens of influential recordings, his version of George Gershwin's "Summertime" being the most famous. Compositions include "Blackstick," "Dans les Rues d'Antibes," "Egyptian Fantasy," "Georgia Cabin," "Les Oignons," "Le Marchand des Poissons," "Petite Fleur"; His pupils included Johnny Hodges, Bob Wilber, Claude Luter

HONORS
Duke Ellington dedicated a movement of his *New Orleans Suite* to Bechet's memory; At Juan-les-Pins, France, a statue was erected in his honor; Commemorative postage stamps issued by the countries of Chad and Gabon

Bix Beiderbecke

YOUNG MAN
WITH A HORN

The shimmering, transcendental tone of Bix Beiderbecke's cornet, and the impressionistic flurries of his piano playing, brought an entirely new palette of musical colors into jazz. In his tragically short 28-year life, he became the first white jazz musician to alter the course of the music and indelibly stamp his personality on a whole school of players. Whereas Louis Armstrong and Sidney Bechet played with an assertive dominance, Beiderbecke's incurably romantic approach filtered his childhood memories into a beautiful and reflective style. It combined the sounds of classical concerts with those of riverboat jazz bands, half-heard across the water as they rounded the great bend in the Mississippi River near his home town of Davenport, Iowa.

Bix was born into the second generation of a German immigrant family in the settlement founded in the Midwest territory that would become Iowa by Colonel George Davenport in the first half of the 19th century. His family was prosperous and middle class, and they continued many

Bix Beiderbecke in 1928 was a star soloist in Paul Whiteman's band. Whiteman played with the San Francisco Symphony Orchestra until he resigned in 1916, after hearing jazz music for the first time in a bar in the so-called Barbary Coast district of San Francisco.

"There was an ethereal beauty of Bix's tone, with its heart-melting blend of pure joyousness and wistful haunting sadness."

—Max Kaminsky, trumpeter, in *My Life in Jazz* (1963)

Leon Bix Beiderbecke

BORN
March 10, 1903
Davenport, Iowa

DIED
August 6, 1931
Queens, New York

EDUCATION
Lake Forest Military Academy, Illinois; expelled in 1922 before graduating; played in several school bands

MAJOR INTERESTS
Cornet, piano

ACCOMPLISHMENTS
One of the most original of all early jazz soloists, featured in bands of Jean Goldkette, Frankie Trumbauer, Paul Whiteman; later, led his own recording groups; published compositions are "In A Mist," "Flashes," "Candlelights," "In the Dark"

MUSEUMS & ARCHIVES
Beiderbecke collections held at the New Orleans Jazz Museum and the Putnam Museum of History and Natural Science in Davenport, Iowa

of the European musical and cultural traditions from their German heritage. Young Bix did not prosper in formal music lessons, but his quick ear and instinctive talent for music meant that he could pick out tunes on the piano with ease. At age 12 he had already made his mark playing the steam organ, or calliope, atop one of the town's river excursion boats. When a similar boat arrived in town from New Orleans, bringing with it Fate Marable's band starring Louis Armstrong on cornet, Bix had his first exposure to jazz.

Around the same time, Bix's elder brother Charles returned from Europe at the end of World War I, where he had found himself fighting against his grandfather's countrymen. He brought back to the family home a disc of the Original Dixieland Jazz Band playing "Tiger Rag." Bix, who had already shown a penchant for playing the cornet, was entranced, and soon began practicing the sounds of jazz on piano and cornet alike during every spare moment. He sat in with various local bands, also getting occasional jobs playing on riverboats, but his inability to read music fluently prevented him from getting his musicians' union card, without which he could not play cornet professionally.

His family did not approve of Bix's interest in jazz, especially as he showed no aptitude for formal education. Their final attempt to drum some schooling into him at Lake Forest Military Academy ended in disaster when he was expelled in May 1922. Instead of returning home, the 19-year-old headed for Chicago, about 35 miles

from Lake Forest, where he had been making unofficial visits to hear and play jazz. He had already met some of the friends and musicians who would be part of his circle in the coming years, including tuba player Min Leibrook and pianist, vocalist, and songwriter Hoagy Carmichael.

His father made attempts to haul Bix back to Davenport, but these were short-lived, and he began his musical career with various bands in and around Chicago, as well as playing on various pleasure boats on the lakes. During one visit to Davenport, however, Bix finally got his union membership by taking the audition on piano; he breezed through by memorizing a couple of light classics.

On a visit to New York, Bix met and learned from Nick La Rocca, the cornetist with the Original Dixieland Jazz Band, whose discs he had so much admired as a youth. In late 1923 he joined a band of Chicagoans in Cincinnati called the Wolverines, with whom he cut his own first discs in February 1924. In the following weeks, the band stayed on the Indiana University campus, where Bix and Hoagy Carmichael spent time together, culminating in Carmichael's "Riverboat Shuffle" being recorded by the band in May.

Later the same year Beiderbecke spent a short time in the big band led by Jean Goldkette, to whom he returned in 1926 to make some of his finest discs. In the interim, Bix teamed up with Frankie Trumbauer, a talented saxophonist who played the cumbersome C-melody instrument with a grace and lightness that matched Bix's

The Wolverines playing at Doyle's Dancing Academy, Cincinnati, 1924. Beiderbecke cut his first discs with this band of Chicago musicians featuring, from left to right, Vic Moore, George Johnson, Jimmy Hartwell, Dick Voynow (standing), Beiderbecke, Al Gandee, Min Leibrook, and Bob Gillette.

cornet playing. Together, Bix and "Tram," as he was nicknamed, played for several months in St Louis before rejoining Goldkette together. Playing arrangements by Bill Challis, the new, light, swinging style of Beiderbecke and Trumbauer matured, and in a sequence of discs cut under Trumbauer's name in early 1927, they captured the very best of their collaboration on tunes like "I'm Coming Virginia" and "Singin' the Blues."

Even during his most creative period with Goldkette and Trumbauer, Beiderbecke had demonstrated a weakness for alcohol. He had once been fit and athletic, playing football and baseball at Lake Forest, but his lifestyle took its toll, and there were signs that he could not maintain the pace at which he chose to live. Until late 1927, however, Bix largely managed to keep his drinking in hand, and to play well on every occasion.

It was after joining the big band led by Paul Whiteman, the "King of Jazz," in which Bix and Trumbauer became just two of a galaxy of featured soloists, that Beiderbecke's health began to break down. Although he may have found the band's cumbersome

arrangements and elaborate routines tedious, he gave every impression of enjoying being a part of Whiteman's well-paid and starry ensemble, taking a fair number of features in their stage shows and recordings. What caused the problems was that he tried to fit in his old lifestyle of after-hours jam sessions, freelance recordings, and bouts of drinking alongside the punishing work schedule of Whiteman's band.

He collapsed with pneumonia in late 1928, and barely recovered before his health gave way again. To his credit, Paul Whiteman was benevolent toward his musicians. He kept Bix on his payroll during several of the months he was unable to play—a period that was lengthened when Bix was attacked and hurt in a brawl. His last recording date for Whiteman in September 1929 was unfinished, and apart from a few isolated visits to the studios with pick-up bands, he passed the last years of his life in an alcoholic haze, unable to rekindle his zest for life or playing. With the help of his close friend, arranger Bill Challis, Bix managed to eke out a living from occasional freelance playing dates when he was well enough, but many of these passed in a

blur of oblivion. Challis persevered in writing out several of Beiderbecke's piano pieces to preserve them for posterity, but he was unable to help his friend back to the limelight, or to health. In a lonely hotel room in Queens, New York, Bix finally died of alcohol-induced pneumonia at the very time that the first jazzman he had heard on the riverboats at Davenport, Louis Armstrong, his only serious rival, was becoming an international star.

DISCOGRAPHY

Bix Beiderbecke and the Wolverines. Timeless CBC 1-013. [Collects the majority of Bix's 1924 discs into one CD.]

Bix Lives! Bluebird ND 86845. [Bix's 1927–30 recordings for Victor with Jean Goldkette and Paul Whiteman.]

Bix Beiderbecke, Vol. 1: Singin' the Blues. Columbia 466309-2. [Part one of Bix's prolific 1927 output with Frank Trumbauer.]

Bix Beiderbecke Vol. 2: At the Jazz Band Ball. [The balance of the Trumbauer sides plus "Bix and His Gang" from 1927–28.]

FURTHER READING

Berton, Ralph. *Remembering Bix*. New York: Harper & Row, 1974.

Deffaa, Chip. *Voices of the Jazz Age: Profiles of Eight Vintage Jazzmen*. Urbana: University of Illinois Press, 1990.

Evans, Philip R., and Linda Evans. *Bix: The Leon Bix Beiderbecke Story*. New York: Prelike Press, 1998.

Schuller, Gunther. *Early Jazz: Its Roots and Musical Development*. New York: Oxford University Press, 1968.

Sudhalter, Richard M., and Philip R. Evans, with William Dean-Myatt. *Bix: Man and Legend*. New Rochelle, N.Y.: Arlington House, 1974.

WEBSITE

http://www.bixbeiderbecke.com
The official site supported by the Beiderbecke family.

Bessie Smith

EMPRESS OF THE BLUES

In a short 1929 movie called *St. Louis Blues*, there is a glimpse of a long-vanished world, as Bessie Smith stars in her only film appearance. Her robust singing voice and her forceful, heartfelt interpretations of the blues can be heard on the 159 records she made during her short life. But it is from her riveting, charismatic presence on film that it is possible to understand something of the vaudeville and theater world she inhabited for most of her life. On screen, she acts as well as sings, but she packs more emotional power into the title song, her one vocal number, than in the lightweight acting role of a wronged wife that surrounds it. The film captures forever something of the essence of her stage presence and unmistakably communicates the aura of a star.

The world of the touring stage show offered an escape from the grinding poverty of the South for many performers such as Bessie, who was born one of seven children in her family's cabin near Chattanooga, Tennessee. In the companies that crisscrossed the United States, playing in a chain of theaters operated by an organization called TOBA (the

Bessie Smith in 1925 with her fashionably bobbed wig and feather boa had earned the title Empress of the Blues. Her reported income of $2,000 a week made her the most successful African-American performer of the time.

Although Bessie Smith's acting and singing in her 1925 movie, *St. Louis Blues,* is dignified and moving, the same could not be said of the film's publicity posters, which used crude racial stereotyping to promote the picture.

Theater Owners' Booking Agency), the worlds of jazz, blues, and vaudeville came together in a fascinating mixture. Jazz musicians acquired the polish and sophistication of the performers who strutted in front of the footlights, while singers simultaneously absorbed much of the nuance and swing of jazz.

Bessie Smith was not a jazz performer herself; she was always a vaudeville and blues singer. But for much of her career she was accompanied by the finest jazz musicians of her generation, from Louis Armstrong and Fletcher Henderson to saxophonist Chu Berry and clarinetist Buster Bailey. The combination of her emotional power as a singer and the musical depth of her accompaniments helped make her discs some of the finest recordings from the pioneer period of jazz.

Her theater career began in 1912, under the wing of another great female blues singer, Gertrude "Ma" Rainey. Indeed, some early stories suggested that Rainey had "kidnapped" Bessie to take the teenager on the road. Throughout the period leading up to 1920, she toured the country, generally returning to a theater called the "81" in Atlanta, Georgia. Many aspiring jazz musicians heard her during this time— the teenage trumpeter Doc Cheatham, for example, actually sat in with her band in Nashville—and by 1922 she either hired her own backup bands or fronted prestigious orchestras like the Atlantic City group led by pianist Charlie Johnson.

Following the sensational success of Mamie Smith (no relation to Bessie), who cut the first blues record, "Crazy Blues," in 1920, Bessie apparently auditioned for several record companies, even cutting a test disc with Sidney Bechet that was never issued. Her first recordings were eventually made in February 1923, and within months she had become a major star. Her disc of "Down-Hearted Blues" sold over three-quarters of a million copies. It is symptomatic of her tempestuous lifestyle that only a few weeks before the session she had been fired from a stage show for fighting with its producer. And, shortly after the recording, she and her husband Jack Gee beat up the pianist on the session, Clarence Williams, for apparently trying to defraud her.

There was soon plenty of money, as Bessie was earning good fees for her discs and hundreds of dollars a week for her theater appearances, amounts that were a fortune in 1923–24. At this stage, welcoming the contrast with her previous hand-to-mouth existence, she accepted most of the offers she received, and worked far harder than she needed. For a time her famous temper was kept in check and she did not overindulge in bootleg alcohol. During the next four years she made a string of exceptional recordings, adeptly handled by producer Frank Walker at Columbia.

To modern ears, some of the accompaniments sound plodding and dated, but Bessie Smith's voice is full and well recorded throughout. The musicians on her best discs include members of Fletcher Henderson's band, notably Louis Armstrong, trombonist Charlie Green, and clarinetist Buster Bailey, whose contributions spur her on to a higher level of performance. She cut virtually all her discs in New York City, but appeared in person there infrequently, mainly continuing to work the provincial circuit where she was well known, but adding new theaters in Cincinnati and Chicago to her itinerary. Eventually, she had her own railroad car and a customized tent made for her show, so that she could appear even where there was no circuit theater.

As the years went on, stories filtered back from the touring circuit that Bessie's temper and her fondness for drink were getting the better of her. She was stabbed in her hometown of Chattanooga, she abandoned her band in Kentucky, and she indulged in several liaisons with dancers and musicians, male and female, which jeopardized her relationship with Jack Gee, even

though they adopted a son in 1926. On one occasion when Jack was accused of stepping out of line, she attempted to shoot him. Finally, in 1928, after he had an affair with another singer, Gertrude Saunders, their marriage broke up.

For almost a year, Bessie's life continued as it had been. She toured, she recorded, and she made her one and only film appearance. However, 1929 was a year in which dramatic changes took place. First, talking pictures, of which Bessie's own film was an example, rapidly began to overtake the popularity of the touring theater circuit, reducing the opportunities for shows like Bessie's to play provincial cities. Second, the Wall Street crash ushered in the Great Depression, which sounded the death knell of much popular entertainment as people scrimped along on slender financial resources in order to remain alive. An artist of Bessie's stature might have survived the Depression, but in the wake of her separation from Jack her dependence on alcohol increased. Just as she began to be feted by white intellectuals, like the writer and photographer Carl Van Vechten, who celebrated African-American show life and performers, her career took a serious turn for the worse.

In 1930 she took to the road again with a show called *Moanin' Low*. It played to small theaters in out-of-the-way places, but it kept her in funds, as did the two shows in which she subsequently appeared in New York City and Philadelphia. At the same time, Jack Gee managed to separate Bessie from Jack Jr., their adopted son, and she had to cope with this emotional trauma while carrying on working. Fortunately she found a new partner, Richard Morgan, who had become wealthy from bootlegging, and this helped soften the blow when she

Bessie Smith

BORN
April 15, 1894
Chattanooga, Tennessee

DIED
September 26, 1937
Clarksdale, Mississippi

MAJOR INTEREST
Blues and vaudeville singing

ACCOMPLISHMENTS
The finest blues singer of her generation, her phonograph records are an enduring monument to her art; accompanists include many pioneer jazzmen; wrote many important blues songs, including "Backwater Blues," "Jailhouse Blues," "Reckless Blues," "Young Woman's Blues." Featured in many touring shows, including *Happy Times* (1930), *Broadway Revue* (1931), *Fan Waves* (1934), *Hot from Harlem* (1934), *League of Rhythm* (1936); appeared in film *St. Louis Blues* directed by Dudley Murphy and featuring James P. Johnson on piano (1929)

HONORS
Down Beat International Jazz Critics Hall of Fame, 1967; commemorative medal issued by American Negro Commemorative Society, 1971; legend of her death formed the basis of the play *Death of Bessie Smith* by Edward Albee (1961)

"I was always impressed by her tremendous power; she had the dynamic range of an opera singer and the same control and power of voice, from the softest pianissimo, and a tremendous pulse in her singing."

—Teddy Wilson, pianist, in *Teddy Wilson Talks Jazz* (1997)

lost her recording contract: In the early 1930s Columbia found there was no market for blues discs. She also accepted lower and lower fees for her theater appearances, but her voice could still work its old magic.

One chance to hear this is in her last recording session, arranged in 1933 by the entrepreneur John Hammond, who paid the musicians out of his own pocket. Bessie's voice is in incomparable form on a selection of vaudeville songs in which she is accompanied by some key swing era musicians, including trumpeter Frankie Newton and trombonist Jack Teagarden.

By 1937, there were signs that Bessie's career would revive, and she was being lined up to make further recordings and possibly another film. She had her drinking under control once more, and although her tours were seldom without incident, she was definitely in the process of making a comeback when she was killed in an automobile accident 75 miles outside Memphis, where she had been appearing.

For years after her death, rumors circulated that she had died as a result of being refused admission to a white hospital and bleeding to death en route to a hospital for black patients. The account of the doctor who attended her disproves this, but he also made clear that her injuries were so severe she had only a slight chance of survival. In the case of a legend, however, rumors are often more potent than facts, and the story of Bessie Smith's death has come to symbolize the segregation of the South in which she grew up.

DISCOGRAPHY

Bessie Smith: Empress of the Blues, The Complete Recordings, Vols, I–IV. Columbia 47091, 47431, 47474, 52838 (each a two-CD set).

FURTHER READING

Albertson, Chris. *Bessie.* New York: Stein and Day, 1972.

Brooks, Edward. *The Bessie Smith Companion.* Oxford, Miss.: Bayou, 1989.

Cowley, John, and Paul Oliver, editors. *The New Blackwell Guide to Recorded Blues.* Oxford and Boston: Blackwell, 1996.

Gourse, Leslie. *Swingers and Crooners: The Art of Jazz Singing.* New York: Franklin Watts, 1997.

Spottswood, Richard K. "Country Girls, Classic Blues and Vaudeville Voices: Women and the Blues" in Lawrence Cohn, *Nothing But the Blues.* New York: Abbeville, 1993.

WEBSITE

http://www.blueflamecafe.com/Bessie_Smith.html
Site with biography and music links.

More Jazz Pioneers to Remember

Freddie Keppard (1890–1933) might well have become the most famous trumpeter in jazz, if he had accepted an invitation to make records in 1916, the year before the Original Dixieland Jazz Band cut their first discs. By then he had already taken an early form of jazz to the West Coast and to Chicago, where he settled during the 1920s. He did not record until the mid-1920s, when he was considered by those who knew him to be past his prime. Nevertheless, his 1926 record of "Stock Yards Strut" reveals a player of huge power and swinging drive, one who must have been a formidable rival to King Oliver and Louis Armstrong. Legend has it that Keppard refused the chance to record because he was worried about his material being copied by others. He was so concerned about rival musicians stealing his material that he apparently played with a handkerchief over his valve hand to conceal his fingering. Recent research suggests that in fact he turned down the deal because it did not pay enough.

Consequently, **Nick La Rocca** (1889–1961), the cornet-playing leader of the Original Dixieland Jazz Band (or ODJB) made the first jazz discs in 1917, with colleagues **Larry Shields** (1893–1953) on clarinet, **Eddie Edwards** (1891–1963) on trombone, **Henry Ragas** (1891–1919) on piano, and **Tony Sbarbaro** (1897–1969) on drums. They took New York by storm after an appearance at Reisenweber's restaurant in 1917, traveled to London, England, in 1919, and made many discs before disbanding in 1925. Ragtime composer J. Russell Robinson replaced Ragas, who died prematurely. The band's discs were influential in beginning the Jazz Age, and many of La Rocca's compositions, like "At the Jazz Band Ball" and "Clarinet Marmalade," became popular "standard" compositions in early jazz. The ODJB's five-piece instrumentation was widely copied in the early 1920s.

Trombonist **Edward "Kid" Ory** (1890–1973) led the first African-American jazz band from New Orleans to make records. He had been a major figure in New Orleans until his Creole Jazz Band traveled to California in 1919, where they recorded "Ory's Creole Trombone" in 1922. He moved to Chicago in 1925, and became a prolific recording artist, working with Louis Armstrong, Jelly Roll Morton, and King Oliver. From the mid-1940s, based on the West Coast once more, he became a leading figure in the New Orleans revival, playing an earthy brand of traditional jazz until his semiretirement in the 1960s.

The clarinetist on many of Ory's discs was **Johnny Dodds** (1892–1940), whose soulful, bluesy clarinet captured much of the African heritage in jazz. His contemporaries,

The Original Dixieland Jazz Band in a characteristic "novelty" pose, in which trombonist Eddie Edwards and cornetist Nick La Rocca share a bucket mute, and even the clarinetist Larry Shields gets in on the act with a mute of his own. Also shown are drummer Tony Sbarbaro and pianist Henry Ragas.

Sincerely Yours,
The "Original Dixieland Jazz Band."

such as **Barney Bigard** (1906–80), **Albert Nicholas** (1900–73), and **Jimmie Noone** (1895– 1944), favored a more ornate, decorative style derived from classical music that became nicknamed "Creole" clarinet playing. On many early records, the technology prevented drums from being used, as the sensitive needles that cut the record grooves in the wax master discs jumped out of place with any loud percussive sounds.

Johnny Dodds's brother, **Warren "Baby" Dodds** (1898–1959), was one of the first drummers to record, although some of his earliest work on disc was playing the domestic washboard with thimbles, a scratchy approximation of a snare drum, originally used by children's "spasm" or "skiffle" bands. In his later recordings Dodds captured the authentic sounds of New Orleans brass bands, with their rolling snares and booming bass drums. He was a great influence on many young white drummers who heard him on Chicago's South Side in the 1920s, as was his fellow New Orleans percussionist **Zutty Singleton** (1898–1975).

The "Austin High School Gang" was the name given to the young white

Chicago musicians, because several of what became a tight-knit group of players had been students there. Members of the group included cornetist **Jimmy McPartland** (1907–91), the man who replaced Bix Beiderbecke in the Wolverines; his brother **Dick McPartland** (1905–57), who played banjo; saxophonist **Bud Freeman** (1906–91); clarinetist **Frank Teschemacher** (1906–32); trumpeter **Wild Bill Davison** (1906–89); pianist **Joe Sullivan** (1906–71); guitarist **Eddie Condon** (1905–73), and drummers **Dave Tough** (1907–48) and **Gene Krupa** (1909–73). Their music was based on the rough-edged collective improvisation of New Orleans jazz, and their style of rugged Dixieland eventually became known as "Chicago Jazz."

Pianist **Lil Hardin Armstrong** (1898–1971) was one of a small number of significant women who were pioneers of early jazz. She not only organized the career of her husband Louis Armstrong before they separated in 1931, but also put together numerous other Chicago jazz bands, including a famous recording group, the New Orleans Wanderers. She continued to lead bands up until her death. Another female Chicago bandleader was **Lottie E. Hightower**, who in addition to leading her Nighthawks was an influential official in the American Federation of Musicians. She and Lil Armstrong often worked together to organize work for other musicians.

Gertrude "Ma" Rainey (1886–1939) was the most significant blues singer after Bessie Smith. She made a large number of recordings, and her studio and touring group (generally named the Georgia Jazz Band, for her home state) employed several well-known jazz musicians over the years. Like Bessie Smith, Ma Rainey toured the vaudeville circuit, and some of her discs, including her famous "Ma Rainey's Black Bottom," capture the salty humor of her stage persona. Among those who played with her band was pianist **Lovie Austin** (1887–1972), who cut many recordings owing to her job as house pianist at Paramount Records, but who also led her own highly effective band, the Blues Serenaders.

Henry "Red" Allen (1908–67) was the most outstanding of the several challengers to Louis Armstrong's role as preeminent trumpeter in jazz in the 1920s and early 1930s. Others included **"Kid" Punch Miller** (1894–1971), **Jabbo Smith** (1908–91), **Lee Collins** (1901–60,) and **Reuben Reeves** (1905–75), but Allen was the player selected by the Victor company to make a series of discs to compete with Armstrong's. Their rivalry was more imagined than real, as they were close friends, and Allen spent many years playing trumpet in Luis Russell's big band during the years it accompanied Armstrong. He also played in the bands of Fletcher Henderson, Lucky Millinder, and King Oliver. In the 1940s he briefly took part in the New Orleans Revival with Sidney Bechet and Jelly Roll Morton. By the 1960s, critics hailed the abstract elements of his style, especially in recordings with clarinetist **Pee Wee Russell** (1906–69), as a vital contribution to modern jazz. His oblique way of attacking notes and jumping from one register to another, and his variety of tone and volume influenced many free jazz players.

The figurehead of the New Orleans Revival in the 1940s was **Willie "Bunk" Johnson** (1889–1949). Johnson was a colorful character whose partially unfounded claims that he was a contemporary of Buddy Bolden, taught Louis Armstrong, and was a major figure in the earliest days of New Orleans jazz were taken seriously by a group of record collectors and critics in the late 1930s and early 1940s. By then Johnson was working on a Louisiana farm, but a subscription fund bought him new teeth and he tentatively began playing again, enjoying a seven-year second career in which he made some influential records. His ragtime-influenced playing was a link to the earliest days of jazz, but much of what of what he told historical researchers was found to be made up of rather tall stories.

Another trumpeter, **Adolphus "Doc" Cheatham** (1905–97), had a career that spanned the first century of jazz. He began in a children's band, the Bright Future Stars, in Nashville before the 1920s, and was still playing once a week in New York at the time of his death. He recorded with Ma Rainey and sat in for Louis Armstrong in Chicago theaters in the 1920s. He spent the swing era in Cab Calloway's band. As an old man, his playing was as rich and powerful as ever, bringing a vanished era of Chicago speakeasies and prohibition vividly back to life. His timing, phrasing and repertoire recalled the Jazz Age itself.

At the height of the Swing Era, big band jazz was America's most popular form of music, appealing both to African-American and white audiences, such as these dancers at New York's Roseland Ballroom in 1941.

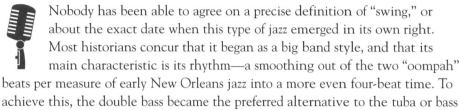

2 Swing Bands and Soloists

Nobody has been able to agree on a precise definition of "swing," or about the exact date when this type of jazz emerged in its own right. Most historians concur that it began as a big band style, and that its main characteristic is its rhythm—a smoothing out of the two "oompah" beats per measure of early New Orleans jazz into a more even four-beat time. To achieve this, the double bass became the preferred alternative to the tuba or bass saxophone, and the guitar was used instead of the more insistent banjo, together giving a lighter, more fluid sound.

Above this even, swinging pulse there were sections of brass and reed instruments: three or four trumpets, two or three trombones, and most of the saxophone family: alto, tenor, baritone, and occasionally bass. These sections had parts written for them in organized arrangements known as "charts," which replaced the improvised sounds of early jazz in which the trumpet stuck to the melody and clarinet and trombone wove variations around it.

Short repeated phrases played by an entire section became known as "riffs." Sometimes all the sections combined to play passages known as head arrangements, so-called because they were worked out by collective experiment and memorized. Later these elements were scaled down to a new style known as "small group swing," in which the brass and reed instruments tended to play melodic lines in unison, interspersed with solos.

The expansion of jazz bands began early in the 1920s, and the Swing Era itself is generally considered to have gotten under way by the start of the 1930s. Perhaps the first big band to receive widespread attention was Paul Whiteman's Orchestra, which as early as 1919 played what became known as "symphonic jazz." Whiteman incorporated the experiments of a West Coast arranger named Ferde Grofé who, along with drummer Art Hickman, had pioneered the idea of big band sections.

At the start of the 1920s, the music that Whiteman produced was a long way from the jaunty syncopated rhythm of the Original Dixieland Jazz Band, let alone the freer, jazzier sounds of King Oliver. Whiteman's band sounded ponderous and genteel by turns; nevertheless, his influence encouraged a number of bandleaders to experiment with similar large forces. This second set of profiles begins with the man who first successfully integrated the authentic African-American rhythms and pitches of jazz with the emergent form of big band music, Fletcher Henderson. Many of the first generation of swing soloists, from Louis Armstrong and Coleman Hawkins to Rex Stewart, Roy Eldridge, and Chu Berry, belonged at various times to Henderson's orchestra, which can truly be said to have launched the swing era.

Fletcher Henderson

THE FIRST GREAT SWING BAND

Balding, scholarly-looking, a college graduate with a degree in math and chemistry, Fletcher Henderson seems an unlikely candidate to be a high-profile bandleader and arranger. However, from the time he led his first large group at the Club Alabam, New York City, in early 1924 until his final full-time orchestra in 1941, Henderson's career spanned the Swing Era. Furthermore, he brought the rhythmic elements of jazz into his 1920s band, developed the idea of the jazz soloist, and subsequently created many of the finest arrangements for Benny Goodman, which made him one of the principal architects not only of that era, but of the jazz big band itself.

Far from having an underprivileged background, Henderson, his younger brother Horace, and their sister Irma grew up in a middle-class African-American family in Georgia. Both parents were musicians and teachers, his father working in a local school and his mother teaching piano. Despite Fletcher's main interests being in the sciences and on the sports field, his family's devoted, even excessive, musical zeal led him to become an accomplished all-round musician. His father's stern attitude—sometimes locking the boy up to ensure he practiced—developed Fletcher's skills to

Atlantic City, New Jersey, was an important center for jazz, and Fletcher Henderson's orchestra lined up on the boardwalk there in July 1932: from left to right are Russell Procope, Coleman Hawkins, Edgar Sampson, Clarence Holiday, Walter Johnson, John Kirby, Henderson, Russell Smith, Bobby Stark, Rex Stewart, J. C. Higginbotham, and Sandy Williams.

a very high level, and he never had difficulty sight-reading, writing music, or hearing exact pitches.

Ironically—despite the fact that he graduated from Atlanta University in a state not renowned for advancing the careers of African Americans—it was when he got to New York City in 1920 that Henderson realized he was unlikely to make his living as a chemist. He found that the barriers for someone of his racial background were formidable. He therefore turned to his musical skills and took a job as a song plugger, playing and demonstrating new songs for the publishing company run by blues composer W. C. Handy and his partner Harry Pace. When Pace and Handy set up a new firm to make phonograph records, Henderson became its musical director. As a consequence, he came to make dozens of discs with blues singers, and went out on the road in the backup band for the label's first star, Ethel Waters.

At a time when Chicago dominated developments in jazz, there was a hunger for similar music in New York City. In the record studios and at many of the city's clubs, Henderson's organizational talents and instrumental skills made him a man in demand. He backed many of the finest blues singers, including Bessie Smith, and as music director for Pace and Handy's Black Swan label, he was able to assemble bands of the city's best musicians. He was already nicknamed "Smack," from the habit of smacking his lips, and also a punning reference to his one-time prowess with the baseball bat.

With a group of recording colleagues, he opened at the Club Alabam in 1924, and later that year transferred to the Roseland Ballroom. Playing there for the hall's affluent white customers for much of the next 10 years, Henderson built the Roseland into a leading venue for jazz in New York and established his band's reputation as the greatest jazz orchestra in the city. From the start, he employed some outstandingly talented players, including Coleman Hawkins on tenor saxophone, drummer Kaiser Marshall, and—most significantly—Don Redman on alto sax and as the band's arranger.

Redman began to develop the pioneering work of the early West Coast arranger Ferde Grofé and his colleague and drummer Art Hickman. He wrote pieces in which the brass and saxophone sections played question-and-answer phrases to one another, or played together in a form of what in classical music is called counterpoint (in which two or more independent melodies are combined). He captured something of the feel of a jazz soloist in the notes he wrote for all the saxophones to play together, but to start with, the band still sounded stilted, lacking the innate swing of its Chicago or New Orleans counterparts. Henderson himself contributed to the band's stiffness. His classical training had not given him any idea of jazz rhythm, and he had to learn how to play in a jazzier way, losing the ragtime stiffness that many New Yorkers equated with jazz. However, his acute ear and what became a legendary ability for talent-spotting came to his aid, and he brought Louis Armstrong from Chicago to inject the missing ingredients into the band.

Armstrong made a greater contribution to Henderson's band than his one-year stay and 48 discs might suggest. There are highlights among their recordings, like "Shanghai Shuffle" and "Copenhagen," but the startling ingredient Armstrong added is evident from a disc like "I Miss My Swiss," where the jerky rhythms of the band suddenly give way to his elegant, flowing cornet improvisations. The band's other soloists, including Coleman Hawkins and trombonist Charlie Green, were quick to realize that this was the way forward, and by the time Louis left, as his successor, Rex Stewart, put it: "Henderson's book [of arrangements]

Fletcher Hamilton Henderson Jr.

BORN
December 18, 1897,
Cuthbert, Georgia

DIED
December 29, 1952
New York, New York

EDUCATION
Atlanta University, Georgia, degree in mathematics and chemistry

MAJOR INTERESTS
Bandleading, arranging, piano

ACCOMPLISHMENTS
Made dozens of discs in early 1920s as blues accompanist and soloist, backing all major singers of the day. Formed big band, 1924; between then and 1929 defined the form and style of the large jazz orchestra. Employed many leading soloists, including Louis Armstrong and Coleman Hawkins. Arrangements for his own band and Benny Goodman include "Down South Camp Meeting," "Wrappin' It Up," "King Porter Stomp," "Sugar Foot Stomp"

Fletcher Henderson in 1941 on a return visit to the Roseland Ballroom, where he had been resident from 1924 to 1934.

was written around Louis's endings and the interplay between Hawk and Louis." Henderson had learned how to combine strong jazz solos with the style of arrangement he and Redman were developing, and the band read the music with far greater freedom after Armstrong's rhythmic approach wore off on the other musicians. Furthermore, the brilliant solo presence of Armstrong had made the band a talking point among musicians and public alike.

Thereafter, Henderson continued to mix excellent arrangements (written after Redman's departure mainly by

Benny Carter and Henderson himself) with high-profile soloists such as Stewart and fellow trumpeters Tommy Ladnier, Henry "Red" Allen, Joe Thomas, and Roy Eldridge, clarinetist Buster Bailey, and trombonists Benny Morton, Claude Jones, and Jimmy Harrison. His preeminent saxophonist was Hawkins, who eventually was replaced by Lester Young (briefly) and Chu Berry.

Despite his obvious talent for playing, arranging, finding talent, and publicity, Henderson was also a chaotic bandleader. At Roseland, with a loyal public, this barely mattered, but on the road, rumor had it that the band never left for the next engagement until so late they would have to drive at outrageous speeds to get there on time. They often failed to do so. Amid this fast-living atmosphere in which the band flaunted its fast sedans and flashy clothes, Henderson himself was severely injured in an August 1928 automobile accident, after which he was even less reliable. He would lose concentration while starting the band off, and was equally disorganized about broadcasts, losing out to less inspired musicians who were prepared to meet their obligations.

Nevertheless, numerous musicians attest that Henderson's band, for all its underlying chaos, was the band everyone wanted to be in because it allowed its soloists the most room to stretch out and play, amid challenging arrangements. The band weathered the Great Depression, but in the 1930s gradually lost its supreme position. To keep going, Henderson sold arrangements to Benny Goodman, who made his version of "King Porter Stomp," among others, nationally famous.

After struggling on as a leader, Henderson finally gave up and joined Goodman as an arranger in 1939, although he tried his hand as a leader again from time to time in the 1940s. His last years were spent as an arranger, until he was left partially paralyzed by a stroke in 1950. Without Henderson's innovations, the jazz big band might not have developed as it did. His main achievement was in successfully combining improvisation and organized arrangements for large bands into a workable model for the future.

DISCOGRAPHY

Fletcher Henderson with Louis Armstrong. EPM FCD 5702.

Fletcher Henderson 1925–1929. JSP 311. [Henderson's best recordings from his period of most rapid development.]

Hocus Pocus: Fletcher Henderson and His Orchestra 1927–1936. Bluebird ND 90413. [21 tracks from Henderson's later bands with Stewart, Hawkins, Eldridge, and Berry.]

Henderson's complete band recordings from 1923–38 are issued in 15 volumes by the French Classics company, with the following numbers (in chronological order of contents): 697, 683, 673, 657, 647, 633, 610, 597, 580, 572, 546, 535, 527, 519.

FURTHER READING

Allen, Walter C. *Hendersonia: The Music of Fletcher Henderson and His Musicians.* Highland Park, N.J.: Walter Allen, 1973.

Chilton, John. *Song of the Hawk.* Ann Arbor: University of Michigan Press, 1990.

Hadlock, Richard. *Jazz Masters of the Twenties.* New York: Macmillan, 1965.

Schuller, Gunther. *Early Jazz: Its Roots and Musical Development.* New York: Oxford University Press, 1968.

Stewart, Rex, *Boy Meets Horn.* Claire P. Gordon, ed. Ann Arbor: University of Michigan Press, 1991.

WEBSITE

http://www.redhotjazz.com/fletcher.html Thorough listing of available discs and other links.

"Fletcher's ideas were far ahead of anybody else's at the time, partly because of all the experience he had with the great soloists in his different bands, and partly because he was such an outstanding musician himself."

—Benny Goodman in *The Kingdom of Swing* (1939)

Duke Ellington

MUSIC IS MY MISTRESS

rom the late 1920s until the 1970s, no other figure in jazz enjoyed so impressive a career as Duke Ellington, whether as bandleader, composer, or instrumentalist. His concern with the shape and form of his compositions took the ideas of Jelly Roll Morton one stage further. Whereas Morton created miniatures to fit the approximately three-minute playing time of early phonograph records, Ellington's pieces stretched out and some soon spanned more than one disc. Although his orchestra never entirely lost its roots as a dance band, it became a magnificent vehicle for his imagination, allowing him to hear his ideas almost as quickly as he could write them down. By the time of his death he had written numerous extended suites and sacred concerts. His talents as a composer, both alone and in partnership with his colleague Billy Strayhorn, created a body of work that has often been compared to his counterparts in the classical field for its breadth, scope, and range.

Edward Kennedy "Duke" Ellington was a suave, almost dandified figure, born in Washington, D.C., just at the end of the 19th century. Ragtime was the music that made the greatest impression on him during his childhood, and although his piano teacher, the aptly named Miss Clinkscales, might have disapproved, he had written his own "Soda Fountain Rag" by the time he was 16.

By his early 20s, Ellington was a well-known figure in his hometown, where he worked with a number of local musicians, including trumpeter Artie Whetsol, saxophonist Otto Hardwick, and drummer Sonny Greer, who were to form the nucleus of his orchestra for many years to come. He already knew that however celebrated he was in Washington, to become really successful in jazz he would have to move to New York City, which he eventually did in 1923, taking with him banjoist Elmer Snowden, who was already a seasoned veteran of the touring life.

In New York, the band settled first at the Hollywood Club and then the Kentucky Club on Broadway, and Duke started the slow process of expanding his group. Right from the start he did so by adding musicians with distinct and individual musical characters until he had a big band made up of players who were all recognizable soloists.

He made records early on with various sizes of ensemble, but his expanded band, in more or less its final form, began recording in earnest in 1926, the year before Duke got his big break and moved into the Cotton Club in Harlem. Run by gangsters, the club featured a dazzling floor show that stressed a jungle theme, with exotic sets, wild African-influenced dancing, and Ellington's music with rolling drums

and moaning brass. Attended largely by well-to-do white audiences who ventured from midtown Manhattan to Harlem for the exciting nightlife, the Cotton Club was a fantastic platform for Duke to develop his career.

Soon, Duke's band began to attract a huge following. The band made records for several different labels and broadcast regularly from the club. Its rhythm section was enhanced by the powerful New Orleans playing of Wellman Braud, who swiftly made the transition from the old-fashioned tuba to the more flexible double bass. Also, the incisive banjoist and guitarist Fred Guy had replaced Elmer Snowden. Saxophonist Rudy Jackson came in alongside Hardwick, and baritone sax player Harry Carney (who was to spend the rest of his long life in Duke's band) also joined. But the vital sound that distinguished the group from any other was the uninhibited trumpet playing of Bubber Miley and the wild growling trombone of "Tricky Sam" Nanton.

Other bands had personalities or star soloists such as Louis Armstrong, great arrangements like Fletcher Henderson's, or slick charm like Paul Whiteman's, but Duke offered his listeners a sound that featured the musical personalities of his instrumentalists, hyped by the "jungle" image of the Cotton Club. By 1931, in four short years at the club, Duke had built his orchestra into the leading big band in the United States; it retained that position until his death in 1974.

With floor shows to accompany, broadcasts to make, and an endless hunger for new music, some bandleaders kept droves of New York's composers working. By contrast, Ellington, with his agent and publisher Irving Mills and collaborators from within his own band, wrote almost all the music he played, giving his orchestra an individual character from the outset. As new star soloists joined, like saxophonist Johnny Hodges, clarinetist Barney Bigard, and trumpeter Cootie Williams, Duke wrote

Duke Ellington usually led his own band, but at this 1939 party on New York's Riverside Drive, he joined in an after-hours jam session. Behind him from left to right are J. C. Higginbotham, Brad Gowans, Juan Tizol, Cootie Williams, Eddie Condon, Rex Stewart, Max Kaminsky, and jam-session organizer Harry Lim. Tizol, Williams, and Stewart were members of Ellington's band at the time.

Billy Strayhorn, standing, and Ellington make last-minute adjustments to a composition. In his autobiography, Ellington summed up his partnership with Strayhorn saying: "Billy Strayhorn was my right arm, my left arm, all the eyes in the back of my head, my brainwaves in his head, and his in mine."

"concertos" for them, which then had lyrics added to become popular songs—Bigard's concerto turning into "Never No Lament," and Williams's into "Do Nothing 'Til You Hear from Me."

In the 1930s, Duke toured extensively, recorded a lot, and experimented with large-scale compositions. His sidemen included new talents: tenor saxophonist Ben Webster brought toughness and lyricism in equal measure, and the tragically short-lived bassist Jimmy Blanton brought a new rhythmic freedom that helped set the bebop revolution in motion in the 1940s. In 1939, pianist and composer Billy Strayhorn joined Duke's entourage, and the two men found they had a natural talent for writing music together. They jointly composed and arranged much of the band's repertoire until Strayhorn's death in 1967.

Ellington's band waned in popularity briefly in the 1950s. But with a remarkable performance of "Diminuendo and Crescendo in Blue," which featured the band's tenor saxophonist Paul Gonsalves, at the 1956 Newport Jazz Festival, Ellington scored a triumph with the public and critics alike, and returned to his position of preeminence. His later orchestras were still built around his star soloists: trumpeters Clark Terry and Cat Anderson, violinist and trumpeter Ray Nance, clarinetist Jimmy Hamilton, and saxophonists Norris Turney, Russell Procope, Harold Ashby, and Harold Minerve, among others.

In his last years, Duke wrote many pieces of sacred music, which he performed in many churches and cathedrals around the world, from London's Westminster Abbey to Grace

Cathedral in San Francisco. He also wrote many other extended suites, inspired by ideas as different as New Orleans music, Shakespeare, and visits to Asia (his *Far East Suite*). When Duke died, his son, trumpeter Mercer Ellington, took over the band until his own death in 1996.

DISCOGRAPHY

Early Ellington: The Complete Brunswick and Vocalion Recordings of Duke Ellington, 1926–1931. MCA GRP 36402 (three-CD set). [67 sides charting the evolution of Ellington's band during its first years at the Cotton Club.]

Early Ellington 1927–1934, RCA Bluebird 86852. [A similar period of Duke's recordings for the Victor label.]

Jungle Nights in Harlem. RCA Bluebird 82499. [More Victor recordings from 1927–32.]

The Duke's Men: Small Groups, Vols. I and II. Columbia 468618, 472994 (both two-CD sets). [Compilation of Duke's small group discs, 1934–39.]

The Blanton-Webster Band. Bluebird 13181 (also RCA 5659-2) (three-CD set). [66 tracks by Duke's important transitional band featuring Ben Webster and Jimmy Blanton.]

Black, Brown, and Beige. RCA Bluebird 86641 (three-CD set). [Tracks from 1944–46, which include two of Ellington's extended suites, the title piece, and the Perfume Suite.]

Ellington at Newport (1956) Complete. Columbia C2K 64932. [1956 Newport Festival set that revived the band's fortunes, newly remastered and in its entirety.]

The Far East Suite. Bluebird ND 87640. [One of Ellington and Strayhorn's most characteristic suites.]

And His Mother Called Him Bill. Bluebird ND 86287. [1967 tribute to Billy Strayhorn, who died that year.]

Second Sacred Concert. Prestige P 24045. [One of the most distinguished examples of Ellington's writing on religious subjects.]

FURTHER READING

Collier, James Lincoln. *Duke Ellington.* New York: Oxford University Press, 1987.

Dance, Stanley. *The World of Duke Ellington.* 1970. Reprint, New York: Da Capo, 1981.

Ellington, Edward Kennedy "Duke." *Music Is My Mistress.* 1973. Reprint, New York: Da Capo, 1976.

Frankl, Ron. *Duke Ellington.* New York: Chelsea House, 1988.

Hajdu, David. *Lush Life.* New York: Simon and Schuster, 1996. [Biography of Ellington's collaborator Billy Strayhorn.]

Hasse, John Edward. *Beyond Category: The Life and Genius of Duke Ellington.* New York: Simon & Schuster, 1993.

Nicholson, Stuart. *Reminiscing in Tempo: A Portrait of Duke Ellington.* Boston: Northeastern University Press, 1999.

Old, Wendie C. *Duke Ellington: Giant of Jazz.* New York: Enslow, 1996.

Stwertka, Eve. *Duke Ellington: A Life of Music.* New York: Watts, 1994.

Tucker, Mark. *The Duke Ellington Reader.* New York: Oxford University Press, 1993.

———. *Early Ellington.* Urbana: University of Illinois Press, 1991.

WEBSITES

http://www.redhotjazz.com/duke.html
Includes links to several discs, filmography.

http:/www.si.edu/aites/exhibits/beyond2.htm
Itinerary of touring exhibit "Beyond Category: The Musical Genius of Duke Ellington" with links to the Smithsonian's main Ellington holdings.

Edward Kennedy "Duke" Ellington

BORN
April 29, 1899
Washington, D.C.

DIED
May 24, 1974
New York, New York

EDUCATION
Armstrong High School, Washington, D.C.

MAJOR INTERESTS
Composing, bandleading, piano

ACCOMPLISHMENTS
Led own orchestra from 1927 to 1974. Compositions include "Mood Indigo," "It Don't Mean a Thing," "Prelude to a Kiss," "In a Mellotone," and "Satin Doll"; longer works include *Black, Brown and Beige, Far East, Latin-American and New Orleans Suites*

MUSEUMS & ARCHIVES
The Duke Ellington Collection is held by the National Museum of American History, Washington, D.C.

HONORS
Frequent *Down Beat* pollwinner in 1950s and 1960s; NAACP Spingarn Medal, 1959; three Grammys for score to *Anatomy of a Murder* (1959). Presidential Medal of Freedom, 1969; French Legion d'Honneur, 1973; numerous honorary degrees and doctorates of music

Cab Calloway

THE HI-DE-HO MAN

Showman, bandleader, singer, and star of musical theater, Cabell "Cab" Calloway rose from modest circumstances to lead one of the highest-paid swing orchestras of the 1930s. His remarkable popularity was broad based and long lasting. This stretched well outside the confines of jazz as he became an all-round popular entertainer during the 1930s and 1940s. Calloway prolonged his widespread appeal when he found a new audience among musical theater enthusiasts in the 1950s and 1960s.

Calloway's father died when Cab was still a child, leaving the family impoverished. Although the young Cab Calloway was intelligent and excelled during his school years at ball games, he preferred the streets and pool halls of Baltimore to formal schooling. As a teenager he typified the streetwise

Cab Calloway fronts his Cotton Club Orchestra in 1942. The line-up includes two musicians who wrote memoirs about their time in the group, bassist Milt Hinton and guitarist Danny Barker.

hustler that he was later to play on stage as the character Sportin' Life in George Gershwin's *Porgy and Bess* (1935). It is often suggested he was the model for the role, and it suited him perfectly.

His older sister Blanche started in show business when Cab was still a young boy, and she cut her first records before he was 18. Partly at her instigation, Cab traveled to Chicago with a touring revue, then decided to forgo any further formal education and stay in the city to teach himself the craft of singing. He developed a highly individual style in which he combined his exceptionally clear diction and robust voice with extremes of range and rapid nonsense syllables. On stage, he moved easily and well, and his natural athleticism helped him to dance in front of a band in a way that quickly drew an audience's attention. On one occasion when he was involved in a "battle of the bands," he saw that his band was in danger of losing, so he reentered the hall by leaping over several chairs and turning somersaults while singing at the top of his voice. This display of outrageous showmanship produced a convincing victory.

Many critics have hailed Calloway's singing as one of the main formative influences in vocal jazz, because his style was so widely imitated. This started soon after the moment in October 1929 that he won a competition at New York's Savoy Ballroom, which led to his fronting, and eventually taking over, a band called the Missourians. Beginning in July 1930, as Cab Calloway and His Orchestra, they made a string of successful records. Soon afterward the band was hired to substitute for Duke Ellington at the Cotton Club in Harlem. During the time when Calloway appeared at this famous New York club, throughout 1931–32 and then for an annual season every subsequent year in the 1930s, he became the most commercially successful African-American bandleader of the age.

He did this first by creating a repertoire of highly individual songs, written for him by such well-known composers as Harold Arlen, Fats Waller, and Harvey Brooks. Many of these contained coded references to the underground world of drugs and sex, disguised under innocent sounding titles like "Minnie the Moocher" and "Kicking the Gong Around," which became immensely popular because of the in-jokes of their lyrics. Second, Calloway created a highly individual stage persona for himself, complete with a costume known as a "zoot suit" that he designed himself. His floppy wide-brimmed hat, flapping trousers, and knee-length jacket were accompanied by a watch with a chain that stretched to the floor. Later he settled

PAN AMERICAN

Calloway in the early 1950s with his two older daughters, Leal (right) and Chris, who still leads a tribute band to her father, keeping his musical legacy alive.

for an off-white evening suit described by one English critic as being "the color of old piano keys." Third, he ensured he had the best possible band to back him up, gradually replacing the original Missourians with younger players who were among the finest musicians

available. He also made the most of the band's frequent broadcasts from the Cotton Club, which brought his singing to a huge audience across the United States, who then went out to buy his records and to hear his live concerts. For its tours, the band often traveled with a full-evening show from the Cotton Club, complete with dancers, singers, and comedians.

Calloway's revue toured in comfort and style, in its own railroad train of Pullman sleeping cars and one that contained Calloway's huge Lincoln automobile. By sleeping in comfort aboard the train, the band avoided the privations of Southern segregated hotels. A short film called *Rail Rhythm*, made in 1934, showed the band traveling on this train.

Throughout the 1930s and early 1940s, Calloway's band contained the finest jazz musicians of the day, including saxophonists Chu Berry, Illinois Jacquet, Hilton Jefferson, and Eddie Barefield; trumpeters Jonah Jones, Dizzy Gillespie, Mario Bauza, and Doc Cheatham; and drummer Cozy Cole. In due course, on the group's record dates, Calloway featured fewer vocals by himself and more solos by his impressive lineup. The band also succeeded in breaking down many of the barriers of racial prejudice, and Calloway was jailed more than once for taking an aggressive stance to defend his own rights and those of his musicians.

Calloway's bandleading career continued during the twilight of the Swing Era, but as it became more and more expensive to keep going, he eventually broke up the band at the end of the 1940s. Shortly afterward, he took up a new career as an actor and singer in musical comedy. He starred around the world as Sportin' Life in *Porgy and Bess* (1952–54), drawing rave reviews from opera and musical critics alike, including a memorable critique of his London theater debut by the English opera expert and critic Lord Harewood. This was a contrast to a 1934 concert by his band in London, when his agitated dance music was greeted with catcalls from the English pit orchestra. In his later years he combined occasional tours as a singer—for which he led a specially assembled band—with returns to the musical stage, including the famous all-black 1967 production of *Hello, Dolly!* and cameo roles in films such as *The Blues Brothers* (1980).

Temperamentally, Calloway was a paradox. His sequence of songs about Minnie the Moocher, which focused on Harlem's drug culture, were wildly successful, despite his own firm antidrug stance concerning his musicians and dancers. He was fond of gambling on horses and of drinking until all hours, but he was a stickler for stage discipline, telling any of his musicians who did not play well after a night on the town, "That was last night—now we're at work!" His stage dances and bandleading gymnastics were the model for other bandleaders of the 1930s, including Lucky Millinder and Tiny Bradshaw, and paved the way for the antics of many a rock and roll singer. His singing influenced many other vocalists, from contemporaries such as Billy Banks, who made some first-rate jazz discs in the 1930s, to more recent rhythm and blues singers like Louis Jordan and Joe Jackson. His legacy lives on in the singing of his daughter Chris, who toured with him often in the 1980s.

DISCOGRAPHY

Kicking the Gong Around. ASV Living Era AJA 5013. [20 tracks by Cab's earliest orchestra from 1930–31.]

Cab Calloway and Co. RCA Jazz Tribune Vol. 58. ND 89560 (two-CD set). [34 tracks by Cab's 1933–34 band, Blanche Calloway's 1931 band, and examples from 1932 of Billy Banks imitating Cab.]

Cruisin' with Cab. Topaz TPZ 1010 [Features a cross section of Calloway's band between 1930 and 1943, including broadcast performances.]

Calloway's complete band recordings to 1941 are issued in ten volumes by the French Classics company, with the following numbers: 516, 526, 537, 544, 554, 568, 576, 595, 614, 625.

Porgy and Bess (Gershwin). CBS S 70007. [Original cast recording with Cab as Sportin' Life.]

Hello, Dolly! RCA GD 81147. [Broadway all-black cast version starring Pearl Bailey and Cab Calloway.]

FURTHER READING

Barker, Danny. *A Life in Jazz.* Alyn Shipton, ed. New York: Oxford University Press, 1986.

Calloway, Cab, and Bryant Rollins. *Of Minnie the Moocher and Me.* New York: Crowell, 1976.

Cheatham, Doc. *I Guess I'll Get the Papers and Go Home.* Alyn Shipton, ed. London and New York: Cassell, 1996.

Hinton, Milt, and David G. Berger. *Bass Line.* Philadelphia: Temple University Press, 1988.

Schuller, Gunther. *The Swing Era.* New York: Oxford University Press, 1989

WEBSITE

http://virginiamusicflash.com/cab.htm

Cabell "Cab" Calloway

BORN
December 25, 1907
Rochester, New York

DIED
November 18, 1994
Cokebury Village, Delaware

EDUCATION
No formal education beyond high school

MAJOR INTERESTS
Singing, bandleading

ACCOMPLISHMENTS
Became a national recording and radio star after taking over leadership of the Missourians, 1930. Cab Calloway's Orchestra became the "highest priced orchestra in the colored show world, drawing $7,000 a week," reported the Baltimore *Afro-American* in 1939. Major hits like "Minnie the Moocher" from 1930, before there were record sales charts; in the chart era, his biggest hit was "Blues in the Night," which made the top ten in 1942. Films include *The Big Broadcast of 1932, Stormy Weather* (1943), *Sensations of '45, St Louis Blues* (1958), *The Blues Brothers* (1980); in the theater, played in *Porgy and Bess* (1952–54), *Hello, Dolly!* (1967)

Benny Goodman

KING OF SWING

No player in the history of jazz has ever surpassed Benny Goodman as a clarinetist. His clear tone with injections of growly excitement, his phenomenally fluent technique, and above all his endless flow of ideas made him the greatest player on his instrument. He could bring a Carnegie Hall crowd to its feet on his final appearances there in the 1980s as effectively as he did almost half a century earlier.

Benny Goodman's meteoric rise to fame is as remarkable as any in jazz, because he grew up in abject poverty in Chicago and created his career on the strength of his talent alone. His parents came from Eastern Europe to the United States in the late 19th century, part of a tide of Jewish migrants anxious about Czarist Russia's anti-Semitic policies. Benny was one of 12 children born after their arrival in the country. His father David scratched a living for himself and his large family, working long hours in the stockyards and later as a tailor, but he took time to ensure that three of his sons, Harry, Freddy, and Benny, took up musical instruments. They played first in the band of their local synagogue and later at a famous Chicago settlement known as Hull House. This was an institution set up to provide for disadvantaged sections of the population, offering tuition in cookery, the arts and—crucially—music. His biographers believe that Goodman, who had started the clarinet at the age of 10, found his inspirational teacher, Franz Schoepp, through the settlement.

Schoepp taught the cream of Chicago's symphonic players, but he also gave lessons to poor black and white students, and Goodman became one of these for about two years around 1920. The lessons gave him a grounding in classical technique. Because of this, and a lifelong commitment to long hours of practice, Goodman seldom had any problems with the technical operation of his instrument; in short, he became a very proficient player before he was properly into his teenage years. At Hull House he played the kind of light classics and concert pieces that most youth bands play. Then in 1921 his family bought a phonograph and he began his lifelong fascination with jazz, when he heard the records of clarinetist Ted Lewis and of the Original Dixieland Jazz Band for the first time.

Before long Goodman was playing jazz himself. Barely out of short pants, he met Bix Beiderbecke and the "Austin High School Gang," cornetist Jimmy McPartland, his banjo-playing brother Dick, and their friends. He was soon dazzling them with his talented playing when they got up bands to play on excursion boats or for local dances. Goodman also

learned from older African-American clarinetists in Chicago, including Jimmie Noone and Buster Bailey, with whom he occasionally shared lessons. In 1925, he set out to Los Angeles to join the band of drummer Ben Pollack. A year later, in December 1926, he made his first records with the Pollack band when it came to Chicago.

Pollack is not one of the best-known figures in jazz, although in 1923 he had been a member of the influential New Orleans Rhythm Kings. His later career involved a tragic decline, spiraling through some years running a "pick-a-rib" restaurant, until he took his own life in 1971. However, in the late 1920s his band was one of the best-known of all white jazz orchestras, with outstanding soloists that along with Goodman included cornetist Jimmy

McPartland and trombonists Jack Teagarden and Glenn Miller. Miller also arranged for the band, as did saxophonist Gil Rodin. After a spell in Chicago, Pollack's group became the house band at New York's Park Central Hotel. At the same time as this residency, they were soon also were playing in a Broadway show and on the radio, and making records. Goodman was suddenly earning more money than all but the very best known stars in jazz. Yet, his success came too late for his father to share, because David Goodman had been killed in a traffic accident a few months earlier. His hardworking father's premature death always haunted Goodman, the years of sacrifice having made possible his musical career and that of his brother Harry, who had joined Pollack as a bassist.

Benny Goodman's 1948 band, a racially integrated group that featured the modern jazz tenor saxophonist Wardell Gray, proved that Goodman was still playing to youthful audiences even as the Swing Era came to an end.

Benny Goodman's first visit to Indianapolis, in May 1939, was sponsored by the Indianapolis Negro Press Club. His interracial quartet, featuring Lionel Hampton, is billed alongside his main orchestra and the singer Martha Tilton.

Goodman did not stay long in Pollack's band. In 1929 he left to spend the next few years as a busy freelancer in the studios and working with cornetist Red Nichols, one of the best-known white jazz musicians in New York at that time. By 1934 Goodman was a veteran recording artist, playing for other leaders as well as making a number of discs under his own name. He hankered to lead his own band, and eventually won the audition to provide a band for a new club called Billy Rose's Music Hall. Thereafter he made more discs and, in December 1934, started a 26-week radio series, *Let's Dance*. During this period of regular work he brought the perfectionist approach of his clarinet playing to the discipline of his orchestra and its musicianship.

The band's discs, particularly those that featured singer Helen Ward, began to sell well, and unbeknown to the band, their radio show acquired a cult following on the West Coast. There it was heard in prime time, owing to the three-hour time difference between California and New York, where it was a late-evening show. The demands of the radio program meant that Goodman was constantly searching for new music to play, which led him to buy some jazzy swing arrangements from bandleader Fletcher Henderson.

After the radio show finished in 1935, the band worked its way to California on a tour that did not do well until it arrived at the Palomar Ballroom in Los Angeles on August 21. Goodman was worried that the tour was going to be a financial disaster, and in place of the smooth dance tunes promoters had required him to play as the band traveled West, he played a set of Henderson's jazz numbers. This was what the crowd expected from listening to the radio shows: their reaction was hysterical, and on a tidal wave of their enthusiasm, Goodman was soon pronounced the "King of Swing" by the press.

From 1936 until 1939, Goodman's band was immensely popular across the United States. Its driving rhythm section, with powerful drummer Gene Krupa and the delicate but swinging piano of Jess Stacy, accompanied trumpeters such as Bunny Berigan, Ziggy Elman, and Harry James, and saxophonists including Bud Freeman, Dick Clark, and Vido Musso. It was, however, Goodman's hot, swinging clarinet and the appealing "girl-next-door" vocals of Helen Ward that underpinned the band's popularity. Ward was eventually replaced by Helen Forrest and later Peggy Lee.

During this period, Goodman decided to showcase his jazz clarinet playing in a small group, originally a trio with Krupa and pianist Teddy Wilson, but from August 1936, a quartet with Lionel Hampton added on vibraphone. Not only was Goodman among the first bandleaders to feature a small group in contrast to his orchestra, but he was the first to feature African-American musicians in an interracial ensemble in live appearances. There had been plenty of examples of mixed bands on recording dates, but Goodman, supported by the enthusiasm of his brother-in-law, the entrepreneur, critic, and record producer John Hammond, pioneered a regular working integrated band. This was also a hallmark of Goodman's landmark concert at New York's Carnegie Hall in January 1938, where members of the Duke Ellington and Count Basie bands joined his own instrumentalists on stage in a rare presentation of swing at a venue famous for classical music.

Success and overwork led Goodman to experience intense back pains in 1940, and he broke up the band to undergo surgery. He was to suffer back problems again, but he regrouped before the year's end, hiring another exceptional big band lineup as well as keeping his interracial small groups going with the mercurial guitarist Charlie Christian and Duke Ellington's former trumpeter Cootie Williams among his recruits.

Although the early 1940s produced some excellent music by Goodman and his band (especially with pianist Mel Powell and drummer Sid Catlett), the military draft, a recording ban imposed by the American Federation of Musicians, and the economic circumstances of the period led Goodman to disband in the mid-1940s. He regrouped in 1947, incorporating many modern jazz or "bebop" musicians in his lineup,

Benjamin David "Benny" Goodman

BORN
May 30, 1909
Chicago, Illinois

DIED
June 13, 1986
New York, New York

EDUCATION
Harrison High School, Chicago; clarinet lessons from Franz Schoepp, band training from James Sylvester at Hull House, Chicago

MAJOR INTERESTS
Clarinet, bandleading

ACCOMPLISHMENTS
Pioneered interracial small groups in his trio and quartet; became the preeminent clarinetist in jazz. Made several films, including *The Big Broadcast of 1937* and *Hollywood Hotel* (1937). Commissioned many classical works, including pieces from Bartok (*Contrasts*, 1939) and Copland and Hindemith, who wrote concertos for him; made many classical discs

HONORS
Frequent *Down Beat* poll winner; New York City's Handel Medal (1966); honorary doctorate from Illinois Institute of Technology (1968); cultural award from State of Connecticut, 1973; citation from New York City mayor John V. Lindsay, 1973

including saxophonist Wardell Gray and trumpeter Doug Mettome, but this orchestra was also short-lived.

For the rest of his life, Goodman led bands intermittently. Much of the time he worked with small groups, only recruiting a big band for special events or tours, like his three State Department–sponsored trips overseas to South America (1961), the USSR (1962), and Japan (1964). Some of his later bands recaptured the fire of his 1930s Swing Era orchestra, but Goodman's own playing altered, taking on a purer, more classical tone, at least in part because he launched a very successful career as a classical soloist. From the late 1930s, he was able to commission new works for clarinet, including Bela Bartok's *Contrasts* (1938) and concertos by Aaron Copland and Paul Hindemith (both 1947). He recorded a number of pieces from the classical repertoire in addition to those works written for him.

From time to time, Goodman took part in reunions, most notably of his famous quartet with Krupa, Hampton, and Wilson; these and his occasional big band appearances kept him active. He never actually retired, but his public appearances slowly became fewer and fewer, although he would call friends to join in his regular practice sessions, still delighting in the classical chamber repertoire as well as small group jazz. When he did appear in public, all his competitive instincts remained intact, and he could still dazzle an audience and his fellow musicians with his technical mastery, proving that he genuinely was the King of Swing.

DISCOGRAPHY

The Complete RCA Victor Small Group Recordings. RCA Victor 09026 68764-2 (three-CD set). [67 tracks by the original Goodman trio and quartet.]

The Birth of Swing (1935–1936). RCA Bluebird ND 90601 (three-CD set). [Charts the rise of Goodman's band from its earliest Victor discs to late 1936.]

Live at Carnegie Hall. Columbia 450983-2 (two-CD set). [The famous Carnegie Hall concert of January 1938.]

Sextet, Featuring Charlie Christian. Columbia 465679-2. [The Goodman small groups with guitarist Charlie Christian.]

Benny's Bop. Hep CD 36. [Mainly broadcast material by Goodman's 1948–49 band, which included several bebop players.]

FURTHER READING

Collier, James Lincoln. *Benny Goodman and the Swing Era*. New York: Oxford University Press, 1989.

Firestone, Ross. *Swing, Swing, Swing: The Life and Times of Benny Goodman*. New York: Norton, 1993.

Rollini, Art. *Thirty Years with the Big Bands*. Urbana: University of Illinois Press, 1987.

Wilson, Teddy. *Teddy Wilson Talks Jazz*. Arie Ligthart and Humphrey Van Loo, eds. London and New York: Cassell, 1996.

WEBSITE

http://www.pbs.org/jazz/biography/artist_id_goodman_benny.htm
Biography and sound file links to Ken Burns's documentary *Jazz*.

Artie Shaw

SYMPHONY IN RIFFS

A lthough Artie Shaw was a clarinetist with a virtuosity that was regarded by many critics as equal to that of Benny Goodman, and although his big band achieved enormous commercial success with hits like "Begin the Beguine," he had a relatively short career in jazz. During the 25 or so years he was an active musician, Shaw experimented restlessly with everything from string orchestras to jazz harpsichords; in the process he introduced some of the most unusual and fascinating tone colors into his swing bands. Like Goodman, he made a stand for racially integrated groups, hiring musicians such as Billie Holiday, Roy Eldridge, and Hot Lips Page to work with some of his many lineups. He was also a man of matinee-idol good looks whose wives included the film actresses Lana Turner and Ava Gardner as well as the novelist Kathleen Windsor. This generated huge amounts of press about him in the gossip columns of the day. He broke up his bands on numerous occasions, seeking privacy and a retreat from the public eye, and finally he retired from music almost completely in the

Artie Shaw fronts his orchestra in 1938, the year of his big hit "Begin The Beguine." Shaw later referred to this hit as "a nice little tune from one of Cole Porter's very few flop shows."

Hollywood screen actress Betty Grable with Shaw in 1939, shortly before he eloped with Lana Turner in February 1940. Grable subsequently married swing bandleader Harry James.

mid-1950s, devoting himself, among other things, to his considerable gifts as a writer.

Shaw was born Arthur Jacob Arshawsky into a Russian Jewish immigrant family in New York City's Lower East Side. His father worked in the garment business, but he lost all his money, forcing the family to move to New Haven, Connecticut, when Arthur was still a young boy. At school there, Arthur was the butt of cruel anti-Semitic attacks, and he turned inward, reading voraciously and listening to music. Although he was not a particularly willing or enthusiastic student, he had considerable powers of self-education. Having decided that he would achieve fame and fortune through music, he taught himself first the saxophone and then the more difficult clarinet. He started playing at the age of 12, and at 15 worked his way home from a visit to Kentucky by playing in a traveling band. On his return, he applied himself to a more formal study of music, which is when he began learning how to arrange and orchestrate. In the late 1920s he played in Cleveland with a band led by Austin Wylie, a violinist, and later in pianist Irving Aaronson's Commanders, with whom he recorded in 1928. By this time he was using the name Arthur Shaw, a recording executive having apparently suggested that "Art Shaw" sounded too much like a violent sneeze.

In due course, Shaw moved back to New York City. After overcoming various setbacks (including having to wait for some months for a union card that would allow him to work), he made a name for himself as a reliable first alto saxophone player in big bands, such as those of Roger Wolfe Kahn and Paul Specht. He also began to show promise as a clarinet soloist, a skill he honed in Harlem jam sessions with the pianist Willie "The Lion" Smith.

In 1933 he dropped out of music for the first time. He spent some months farming in Pennsylvania, as well as trying to write a book about Bix Beiderbecke, who had died in 1931. On his return to New York the following year, he specialized mainly on clarinet and made many recordings as a freelancer, including sessions with the xylophonist Red Norvo and the singer Mildred Bailey, Norvo's wife.

It was the chance to present his own group at a swing concert in June 1936 at the Imperial Theater in New York City that started Shaw's career as a bandleader. Typically, he chose an unusual instrumentation for the time: a string quartet, plus a jazz rhythm section of guitar, bass, and drums, as well as his own clarinet. At the concert, Shaw played only one piece, "Interlude in B Flat," but its success led to him setting up a regular band, which included strings, one saxophone, two trumpets, a trombone, and a rhythm section.

This band made a few recordings, a number of them featuring Shaw's clarinet, the strings, and the rhythm section, which, on pieces like "Streamline," created a new and original sound in jazz. Shaw used his considerable charm and personality to hold together a group that initially got little work but eventually began to achieve popularity, especially through weekly broadcasts from the Roseland State Ballroom in Boston. However, the band with its unusual lineup was not sufficiently popular to hold out commercially against more conventional groups, so it was replaced in April 1937 by a swing band instrumentation that replaced the violins, viola, and cello, with trumpets, trombones, and saxophones.

Shaw had written most of the arrangements for his first band, but in his new lineup he employed Jerry Gray, who had been one of his violinists, to write for him. Gray produced their first big hit, an arrangement of Cole Porter's "Begin the Beguine," in 1938, and for 18 months the band toured and recorded prolifically. It was during this period that Billie Holiday was the band's vocalist, breaking the color bar in a different way from Benny Goodman. While Goodman's interracial trio and quartet appeared as a separate group from his all-white orchestra, Shaw employed Holiday as the singer with his full big band, and he followed this up by hiring many fine African-American instrumentalists within his main lineup.

In late 1939, however, Shaw suddenly told the world he was retiring. He disappeared to Mexico for several months, leaving tenor saxophonist Georgie Auld to lead his former band on the remaining engagements. He returned to the United States halfway through 1940, and in order to fulfill his record contract, he took a band into the studios again, where they made another hit record, "Frenesi." The success of his discs led Shaw to reconsider his decision to retire, and he once more put together a touring band, which this time combined a large string section with a full-size jazz orchestra. Some of their recordings, including his "Concerto for Clarinet," are among his finest work. At the same time, he led a small group called the Gramercy Five (which was a misnomer, since there were generally six, and occasionally seven musicians including Shaw.) In this band, pianist Johnny Guarnieri transferred to the harpsichord, and its spiky, clattery sound combined in a percussive way with the guitar, bass, and drums. Once more, Shaw's ear for an unusual sound caught on with the public, and the sextet's discs, such as "Summit Ridge Drive," became very popular.

Artie Shaw (Arthur Jacob Arshawsky)

BORN
May 23, 1910
New York, New York

EDUCATION
High school in New Haven, Connecticut, where he played in the band

MAJOR INTERESTS
Bandleading, clarinet, writing

ACCOMPLISHMENTS
One of the principal bandleaders of the swing era, and one of the finest virtuoso clarinetists in jazz. A pioneer of featuring African-American musicians in his predominantly white swing bands. Played parts of the classical repertoire with equal skill. Published autobiography, *The Trouble with Cinderella*, 1952, a collection of short stories, *I Love You, I Hate You, Drop Dead*, 1965. Appeared in numerous films, including *Dancing Co-ed* [*Every Other Inch a Lady* in Great Britain] (1939) and *Second Chorus* (1940)

> *"It was the feeling of wanting to play that gave the Artie Shaw band its great punch. The contagion of enthusiasm and inspiration leaps from one musician to catch fire with another, as it did in the case of 'Begin the Beguine.'"*
>
> —Max Kaminsky in My Life in Jazz (1963)

Yet again, Shaw felt the pressure to disband. He broke up both his small group and orchestra, only to re-form in late 1941. His short-lived new group included the brilliant trumpeter Hot Lips Page, who sang and played one of the best-ever versions of the song "St. James Infirmary" with the band. In early 1942, Shaw once again disbanded, this time to join the U.S. Navy, and in due course he became the leader of a service band that entertained troops throughout the Pacific area during World War II. His musicians told of the scenes of wild enthusiasm that greeted their performances for U.S. troops. Eventually, Shaw was released from the navy for health reasons in late 1943 and returned to civilian life.

He led a number of groups in the mid-to-late 1940s and continued to play off and on until about 1955, when he moved to Spain. Some of his last recordings were not issued at the time, and did not appear until the 1990s, by which time Shaw had made a brief return to playing. He performed a few times in the 1980s, then lent his name to a number of re-creations of his earlier groups, some led by Dick Johnson, and one, in London, conducted by himself but featuring clarinetist Bob Wilber playing Shaw's original parts.

Although Shaw had retired more or less for good from music in the 1950s, he offered his perceptive opinions on music in occasional television or film interviews and continued to write books and plays. His autobiography, *The Trouble with Cinderella*, is a particularly shining example of a musician telling his own story in a vivid and absorbing writing style, every bit as distinguished as his fluid sound on the clarinet.

DISCOGRAPHY

In the Beginning. Hep CD 1024. [Collection of Shaw's earliest discs from 1936.]

Begin the Beguine. RCA Bluebird ND 82432. [Anthology by Shaw's best known bands from 1938 to 1941.]

The Complete Gramercy Five Sessions. Bluebird ND 87637. [All the small group recordings from 1940 to 1945.]

Blues in the Night. Bluebird ND 82432. [The best of Shaw's discs with Hot Lips Page and Roy Eldridge as featured trumpet soloists.]

The Last Recordings. Musicmasters 65071-2 (two-CD set). [Shaw's final small groups from 1954.]

FURTHER READING

Kaminsky, Max. *My Life in Jazz*. New York: Harper & Row, 1963.

McCarthy, Albert. *Big Band Jazz*. New York: G. P. Putnam, 1974.

Shaw, Artie. *The Trouble with Cinderella: An Outline of Identity*. 1952. Reprint, New York: Collier, 1963.

Schuller, Gunther. *The Swing Era*. New York: Oxford University Press, 1989.

White, John. *Artie Shaw: Non-Stop Fight*. Hull, England: Eastnote, 1998.

WEBSITE

http://www.artieshaw.com
Official website with biography and links to the current Shaw orchestra, which plays his music with his approval and guidance.

Jimmy Dorsey Tommy Dorsey

THE FABULOUS DORSEYS

Not every big band leader in the 1930s was a brilliant instrumentalist. Cab Calloway, Lucky Millinder, and Bill McKinney, once a drummer, were all conductors rather than players, but both Jimmy and Tommy Dorsey were masters of their instruments. Jimmy was a technically advanced saxophonist, while Tommy combined a smooth trombone ballad style with the ability to play hot jazz solos. Their careers were inextricably linked, although when they led a band together there were frequent fights. Even when each became a bandleader in his own right, they remained mutually respectful, and they finally reconciled at the end of the swing era.

Thomas F. Dorsey, father of Jimmy and Tommy, was originally a miner, but he was musically talented and became director of the Elmore Band in Shenandoah, Pennsylvania, which lies in a valley between the Blue Mountains and the Appalachians, in the heart of a coal mining area. He taught music for a living, specializing in brass instruments.

Very early in life, as soon as their teeth were strong enough for brass playing, both the Dorsey boys began lessons on the cornet. Jimmy was in the Elmore band from the age of seven, and Tommy joined him just a year or two later. Egged on by their enthusiastic father, both boys experimented with several instruments. Jimmy tried the slide trumpet (a kind of soprano trombone) before settling on

The Jimmy Dorsey Orchestra on the set of the 1944 movie *Hollywood Canteen.* The orchestra came to fame during an 18-month stint on Bing Crosby's Kraft Music Hall radio series in 1936–37.

James "Jimmy" Dorsey

BORN

February 29, 1904
Shenandoah, Pennsylvania

DIED

June 12, 1957
New York, New York

EDUCATION

Taught by his father, Thomas F. Dorsey

MAJOR INTERESTS

Clarinet, saxophone, bandleading

ACCOMPLISHMENTS

Reached new technical standards on clarinet and saxophone, becoming one of the most proficient players of the 1920s. Made dozens of freelance discs in the 1920s and 1930s, including "I'm Just Wild about Harry" and "Oodles of Noodles," that were widely imitated. Recorded prolifically with Dorsey Brothers Orchestra and then his own band; 23 Top 10 hits in the United States between 1940 and 1944, including number-one successes "Amapola" and "My Sister and I." Appeared in many movies including *The Fleet's In* (1942), *Lost in a Harem* (1944), and *The Fabulous Dorseys* (1947)

HONORS

Subject of a reconstruction of his band in the show *Jazz Bands Are Back*, Brooklyn Academy of Music, 1980

saxophone and clarinet, while Tommy took up the trombone, although he still played trumpet occasionally throughout his life and could also turn his hand to the clarinet.

Jimmy had a fairly easygoing character; he played in a variety of different styles, and various types and sizes of groups. He was as happy in a symphony orchestra as in a big band, and he was always puzzled when his jazz-playing colleagues found it hard to adapt from one setting to another as easily as he did himself.

By contrast, Tommy had a complex personality, dating from the perfectionism expected of him by his father and his own burning desire to succeed. He could be fiercely loyal to those whose ability he respected, but he often lost his temper and fired musicians irrationally and quickly. When he died, former colleagues were amazed to discover just how many players had passed through his band.

Before they were into their 20s, Jimmy and Tommy had both decided on musical careers, and that they would work together. Despite their training in brass band music and the classics, they wanted to play jazz, and did: first in the Novelty Six and the Wild Canaries, and later in the Scranton Sirens, led by Billy Lustig. They managed to play together for much of the 1920s, ending up in the giant orchestra led by "King of Jazz" Paul Whiteman. On the way, they worked in the California Ramblers, and later in Jean Goldkette's band.

During this decade, the brothers became two of the most prolific freelance recording artists in history. Jimmy made countless sessions with his Goldkette colleagues, of whom the most famous was Bix Beiderbecke. Contemporary reed players were dazzled by Jimmy's prowess. Some of his technical innovations, like the rapid alternation

of different fingerings for the same note to give a variety of tone, became important elements in the technique of players like Lester Young.

Meanwhile, Tommy was already combining a hard-swinging Dixieland style with smooth ballad playing. He did not think of himself as primarily a jazz player, and later happily stood aside to let others play hot jazz solos. Yet his ability was highly regarded. As well as playing on many of Beiderbecke's discs, he also appeared on several interracial recording sessions, including some with the famous Billy Banks Rhythmakers. He cut his best trumpet records in the late 1920s, and was sometimes mistaken for King Oliver.

Both brothers occasionally fronted pickup studio bands, but in the spring of 1934 they put together a full-time big band of their own: the Dorsey Brothers Orchestra. In June 1935, a violent quarrel flared up between the brothers, resulting in Tommy stalking off the bandstand more or less for good. Jimmy took over the reins, leaving Tommy to form his own orchestra.

In its short life, the Dorsey Brothers Orchestra achieved some important innovations. Its arranger, Glenn Miller, was already trying to achieve a unique sound. Miller wrote for an unorthodox lineup of one trumpet, three trombones, and three saxes, which produced a slightly muddy ensemble, with all the instruments in a similar range, but it led to some convincing "big band Dixieland," an idea that appealed to the band's singer, Bob Crosby. Mercilessly criticized by Tommy Dorsey for not being as good as his famous brother Bing, Bob adopted this Dixieland style when he left to lead his own orchestra. Tommy himself created a band-within-a-band, the Clambake Seven, to play small-group Dixieland as part of his act and on recordings.

> *"Working with Tommy Dorsey was like working on a hot stove that might explode at any moment—and always did."*
>
> —Max Kaminsky in *My Life in Jazz* (1963)

Aside from Benny Goodman, few other white bands were really trying to play hot jazz in the manner of the great black orchestras at this time. The Dorsey Brothers Orchestra's discs suggest it played a big part in ushering in the Swing Era, and in opening up the market for other white swing bands.

The split of the brothers' orchestra created one of the most promising such Swing Era bands under Tommy's leadership. Initially it was primarily a dance band, but its versatility was important. While Jimmy followed a more commercial route, Tommy's band could play jazz as hot as anything around, while his ballad playing and an astute choice of vocalists gave him a string of best-selling hits. Tommy always hired jazz players as the core of his band, even though he built his reputation around ballads like his theme tune "I'm Getting Sentimental Over You." This led to his nickname "the Sentimental Gentleman of Swing."

Tommy insisted on punctuality in his musicians, and he was also particular about the band uniforms, in which he invested equal portions of pride and money. There were blue uniforms for matinees and brown uniforms for the evenings. Pianist Joe Bushkin turned up late and hung over for one matinee still wearing the brown suit from the night before. As he slid onto the piano stool, Dorsey stopped the band and announced acidly: "You *used* to play for us."

In the early 1940s, Tommy hired a singer who rapidly shot to stardom. All Frank Sinatra's best early discs were cut with the band, and he later attributed his relaxed ballad singing style to imitating the smooth sounds of Tommy's trombone. Dorsey also recruited arranger Sy Oliver from Jimmie Lunceford's orchestra to inject vigor into the band. This was an inspired move, and with Oliver's help, Dorsey recruited new sidemen capable of playing Oliver's demanding charts.

When Sinatra left, Oliver himself took over singing duties and brought in other star African-American musicians like trumpeter Charlie Shavers, creating one of the best mid-1940s big bands and a model of interracial cooperation. Like many other bands of the time, Tommy experimented with string sections and "orchestral" effects, but he retained the potent combination of swing and sentiment that had brought him success, helped by the spectacular jazz drumming of Buddy Rich from 1939 to 1942.

Jimmy Dorsey continued to lead the band that he had originally fronted with his brother. He had a number of hits, although these featured his star vocalists Helen O'Connell and Bob Eberle rather than his own virtuoso reed playing. Nevertheless, Jimmy remained interested in all technical advances in saxophone playing, marveling at the innovations of bebop pioneers like Charlie Parker and

Thomas "Tommy" Dorsey

BORN

November 19, 1905
Shenandoah, Pennsylvania

DIED

November 26, 1956
Greenwich, Connecticut

EDUCATION

Taught by his father, Thomas F. Dorsey

MAJOR INTERESTS

Trombone, trumpet, bandleading

ACCOMPLISHMENTS

Many freelance sessions, 1920s–early 1930s, including playing trumpet with guitarist Eddie Lang. Formed band with brother Jimmy, 1934; own band, 1935. First chart hit of nearly 200 was "Treasure Island" with vocalist Edythe Wright, 1935; others included "Marie," "Song of India," "Indian Summer." Frank Sinatra's many hits with the band included "Polka Dots and Moonbeams," "I'll Never Smile Again" (1940). Briefly involved in music and magazine publishing; owned a ballroom. Worked for Mutual Radio Network, mid-1940s, later had own CBS-TV series. Movie appearances include *Ship Ahoy* (1942), *Broadway Rhythm* (1944), *A Song Is Born* (1948), *The Fabulous Dorseys* (1947)

Frank Sinatra, who sang with the Tommy Dorsey band from 1940 to 1942, is flanked by Tommy Dorsey on his left and Jimmy on his right.

DISCOGRAPHY

Dorsey Brothers Orchestra

Harlem Lullaby. Hep CD1006. [Studio sessions from 1933 under both brothers' names before they founded their full-time orchestra.]

Jimmy Dorsey

Contrasts. MCA GRP 16262. [The best of Jimmy's own orchestra from after Tommy's departure, with tracks from 1936–43.]

Tommy Dorsey

Yes, Indeed! Bluebird ND 904499. [An excellent cross section of Sy Oliver's arrangements for the band, 1939–45.]

The Music Goes Round and Round. Bluebird ND 83140. [A wider-ranging anthology, 1935–47.]

The Post-War Era. Bluebird 07863 66156-2. [The best of Tommy's work, 1946–50.]

FURTHER READING

Bockemuehl, Eugene (Gene Bockey). *On the Road with the Jimmy Dorsey Aggravation 1947–49.* San Diego, Calif.: Gray Castle, 1996.

Kaminsky, Max. *My Life In Jazz.* New York: Harper & Row, 1963.

McCarthy, Albert. *Big Band Jazz.* New York: G. P. Putnam, 1974.

Sanford, Herb. *Tommy and Jimmy: The Dorsey Years.* 1972. Reprint, New York: Da Capo, 1980.

Schuller, Gunther. *The Swing Era.* New York: Oxford University Press, 1989.

Simon, George T. *The Big Bands.* 4th edition. New York: Schirmer, 1981.

Stockdale, Robert L. *Jimmy Dorsey: A Study in Contrasts.* Lanham, Md.: Scarecrow, 1999.

WEBSITES

http://www.redhotjazz.com/jimmy.html

http://www.redhotjazz.com/tommy.html

Connected sites with brief biographies and many recording links.

commissioning arrangements from Dizzy Gillespie.

The press fueled the story of the feud between the brothers, who only occasionally appeared together in public until 1947, when they reunited for the movie *The Fabulous Dorseys.* This forced them to cooperate in a straightforward "bio-pic" (with a splendid brief appearance by Art Tatum) on the same formula as the recently released Benny Goodman and Glenn Miller stories.

As the Swing Era drew to a close, each Dorsey led his own band into the early 1950s. Economic pressures eventually forced them to reunite in May 1953 as the "Tommy Dorsey Orchestra featuring Jimmy Dorsey." Three years later, Tommy, who for much of his career had given up his formidable drinking habit to focus on successful bandleading, choked to death in his sleep. Jimmy kept things going on his own for a few months longer until he succumbed to cancer, handing the orchestra over to Lee Castle during his final weeks.

Jimmy Dorsey's main reputation was made in the 1920s, and his lightning skills on clarinet and alto sax influenced almost all the first generation of jazz reed players. Later, his influence waned, although he never lost his formidable instrumental talent. History has been kinder to his brother Tommy, partly because of the greater jazz content throughout his work, and partly because of his immensely influential approach to ballad playing.

Count Basie

ROMPIN' AT THE RENO

Although Count Basie was a remarkably talented pianist in the bustling New York "stride" style of men like James P. Johnson and Fats Waller, as a bandleader he pioneered one of the most economical piano techniques in jazz, often adding no more than a few sparse chords to the smooth forward motion of his rhythm section. His piece "The Kid from Red Bank," which commemorates the area in New Jersey where he was raised, has an uncharacteristically athletic piano part, perhaps recalling his earliest years as a pianist.

William "Count" Basie's birthplace was within striking distance of New York City, and as a youth he came under many of the same influences as his contemporary Thomas "Fats" Waller, who lived across the Hudson River in the Harlem area of New York itself. Early in their careers both men played (at different times) for the same vaudeville acts. Waller instilled in Basie his lifelong love of the organ by encouraging Bill to sit alongside him at the console of the

Trumpeter Buck Clayton takes a solo with Count Basie's band at the Famous Door, New York, in July 1938. In 1936, Clayton had returned from a two-year stay as a bandleader in Shanghai when he met Basie in Kansas City and was recruited to join the band.

Count Basie brought the competitive jam session atmosphere of Kansas City to New York by taking on other swing bands, such as Chick Webb's Orchestra, in public "battles."

instrument in Harlem's Lincoln Theater, where Waller was the resident musician from his early teens.

By the early 1920s, Basie could hold his own among the elite group of Harlem stride pianists, and right through his life he could still outplay virtually any challenger in the style—even such virtuosi as Oscar Peterson. However, whereas most such pianists stayed around New York City to play for rent parties, Basie followed his vaudeville instincts and went on the road with a series of revues, those of singers Katie Crippen and Gonzelle White among them. There he learned the crafts of showmanship and how to work an audience first hand. When Gonzelle White's show arrived in Kansas City, Basie stayed there due to illness. When he set about restarting

his theater career, he came to realize that he could be a valuable asset to the "territory bands" based in the city. These were big bands with evocative names that toured the South and Midwest, playing for provincial audiences far from the big cities of New York and Chicago, and they developed a hard-swinging style that was largely independent of developments in those cities.

Before long Basie was in Dallas with bassist Walter Page and the Blue Devils. Then he spent a number of years working with Bennie Moten, either in Moten's own band, or leading a second band under Moten's name in places like Little Rock, Arkansas. When Moten died during a tonsillectomy, Basie—assuming the nickname "Count"—took over many of the musicians and incorporated them into his

William "Count" Basie

BORN
August 21, 1904
Red Bank, New Jersey

DIED
April 26, 1984
Hollywood, California

EDUCATION
Left school after junior high; took piano lessons from Mrs. Vandevere in Red Bank, New Jersey

MAJOR INTERESTS
Bandleading, piano

ACCOMPLISHMENTS
Led one of the longest-lived and most consistent big bands in jazz history; brought the "Kansas City sound" to New York City, incorporating a strong blues feeling. His later band was a model of precision playing, adorned by his own minimal piano style; their performances of "One O'Clock Jump," "Jumpin' at the Woodside," "Doggin' Around," "Jive at Five," and "Blue and Sentimental" epitomized the Basie sound and were widely imitated. Backed many singers, notably Jimmy Rushing, Helen Humes, and Joe Williams

HONORS
Won many *Down Beat* critics' and readers' polls for big band throughout the 1960s

"He'd pit two different people against one another to keep things going. He was one of the first bandleaders to start two tenors battling each other."

—Marshal Royal in *Jazz Survivor* (1996)

own band, which began broadcasting from the Reno Club in Kansas City. At this point, Kansas City was a wide-open town with an administration that actively encouraged nightclubs, dance halls, and the consumption of alcohol. There were countless small clubs, and several prestigious larger ones, among which there was plenty of opportunity for musicians. The city developed a keen competitive atmosphere among players, who would meet for long competitive jam sessions known as "cutting contests," at which players tried to assert their supremacy over one another. Most of the most successful jam session players wound up in Basie's band.

Their radio broadcasts from the Reno were heard by critic and record producer John Hammond. With his assistance, Basie's band, including its star soloists tenor saxophonists Lester Young and Herschel Evans, trumpeter Buck Clayton, and a rhythm section of guitarist Claude Williams, bassist Walter Page, drummer Jo Jones, and Basie himself, hit the road for a national tour. Once the band had finally arrived in New York City by late 1936, with a Decca recording contract and a residency at the Roseland Ballroom, it made a huge impression and became one of the country's leading big bands.

Basie made the most of the contrasting styles of his saxophonists: the bustling hot style of Evans versus the laid-back clarity and beauty of Lester Young's playing. The band was one of the first to feature two tenors alongside one another, recreating some of the excitement of those long after-hours jam sessions the band had enjoyed at the Reno. There were soon competitive tensions in the trumpet section as well, when Buck Clayton was joined by Harry "Sweets" Edison. The trombone soloists included Vic Dickenson, Dicky Wells, and Eddie Durham, who was also a pioneer of the electric guitar in jazz.

In a short time, Basie was a star. His "all-American rhythm section," which soon included guitarist Freddie Green along with Walter Page and Jo Jones, redefined the sound of the big band, and his recordings like "One O'-Clock Jump" and "Jumpin' at the Woodside" sold well. In true Kansas City style, the band also featured singer Jimmy Rushing, who had worked the same circuit as Basie himself. Rushing specialized in the robust type of blues, sung loudly over the band and known as blues shouting. He was also a fine ballad singer and included the occasional protest song in his repertoire, such as "It's the Same Old South." In the studios, Basie proved his versatility with a sequence of small-group sides by his Kansas City Five or Seven.

Basie kept his orchestra going right through the 1940s, scaling down to a smaller group in the early 1950s but soon reestablishing a big band at a time when the economic climate made this a tough proposition. This new group—known as Basie's "New Testament" band—radically altered the history of large jazz orchestras again, with the innovations of trumpeter Joe Newman and saxophonists Frank Foster and Frank Wess playing just as important a part in 1950s jazz as Basie's pioneering band had done in the 1930s. This time, the main achievement was the seamless incorporation of modern jazz or bebop soloists into the swing formula of the rhythm section, coupled with a phenomenal discipline among the brass and reed sections which made a 15-piece group sound almost like one person in its ability to phrase and breathe.

So well drilled was Basie's band, it was frequently used as the perfect accompaniment for jazz singers like Ella Fitzgerald and Sarah Vaughan as well as popular stars like Tony Bennett. It played in films, providing soundtracks, or hilarious takeoffs, as in Mel Brooks' spoof cowboy movie *Blazing Saddles* (1974).

Basie lived on the road, and his autobiography is very largely a catalog of his travels. Just like Louis Armstrong, he overcame illness to resume a tough touring schedule in his last years. His last concerts were conducted from a wheelchair, but he never gave up his touring life, a habit born early in his career when he opted for the vaudeville circuit in preference to the safety of New York City. He died in California after taking ill during a concert in Vermont.

DISCOGRAPHY

The Original American Decca Recordings. MCA GRP 36112 (three-CD set). [All the discs made for Decca in the band's first recording contract, 1937–39.]-

The Essential Count Basie, Vols. 1–3. Columbia 460061, 460828, 461098. [Three albums covering the best of Basie's work for Columbia, 1939–41.]

Brand New Wagon. Bluebird ND 82292. [1947 recordings that feature many of the original band plus newer soloists, including tenor saxophonist Paul Gonsalves.]

The Complete Atomic Mr. Basie. Roulette CDP 7932732. [The finest recording by Basie's "New Testament" band, 1957.]

Fun Time. Pablo 2310-945. [A late edition of the band at the Montreux Festival, 1975.]

FURTHER READING

Basie, Count, as told to Albert Murray. *Good Morning Blues: The Autobiography of Count Basie.* London: Heinemann, 1986.

Clayton, Buck. *Buck Clayton's Jazz World.* New York: Oxford University Press, 1986. [Autobiography of Basie's star sideman of the 1930s.]

Dance, Stanley. *The World of Count Basie.* 1980. Reprint, New York: Da Capo, 1985.

Royal, Marshal, with Claire P. Gordon. *Jazz Survivor.* London and New York: Cassell, 1996. [Autobiography of a key member of the "New Testament" band of the 1950s.]

Sheridan, Chris. *Count Basie: A Bio-discography.* Westport, Conn.: Greenwood, 1986. [Major reference book with details of every session recorded by Count Basie.]

WEBSITE

http://www.geocities.com/Bourbon-Street/5491/cbasie.html
Lengthy biography plus audio links.

Ella Fitzgerald

FIRST LADY OF JAZZ

Until the arrival of Ella Fitzgerald on the jazz scene in the 1930s, singers with jazz bands had stuck meticulously to the melody and lyrics of their songs and relied on their accompanying musicians to create whatever jazz content was needed. With her debut, such an approach to singing immediately seemed stale and old-fashioned, for here was a singer who treated her voice like a musical instrument, and who was as inspired an improviser as the best jazz soloists of her day. She bent notes, altered melodies—and often the lyrics themselves—sometimes scurrying off into a sequence of nonsense syllables or "scat" singing, as her ideas poured forth in her beautiful, clear voice.

Like so many jazz and blues musicians, Ella Fitzgerald was born in the southern United States and went on to make her career in the North. She was born in Virginia, at Newport News, but her father was gone from the family, either dead or permanently away from home, before she was three years old. Her mother, Tempie, moved with Ella to find work, settling in the suburb Yonkers, New York, in the valley that runs north from Manhattan.

From early in her career, Ella Fitzgerald was able to sell out concert halls all over the world, as she did for this appearance with tenor saxophonist Illinois Jacquet.

Ella Fitzgerald at Café Society, New York, in July 1951. At the time of this performance, Fitzgerald was on the verge of international stardom, and she would soon launch her professional relationship with Norman Granz and Verve records.

"Fitzgerald makes melodies . . . soar through skies of aural heaven. Her voice, even on first hearing, is quite the loveliest in all music."

—Will Friedwald in *Jazz Singing* (1990)

Yonkers was then, and still is, a contradictory place. The buildings that peep through the trees overlooking the Hudson River are large houses, built in the local clapboard style, with all the trappings of the prosperous suburbs of White Plains and Bronxville, which also lie on commuter railroads north of Manhattan. By contrast, below them, inland from the river, is the sprawling town where Ella grew up, surrounded by a poor neighborhood made up of Spanish, Italian, and African-American communities. This is where Ella attended public school and it is also where her half-sister Frances was born in 1923.

Ella took part-time jobs while she was still in school, since her mother's work as a laundress paid very little. However, at 16 she began to win talent competitions as a singer, the most prestigious of them being at the famous Apollo Theater in Harlem. She seemed well on the road to success when suddenly her mother died. This left Ella shuttling between an aunt in Harlem and an orphanage, just as her career was beginning. She was unable to complete the documentation for her first radio contract because she was too young to sign it herself, and she had no legal representative who could sign for her.

She did not always win contests. One at another Harlem theater, the Lafayette, ended in disaster when her accompanist did not follow her into a change of song, and played the wrong part to back her up. Yet before long, the bandleader Tiny Bradshaw, who featured her at the end of his shows on the touring circuit of African-American theaters, was able to introduce her as "the girl that's been winning all the contests." Then, famously, those members of the audience who were putting on their hats and coats were seen to take them off again and slowly sit to hear Ella's miraculous voice.

Fortunately, soon after this, her talents were spotted by Bardu Ali, who was a dancer, singer, and master of ceremonies at the Savoy Ballroom in Harlem, where drummer Chick Webb led a big band. Bardu, whose own act included chasing half-clothed girls around the stage with a whip, persuaded Chick to take Ella on as his singer, and after she traveled with the band to play a dance at Yale University and won the hearts of the students, she joined the band permanently.

Chick Webb himself had conquered adversity to become one of the most respected drummers and bandleaders in jazz. Injured in a childhood fall, he suffered from tuberculosis of the spine, which left him unable to grow properly and suffering from progressive paralysis. The diminutive bandleader was enchanted by Fitzgerald. To allow her to work with his band while she was still only 17, Webb became her legal guardian. This proved to be a mutually beneficial relationship.

Chick Webb had extraordinary musical gifts. Not only was he a brilliant drummer whose solos combined technical proficiency with great showmanship, but he had a phenomenal musical memory that allowed him to remember entire arrangements. He could hum any of his band parts from memory. His orchestra was very well disciplined, because he could immediately spot any deviations from the written charts. He employed star soloists, like the trumpeters Taft Jordan and Mario Bauza and the trombonist Sandy Williams. In this company, Fitzgerald flourished, learning the trade of big band singing from one of the finest leaders in New York. In the many "battles of bands" that the Savoy staged to draw in audiences, Webb usually won, and Ella was one of the weapons in his arsenal.

When Webb died suddenly in 1939, Fitzgerald took over the band, which she ran for three years before deciding she would work mainly as a solo singer. Following a number of hit records that she had made with Webb, her career looked very promising, but what elevated it from modest success to international stardom was largely the work of two people.

One was Milt Gabler, a record producer at Decca and also the proprietor of the Commodore jazz label, who lavished unusual care on Fitzgerald's recordings, as he also did for artists such as Louis Armstrong. The other was Norman Granz, the impresario who came up with the idea of the touring Jazz at the Philharmonic concerts and owned the Verve record label.

Launched by the acclaim she received from Granz's concerts, which toured all over the world, and supported first by a series of successful records first on the Decca label, then by a series on Verve, Fitzgerald became a world-famous star. Her best-known and -loved discs are a series of albums called "songbooks" on which she interprets the songs of particular composers. First accompanied by Buddy Bregman's orchestra, then by that of Nelson Riddle, Fitzgerald made albums of songs by Gershwin, Cole Porter, Rogers and Hart, Harold Arlen, and many others, including Duke Ellington. On the Ellington record she was accompanied by Duke himself.

Fitzgerald's career continued to be a whirlwind tour of the world's stages, concert halls, and recording studios until failing sight gradually slowed down her career in the 1980s; she retired in the 1990s. She was married at various times, notably to bassist Ray Brown, who played in her accompanying trio in the early 1950s.

What distinguished Fitzgerald's singing from that of her contemporaries was her faultless diction, her perfect sense of pitch, the sweetness of her voice, and her ability to improvise like a saxophonist or trumpeter. Like Louis Armstrong, she reached a public far beyond those who were interested in jazz. Her ability to interpret the great repertoire of popular songs made her a household name, and she is regarded as one of the greatest singers of the 20th century, as well as the preeminent jazz vocalist.

DISCOGRAPHY

The Early Years. Decca GRP 2-618 (two-CD set). [Recordings from 1935–37 during the time Fitzgerald sang with Chick Webb's band, which later became her own.]

Pure Ella. MCA GRP 16362. [Fitzgerald with pianist Ellis Larkins in a CD reissue of two of her greatest albums from the 1950s, including *Ella Sings Gershwin*.]

Best of the Songbooks., Verve 519804-2. [Anthology from the 18-CD set of Fitzgerald's complete songbooks, covering Arlen, Gershwin, Mercer, Rodgers and Hart, Kern, Porter, Berlin, and Ellington.]

Ella and Louis Again, Vols, 1 and 2. Verve 825373-2 and 825374-2. [1957 meeting of Fitzgerald and Louis Armstrong, offering a fascinating comparison of their vocal styles.]

Ella Swings Lightly. Verve 517535-2. [Fitzgerald with a cross section of West Coast jazz musicians in 1958.]

FURTHER READING

Friedwald, Will. *Jazz Singing*. 1990. Reprint, New York: Da Capo, 1996.

Gourse, Leslie. *The Ella Fitzgerald Companion: Six Decades of Commentary*. New York: Schirmer, 1998.

Haskins, Jim. *Ella Fitzgerald: A Life Through Jazz*. London: New English Library, 1991.

Kliment, Bud. *Ella Fitzgerald, Singer*. New York: Chelsea House, 1988.

Nicholson, Stuart. *Ella Fitzgerald*. London: Gollancz, 1993.

WEBSITE

http://www.geocities.com/meggledy

A fan site, but with a very full biography and discographical information.

Ella Fitzgerald

BORN
April 25, 1917
Newport News, Virginia

DIED
June 15, 1996
Beverly Hills, California

EDUCATION
Benjamin Franklin Junior High School, Yonkers, New York

MAJOR INTEREST
Singing

ACCOMPLISHMENTS
Became a celebrity through the popularity of her early discs like "A-Tisket, A-Tasket" (1938) and "Undecided" (1939). Leading her own band and as a soloist, she became recognized as the leading singer in jazz from the early 1940s, a position she held until her retirement in the 1990s. Several discs in *Billboard* charts during the 1940s. Principal member of Norman Granz's Jazz at the Philharmonic touring concert shows, and for three decades produced a sequence of first-rate discs, most of her songbook albums making the U.S. charts. Appeared in several films including *Pete Kelly's Blues* (1955), *St. Louis Blues* (1958), and *Let No Man Write My Epitaph* (1960)

HONORS
Won *Down Beat* readers' and critics' polls as leading singer for many years, including an unbroken run from 1953 to 1970; Grammy Award in 1980; honorary doctorate from Yale in 1986

Billie Holiday

LADY DAY

Billie Holiday is remembered by her millions of fans as one of the finest of all jazz singers, although her heartfelt interpretations of songs fall at the opposite end of the spectrum from Ella Fitzgerald's joyous improvisations. This is because Holiday was also one of the most sublime interpreters of the blues. Many people feel that to sing the blues effectively the singer must have firsthand experience of pain and sadness. Holiday's life was tinged with constant sadness, and she made every performance sound as if she had lived through the melancholy lyrics of the songs.

"Mom and Pop were just a couple of kids when they got married," she says at the start of her autobiography. "He was eighteen, she was sixteen, and I was three." In fact this was not quite true: her parents were never married, and her father, Clarence Holiday, who played guitar in big bands like McKinney's Cotton Pickers and Fletcher Henderson's Orchestra, left home soon after she arrived. Billie began her life as an impoverished child in a one-parent family, with her mother struggling to pay the bills by working as a maid

Billie Holiday, with guitarist Jimmy McLin, in the studio on April 20, 1939, when she recorded one of her best-known songs, "Strange Fruit." Columbia declined to record the melancholy song, but Milt Gabler the owner of the small label Commodore gladly agreed to the studio session.

> *"Billie Holiday was working opposite us, sounding so good like her heart was breaking on every tune. She was a rowdy, big hearted, soulful woman; carried round a pair of those little dogs you put sweaters on."*
>
> —Hampton Hawes, pianist

Billie Holiday
(Eleanora Fagan, Elinore Harris)

BORN
April 7, 1915
Philadelphia, Pennsylvania

DIED
July 17, 1959
New York, New York

EDUCATION
Little or no formal schooling

MAJOR INTEREST
Jazz and blues singing

ACCOMPLISHMENTS
Made dozens of recordings, 1933–59; through long association with pianist Teddy Wilson and later with Verve, her discs fall into two main periods: her youthful, joyous recordings, and her later more worldly tracks; wrote or co-composed many songs, including "Fine and Mellow," "God Bless the Child," "Billie's Blues," "Lady Sings the Blues," "Don't Explain," and "Our Love Is Different"

HONORS
U.S. commemorative postage stamp, 1994. Plays about her include *Lady Day at Emerson's Bar and Grill* by Lanie Robertson, *Yesterdays* by Reenie Upchurch, *Lady Day* by Stephen Stahl, and Archie Shepp's avant garde *Lady Day—A Musical Tragedy*; inspired poems by Frank O'Hara and Langston Hughes, and several novels

many miles from their home in Baltimore, where they had settled when Billie was still an infant. As a consequence, Billie—who was known at that time by various spellings of her first name, Elinore and Eleanora, and the last names of her mother and her occasional stepfather, Harris and Fagan—ran wild. She was sent to an institution, where she was treated cruelly, and after she left, aged only 12, she began working as a prostitute.

It seems that it was then, while in her very early teens, that she started to sing in public in Baltimore, but her career began in earnest when she followed her mother to New York City a year or two later. By then, she had learned many of the songs made famous by the discs of Louis Armstrong, among others. These were what she sang when she began to appear in various Manhattan clubs, such as the Nest or Pod's and Jerry's.

Holiday was exceptionally good looking, and because she was truly a remarkable singer, she became famous as she moved from table to table in these small clubs collecting tips. While she was singing at the Harlem club Smalls' Paradise, she was heard by the entrepreneur John Hammond, who quickly recognized her talents and arranged for her to make some recordings with his friend and future brother-in-law, Benny Goodman.

Before long Billie Holiday was a popular fixture at the Apollo Theater and was making discs with Teddy Wilson's band. These were so-called race records, aimed at the African-American audience, through jukeboxes as well as in millions of African-American homes. Between 1935 and 1940, Billie performed on a substantial number of these recordings, many of them featuring solos by Count Basie's sidemen Lester Young and Buck Clayton, and they became recognized as exceptional, finding a public far beyond the race market.

On some records she sang the blues. On others, she interpreted jazz songs, but all of them revealed her as a great singer with a unique voice. With Young she also formed an abiding friendship, and their deep affection for each other is evident on many of the discs. Young was also responsible for her nickname, "Lady Day." The recordings stand out from those made by other singers of the period partly because of Holiday's skilful interpretations of the lyrics and partly because of the perfect balance between her singing and the contributions of the jazz soloists. She did not sing "scat" choruses, using the "instrumental" approach of Ella Fitzgerald. Instead, she subtly altered the timing of her lyrics—a pause here, a slight speed-up there—to bring out new levels of meaning in what she sang. She also minutely altered the pitch of the melodies, making each one seem as if it was her own personal statement rather than a tune written by another composer. Several of the

Billie Holiday in 1947 with her dog "Mister." Holiday's dogs were a source of solace throughout her often-difficult life.

drove her in his own car to engagements, he eventually capitulated by hiring the white singer Helen Forrest, who gradually took over the singing duties. Holiday finally left after refusing to use the kitchen entrance to the Lincoln Hotel in New York City, where she was appearing with Shaw's band. Her experiences of racial prejudice gave a bittersweet quality to what was to become her most famous song, "Strange Fruit," on the subject of a Southern lynching.

Holiday was always at home on stage at the Apollo, playing to a black audience, and she was to become equally at home in the Café Society, run by Barney Josephson as a racially integrated club. She could still an audience with the power of her singing, and her stage presence, with a gardenia in her hair and a white dress down to the floor, was mesmeric. Offstage she was easily identifiable by the fact she would often carry a pet chihuahua under her arm.

In 1941, when Holiday married her first husband, Jimmy Monroe, after a succession of lovers, a shadow was cast over her life that never truly disappeared. Monroe, who was a fashionable man about town, smoked opium. He introduced Holiday to the drug. She had always smoked a little marijuana, and she liked to drink, but opium led her quickly to heroin. She was soon addicted, and the rest of her life was a battle against narcotics. The large sums of money she made all disappeared after drugs, cures, loans to friends, and high living took their toll.

From time to time, Holiday kicked her habit or had it under control. In 1947, she was sent to prison for possession of heroin. When she reemerged, the New York City police would not

songs she made famous she either wrote or co-wrote herself.

In 1937 she toured with Count Basie's band. The following year, in a pioneering move, she became the first African-American female singer to tour with a white band, the orchestra led by Artie Shaw. Working with Shaw meant that Holiday often encountered racism on the road and in theaters and dance halls. She was barred from several of the hotels and restaurants that the band used. Although initially Shaw campaigned hard for her rights and

issue the cabaret card she needed to appear in clubs, and so she had to appear in big venues, record, or travel, to make a living.

Her new manager and lover, John Levy, managed to get her work at one New York club, the Ebony, but this was an exception. Often her subsequent appearances were tinged with notoriety. She was arrested again with Levy for possession of opium. The court believed she had been framed by Levy, whom she at one point had intended to marry and occasionally referred to as her husband. Once more, she reemerged, picked up her career, and toured Europe, as well as making a series of recordings for Norman Granz's Verve label. These lacked some of the vigor and life of her early discs with Teddy Wilson, although most of them featured the quicksilver piano of Oscar Peterson, but Holiday's experiences had brought a world-weary timbre to her voice that made it attractive in a different way from her youthful recordings.

In Europe she was greeted by an adoring public, and during her second marriage, to Louis McKay, whom she married in Mexico in 1957 after finally divorcing Monroe, she achieved some measure of fame and stability. But in 1959, separated from McKay after she once again returned to drug use, she died in the hospital, alone and almost penniless. To raise some money, she had collaborated with journalist William Dufty to write her life story, *Lady Sings the Blues,* which was later filmed with Diana Ross as Holiday. The 1972 movie is a highly fictionalized account of Holiday's life, but it does accurately reflect that despite appalling hardships and self-imposed problems with narcotics, she managed to become one of the best-loved singers in jazz history.

DISCOGRAPHY

The Quintessential Billie Holiday, Vols. 1–9. Columbia 450987-2, 460060-2, 460820-2, 463333-2, 465190-2, 466313-2, 466966-2, 467914-2, 467915-2. [All of Holiday's Columbia recordings. 1933–42, under her own name and with Teddy Wilson.]

The Complete Original American Decca Recordings. MCA GRP 26012 (two-CD set). [Discs made between 1944 and 1950.]

Lady in Autumn. Verve 849434-2 (two-CD set). [Anthology drawn from her final years, covered in full on a 10-CD set, *The Complete Billie Holiday on Verve 1945–1949* (Verve 517658-2).]

FURTHER READING

Chilton, John. *Billie's Blues.* London: Quartet, 1975.

Clarke, Donald. *Wishing on the Moon: The Life and Times of Billie Holiday.* New York: Viking, 1994.

Gourse, Leslie, ed. *The Billie Holiday Companion: Seven Decades of Commentary.* New York: Schirmer, 1997.

Holiday, Billie, with William Dufty. *Lady Sings the Blues.* 1956. Reprint, London and New York: Penguin, 1992.

Kliment, Bud. *Billie Holiday.* New York: Chelsea House, 1990.

Margolick, David. *Strange Fruit: Billie Holiday, Café Society, and an Early Cry for Civil Rights.* New York: Running Press, 2000.

Nicholson, Stuart. *Billie Holiday.* London: Gollancz, 1995.

Vail, Ken. *Lady Day's Diary.* Chessington, England: Castle, 1996.

WEBSITE

http://www/pbs.org/jazz/biography/artist_id _holiday_billie.htm

Biography, music samples, and links to Ken Burns's documentary *Jazz.*

Lester
Young

"THE PRESIDENT"

Holding his tenor saxophone out at an unusual 45-degree angle, wearing a porkpie hat on his head and an immaculate pinstripe suit, with an other-worldly expression in his eyes, Lester Young cut a memorable figure. His wistful, light, airy saxophone solos combined great melodic beauty with technical facility in equal measure and were quite unlike those of any saxophonist who preceded him. Although he was briefly with Fletcher Henderson's Orchestra, it was Young's association with Count Basie that brought him to public attention and provided a launch pad for his subsequent solo career, which became progressively tinged with tragedy.

Like his old friend Billie Holiday, Young's latter-day playing seemed to express his world-weary experience of life, and its haunting beauty was at odds with his own self-destruction through alcohol. Yet his playing touched the hearts of many fans around the world, and he was often

Lester Young demonstrates his unorthodox method of holding the tenor sax at a jam session in the Village Vanguard club, New York, in December, 1940.

voted into top place in listeners' polls. His technical innovations, along with those of Coleman Hawkins, paved the way for modern jazz.

Although Young was born in Woodville, Mississippi, he spent his first 10 years growing up in and around the musical melting pot of New Orleans. His father, Willis Handy "Billy" Young, was a member of one of the city's close-knit musical families, and like most of his cousins, played several instruments. In due course, Lester joined a band led by his father that was mainly made up of family members, and they toured widely, even after the family moved first to Memphis and then to Minneapolis. Lester began by playing drums, then moved to alto saxophone. His brother, the drummer Lee Young, remembered that Lester never bothered to learn the correct way of holding drumsticks, and he was slow to learn to read music, preferring to rely on his acute musical ear. Eventually, challenged by his father to play a score from sight, and failing, he went off and taught himself to read fluently. The boys' father was a stern taskmaster, and although even as a child Lester was unwilling to conform to discipline, the experience of working in a family environment steeped in music rubbed off on him.

In due course, Lester made the transition to tenor saxophone, but not before he had started to make a reputation for himself on the alto. Later colleagues who heard him in those early days say that his alto style had a harder tone and more "bite" to it than his subsequent mellow sound on the tenor. Interestingly for an African-American player, Young's role models were white. Chief among them were alto saxophonist Jimmy Dorsey and Bix Beiderbecke's colleague Frank Trumbauer, who played the hybrid C-melody saxophone, which has a higher pitch than the tenor. Both players were dazzlingly proficient and introduced innovations in fingering and speed of execution. Perhaps

because Young had been an altoist himself, and because he enjoyed the playing of these two saxophonists, his tenor sound always had something of an alto feel about it. It was clearer and cleaner than that of most of his contemporaries, and his reputation as a man with an original sound began to spread when he joined the territory band known as the Thirteen Original Blue Devils in 1932.

The following year, Young settled in Kansas City, where he played in a variety of bands but also took part in the same free and easy musical atmosphere that had launched Count Basie's career. Like many Kansas City players, Young reveled in the all-night jam sessions that allowed him to unfurl his ideas in chorus after chorus of imaginative improvisation. He even joined Basie's first band at the start of 1934, but in late March he left to travel to New York City and play with Fletcher Henderson. Although some critics raved about his unusual sound, Henderson's band members hated it, and instigated a whispering campaign against Young. Always a sensitive character, the saxophonist was deeply hurt and left the band to return to Kansas City, working his way by playing with a few other orchestras en route.

Although Young was given to mixing startling profanities into his ordinary speech, he was a gentle soul who retreated into a private language or resorted to drink and marijuana when faced with criticism. His personal argot became part of jazz legend, and many of his terms and nicknames for fellow musicians were widely adopted. Billie Holiday, for example, became "Lady Day," while trumpeter Harry Edison was nicknamed "Sweets." His association with both these musicians began when he returned to New York City as a member of Count Basie's Orchestra in the final weeks of 1936.

On his way to New York, when the band stopped off in Chicago, Young cut his first discs, with a small group

Lester Willis Young

BORN
August 27, 1909
Woodville, Mississippi

DIED
March 15, 1959
New York, New York

EDUCATION
Little formal schooling, but thorough musical education from his father, bandleader Willis Handy Young

MAJOR INTEREST
Tenor saxophone

ACCOMPLISHMENTS
His first recorded solos, "Lady Be Good" and "Shoe Shine Boy," became widely imitated by jazz saxophonists all over the United States. A star soloist in Count Basie's band; influenced the beginnings of modern jazz through his fluent improvisational style, light tone, and solo technique, using fragments of melody rather than harmonies as the starting point for improvisation. Adorned numerous records by Billie Holiday and Teddy Wilson with remarkable solos; went on to be a touring soloist and bandleader, still capable of playing with exquisite beauty and imagination up until his early death

HONORS
Won *Down Beat* poll, 1944; *Esquire* silver award 1945, 1947; posthumously elected to *Down Beat* Hall of Fame

Members of the Count Basie and Bob Crosby band jam together in 1941. The two tenor saxophonists in the center are Eddie Miller and Lester Young, wearing a hat.

known as Jones-Smith Incorporated, which was a quintet of Basie musicians. His inventive solos on these recordings were the first of many that he was to record with Basie, and Young's playing became one of the stellar attractions of Basie's full band. In it, he was paired with his friend and fellow tenor player Herschel Evans. Their contrasting styles were displayed in tenor "battles" between the two players—Evans's blustery sound, which owed a lot to Coleman Hawkins, making Young's ethereal solos sound even more radically different from the rest of the band's robust playing.

From January 1937 until December 1940, when he abruptly left Basie,

Young was a star soloist in one of the finest big bands of the period. In addition, he appeared on many small-group records with Teddy Wilson and Billie Holiday among others, his close friendship with Holiday adding an emotional depth to their work together. This period was the high point of his personal and professional life.

After leaving Basie, Young struck out on his own, leading a band and later sharing the leadership of a second group with his brother Lee. This lasted for a year or two before Young rejoined Basie in 1943. Within the organizational fold of Basie's group, Young's eccentric personality found a niche. He dressed with the same snappy style

> "*Lester's greatest contribution was to widen immeasurably the very horizons of jazz creativeness: melodic invention.*"
>
> —Rudi Blesh in *Combo USA* (1971)

as his fellow musicians, contributed his outstanding solo playing to the band's discs, concerts, and club dates, talked his highly personal type of slang, and indulged in alcohol and soft drugs as a palliative for time spent traveling or waiting to play music. He was also married at this point, for the second time in his life, and kept his relationship going despite the late hours kept by Basie's band.

This harmony was shattered when on September 30, 1944, he was drafted into the U.S. Army. His personality was unable to come to terms with the discipline and structure of army life, and the triumph of winning the *Down Beat* poll that year as best saxophonist was blotted out within weeks by a humiliating court martial and subsequent period of imprisonment for drug offenses.

By the end of 1945, Young was a free man. He returned to playing, but was never the same again. His playing took on an increasing sense of foreboding and melancholy, his once-clear tone often sounding husky and plaintive. He generally worked as a soloist, either with local rhythm sections or in touring shows like Norman Granz's Jazz at the Philharmonic packages, where he was one of a string of featured players backed by Oscar Peterson's trio or a similar high-profile group.

From 1946 until 1957, Young made regular tours for Granz, earning a considerable amount of money and retaining his popularity with a public who were often hearing live jazz for the first time. Yet Young himself became increasingly disillusioned. His marriage broke up after he left the army, and subsequent relationships were stormy. He spent much time living in lonely hotel rooms with only his tenor sax, a phonograph, and a bottle of whisky for company. He saw other players such as Stan Getz and Paul Quinichette adopt his style and become stars, and he saw modern jazz players like Charlie Parker adapt his ideas into a new style of jazz altogether. For a sensitive man like Young, this was hard to bear.

He was frequently hospitalized, often because of his addiction to alcohol, and although he could summon up some of his old enthusiasm for returns to playing, always facing the outside world in smart suits and with well-cut hair, his outer neatness concealed a soul in turmoil. In the spring of 1959, an ill and broken man, he made one last effort, appearing for a season in Paris. His playing on his last recordings from that visit shows his unique musical imagination had survived, but that was almost all. Within 24 hours of landing on American soil, he was dead. In his own mind, he had been overtaken by younger players, although all of them would have unhesitatingly acknowledged that they owed a huge amount to him, and that for them he would always be, in his own words "the Pres"—president—among saxophonists.

DISCOGRAPHY

Count Basie: The Original American Decca Recordings. MCA 36112. [Three-CD set of Young's earliest work for Basie.]

Count Basie 1939, Vols. 1 and 2, and *Count Basie 1939–1940.* Classics 513, 533, 563. [These three CDs contain Young's other work from the Basie period, including the Kansas City Five and Seven small groups on which he plays clarinet.]

The Quintessential Billie Holiday, Vols. 3, 4, 5, 6, 8, and 9. Columbia 460820-2, 463333-2, 465190-2, 466313-2, 467914-2, 167915-2. [These contain Young's best work for Billie Holiday and Teddy Wilson.]

Lester Young: The Master Touch. Savoy SV 0113.

Lester Young: The President Plays. Verve 831 670.

Lester Young: Pres and Teddy. Verve 831 270 [Final collaboration with Teddy Wilson, 1956.]

FURTHER READING

Buchmann-Møller, Frank. *You Just Fight for Your Life: The Story of Lester Young.* New York: Praeger, 1990.

Gelly, Dave. *Lester Young.* New York: Hippocrene, 1984.

Porter, Lewis. *Lester Young.* Boston: Twayne, 1985.

WEBSITE

http://www.pbs.org/jazz/biography/artist_id_young_lester.htm

Site with life story, music links, and connections to Ken Burns's documentary *Jazz*.

Coleman Hawkins

THE FATHER OF THE TENOR SAXOPHONE

The image of a tenor saxophonist is a commonplace way to represent the whole idea of jazz. The instrument is so widespread throughout the music that its sound and appearance are synonymous with the music itself. This is largely due to the impact of one man: Coleman Hawkins. He took the tenor saxophone from being a novelty instrument in the early 1920s and made it into a strong, individual solo voice. His full, rounded tone and rhapsodic improvisations, based on the harmonic structures of the pieces he played, became the model for the majority of jazz saxophonists in the 1930s.

From the 1940s onward, at a time when the lighter tone and melodic phrasing of Lester Young had an influential effect on many of the first modern jazz saxophonists, Hawkins adapted his own playing in different ways to become a convincing modern jazz soloist himself. His sure-footed harmonic knowledge enabled him to keep pace with the chordal innovations of musicians such as the pianist

Tenor saxophonist Coleman Hawkins plays with his young trumpeter Miles Davis, who began sitting in with him at the Downbeat club on 52nd Street, New York City, when Hawkins's regular trumpeter, Joe Guy, failed to show up.

"Almost all of the recordings he made throughout a 45-year period were outstanding examples of improvisation, but among them were masterpieces by which all tenor saxophone solos will forever be judged."

—John Chilton in *Song of the Hawk* (1990)

Coleman Randolph Hawkins

BORN
November 21, 1904
St. Joseph, Missouri

DIED
May 19, 1969
New York, New York

EDUCATION
Industrial and Educational Institute, Topeka, Kansas

MAJOR INTEREST
Tenor saxophone

ACCOMPLISHMENTS
Joined Mamie Smith's Jazz Hounds to tour the United States while still a teenager, playing C-melody saxophone. Recorded with Fletcher Henderson, August 1923; joined Henderson's band, 1924–34. Became the most influential tenor saxophonist in jazz during the 1920s and 1930s with a string of records for Henderson and as a freelancer. In 1939, made famous disc of "Body and Soul"; subsequently worked as bandleader and soloist. Made pioneer bebop recordings in 1944; took a bebop band to California in 1945; continued to tour and record until the late 1960s

Thelonious Monk and the trumpeter Miles Davis, both of whom played in his band, and he had already developed formidable speed in his playing. He spent the last two decades of his life as a celebrated international soloist, touring the world.

Hawkins' study of music began early. He grew up in St. Joseph, Missouri, where his parents made sure that he had lessons on the piano and cello. When he was nine, Coleman was given a C-melody saxophone, and this became his major instrument. He told friends that until that time his mother had had to lock him in his room to practice, but once he had the saxophone, she had to tear him away from it to take breaks for meals and sleep. He began playing popular songs with a small group of young musicians in and around St. Joseph when he was not much more than 12 years old. Not long after, when he was attending the Industrial and Educational Institute in Topeka, Kansas, about 80 miles from home, he began playing cello and saxophone in a band organized by Jesse Stone, later a famous big band arranger and composer and a pioneer of rhythm and blues.

The Topeka institute was similar to those attended by musicians such as Teddy Wilson in Tuskegee, Alabama, and Dizzy Gillespie in Laurinburg, North Carolina. It offered African-American students a broad-based education with a strong vocational emphasis. Music was encouraged at these colleges, and Hawkins developed well on both cello and saxophone, which his mother had initially encouraged him to leave at home.

From Topeka, Hawkins often traveled to Kansas City to play his saxophone. It was there in 1921 that he first played in the band led by blues singer Mamie Smith. He impressed all the members of this traveling vaudeville ensemble with his musicianship, and the following year, when they passed through Kansas again, the young Hawkins joined the band, Mamie Smith agreeing to become the 17-year-old's legal guardian.

Hawkins stayed with Mamie Smith's Jazz Hounds for about a year, appearing in vaudeville theaters from New York to California as the band worked its way across the country. He also cut his first records, although on most of them it is hard to pick out his playing. Then, in 1923, he became a freelancer in New York, and before long met Fletcher Henderson, who hired Hawkins to play tenor sax in his orchestra. Hawkins's tenure from 1924 until 1934 in Henderson's high-profile band saw him progress from the jerky, almost ragtime-influenced saxophone style of the early 1920s to his full-toned, free-improvising style of the following decade. Hawkins was at the cutting edge of musical development during those years. Indeed, not only was he always capable of playing whatever style was currently popular, but for most of his time in Henderson's band

On his return from Europe, Hawkins took a nine-piece band into this famous club, one block from 52nd Street. During this residency, he recorded his solo "Body and Soul," which became a best-selling disc and was hugely influential.

he was largely responsible for instigating the current fashion.

This was partly due to the fact that Henderson's musicians spent a considerable amount of time making records. Through recording, Hawkins's stylistic developments reached a wide public, far beyond the New York crowds that clustered to hear the band, first at the Club Alabam, and then at the Roseland Ballroom. He was in Henderson's orchestra at the same time as Louis Armstrong, and he was one of the first musicians to transfer Armstrong's fluid musical lines and rhythmic freedom to the saxophone successfully. In a string of remarkable solos, from "The Stampede" in 1926 to "Can You Take It?" in 1933, Hawkins developed his abilities to construct logical and impressive solos, exploring the underlying harmonic structures of each tune and packing his playing with a strong

emotional content. He also produced compositions for the band, some of them incorporating unusual scales and harmonies as further evidence of his restless musical imagination.

By 1934 Hawkins had established himself as a star, and he decided to leave Henderson and strike out on his own. Unusually, he decided to do so by traveling to Europe, having been engaged as a soloist by English bandleader Jack Hylton. He was to spend five years in Europe, playing not only in England but in France, Holland, Belgium, and Switzerland, and in most cases appearing as a star soloist. This gave him valuable playing experience open to few of his contemporaries who had remained in the United States in various big bands. Whereas the average big band soloist got to play a few measures here and there in a whole evening of playing, Hawkins—often working with just piano, bass, and drums—played for hour after hour, and this developed his talents to a formidable extent.

When he returned to the United States in 1939, he cut his famous disc of "Body and Soul," perhaps the most famous tenor saxophone solo in jazz. From that point onward he worked either as a bandleader or as an individual star, and never returned to the ranks of another leader's band.

In the mid-1940s, as the modern jazz ideas of Dizzy Gillespie, Charlie Parker, and Thelonious Monk took hold of the New York scene, Hawkins enthusiastically incorporated them into his work. He formed a succession of groups that included bebop musicians, and organized some recording sessions that featured Dizzy Gillespie and Max Roach. Hawkins himself never wholly absorbed all the stylistic nuances of bebop, not least because his own highly personal approach to jazz was so well formed by the mid-1940s. Nevertheless, he managed to command the respect of all generations of musicians with the passion, intensity, and sheer musicality he brought to his playing.

Like many players of his generation, he toured with Norman Granz's Jazz at the Philharmonic shows, and he made records as a freelancer with Count Basie, Duke Ellington, and a host of other leaders. He was popular on the international festival circuit, and for some time in the 1950s co-led a band with trumpeter Roy Eldridge, who matched him for competitive instinct and originality. By the 1960s, he generally worked as the leader of a quartet, and was a popular attraction in New York City, Chicago, and London.

Throughout his life, Hawkins had great style, and he never lost the Fletcher Henderson Orchestra's habit of dressing well and fashionably, coupled with what was, for the most part, a charming manner. He was well versed in all kinds of music, and had a large collection of classical records. It came as something of a shock to those who knew him that in his last few years, possibly because he had become bored with jazz, he let some of these high standards slip, growing a straggly beard and becoming increasingly dependent on alcohol. He retreated to his apartment, only being tempted out to play an occasional concert or tour, and on each appearance seeming weaker and older than the one before. Despite contracting pneumonia on a tour to Europe, he rallied and produced some fine recordings, but the end was close. Hawkins never fully recovered from the rigors of that last tour, dying of malnutrition and the effects of pneumonia not long afterward.

DISCOGRAPHY

Coleman Hawkins 1929–1934, 1934–1937, 1937–1939, and *1939–1940.* Classics 587, 602, 613, 634. [These offer a cross section of the saxophonist's best work from his Fletcher Henderson days (although not with Henderson's own band), through the European period, and beyond his triumphant return to the United States with "Body and Soul."]

Hawkins' work with Henderson can be found on the first 12 Classics volumes listed in the discography with the Fletcher Henderson profile earlier in this chapter.

Body and Soul. RCA Bluebird ND 85717. [Hawkins' sessions from 1939 to 1956.]

Hollywood Stampede. Capitol B21Y-92596-2. [Modern jazz experiments with trumpeter Howard McGhee.]

The Genius of Coleman Hawkins. Verve 825673-2. [Hawkins in 1957 with the Oscar Peterson Quartet.]

The Hawk Flies High. OJC 027.

Hawkins! Eldridge! Hodges! Alive! At the Village Gate. Verve 513755-2. [A good example of Hawkins' collaboration with Eldridge from 1962, with the added bonus of Ellington alto sax star Johnny Hodges.]

FURTHER READING

Chilton, John. *Song of the Hawk: The Life and Recordings of Coleman Hawkins.* London: Quartet, 1990.

McCarthy, Albert. *Coleman Hawkins.* London: Cassell, 1963.

WEBSITE

http://www.redhotjazz.com/hawkins.html
Short biography with picture and music links.

More Swing-Band Leaders and Soloists to Remember

To many Americans, **Paul Whiteman** (1890–1967) was the King of Jazz, and his ponderous big band the archetypal swing orchestra. Son of a prominent Denver musician, Whiteman initially became a symphonic viola player. In the Navy during World War I, he began leading a band that provided dance music for evening events. This inaugurated his successful career as a bandleader. He claimed to have discovered jazz by hearing a street band in New Orleans led by "Stalebread" Lacoume, and as the 1920s began, Whiteman's band incorporated jazzy syncopations into its dance repertoire. At its best, in the late 1920s, with musicians like Bix Beiderbecke, Frank Trumbauer, and Eddie Lang in its ranks, Whiteman's orchestra recorded some convincing jazz. More often it was a huge, unwieldy band that played stuffy dance music. Nevertheless, Whiteman left an enduring legacy, because in addition to his best jazz discs, he initiated the style of arranging that was developed by Fletcher Henderson and Duke Ellington, and commissioned stimulating music from several contemporary American composers. The best-known such piece was George Gershwin's *Rhapsody in Blue*, which the composer played with Whiteman's band at the New York premiere in 1924.

Many of the finest jazz players who joined Whiteman's band also worked in one or more of the orchestras organized from Detroit by the entrepreneur **Jean Goldkette** (1899–1962). Although Goldkette had trained as a classical pianist, his talent was in managing bands, and the groups he assembled to tour the Midwest, especially his "Victor Recording Orchestra," were always good and often exceptional. The Dorsey Brothers and Bix Beiderbecke worked for Goldkette. From his base at Detroit's Graystone Ballroom Goldkette also helped to manage McKinney's Cotton Pickers, the city's legendary African-American big band. Another of his ventures, a group called the Orange Blossoms, became one of the most famous jazz orchestras of the 1930s when renamed the Casa Loma Orchestra, under the leadership of one of Goldkette's former sidemen, saxophonist **Glen Gray** (1906–63).

McKinney's Cotton Pickers was a band renowned for tight discipline and clever arrangements. In addition to a stable and talented regular personnel, it owed much of its sound to two exceptional directors, **Don Redman** (1900–64) and **Benny Carter** (born 1907). Both men had also worked for Fletcher Henderson, and used McKinney's as an extension of their ideas about transferring the flowing melody lines of an individual soloist to the brass and reeds of a full

jazz orchestra. Carter went on to lead his own small groups and big bands, and is recognized as one of the major instrumental and arranging talents in jazz. He played all the reed instruments as well as trumpet, but specialized on alto saxophone. He was still winning Grammy awards for his compositions and arrangements when well into his 80s.

Trumpeter Doc Cheatham heard McKinney's Cotton Pickers on a primitive radio set while he was in Europe, thousands of miles away from Detroit, and vowed that this disciplined ensemble was the band he wanted to join; he did so after his return to the United States. Cheatham had been on tour with a band led by **Sam Wooding** (1895–1985). Originally formed to accompany a touring revue called the Chocolate Kiddies, Wooding's band spent many years in Europe, in 1925–27 and again in 1927–31. It

brought authentic African-American jazz for the first time to audiences from Istanbul to Barcelona (where the band recorded) and also played for long seasons in Berlin and Paris. Among Wooding's stars were trumpeter **Tommy Ladnier** (1900–39) and clarinetist **Garvin Bushell** (1902–91), who wrote a wry and witty memoir of his experiences. His musicians were treated like royalty in Europe, so Wooding had no inclination to return to the United States. When he did so, after the onset of the Great Depression, he found popular tastes had moved on, and he was never able to regain his position as a popular bandleader. He eventually broke up his band in 1935. He returned to music school and, after becoming a teacher, led gospel choirs and founded his own record label.

Drummer **Chick Webb** (1909–39) had a brief career for a different reason.

Swing Era stars jam at the Hickory House in New York in 1938. The stick-juggling drummer is Lionel Hampton, and the other musicians are, from left to right, Marty Marsala, Joe Bushkin, Artie Shapiro, Ray Biondi, and Joe Marsala.

He contracted tuberculosis of the spine, which restricted his growth and finally made him too ill to play. He is regarded as one of the finest drummers and bandleaders of the swing era. In addition to fronting the house band at New York's Savoy ballroom for much of the period from 1927 until his death in 1939, he employed Ella Fitzgerald in 1934 to sing with the band. Their records and broadcasts became widely popular, but musicians and Harlem audiences knew that Webb's real skill was to vanquish all challengers in the "cutting contests" held at the Savoy. In these events, the crowd voted for the band that outplayed all others, and Webb was consistently able to defeat challenges from virtually every other band of the day.

Lionel Hampton (born 1909), also a master of the cutting contest, began his career as a drummer in Chicago. After moving to California and earning the billing the "world's fastest drummer," he took up vibraphone and the piano, which he played using two fingers like vibraphone mallets. Hampton was recruited to play in Benny Goodman's quartet in 1936. He became internationally famous, not least for a series of informal record dates he led in which he corralled members of many famous big bands into jamming together in front of a microphone, spurred on by the relentless power of his own playing. He continued to tour and record through the 1990s.

Among the players recruited by Hampton for his recordings was alto saxophonist **Johnny Hodges** (1907–70). For the bulk of his career, from 1928 until his death, Hodges played in Duke Ellington's orchestra (apart from a few years in the early 1950s), also leading small groups from Ellington's band on a series of discs of his own. These have a less spontaneous feel than Hampton's studio sessions, but display Hodges' flawless tone, mastery of fast swing tempos, and above all his skill as a blues player. He was the dominant altoist in jazz until the advent of modern jazz, or bebop, and the arrival on the scene of Charlie Parker.

The swing trumpeter **Roy Eldridge** (1911–89) is generally regarded as the musical link between Louis Armstrong and the modern jazz innovations of Parker's contemporary, Dizzy Gillespie. Eldridge was a formidably competitive player, a trait that he later used to his advantage as a soloist with the touring Jazz at the Philharmonic concerts of the 1940s and 1950s. He gained his experience in the big bands of Teddy Hill and Fletcher Henderson, then began leading his own band in Chicago, which broadcast across the United States and featured his fiery, energetic trumpet playing. He went on to join the swing bands of Gene Krupa and Artie Shaw. Other important swing trumpeters included two men who both worked in the Benny Goodman Orchestra, **Bunny Berigan** (1908–42) and **Harry James** (1916–83).

Perhaps the swing band most admired by other musicians (even those who grudgingly referred to its disciplined section players as "trained seals") was the orchestra of **Jimmie Lunceford** (1902–47). He was a well-schooled musician who valued precise musicianship combined with slick presentation. The innovative arrangements of his trumpeter **Sy Oliver** (1910–88) created atmospheric effects—a typical example is his "Organ Grinder Swing," which used celesta (a keyboard instrument played with hammers) and woodblocks. The band broke up after Lunceford died from food poisoning at Seaside, Oregon, but by then Oliver had moved to the Tommy Dorsey band, and Lunceford's creative originality was on the wane.

The majority of the large swing orchestras ran into financial trouble in the years following the end of World War II in 1945. Some of the biggest names, like Duke Ellington, kept going. Count Basie and Cab Calloway scaled down their bands, and other leaders like Artie Shaw and Benny Goodman only led their bands intermittently. One leader who kept going throughout the 1940s was reed player **Woody Herman** (1913–87). His "Band That Played the Blues," and the First and Second "Herds" that followed, marked a slow but significant integration of the modern jazz style of bebop into the sound of a big swing band, following the pioneering work of Dizzy Gillespie, who wrote arrangements for Herman. Star soloists with the band included saxophonists Stan Getz, Zoot Sims, Al Cohn, and Serge Chaloff (nicknamed the Four Brothers) and its most celebrated arrangements were written by Neal Hefti, Ralph Burns, and Shorty Rogers. In the years that followed, the various bands of **Stan Kenton** (1911–79) experimented further with the fusion of classical instrumentation, Cuban rhythms, and progressive ideas about writing and arranging. Although not all these experiments bore fruit, many of his bands made exceptional records, combining outstanding soloists with the hard-swinging values of an earlier era.

Virtually every swing band employed a female singer. Ellington featured **Ivie Anderson** (1905–49), Shaw hired Billie Holiday, and Goodman featured several vocalists, of whom **Helen**

Ward (1916–98), who sang with his 1934–36 band, was the most popular. She cultivated a "girl next door" image that sat easily with her accomplished grasp of the music itself. Especially popular with college students, she was one of the first jazz singers to break through to success with the youth culture of the 1930s.

One of Helen Ward's successors with Goodman was **Mildred Bailey** (1907–51), who had earlier sung with her then-husband, vibraphone player **Red Norvo** (1908–99), the pair earning the title "Mr. and Mrs. Swing." Bailey was among the first white singers to master the inflections of African-American song, and to mix blues feeling with jazz improvisation. Whether singing "scat" nonsense lyrics or tenderly delivering the words of a ballad, Bailey epitomized the sophisticated blend of popular song, jazz, and the blues that was at the heart of the big band swing era.

Mildred Bailey in a publicity shot for her hit song "Rockin' Chair."

Teddy Wilson said of Art Tatum's hands: "they could go out to any distance he needed, almost as if they were made of rubber, he was so relaxed and fluid in his playing."

3 The Piano Giants

In many ways, the story of jazz piano is a microcosm of the story of the development of jazz itself. The pianists who played in pioneer jazz bands kept abreast of every new fashion in the music, so that they could fit effectively with brass or reed soloists. What they played when let loose on their own often mirrored the music they were used to playing in an ensemble setting. In spite of this development, the solo jazz piano tradition stands just a little to one side of the main history of jazz, and has a rich and rewarding story of its own.

The transition from ragtime to early jazz is most apparent in the work of pianists that is preserved on piano rolls, on early discs, and in notated sheet music. It was only a few steps from the jaunty, syncopated ragtime of Scott Joplin to the more subtle swing of Jelly Roll Morton's piano pieces such as "The Pearls" or "Grandpa's Spells," yet Morton's music is undeniably jazz. It has a freer rhythmic feeling, the left-hand beat is more varied, and there is a sense of improvised melody lines in his flowing right-hand figures that is absent in the angular tunes of Joplin's best-known rags. Morton later transferred many of his compositions to arrangements for an entire band, but some, notably "Finger-buster" (or "Fingerbreaker"), are such virtuoso displays of piano technique they have remained firmly inside the solo piano repertoire.

It was not only New Orleans pioneers like Morton who influenced jazz piano. There were two hugely significant types of solo keyboard style that matured in the cities of Chicago and New York. These were boogie woogie and stride, respectively. In Chicago, players like Meade "Lux" Lewis, Albert Ammons, and Jimmy Yancey developed a rolling style called boogie woogie. It did not begin in Chicago but grew up all over the South and Midwest. Yet almost all the key players migrated to Chicago, and it was there that the style really took hold. Boogie woogie is rooted in the blues, and so the most common form of boogie composition is based on the standard 12-measure blues, but with a regularly repeated bass line. Some of these bass lines are built on a slow, single-note pattern called an "ostinato." Others have rolled or repeated chords, which gave rise to the style's Southern nickname, "the horses," because of the relentless "galloping" sound of the player's left hand. Many boogie woogie pieces imitate

IN THIS PART

ALBERT AMMONS

FATS WALLER

EARL HINES

MARY LOU WILLIAMS

TEDDY WILSON

ART TATUM

OSCAR PETERSON

the sound of trains—Meade "Lux" Lewis's "Honky Tonk Train Blues," for example—and there is almost always a sense of urgency and movement about the style.

As thousands of African Americans from the South and Midwest poured into Chicago during the 1920s, many of them into overcrowded housing, the social conditions were right to foster a form of entertainment limited to solo piano. This was the so-called rent party, at which a family who lacked the money to pay the rent would host a party, charging admission to pay for a pianist, food, and drink, and keeping the profits to pay the landlord. Pianos were quite common in tenement buildings, and boogie woogie developed as a powerful crowd-pleasing style that would cut through the hubbub of a party, keep people entertained, and be suitable for singing and dancing. The singing was generally the blues, and the dancing could take place at any tempo provided by the pianist.

Just such a social tradition grew up in New York City as well, especially in Harlem, where there had been a similar influx of rural African Americans; by 1920, housing built for 60,000 was accommodating 300,000. However, the music played at rent parties in Harlem was different from Chicago boogie woogie. Stride, as it came to be known, was superficially closer to ragtime, partly because many of its inventors were themselves originally ragtime pianists—the so-called Eastern ragtimers from the coast between the Carolinas and New York. These included men like Eubie Blake from Baltimore, James P. Johnson from New Jersey, New Yorker Fats Waller, and Willie "The Lion" Smith, who was born in Goshen, New York, and raised in Newark, New Jersey.

Instead of the rolling ostinato left-hand patterns of boogie woogie, these stride players took the "oompah" bass of ragtime and developed it. They stretched their left hands beyond a simple octave to 10ths and 13ths on the keyboard, inserting subtle countermelodies alongside the walking or "striding" alternation of a bass note on beats one and three of a measure, and a chord on beats two and four. Furthermore, they created intricate right-hand phrases intended to form a kind of improvisational language that could be put together in a variety of contexts to form dazzlingly effective solos.

The Harlem stride players took much of their inspiration from classical pianists, whereas the Chicago boogie woogie musicians were inspired by the heart and soul of the rural blues. Between these twin stylistic poles, the solo jazz piano tradition of the 1920s and 1930s developed, providing a platform for new ideas. Some of these ideas included Earl Hines transferring to the keyboard the linear improvised melodies of brass and reeds in his "trumpet" style of piano playing; Teddy Wilson taking this a stage further into his sparse, single-line melodies that paved the way for bebop; and Art Tatum bringing the virtuoso technique of the concert pianist into jazz improvisation, without ever losing the compelling swing and energy of stride.

Albert Ammons

A LEFT HAND LIKE GOD

here has been plenty of speculation as to why it was that boogie woogie took quite such a strong hold over piano jazz and blues in 1920s Chicago. Certainly the impact of Alabama-born Clarence "Pine Top" Smith, both in person and in his 1928 recreation on disc of a characteristic rent party piece, "Pine Top's Boogie Woogie," was important. So was the playing of other musicians like Cripple Clarence Lofton, who dominated the rent-party scene from about 1917, and "Cow Cow" Davenport, who arrived in the city in 1925 from the touring theater circuit. Yet there seems to have been something in the feel of Chicago itself that fueled boogie woogie, perhaps most obviously the

---

The Milwaukee Rhythm Club

Presents Its Second Concert

featuring

Albert Ammons And His Rhythm Kings

Sunday Afternoon, September 20th, at 3:00   *1936*

VENETIAN ROOM
HOTEL ASTOR
JUNEAU AVE. AT MARSHALL

The year of this 1936 concert in Milwaukee, Ammons and his band the Rhythm Kings made their first records, including a version of "Pine Top's Boogie Woogie." Ammons, Meade Lux Lewis, and Pine Top Smith, three leading boogie woogie pianists, lived in the same rooming house in Chicago during the late 1920s.

Albert Ammons, on the left, and Meade "Lux" Lewis were lifelong friends and they are considered the greatest practitioners of the boogie woogie piano style.

rhythms of the elevated railroad or "El" that ran alongside so many of the city's buildings. Amid its constant noise, the rumbling of trains and clicking of points, a forceful, rhythmic piano style that echoed its clatter caught on, and no pianist captured that powerful repetitive rhythm more effectively than native Chicagoan Albert Ammons.

The Ammons family was musical, and Albert's father James had played boogie woogie himself in his home area of Kentucky before moving to Chicago. Even though the family relocated from apartment to apartment quite frequently, their prized possession was a player piano, which went everywhere with them. Albert was a large, active boy who played softball and became a drummer in the Illinois Home Guard during World War I. He became an accomplished pianist, both by studying

punched-paper rolls that operated the piano keys as they worked their way through the instrument, and by playing alongside his father and a school friend two years his senior, Meade "Lux" Lewis. Lux got his curious nickname by imitating the mannerisms of a comic strip character, the "Duke of Luxembourg." Lewis was also adept at recreating railroad noises at the keyboard, not least because "Big Bertha" freight locomotives on the New York Central roared past the windows of his home on South La Salle Street.

As teenagers, Ammons and Lewis fell into a routine of practicing together, and this continued when they both found jobs as drivers for the Silver Taxicab Company. To ensure the two pianists returned to base after delivering their fares, the company installed a piano in their offices, so that the drivers

Albert C. Ammons

BORN
September 23, 1907
Chicago, Illinois

DIED
December 2, 1949
Chicago, Illinois

EDUCATION
No formal musical education

MAJOR INTERESTS
Jazz piano, bandleading

ACCOMPLISHMENTS
One of the Chicago's leading boogie woogie pianists; helped popularize boogie woogie at New York's Café Society from 1939, often in partnership with Pete Johnson and Meade "Lux" Lewis; recorded a core repertoire of boogie woogie pieces as soloist, duetist, and bandleader

"Boogie woogie consists of playing with the left hand and just improvising with the right. The left hand tells the real story."

—Albert Ammons in a 1943 interview with the *Milwaukee Journal*

could always be found when they were needed. After a day's driving around the city, the young men worked steadily at rent parties. In the mid-1920s both Lewis and Ammons left Chicago briefly, and each worked for a spell in both South Bend, Indiana, and Detroit. While Lewis undertook a variety of jobs, including—briefly—being a brothel-keeper, Ammons worked steadily as a pianist. Because he had facility in every key (whereas the self-taught Lewis was a more limited player) he was able to work both in small groups and as a soloist. Ammons never read music proficiently, but he had a quick ear and was a sensitive accompanist.

This meant that even with the onset of the Great Depression in 1929 he had work. He played in a band on long-haul passenger trains that ran southward to Memphis and New Orleans. Among the band's lineup was trumpeter Punch Miller, at one time considered a rival to Louis Armstrong. Ammons played for dancers in Chicago's Lincoln Gardens, and he ended up as a member of a couple of popular local bands led by Francis Moseley and William Barbee. Barbee's Headquarters Orchestra employed Ammons as a second pianist, and although he never abandoned his rugged boogie woogie left hand, it was in this band that he learned to play a lighter swing-style accompaniment.

This style was similar to the playing of Earl Hines.

Ammons went on to play with Louis P. Banks's band before founding his own group in 1934. This was called the Rhythm Kings, and its lively lineup included the local bassist Israel Crosby. With his pulsing double bass backing up the pounding left hand of Ammons's boogie piano, they created a uniquely powerful rhythm section along with drummer Jimmy Hoskins. Together, they successfully transferred the boogie woogie piano style to a full band setting, and were described by critic Bill Russell as sounding like a much larger band—15 pieces rather than 6. It was with this band that Ammons made his first discs in 1936, and although only four sides were cut, they were hugely influential, especially "Boogie Woogie Stomp."

Later that year, the Rhythm Kings broke up, and Ammons reverted to playing solo, which he was still doing when he moved to New York City in 1938. Prompted by John Hammond's enthusiasm for the playing of the Kansas City pianist Pete Johnson, New York audiences were discovering the boogie woogie style. Ammons, together with Johnson and his old friend Meade "Lux" Lewis, began working at Barney Josephson's Café Society in Greenwich Village. This was a venue that encouraged a racially mixed clientele, was loved by the artistic bohemian set of the Village, and where there was the highest quality jazz seven nights a week. For several years, Ammons worked there, either as a duo with Johnson or by adding Lewis to make up a trio. He suffered a mild setback when he severed the top of a finger in a kitchen accident in 1941, but carried on playing soon afterward until a nervous collapse brought on by overwork sent him home to Chicago for a time.

Well before this, Ammons was heard by the German immigrant Alfred Lion, a jazz enthusiast who had left Nazi Germany to come to New York City, where he founded a new record company, Blue Note. Ammons cut "Boogie Woogie Stomp," the very first disc for Blue Note records, in January 1939, starting an epic new chapter in the history of recorded jazz with the birth of a label that went on to document the transition from swing to modern jazz with an enthusiasm and attention to detail unmatched by any other. Lion also recorded Ammons playing in a duo with Lewis. Their trio with Johnson (as well as some duos with Ammons and Johnson) was also preserved on discs they made for various other labels.

In the mid-1940s, after traveling to various parts of the United States, Ammons returned to his hometown of Chicago, where he resumed his round of local clubs, playing at the Beehive and similar venues. Although he suffered from a form of paralysis, he could still be heard in clubs and concerts until not long before his death at the early age of 42. His musical legacy continued in the playing of his son, saxophonist Gene Ammons, who combined a formidable grasp of modern jazz ideas with the heart and soul of his father's best work.

Albert Ammons was the most broadly based of his generation of boogie woogie pianists, easily making the transition from solo to band, and working effectively alongside other pianists in duos or trios. He may have lacked the ability to create pictures in sound like Lewis or the plaintive blues feeling of his fellow Chicagoan Jimmy Yancey, but he was the most consistently powerful of his contemporaries. His recordings, although few in number, are a lasting memorial to the sounds of the Chicago rent parties of the 1920s.

DISCOGRAPHY

Albert Ammons 1936–39. Classics 715.
Barrelhouse and Boogie. RCA Bluebird ND 88334 (various artists). [Includes nine duets with Johnson and examples of Yancey and Lewis playing solo.]

FURTHER READING

Silvester, Peter. *A Left Hand Like God: A Study of Boogie Woogie*. London: Quartet, 1988.

Oliver, Paul. *The Story of the Blues*. 1969. Reprint, Radnor, Pa.: Chilton, 1982.

WEBSITE

http://homepages.munich.netsurf.de/ Andreas Busch/boogie.index.html
Site with wide coverage of boogie woogie piano, with biographies and pictures of several musicians, including Ammons.

Fats Waller

THE CHEERFUL
LITTLE EARFUL

Almost everything about Fats Waller was larger than life. He weighed 285 pounds, stood six feet tall, and had a giant's appetite for food, drink, and the good life. In his short life, he made hundreds of records, wrote dozens of songs, and became loved by millions. He was also one of the most influential pianists in the history of jazz, the composer of several Broadway shows, and a radio and film star.

Thomas Wright "Fats" Waller was always a New Yorker, through and through. His family lived in Harlem, on 134th Street, when he was born—the seventh of eleven children, of whom five survived. The family was united by religion. Thomas's father, Edward, was a lay preacher who would stand on street corners and hold forth on the evils of sin. Fats' life was continual conflict between the values of his family—faith, a love of the church organ, charity and kindness to others—and the call of Harlem's low life: drink, women, music, and having fun. The low life eventually won.

The family owned a piano and Fats studied the classics, playing at school and for his friends. When his mother died suddenly, Fats moved out of the family home at age 16 to live with a school friend, Russell Brooks. Russell's home had a player piano, and Fats spent hours slowing down the

Fats Waller had great comic gifts as well as musical talent, and this 1938 photograph catches him "mugging" for the camera.

mechanism and laboriously teaching himself to play ragtime pieces by ear, sometimes stopping the rolls midway to work out how to finger the difficult passages.

He sought lessons from James P. Johnson, one of the main creators of a new school of jazz piano playing called stride, the style Fats was to make his own. Fats also followed up his childhood fondness for the organ by getting to know the organist in the neighborhood's Lincoln Theater, who played accompaniment to silent movies and stage shows. It was not long before Fats substituted there, entertaining his school friends by playing the organ for the movies they attended every weekend.

James P. Johnson introduced Waller to Harlem rent parties. More important, Johnson introduced Fats to Leroy's Club on 135th Street, where the young man soon was sitting in for Willie "The Lion" Smith, the house pianist. Smith nicknamed Fats "Filthy" after the greasy suit he was wearing, and the name stuck during Fats' career in the 1920s.

Waller was soon a familiar character around the streets of the area, since he also worked as a delivery boy, concealing bottles of bootleg liquor about his ample body as he sped around delivering more innocuous looking groceries. That job did not last long, because he was soon taking home a reasonable wage as organist at the Lincoln Theater. Occasionally Fats would fail to look up at the films he was supposed to be accompanying, and on one occasion his romping good-humored pieces accompanied sad scenes of a funeral. Also, as a teenager he discovered alcohol, and was frequently admonished for leaving empty gin bottles in the pipework of the organ.

His income was needed, for in late 1920, still only 16 years old, he married. This was a rash decision that cost him dearly over the years. His youthful bride, Edith Hatchett, the mother of their son, Thomas Junior, grew apart from him quickly, and the couple separated in 1923, by which time Fats was on the road with a traveling revue. For Hatchett, their separation turned into a lifelong pursuit of alimony that Waller frequently neglected to pay.

At 19, Fats had yet to become the boisterous, confident performer familiar from his 1930s records. What the touring revue—an act called Liza and her Shufflin' Sextet—gave him was nightly experience working in front of an audience. By 1929, when he made many of his best piano solo recordings, Waller was already an experienced show composer with many songs to his credit, and had learned his craft the hard way, on the road.

He lived the life of a Tin Pan Alley composer, in other words selling his songs to the various music publishers located near Broadway in Manhattan. Fats and his lyric-writing partner Andy Razaf, a descendant of the royal family of Madagascar, often sold the same song several times in one day and drank the proceeds by nightfall. By the end of the 1920s, Waller had written several shows, of which the most famous were *Shuffle Along* and *Hot Chocolates*. The latter included "Ain't Misbehavin'," the song that made both Louis Armstrong and Cab Calloway into stars.

In 1929, Waller recorded a series of piano solos that showed he had a rather different compositional talent, the ability to write brilliantly for the approximately three-minute playing time of what was then the standard phonograph record, the 78 rpm disc. His tunes, such as "Handful of Keys," have become classics of jazz piano, celebrated for their perfect construction and balance. He also played on many records with other groups, including those of Fletcher Henderson and Thomas Morris.

When the Wall Street crash came, in October 1929, the market for freelance recording artists and show composers collapsed; Waller was suddenly facing a grim future. By then, his second marriage, to Anita Rutherford, was a stabilizing influence on him, but since they had produced two sons, he had to find a regular source of income to support his family.

Waller decided that radio was the answer. While he still played in clubs and theaters, he spent the period from 1930 to 1934 working as a broadcaster, mainly from Cincinnati. He perfected the jocular microphone technique as a vocalist and announcer that was to stand him in good stead for the hundreds of records he made from 1934 onward with his own sextet, the Rhythm.

Fats had been back in New York for only a short time when RCA Victor signed him up to make the first of these Rhythm records. The group became the band Waller used both to record and tour for the remaining nine years of his life. Its very first discs included schoolboy guitarist Al Casey and trumpeter Herman Autrey, both of whom stayed for most of Fats' dozens of future sessions.

The pattern was set from the start: Waller lampooned his way through vocals, often on material with such trite lyrics and simplistic melodies that nobody else would record it. His little group added such swing and feeling

that even the most hardened listeners would soon be tapping their feet. The sextet also formed the core of an occasional big band.

In the early 1930s many engagements were ruined by process servers arriving to slap Waller in jail until the latest alimony payments were made, or by Fats himself deciding on a whim to head for New York, whether or not the tour was over. His manager, Ed Kirkeby, began to have trouble booking the band, despite the success of its discs.

The solution to Kirkeby's problem came in two tours in Europe, for which he asked a ridiculously high fee for Waller's performances and which, to his surprise, was accepted. Waller visited Britain in the summers of 1938 and 1939, but the latter tour was cut short by the outbreak of World War II. During his visits to England he made several discs, including his piano masterpiece, the "London Suite," which—although it survived the wartime bombing of Britain only as a scratchy set of test recordings—is Waller's most accomplished piece of extended piano playing.

Back in the United States, Fats made movies, dozens more records, and wrote another musical, but the strain of his lifestyle was beginning to tell. He drank huge quantities of alcohol. He went with little sleep for days. He indulged in giant food binges and constantly moved from party to party, even though he told his friends he would slow down, compose more, play less, and stop touring. The pressure of constantly being expected to be funny told on him too, and his later discs have some leaden jokes that hint at desperation.

The planned peace and quiet never came. Just before Christmas 1943, Fats was traveling home by train from the

Thomas Wright "Fats" Waller

BORN
May 21, 1904
New York, New York

DIED
December 15, 1943
Kansas City, Missouri

EDUCATION
Public School 89, in Harlem, until age 14; informal piano lessons from James P. Johnson

MAJOR INTERESTS
Jazz piano, singing, composing, bandleading

ACCOMPLISHMENTS
Over 400 recordings as pianist and singer; composed or co-wrote the musicals *Keep Shufflin'* (1928), *Hot Chocolates, Load of Coal* (both 1929), *Early to Bed* (1943). Appeared in the films *Hooray for Love, King of Burlesque* (both 1935), *Stormy Weather* (1943). Copyrighted hundreds of songs, including "Ain't Misbehavin'," "Black and Blue," and "Honeysuckle Rose." Made Carnegie Hall debut in James P. Johnson's classical rhapsody *Yamekraw* (1928)

Fats Waller's funeral at the Abyssinian Baptist Church in Harlem halted traffic with huge crowds amassed for three blocks in every direction, and thousands more people lining the route out to the crematory on Long Island.

West Coast. He had suffered a bout of pneumonia, but nevertheless finished his engagement, attended an all-night party, and caught the long-haul express train back East. Just as the train got to Kansas City, Waller's big heart gave out. He died in the arms of his manager and friend Ed Kirkeby.

Harlem turned out in droves to remember him, and his family friend, the Reverend Adam Clayton Powell Sr., gave the eulogy at a packed funeral. At the memorial concert, groups of grim-faced musicians stood about, then one remembered a funny story about Waller, then another, until soon everyone was roaring with laughter. He would not have wanted it any other way.

DISCOGRAPHY

Turn on The Heat—The Fats Waller Piano Solos. RCA Bluebird ND 82482-2 (two-CD set). [40 tracks, including "Handful of Keys," "Valentine Stomp," "Smashing Thirds," "Honeysuckle Rose."]

Fats and His Buddies. RCA Bluebird 90649 (CD). [Fats' earliest recordings.]

The Middle Years, Part One: 1936–38. RCA Bluebird 07863 66083-2 (three-CD set). [70 tracks, including *Blue Turning Grey Over You.*]

London Sessions 1938–1939. EMI/Pathé Jazztime 251271-2 (CD). [Includes "London Suite."]

The Last Years: 1940–1943. RCA Bluebird ND 90411 (three-CD set). [63 tracks, including "Original E-flat Blues," "Buck Jumpin'," Jitterbug Waltz," "Ain't Misbehavin'."]

FURTHER READING

Kirkeby, Ed, with Duncan P. Scheidt and Sinclair Traill. *Ain't Misbehavin': The Story of Fats Waller.* New York: Da Capo, 1966. [Includes complete discography.]

Shipton, Alyn. *Fats Waller: The Cheerful Little Earful.* London: Continuum, 2001.

Vance, Joel. *Fats Waller: His Life and Times.* Chicago: Contemporary, 1977.

Waller, Maurice, and Anthony Calabrese. *Fats Waller.* New York: Macmillan, 1977.

Wright, Laurie. *Fats in Fact.* Chigwell, Essex, England: Storyville, 1992.

WEBSITE

http://www.redhotjazz.com/fats.html
Biography, pictures, and very thorough recordings and film lists with links to video and audio clips.

Earl "Fatha" Hines

TRUMPET STYLE
ON PIANO

Some jazz pianists are members of a "school" of players, sharing and developing a style through collective experimentation and competition. Ragtimers like Scott Joplin and James Scott are in this category, as are Harlem stride pianists like Fats Waller and James P. Johnson. A handful of other players are genuinely original talents, their individuality owing little to any prevailing movement or fashion. Earl Hines was one such player, a remarkably innovative musician from the 1920s until his final concerts in the 1980s. Few other pianists could imitate his dazzling technique or the speed of his invention, which made him the ideal accompanist in the 1920s for Louis Armstrong. As Armstrong created a solo role for the trumpet within his bands, Hines proved that the piano could do the same. He steered a midway course between the set-piece solos of stride players like Waller and the unsophisticated accompanying role of band players like Lil Hardin Armstrong. When he chose to play unaccompanied, his fertile imagination freed him from the restrictive rhythms and left-hand patterns adopted by other pianists, and he could outplay most challengers until the end of his long life.

Earl Hines was born in a suburb of Pittsburgh called Duquesne, into a musical family. His father, Joseph, was a

"Hines never lost his touch, although he could carry the volume up to the point where he might break a string on the piano," wrote Teddy Wilson about Earl Hines, seen here at the Savoy Ballroom, New York, in 1939.

Hines, complete with his trademark wig and square glasses, gives a concert at the Marquee Club, London, in 1966. Hines had also toured England in the late 1950s in a sextet that included the trombonist Jack Teagarden.

cornetist, his mother played the organ, and his sister Nancy was, like Earl, a pianist, who went on to lead her own bands. Earl started serious study of the piano when he was only nine, and this eventually took precedence over his formal education. He left Schenley High School to go straight into the band that backed a local baritone singer named Lois Deppe. Hines toured and recorded with Deppe, and spent the money he earned from his first discs on more piano lessons. Deppe, for his part, recognized Hines's talent, and to help him develop, organized jobs for him that involved bandleading and directing as well as simply accompanying at the piano.

After a tour with Deppe in 1923, Hines moved to Chicago. He quickly found work with some of the city's leading bandleaders, including Carroll Dickerson and Erskine Tate. Both men provided backing for Louis Armstrong at various times. Consequently Hines became a regular accompanist for Armstrong, joining his studio recording bands whenever possible, and cutting some very influential discs with Armstrong's Hot Five. His playing was nicknamed the "trumpet" piano style, since his right-hand phrases mimicked the melodies of the trumpet in early jazz bands, playing in octaves: his thumb and little finger hitting the same note an octave apart on the keyboard.

Earl Kenneth Hines

"The technique he used gave great force to the solo piano in the big band before the days of amplification . . . his octave technique was original, brilliant, and clear, even above full ensemble backgrounds."

—Teddy Wilson, pianist, in *Teddy Wilson Talks Jazz* (1996)

BORN
December 28, 1903
Duquesne, Pennsylvania

DIED
April 22, 1983
Oakland, California

EDUCATION
Schenley High School, Pittsburgh; various piano teachers, including jazz players Jim Fellman and Johnny Watters

MAJOR INTERESTS
Piano, bandleading

ACCOMPLISHMENTS
Created the "trumpet style" of jazz solo piano; made a series of influential recordings with Louis Armstrong in late 1920s and again in 1948–51. Led his own big band throughout 1930s and most of 1940s; returned to the world concert circuit, 1960s–1983 as pianist and leader of his own quartet. Compositions include "A Monday Date," "Deep Forest," and "Fatha's Blues"

HONORS
Downbeat Critics' Hall of Fame, 1965; won critics' poll as best pianist, 1967, 1969, 1970, 1972, 1973; numerous other awards

Erskine Tate, a violinist whose band provided the music for the Vendome movie theater, employed Hines both to play piano and to conduct the band. Hines sat at one piano, and when he got up to conduct, band member Willie Hamby took over at a second piano. The band identified the arrangements they used to accompany the silent movies of the time with numbers on their sheet music. Hines would call out the number of the next sequence to his musicians as they played so that they could move at the appropriate moment from "sad" to "happy" or from "calm" to "storm," for example.

Between movie shows, guests would join in with the band. These guests included Armstrong and visiting pianists like Fats Waller, who would take Hamby's seat at the second piano and play thrilling duets with Hines, who acquired the nickname "Father" or "Fatha."

Hines inaugurated his own big band at a new club, the Grand Terrace, on December 28, 1928. This was the start of a residency that ran for over a decade, during which Hines became a recording star in his own right and employed some of Chicago's best musicians. He was quoted as saying the Terrace could not afford to pay for established stars, so he had to find new ones. In doing so, his band made the reputations of trumpeter Walter Fuller, saxophonist Budd Johnson, and two of the most swinging drummers in jazz, Wallace Bishop and Alvin Burroughs. Although the club was controlled by criminals, notably Al Capone, even decades later Hines could never bring himself to criticize Capone, always recalling how generous the mobsters had been to himself and the musicians, and turning a blind eye to their brutal crimes.

At the end of the 1930s, the Grand Terrace closed, but Hines led his big band for another few years, touring the country, and employing many stars of the new trends in jazz such as Dizzy Gillespie and Charlie Parker. Hines hated the bebop music they played, but he knew that the younger black audiences wanted it, so he let Parker and Gillespie play their own arrangements from time to time. Eventually, led by singer Billy Eckstine, whom Hines had made famous with his "Stormy Monday Blues" and "Jelly, Jelly," they left and formed a new bebop-style big band. Hines continued with his own orchestra, briefly hiring a string section and harpist, before conceding that the era of big bands was over in the late 1940s.

In 1948, Hines joined Louis Armstrong's All Stars, replacing founding member Dick Cary and traveling to Nice, France, for the first great post–World War II jazz festival. Although his reunion with Armstrong briefly rekindled the chemistry that had made their 1920s work so exceptional, it was never easy for him to accept a subordinate role to Armstrong after so many years as a leader himself, and he left after three years. He passed the 1950s in obscurity, mainly playing with small bands in California alongside other fallen giants like cornetist Muggsy Spanier, a fiery Chicagoan who eked out a living on the West Coast.

The final phase in Hines' career was to begin in the 1960s when he was rediscovered by jazz fans like the German writer Joachim Berendt and English-born critic Stanley Dance. During the last years of his life, promoted by their enthusiastic support, he once more toured the world as a star. People marveled at his undiminished abilities, although some jazz purists who yearned to hear him recreate his earlier triumphs felt Hines' act was vulgar, concentrating on flashy showmanship instead of on the instrumental and improvisational brilliance of which Hines was capable. Nonetheless, Hines left a legacy of recordings that show that he was truly one of the greatest pianists in jazz, right up until his 80th year.

DISCOGRAPHY

Louis Armstrong and Earl Hines, Vol. IV. Columbia 466308-2. [Best of the Armstrong–Hines collaborations from the 1920s.]

Earl Hines Collection: Piano solos 1928–1940. Collector's Classics COCD 11.

Piano Man. RCA Bluebird ND 86750. [Big band tracks, 1939–40.]

Tour De Force. Black Lion BLCD 760140. [Piano solos from 1972, showing Hines's later style.]

FURTHER READING

Balliett, Whitney. *Such Sweet Thunder.* New York: Bobbs-Merrill, 1966.

Dance, Stanley. *The World of Earl Hines.* New York: Scribners, 1977.

Hadlock, Richard. *Jazz Masters of the 1920s.* New York: Macmillan, 1965.

Schuller, Gunther. *The Swing Era.* New York: Oxford University Press, 1989.

Wilson, Teddy. *Teddy Wilson Talks Jazz.* Arie Ligthart and Humphrey Van Loo, eds. London and New York: Cassell, 1996.

WEBSITE

http://www.redhotjazz.com/hines.html
Biography, pictures, and many music links.

Mary Lou Williams

SIX MEN AND A GIRL

T he first female instrumentalist and composer to become an internationally celebrated jazz arranger, pianist, and eventually bandleader, was Mary Lou Williams. Her accomplished solo piano playing, which drew equally on boogie woogie and stride influences to form a convincingly original style, would have been sufficient for her to become famous. Yet added to that, she possessed strong arranging skills and the ability to construct memorable, swinging compositions for ensembles that ranged from trios to big bands.

In the early days of Chicago jazz, there were several women who made their mark on the music either as pianists or organizers; they included Lil Hardin Armstrong, Lovie Austin, and Lottie Hightower. However, none of these female pioneers of jazz rivaled the all-round accomplishments of Williams, who first came to fame on the touring theater circuits and with the territory bands of the Midwest.

Although she was born in the South, Williams grew up in Pittsburgh, where, in her early teens, she saw Lovie Austin in person at a theater on Frankstown Avenue. She was so impressed at the sight of Austin accompanying the show

Mary Lou Williams at the keyboard in New York, 1949. In addition to playing with male groups, Williams led an all-woman band in 1945–46 that included the talented guitarist Mary Osborne.

"Mary Lou's playing is real. Earthy. Running through all the emotions, it speaks volumes, for there is much in the creator that comes out in the music."

—Marian McPartland in *All in Good Time* (1987)

with her left hand while copying out music for a new song with her right, that the young girl vowed that playing and composing was what she wanted to do in life. By then, Williams was already making a name for herself playing boogie woogie in gambling joints frequented by her stepfather, Fletcher Burley. She even borrowed his name for her appearances, being known as Mary Burley. In addition to boogie woogie, she had learned to play the difficult solos of Earl Hines and Jelly Roll Morton by listening carefully to their phonograph records. She soon came to know Hines and to hear him in person, because while she was still at school he was still playing with singer Lois Deppe in and around the Pittsburgh area.

Mary Lou bumped into Hines again a year or two later in Chicago, where he was working alongside Louis Armstrong. By this time, Williams had joined a touring theater troupe led by the unusually named Buzzin' Harris, to play piano for a show called *Hits and Bits*. Initially she worked with Harris just during her summer vacation, returning afterward for another year at high school. Nevertheless, she had acquired a taste for the life she was subsequently to lead, and she met numerous jazz musicians of importance, from Armstrong and Hines to her future husband, John "Bearcat" Williams, nicknamed for his wild baritone saxophone style.

John Williams was leading the band for Buzzin' Harris when Mary Lou rejoined the show the following year. Her stepfather had become ill, so to support the family she quit school and went back on the road. John Williams' Syncopators, later known as his Synco Jazz Band, were a show in themselves. Trumpeter Doc Cheatham was in the lineup for a while, and his main memory of the band (before a well-to-do uncle pulled him out of the group in St. Louis and sent him back to Nashville) was that even though they were African Americans, they had to play with black makeup on, like 19th-century minstrels.

Then the band had a lucky break. They were stranded in Cincinnati with no further bookings at the end of a tour when they were summoned to accompany the dancers Seymour and Jeannette on the prestigious Keith–Orpheum theater circuit. Overnight, they became almost the only African-American act employed by this management, and their success in playing predominantly for white audiences reflected their considerable musical skill. Even when Seymour died (apparently from a heart attack brought on by his strenuous dance routines), the band continued to work the circuit, eventually arriving in New York City, where Mary Lou met three of her pianist heroes: Fats Waller, Clarence Williams, and Jelly Roll Morton. She much preferred Waller's boisterous bonhomie to Morton's stern tone of instruction.

While they were in New York, Mary Lou and John Williams decided to marry. They traveled to Memphis to have the wedding at his parents' home. Once they had arrived in the South, they formed a new band, which lasted until John was summoned to join a territory band led by "T" Holder in Oklahoma. The Williams' new band had several dates to play after he had departed, so at the age of 17 Mary Lou became the leader for the following few weeks, hiring a scholarly looking local schoolteacher named Jimmie Lunceford to fill in for John on saxophone. By the time she left for Oklahoma to join her husband, Lunceford was already well on the way to forming what became his famous orchestra.

Although Mary Lou played occasionally with Holder's band, the group had another pianist, so she had little to do in the evil-smelling oilfield town of Oklahoma City, and when her stepfather suddenly died, she returned to Pittsburgh. By the time she rejoined her husband, the band's bassist, Andy Kirk, had taken over the group, renamed it the Clouds of Joy, and landed a plum job in a Kansas City ballroom. In due course, Mary Lou—who by then had cut her first solo discs for Decca under her married name of Mary Lou Williams—became Kirk's pianist. She had also painstakingly learned how to arrange for the band, first by dictating her ideas to Kirk, then by writing them down, and finally, by trial and error, establishing the range of each instrument and what it was technically possible to play. Many critics take the view that although Kirk fronted and managed the band (retiring from playing to wield a baton in the mid-1930s), the band's overall sound and style were in effect her creation.

For 11 years, from 1931 to 1942, she was the sole pianist in Kirk's band, at a time when it became one of the leading big bands in the United States. Williams acquired a strong reputation for compositions like "Messa Stomp" and "Walkin' and Swingin'." During this time her arrangements also began to be played by a number of other bands that commissioned charts from her. One reason she was able to produce pieces for other leaders was that until it achieved a national hit with "Until the Real Thing Comes Along" and was able to spend more time in New York, Kirk's band was endlessly traveling. As with other territory bands, this involved covering huge distances across the South and Midwest, with occasional forays into Canada. With the natural gift of perfect pitch, Williams did not need a piano to compose, and taught herself how to write music on long bus and train journeys around the country. While with Kirk she also made occasional recordings under her own name leading a band she called Six Men and A Girl, and her more conventionally titled Kansas City Seven, in 1940.

Traveling eventually became too much for her; in addition, her marriage to John Williams ended. Mary Lou Williams went home to Pittsburgh, and was soon joined by one of Kirk's trumpeters, Harold "Shorty" Baker, who became her second husband. Together they started a band in 1942, which was short-lived when Duke Ellington recruited Baker in the fall of the same year. For a year or so, Mary Lou traveled with the entourage, writing a number of pieces for Duke's band. She

Mary Lou Williams
(née Mary Elfrieda Scruggs, also known as Mary Burley)

BORN
May 8, 1910
Atlanta, Georgia

DIED
May 28, 1981
Durham, North Carolina

EDUCATION
Lincoln School, East Liberty, Pittsburgh; Westinghouse Junior High School, Pittsburgh

MAJOR INTERESTS
Piano, composing, arranging

ACCOMPLISHMENTS
Played in and arranged for Andy Kirk's Clouds of Joy, 1931–42; subsequently arranged for numerous others, including Duke Ellington, and led her own bands. Started charity, Bel Canto Foundation, for needy musicians. Composed several masses: *Mass* (1966), *Mass for the Lenten Season* (1968), *Music for Peace* (renamed *Mary Lou's Mass*; 1970–71). Held posts at University of Massachusetts, Amherst, 1975, and Duke University, North Carolina, 1977

HONORS
Mary Lou Williams Lane is named for her in Kansas City, Missouri; honorary doctorates from Fordham University, Manhattan College, Loyola University, New Orleans; Guggenheim Fellowship, 1973

This manuscript of one of Mary Lou Williams's arrangements for Andy Kirk was written during her long years on the road. Kirk's Clouds of Joy recorded this number on December 9, 1936, under the title "She's the Lady Who Swings the Band."

was one of the very few composers other than Billy Strayhorn and Ellington himself who wrote regularly for the band, and certainly the only female arranger Duke used.

Leaving the road again, she settled in New York City, where she began working at the Café Society in Greenwich Village in November 1944. She was one of a number of female pianists to play there: the West Indian musician Hazel Scott was another regular feature on the club's programs. Settled in one place, Williams, who still used her former husband's name, began to compose extended pieces, in addition to playing

a variety of clubs and undertaking the odd tour in her own right, or with Benny Goodman. She also found herself drawn into the emergent modern jazz movement, befriending pianists Bud Powell and Thelonious Monk. She did not abandon the recognizable swing and blues elements in her own playing, even though she did add some of the newer bebop harmonies and phrasing to her work.

As the 1950s dawned, she became increasingly preoccupied with religion; this coincided with her decision to spend a couple of years outside the United States. She lived in Britain and

France in 1952–54, dictating her life story to Max Jones for publication in the *Melody Maker* magazine while she was there. On her return to the United States she taught and undertook charity work before returning to the stage in 1957, the year in which she converted to Roman Catholicism.

Thereafter, Williams divided her time between developing as an increasingly virtuoso and unusual piano soloist, and composing large-scale religious pieces, many of them performed by community or youth choirs. One reason she continued to play during a time when she was preoccupied with religious questions was the guidance of her mentor and manager, a Jesuit priest named Father Peter O'Brien. He helped her develop a philosophical approach to her role in "saving" jazz—setting an example for others to follow while at the same time seeking out young and original players with something new to say. She felt strongly that there was little point in recreating what had already been played. "I'm looking for a new style in jazz, which will have to be played by someone very young," she said. Her religious pieces included settings of words by another Catholic mentor, the Reverend Anthony Woods, who believed that Williams thought "jazz was becoming superficial, losing its spiritual feeling." Her recordings from her final years are anything but superficial and are full of the spirituality Woods found wanting. Williams's own playing is among the most technically assured of all her recorded work. She was asked to play at home and abroad in everything from clubs and concerts to full-scale festivals during her last years. She also found herself in demand as a teacher, and combined university teaching about jazz and its history with her twin careers as performer and composer.

DISCOGRAPHY

Mary Lou Williams 1927–40. Classics 630.

Mary Lou Williams 1944. Classics 814.

Andy Kirk and His Clouds of Joy, 1936–40: Kansas City Bounce. Black and Blue 59.240.

Mary Lou Williams Zodiac Suite, *Town Hall, December 1945*. Vintage Jazz 1035. [Williams' first extended composition, and until her Catholic masses are reissued, the only long piece of hers recently in catalog.]

Mary Lou Williams Live at The Cookery. Chiaroscuro 148. [A 1970s club set.]

FURTHER READING

Dahl, Linda. *Morning Glory: A Biography of Mary Lou Williams*. New York: Pantheon, 1999.

Jones, Max. *Talking Jazz*. London: Macmillan, 1987.

Kirk, Andy. *Twenty Years on Wheels*. Amy Leed, ed. Ann Arbor: University of Michigan Press, 1989.

Lyons, Len. *The Great Jazz Pianists*. New York: Morrow, 1983.

McPartland, Marian. *All in Good Time*. New York: Oxford University Press, 1987.

WEBSITE

http://www.kennedy-center.org/programs/jazz/womeninjazz/1stlady.html

Biographical notes and pictures, giving a very personal view of William's life.

Teddy Wilson

GENTLEMAN OF SWING

Both Teddy Wilson's playing and the man himself could be described by the words "elegant" and "charming." He had an effortless fluency about his piano solos, and his presence in a band guaranteed a swinging rhythm. His supreme talent was in directing a studio band, proved by a host of small group recordings in the 1930s. These created perfect accompaniments for singers from Billie Holiday to Ella Fitzgerald and employed the cream of New York's jazz musicians, who clamored to record for him despite lowly fees of about $5 a tune.

Teddy Wilson's story is not one of a rapid rise from rags to riches, but of a measured progress toward realizing his childhood promise. Teddy and his elder brother Gus were born into a well-educated family; their parents taught at a college for black students, Tuskegee Institute in Alabama. Gus played trombone and Teddy studied piano and violin. Their talents were helped along because both boys lived at

A 1952 musicians' reunion at Teddy Wilson's piano. Benny Goodman leans forward with a cigarette: to his right is Gene Krupa, who, with Wilson, made up the original Goodman Trio.

the school and took extra music lessons during vacations. Teddy's piano teacher, Mrs. Sims, developed his sight-reading and a love of the classics, and Teddy gave occasional classical concerts even after he had made a reputation as a jazz player. Teddy also joined the marching band that supported the college's football team.

More importantly, a former pupil at the school, John Lovett, was not only a fine pianist but also a collector of jazz recordings. While Fats Waller was learning from other pianists in the after-hours joints of New York City, in faraway Alabama, Teddy Wilson was learning his jazz from Lovett's stack of discs. He discovered not only those by Waller, but the solos of Earl Hines and Duke Ellington, plus band tracks by Bix Beiderbecke and Louis Armstrong. Using a phonograph with adjustable speed, Teddy taught himself to play his favorite solos, matching the pitch of the disc to the school piano. He developed his remarkable musical ear by writing down what he heard or simply imitating recordings at the keyboard. This gave him an encyclopedic knowledge of the discs that arrived by mail order, and a sense of how a 78 rpm record ought to sound—the basis of his mastery of the three-minute playing time when he later came to lead his own studio bands.

Wilson heard his first live jazz on a vacation in Detroit, where he marveled at the sounds of Fletcher Henderson and McKinney's Cotton Pickers. This inspired him to become a jazz musician. His mother asked him to spend a year in college, so he studied music for three semesters at Talladega College in Alabama, then set off with his brother Gus to Detroit, where they both worked for bandleader Bob Cruset.

Eventually, a traveling orchestra led by "Speed" Webb passed through town and the brothers joined it. Webb was a musical talent spotter who hired many fledgling stars, including trumpeter Roy Eldridge and trombonist Vic Dickenson. With Webb, Wilson got his first taste of touring, playing throughout the Midwest and New England.

He stayed in Toledo, Ohio, to replace Art Tatum in a small group led by Milt Senior when Tatum went on to play a daily show on the local radio station. After hours he and Wilson got together regularly, and the young pianist absorbed much of Tatum's style by observing him. Tatum and Wilson took on all comers in many all-night cutting contests in Toledo.

In due course, Senior's band broke up in Chicago. Wilson realized that he could get plenty of work in Chicago's thriving jazz scene, and he joined Louis Armstrong's big band. He also worked regularly opposite Earl Hines, from whom he learned a lot. While he was with Armstrong, Wilson's playing on the band's broadcasts was heard by the entrepreneur and record producer John Hammond, who liked the sound of this fleet-fingered, swinging pianist. Hammond played a major part in Wilson's life during the mid-1930s. His first generous act was to introduce Wilson to Benny Carter, who brought him to New York to cut a number of records.

Settled in New York City, with a well-paying job with bandleader Willie Bryant to sustain him, Wilson began to absorb the city's unparalleled musical life. Through Hammond's influence he heard Arturo Toscanini conduct the New York Philharmonic Orchestra and met several great classical pianists, but by far the most significant introduction was when Hammond took the young pianist up to Harlem to hear Billie Holiday singing at Jerry's Bar.

There was an immediate musical chemistry between Holiday and Wilson, which prompted Hammond to set up the first recording date of what became a long series. "We must have made some 200 sides together," recalled Wilson. "I organized the bands and helped Billie select the songs she was to

Theodore Shaw "Teddy" Wilson

BORN

November 24, 1912
Austin, Texas

DIED

July 31, 1986
New Britain, Connecticut

EDUCATION

Tuskegee Institute, Alabama; studied music at Talladega College, Alabama

MAJOR INTERESTS

Piano, bandleading

ACCOMPLISHMENTS

Backed many singers, notably Billie Holiday on over 200 discs. Led own big band and sextet, 1940s, before touring the world as a soloist and with a trio. Ran own piano school in New York City, taught at several colleges there. Appeared in the films *Hollywood Hotel* (with Benny Goodman, 1937), *Boogie Woogie Dream* (1941), *Something to Shout About* (1943), *Make Mine Music* (with Goodman, 1945), and *The Benny Goodman Story* (1955)

HONORS

Honorary doctorate, Berklee School of Music, Boston; numerous awards for recording; Gold Disc for collaboration with Dutch Swing College, 1974; elected to Newport Jazz Hall of Fame, 1975

Wilson's short-lived big band made an appearance at the Apollo Theater in the fall of 1939. This advertisement for the show quotes Benny Goodman, though his name is misspelled, calling Wilson "America's greatest swing pianist."

sing. I would sketch the main body of the music, leaving the rest to be improvised apart from the vocal chorus."

From his avid listening as a boy, Wilson thoroughly understood the limitations and potentials of the three-minute phonograph record, producing an inspired blend of improvised solos, neatly arranged ensembles, and decorative backing for singers. Billie Holiday was followed by several other singers, including Helen Ward, Nan Wynn, Ella Fitzgerald, and—putting his trumpet aside for long enough to squeeze out a vocal—Roy Eldridge.

It was not the tiny standard session fee that brought the likes of Benny Goodman, Harry James, Roy Eldridge, and Ben Webster into the ranks of Wilson's little groups. "It was only in those sessions that those artists could play with a group that was at their own level," wrote Wilson. He explained

that for musicians who appeared for only a few measures of each arrangement in their usual big band performances, the chance to play entire solo choruses was a luxury.

However, it was another of John Hammond's ideas that saw Wilson reach his greatest fame in a far smaller group than his own recording bands. In 1935, at a party held by the singer Mildred Bailey, Wilson played piano for a few numbers and was joined by Benny Goodman. With an amateur drummer keeping time, they romped through a set of well-known swing tunes. John Hammond immediately persuaded Benny Goodman that he should record the trio, but with Gene Krupa in place of the amateur to play drums.

Although the trio recorded in 1935, it was not until Easter 1936 that it was launched as a ful-fledged part of the Goodman organization, making it

> *"My Trio and Quartet with myself, Teddy, Lionel and Gene was the first interracial music group and marked an important milestone in race relations in the U.S."*
>
> —Benny Goodman in his 1978 introduction to *Teddy Wilson Talks Jazz*

the first racially integrated jazz group to work full time in the United States. A few months later, with the addition of Lionel Hampton on vibraphone, the trio became a quartet and for three years it was one of the highest profile groups of the Swing Era. Teddy Wilson had gone from being a well-known leader of record sessions to a national star.

In 1939, after three years at the top of his profession, Wilson set up his own big band. It had a blend of strong soloists, neat arrangements, and forceful ensemble work that immediately recalled the best of Wilson's small group recording dates. Its recordings attest to a hard-swinging group that clearly shows why it was a favorite with crowds at the Golden Gate Ballroom where it played. However, the big band was not a commercial success and folded by the spring of 1940. Wilson then led a septet for three years, whose recordings continued the fine work he had done in the studios during the 1930s. His stars included Jimmy Hamilton and Ed Hall on clarinet, Bill

Coleman and Emmett Berry on trumpet, Benny Morton on trombone, and J. C. Heard on drums. In due course Ed Hall took over the band and continued to lead it for several more months after Wilson rejoined Goodman.

Wilson was a popular addition to the Goodman small groups, and he was to make several more appearances with his former boss over the years. Among the most memorable was a trip to Russia, but there were also numerous Quartet reunions, which even went on into the 1980s, with Panama Francis taking over on drums after Krupa's death.

However, Teddy Wilson never again achieved the quality and quantity of his work in the 1930s. That was his finest hour, and nobody else came near his consistency as a recording artist and studio bandleader. Nevertheless, he continued to work all over the world until the mid-1980s, cutting scores of albums from solo discs to collaborations with international groups. He was immensely popular in Europe and in Japan and toured incessantly.

He recorded for the entrepreneur Norman Granz, who produced reunions with Lester Young and Benny Carter that are among the finest examples of Wilson's playing from the 1950s. In addition, there was plenty of radio work, and teaching appointments in New York that allowed him to enjoy witnessing his pupils progress to successful careers of their own. He was always conscious of his legacy to the next generation, and found his greatest solace in old age touring with his sons. With Theodore on bass and Steven on drums, the family formed a trio that brought all the best of Wilson's musical values to the concert stages of the 1980s and proved that, in his family at least, those values were strongly upheld.

DISCOGRAPHY

Teddy Wilson's complete small group recordings up to 1941 are issued in eight volumes by the French Classics company, numbers 508, 511, 521, 531, 548, 556, 571, 620.

Benny Goodman: The Complete RCA Victor Small Group Recordings. RCA Victor 09026 68764-2 (three-CD set). [67 tracks by the original Goodman trio and quartet.]

With Billie in Mind. Chiaroscuro CRD 111. [Collection of solo piano tracks from 1972.]

Three Little Words. Black and Blue 233 094. [A 1976 trio with Milt Hinton and Oliver Jackson.]

FURTHER READING

Collier, James Lincoln. *Benny Goodman and the Swing Era.* New York: Oxford University Press, 1989.

Firestone, Ross. *Swing, Swing, Swing: The Life and Times of Benny Goodman.* New York: Norton, 1993.

Nicholson, Stuart. *Bille Holiday.* London: Gollancz, 1995.

Wilson, Teddy. *Teddy Wilson Talks Jazz.* Arie Ligthart and Humphrey Van Loo, eds. London and New York: Cassell, 1996.

WEBSITE

http://www.duke.edu/~oa2/TeddyWilson

Features Wilson's biography, links, pictures, and music samples.

Art Tatum

GOD IS IN THE HOUSE

I n the whole history of jazz there has never been a virtuoso pianist to match Art Tatum. His flawless technique and his combination of driving swing with outstanding invention are unrivaled, although his towering influence drew many pianists from all walks of jazz toward his stylistic innovations. Underpinning most of his work was a strong left hand modeled after the stride style of Fats Waller. To this, Tatum added the kinds of harmonies favored by Earl Hines, but instead of Hines's stabbing "trumpet" style right-hand octaves, he adopted fleet, nimble melodic patterns comparable to those of his friend Teddy Wilson.

Perhaps because he suffered from defective eyesight and needed continuous tactile contact with his instrument, Tatum developed a type of cascading run that rippled down the whole extent of the piano keyboard at dazzling speed. Some critics have suggested that this assisted him in navigating beyond his field of vision, but that does not explain the

Art Tatum at the Vogue Room, New York, in the mid-1940s.

uncanny precision of his split-second leaps from the center to the outer reaches of the keys to begin his downward spirals. Whatever his motivation, Tatum's devastating speed and precision in these trademark runs marked him out from all other pianists of his era.

Toledo, Ohio, where Art Tatum was born in 1909, the second of four children, is a city that had no more than a walk-on part in jazz history. Equidistant between Detroit and Cleveland, at the southwestern tip of Lake Erie, it was a staging point for touring territory bands, especially those from Detroit. Toledo had a few bands of its own, such as the small group run by saxophonist Milton Senior. Yet there seems to be no reason other than the fact it was a convenient stopping-off place, well connected by rail, road, and water, that any kind of jazz life grew up there at all.

Art's father, who worked as a mechanic, and his mother Mildred, were founding members of the local Presbyterian church. It has been suggested that both parents were musical, but Tatum's biographer, James Lester, found no evidence of this, and believes that it was through the church that Tatum began his love affair with music. He was also passionate about sports, but both his musical and sporting ambitions were hampered by the virtual absence of sight in one eye and progressive deterioration in the other. Born with cataracts, the infant Tatum was also affected by an attack of measles, which further damaged his vision, and the improvements brought about by numerous childhood operations were undone in a moment when a mugger injured Tatum's eyes during his late teens.

Despite his sight problems, Tatum became an enthusiastic and accomplished pianist early in his life, quickly abandoning a short-lived period as a violinist. He had some formal lessons, but much of what he learned came from listening to the full spectrum of music that he heard around him, from recordings and broadcasts of everything from the classics to musical theater, and from marches and rags to early piano jazz. Like many of his contemporaries, Tatum learned from piano rolls, imitating the fingering of the depressed keys on a player piano; before long he was playing around town, at friends' houses, and at the Y.M.C.A.

With a dozen or more small clubs and plenty of social societies to play for, work was plentiful when Tatum began to make his living as a musician. Almost from the start he demonstrated an exceptional talent. Visiting musicians who heard him in his late teens marveled at his abilities. We know from Rex Stewart's account of Fletcher Henderson's band going to listen to the young man in the mid-1920s that not even an established professional like Henderson was prepared to take the stand after Tatum had finished. His playing was already too brilliant and too original for others to compete with him. Yet he did not feel ready to accept the encouragement of many of his contemporaries to go to New York City and try his hand against the acknowledged piano masters. Not even Duke Ellington's eloquent flattery was successful.

Nevertheless, within the jazz community word started to spread about this phenomenally talented player from Toledo, a rumor assisted, about the time Tatum entered his 20s, by the fact that he recommended another young pianist, Teddy Wilson, to take his place in Milton Senior's band. This freed Tatum to play on a daily broadcast on the local radio station, WSPD, which was in due course relayed to the nation over the Blue Network.

Radio was an ideal forum for Tatum. However, whereas Fats Waller used it to develop as an all-round entertainer, quipping and singing alongside his playing, Tatum took the opportunity to hone his solo skills even further, to the extent that for the rest

Art Tatum

BORN
October 13, 1909
Toledo, Ohio

DIED
November 5, 1956
Los Angeles, California

EDUCATION
Jefferson School, Toledo, where he learned braille; Columbus School for the Blind; Toledo School of Music; piano lessons in Toledo from Overton G. Rainey

MAJOR INTEREST
Piano

ACCOMPLISHMENTS
Developed the art of solo jazz piano from the basic stride style; made dozens of innovative recordings; appeared on film and television, especially the movie *The Fabulous Dorseys* (1947)

HONORS
Art Tatum Day, Toledo, 1988; section named after him in local Toledo library; month-long Toledo Art Tatum Festival, 1991

"Tatum can woo a willing listener step by step from surface sounds down to the heart of his kaleidoscopic imagination."

—John S. Wilson in the *New York Times*

of his career he was always at his best as a soloist rather than in a band context. Owing to this specialization, he pushed the boundaries of unaccompanied jazz piano playing much further in terms of technique than did his contemporaries who doubled as bandleaders, such as Fats Waller and James P. Johnson. What Tatum managed to do was to introduce complex additional harmonies known as passing chords into every measure of most of the pieces he played. He melded these along with many types of ornaments and flourishes borrowed from the classical tradition into a bravura style in which the melody—even if it was paraphrased from time to time—remained intact. No matter what piece he played, within a few bars any listener could pick out the tune.

Even so, it was not as a soloist but as an accompanist to the singer Adelaide Hall that Tatum first took to the road and ended up in New York City, where he cut his first records with her in 1932. Hall was accompanied by two pianists playing four-handed duets that gave an orchestral depth to her backing. For some of the time, the other pianist was the eminent stride player Joe Turner. Turner recalled with admiration how Tatum persuaded him to play his piano arrangement of George

Gershwin's song "Liza," and then how Tatum almost immediately sat down and reproduced it note-perfectly himself, demonstrating his incredible musical memory.

Turner was not the only New York stride pianist to be impressed by Art Tatum. Before long, in addition to his theater engagements with Hall, Tatum became a regular fixture at the 1930s after-hours clubs where pianists got together to challenge one another as they had done a decade before on the rent party circuit. He had soon made a deep impression on James P. Johnson, Willie "The Lion" Smith, and Fats Waller. In Fats he found something of a soul mate, since they shared an appetite for vast quantities of alcohol as well as a zest for life and the piano. There are riotous accounts of these two overweight pianists dressing up as Bessie Smith and Mary Lou Williams to perform an outrageous drag act for their fellow entertainers while both were in Hollywood in the mid-1930s. Although their styles were very different, there was great mutual respect between the two men. Tatum told listeners that Fats' music was "where he came from," whereas Fats once noticed Tatum arrive in the audience while he was playing at New York's Yacht Club on 52nd Street, and solemnly announced: "I just play the piano, but God is in the house tonight."

Nevertheless, there was a negative side to their relationship. Just as Fats sowed the seeds of his eventual physical collapse by too much high living, Tatum displayed the early warning signs of diabetes but ignored them, continuing to drink and stay up all

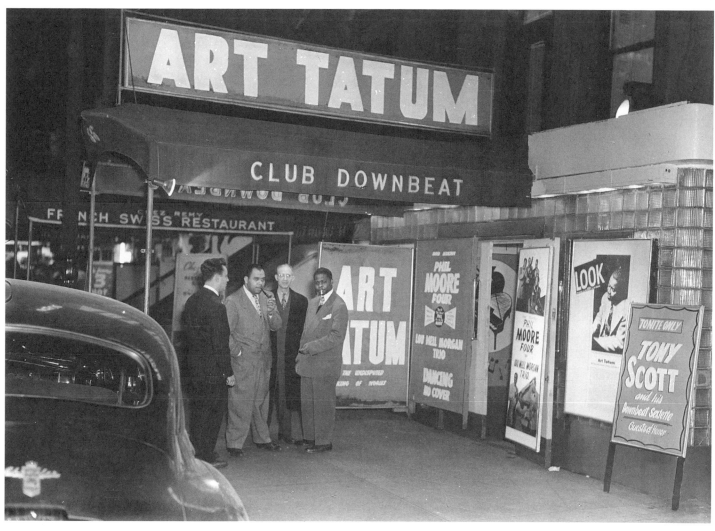

night, which eventually took its toll. Like Waller, Tatum also had a complex personal life. His son Orlando was born around 1932 to a Toledo girlfriend. Father and son remained distant, and in the mid-1930s, Tatum married for the first time, to Ruby Arnold, who accompanied him to London in 1938 on a short solo tour.

Tatum returned to New York and the smallish clubs of 52nd Street, where he played as a solo pianist opposite many of the famous bands of the day. He also cut over 50 solo piano discs between 1933 and 1940, establishing

once and for all his mastery of pieces like "Tiger Rag" along with jazz interpretations of light classics like Massenet's *Elegie*. He made a small number of band recordings in 1937 and 1941, but generally he seemed cramped in an ensemble until in 1943 he hit on the idea of using a trio similar to that used by Nat King Cole: piano, guitar, and bass. The two string instruments gave an underpinning of the basic rhythm and chords, but gave Tatum free rein to improvise around them. Some musicians who played for a short while with the trio, like bassist

Art Tatum, far right, played long residencies at the Downbeat Club on 52nd Street from 1944 to 1946, and he was one of the street's largest draws along with Coleman Hawkins and Billie Holiday.

Truck Parham and guitarist Al Casey (who had worked with Waller), found Tatum's mastery of chords and his impressively fast tempos too much of a challenge. But, with either Tiny Grimes or Everett Barksdale on guitar and Slam Stewart on bass, the trio settled into a regular working lineup on and off during the next 10 years.

With the challenge of modern jazz arriving in the mid-1940s, Tatum made a subtle change to his routine. Instead of playing in nightclubs on New York's 52nd Street, or the equivalent in other big cities, in 1944 he appeared in concert at the Metropolitan Opera House. He subsequently played a whole series of solo recitals in 1946–47 that in due course took him to many of the major halls in the United States. At a time when many other players of swing or older styles of jazz found work hard to come by, Tatum's move to the concert stage created a new audience for his virtuoso technique. He later played in some of Norman Granz's first Jazz at the Philharmonic touring concert shows, and in West Coast concerts for entrepreneur Gene Norman.

Despite the fact he appeared in concert halls all over the country, Tatum never featured highly in the listeners' polls of the late 1940s. His great popularity was created in an earlier era, and he largely remained faithful to the swing repertoire. Although, after initially disparaging beboppers like Bud Powell, he respected the technical prowess of the "new jazz" players, especially after seeing Powell play an entire piece at breakneck speed with only his left hand, to prove to Tatum it was possible. Despite his own prowess, Powell was in awe of Tatum and adopted much of Tatum's style in his rapid runs and reflective ballads.

Tatum did not give up going to after-hours clubs where he could hear, and compete with, up-and-coming pianists, especially in Los Angeles, where he spent increasing amounts of time and lived with his second wife, Geraldine Williamson, from late 1955. Even so, he had reached his zenith as an artist and his style did not materially alter as he moved into the 1950s.

Fortunately Norman Granz decided to preserve Tatum's mature style on disc. Starting in late 1953 he recorded over 120 solos for his Pablo label, along with a similarly comprehensive series of Tatum in informal ensembles that seldom inhibited his natural style. The series ended in 1956, just as there were plans for Tatum to play more concerts alone and with his trio. Sadly, this cycle of appearances had barely begun—following a triumphant Hollywood Bowl concert—when Tatum was forced to withdraw. His lifestyle, with too little sleep and too much alcohol, had irreparably damaged his system; he contracted blood poisoning from chronic kidney disease. He died less than a month after his 47th birthday, tragically young for so talented a figure. In his short life he had moved the art of solo jazz piano forward significantly. His legacy was carried forward into the mainstream jazz style by Oscar Peterson, and into modern jazz by Bud Powell. Some critics felt Tatum's style was overly decorative and without substance—charges later leveled at Oscar Peterson—but musicians themselves had no doubts: when Norman Granz titled his immense series of recordings "The Genius of Art Tatum," he was right.

DISCOGRAPHY

Complete Brunswick and Decca Recordings, 1932–1941. Affinity AFS 1035 (three-CD set). [Contains the majority of Tatum's earliest recordings.]

Art Tatum 1940–44. Classics 800. [Includes a masterly 1941 small band with Joe Thomas and Edmond Hall.]

Complete Capitol Recordings of Art Tatum. Capitol 821325-2 (two-CD set). [Includes trio with Everett Barksdale and Slam Stewart.]

Complete Pablo Solo Masterpieces. Pablo 4404 (seven-CD set). [1953–56 solo performances.]

Complete Pablo Group Masterpieces. Pablo 4401 (six-CD set). [Same period as piano solo edition.]

FURTHER READING

Balliett, Whitney. *Ecstasy at the Onion: Thirty-one Pieces on Jazz*. Indianapolis: Bobbs-Merrill, 1971.

Lester, James. *Too Marvelous for Words: The Life and Genius of Art Tatum*. New York: Oxford University Press, 1994.

WEBSITE

http://angelfire.com/ca/pianogod

Short biography, picture and audio files on this "Art of Tatum" website.

Oscar Peterson

THE ART OF THE TRIO

Although his career has stretched from the 1940s into the 21st century, Oscar Peterson's playing is an encyclopedic summary of everything that happened in jazz piano up to and including Art Tatum, plus a lot of more recent influences. He belongs in this section because he is the musical heir of Tatum, and while he became an adept and versatile accompanist to modern jazz players like Dizzy Gillespie, the core of his playing is about maintaining and giving a contemporary feel to the values of an earlier era. Peterson has what fellow pianist Roger Kellaway described as "the will to swing," a phrase so apt that it was borrowed as the title of the major biography of Peterson by his fellow Canadian, Gene Lees. Furthermore, Peterson's phrasing and improvisatory lines contain the sound of gospel and blues, giving a depth to his playing that is firmly connected to underlying African-American traditions as well as to stylistic currents in jazz itself.

Producer Norman Granz, left, supervises a 1957 record session with Oscar Peterson, who was Granz's favorite accompanist, on piano; Buddy Rich on drums; and Buddy De Franco on clarinet. Peterson had a lengthy and prodigious recording career with Granz's Verve records.

Oscar Peterson plays solo piano in 1959, about the time he formed his greatest trio with Ray Brown on bass and Ed Thigpen on drums.

Encyclopedic as his knowledge of jazz piano is, let alone his ability to demonstrate it in performance, on disc, and in hundreds of broadcasts, Peterson is also a tremendous contributor to the development of the playing of unaccompanied solo piano. The ideal compromise between such solos and his ensemble style can be found in a trio context, where he has combined his prodigious technique with clarity of thought and execution comparable to the finest pianists in classical music. Peterson's trios with guitar and bass, or bass and drums, set the standard by which other trios were measured for more than half a century.

Whereas Art Tatum was at his most sublime playing unaccompanied, Peterson is a comparably accomplished ensemble player. He has an almost telepathic ability to share his ideas with fellow musicians, and he is also a supremely sympathetic accompanist, shading the balance and nature of his playing to offset the skills of the soloist as effectively as possible. He believes this results from his many years touring with the all-star soloists of Norman Granz's Jazz at the Philharmonic concert packages: "I learned a lot about accompaniment, and how everyone wanted something different," he told the author. "Lester Young, for example, wanted a kind of floating feeling, rooted in the basic time of the piece, whereas Dizzy Gillespie wanted a more sock-it-to-me aggressive kind of backing." As a consequence of the touring concerts, Peterson became Granz's preferred studio accompanist for his prolific Verve and Pablo record labels. Because he provided such sympathetic backing, the personality of the soloist shone through, from introverted singers like Billie Holiday to outrageous extroverts like trumpeters Clark Terry and Roy Eldridge.

Oscar Peterson grew up in the French-speaking part of Canada, among the minority black population of Montreal, where his father, of Caribbean background, was a Pullman porter on the Canadian railroad. Perhaps because he spent several days at a time away at his job (it took four days to cross Canada by train in the 1920s) and was then home for a similar spell of time, Peterson's father, a self-taught organist, took a strong interest in his children's musical education. He listened to their exercises when he was home and set tough tasks for them to learn while he was away. Oscar's older sister Daisy helped him to learn, although whereas she diligently practiced, as a boy Oscar had the innate ability to learn fast with far less dedicated application.

Oscar also discovered jazz, as the great American musicians of the day came to Montreal, a city whose French language and artistic climate earned it the nickname "Little Paris." "Duke Ellington, Count Basie, and later players like Nat King Cole all played in my hometown," Peterson recalled, "and there was a great air of musical expectancy about what we would hear at each of their performances."

Peterson's attitude toward the piano changed as he grew older and took lessons from some distinguished players who saw his potential. He won a contest that brought him to a radio audience as a teenager and began a broadcasting career that has continued throughout his life. He was already an established professional musician, with his own trio and a few local recordings behind him, when Norman Granz

heard him in 1948 at the Alberta Lounge in Montreal. Granz encouraged Peterson to travel to New York City for his debut at Carnegie Hall in September 1949.

To avoid work permit problems, Peterson was in the audience for the concert, and called up on stage by Granz, who put him on as a duo with bassist Ray Brown, thus beginning a musical partnership that has survived half a century. Audiences marveled at Peterson's swing, his dexterity, and above all his energy. After recording as a duo with Brown, Peterson added a guitar, initially played by Barney Kessell, and then, after a few changes, Herb Ellis, establishing a group that was a cornerstone of much 1950s jazz in concert and on record. The model was the piano-bass-guitar trio of Nat King Cole, as it had been for Art Tatum, but Peterson relentlessly pushed the band's musical horizons outward. He created an individual style in which the musicians worked much more as a fully integrated group than Tatum's trios, which were always vehicles for the leader's phenomenal piano skill, or Cole's, which featured his singing.

Later, Peterson substituted a drummer for guitar, with Ed Thigpen and Bobby Durham individually enjoying long stays in the trio, and bassist Sam Jones took over from Ray Brown, although Peterson and Brown were often reunited in the recording studio. They made numerous albums with other Jazz at the Philharmonic alumni, including trumpeters Roy Eldridge and Dizzy Gillespie, saxophonists Benny Carter and Stan Getz, and a range of singers including Ella Fitzgerald and Billie Holiday. Peterson's later trios—which had an equally packed recording

Oscar Emmanuel Peterson

BORN

August 15, 1925
Montreal, Canada

EDUCATION

Early piano lessons from Lou Hooper, then from Paul de Marky while attending Montreal High School

MAJOR INTEREST

Piano

ACCOMPLISHMENTS

Won Canadian Broadcasting Corporation contest at 14; prolific recording career since 1946. Regular appearances as television presenter of jazz programs since 1974 with award-winning Canadian *Oscar Peterson Presents* series. Many compositions, including *Canadiana Suite*, 1965

HONORS

Frequent poll winner, including *Downbeat* readers' poll 14 times, 10 *Playboy* Musicians' Musicians awards; Toronto Civic Medal, 1971; honorary doctorates from Carleton University (1973), Queen's University (1976), Concordia University (1979), Sackville University (1980), McMaster University, Victoria University (both 1981), York University (1982), Northwestern University (1983), University of Toronto, Laval University (both 1985); Companion of the Order of Canada, (1984); four Grammy awards, including *The Trio* (1975); Canada's Glenn Gould Prize (1993)

"Oscar Peterson must be considered more than an influence. He has become an institution."

—Gene Lees in *Oscar Peterson: The Will to Swing* (1988)

career backing the likes of such soloists as trumpeters Clark Terry and Freddie Hubbard—included guitarists Joe Pass, Lorne Lofsky, and Ulf Wakenius, bassist Niels-Henning Ørsted Pedersen, and drummers Louis Hayes and Martin Drew.

Peterson played some solo tours in the early 1970s, and from time to time he has explored a variety of other settings for his playing and compositions, but he has generally worked in a trio or, from the late 1980s, a quartet for the majority of his career. He has composed prolifically, from full-length suites to concert favorites like his "Nigerian Marketplace."

In 1993, Peterson suffered a stroke. With characteristic fortitude he returned to playing, depending more heavily on his right hand, but still taking on a challenging playing, recording, and teaching schedule. He has done much to foster young musicians, notably the pianist Benny Green, who was named Peterson's official protege in 1993. Peterson says of his teaching at York University in Ontario, Canada: "I don't believe you can actually teach jazz—all you can do is advise. I hold seminars, I bring in the quartet for workshops, I use videos, but all to give youngsters a grounding in what jazz is about, and to learn and listen with respect to those that have gone before them in the jazz tradition."

DISCOGRAPHY

The First Recordings. Indigo IGOCD 2070. [1945–46 trio/quartet sessions from Montreal.]

Jazz at the Philharmonic, Hartford 1953. Pablo Live 2308240. [Representative JATP concert displaying Peterson's

versatile accompaniment to a range of all-star soloists.]

The Song Is You: The Best of the Verve Songbooks. Verve 531558. [Peterson's trios, 1952–59, with Barney Kessell, Herb Ellis, Ray Brown, and Ed Thigpen.]

The Ultimate Oscar Peterson. Verve 539786. [Anthology, 1956–64, with guests Clark Terry and Milt Jackson.]

Exclusively for My Friends. MPS 513 830 (four-CD set). [Peterson's 1960s trio with bassist Sam Jones and drummers Bobby Durham and Louis Hayes.]

The Trio., Pablo 231070. [1970s trio with guitarist Joe Pass and bassist Niels-Henning Ørsted Pedersen.]

Jousts. Original Jazz Classics OJCCD 857. [Duos with trumpeters Harry Edison, Roy Eldridge, Jon Faddis, Dizzy Gillespie, and Clark Terry.]

Live at the Blue Note. Telarc CD 83304. [One of four-CD series recorded in 1990 with old colleagues.]

Oscar in Paris. Telarc CD 83414 (two-CD set). [A 1997 Paris concert.]

FURTHER READING

Lees, Gene. *Oscar Peterson: The Will to Swing*. 1988. Reprint, New York: Cooper Square, 2000.

Lyons, Len. *The Great Jazz Pianists*. New York: Morrow, 1983.

Palmer, Richard. *Oscar Peterson*. New York: Hippocrene, 1984.

Peterson, Oscar. *A Jazz Odyssey*. New York: Continuum, 2002.

WEBSITE

http://www.oscarpeterson.com/op

The pianists' own official and very comprehensive website.

More Jazz Pianists To Remember

One of the longest-lived of all jazz pianists was **Eubie Blake** (1883–1983). He was born in Baltimore just as the ragtime era began, began playing in public in the 1890s, and wrote the first of his many rags in 1899. He later became a popular song composer, writing several shows with singer and bandleader **Noble Sissle** (1889–1975). Revues like their *Shuffle Along* (1921) had a great impact on African-American music of the 1920s, and their songs, including "I'm Just Wild About Harry," became hits. More importantly, Blake wrote a number of jazz standards, including "Memories of You" (1930). As a pianist he never shed the jerky syncopations of ragtime, but he turned this to his advantage, and in his old age demonstrated the music that had been heard in bars and sporting houses at the start of the 20th century, predating almost all the main styles of piano jazz.

Like Blake, who influenced him, **James P. Johnson** (1894–1955) was an accomplished show composer. As well

Ragtime pianist Eubie Blake, pictured shortly before his 100th birthday, performed for decades after most people have retired.

as matching many of Blake's accomplishments, Johnson was a prime mover in the New York stride school of piano. He learned to play "shout" pieces, numbers that used strong simple phrases to help his playing cut through noisy dance halls, in which his repetitive right-hand figures sang out over a strong ragtime-influenced bass. In due course this became stride, in which the right-hand figures became more decorative, and the left more varied than the alternating bass notes and chords of ragtime. Johnson wrote some of the most influential stride compositions, including "Carolina Shout" (1917), and his hit songs and dances included "The Charleston," "Old Fashioned Love" and "Stop it, Joe!" He wrote two symphonies and a piano concerto, a one-act opera, and the piano fantasy *Yamekraw*, which had orchestration by fellow composer William Grant Still and was first performed by Fats Waller at Carnegie Hall in 1927. The piece has occasionally been revived and was recorded in the 1990s by **Marcus Roberts** (born 1963).

William Henry Joseph Bonaparte Bertholoff Smith, better known as **Willie "The Lion" Smith** (1897–1973), is the other major figure in stride piano. Of mixed Jewish and African-American parentage, Smith cut a dashing figure, with his characteristic derby hat, large cigar, and gold watch chain. His nickname was earned during World War I service in France, and his reputation was made in 1920s Harlem, where his delicate filigree compositions like "Echoes of Spring" and "Morning Air" contrasted with the more vigorous works of Waller and Johnson. As a player Smith was very much the equal of the other two, both as a soloist and

in the small recording band he led in the 1930s called his "Cubs." His longevity made him a celebrated figure in the New York jazz scene of the 1960s, where he still played regularly.

The younger white pianist **Ralph Sutton** (born 1922) has kept the stride tradition living into the 21st century. He first heard jazz played on the radio by Fats Waller and learned to copy the style himself before coming to New York City to play with trombonist Jack Teagarden. For many years he was the house pianist at the Greenwich Village club named for and run by guitarist Eddie Condon, where Willie "The Lion" Smith occasionally took his place. He later played in the World's Greatest Jazz Band before starting on a long and distinguished solo career.

The link between players of Waller's generation and Sutton was Chicagoan **Joe Sullivan** (1906–71). Sullivan made his name among the white musicians of the Chicago Austin High School Gang (see Part 1). His playing combined elements of stride with boogie woogie, Earl Hines's "trumpet" style, and the bravura of classical pianists. His famous composition "Little Rock Getaway" exemplifies this eclectic mixture over a strong boogie foundation.

One of the most influential early figures in boogie woogie itself was **Clarence "Pine Top" Smith** (1904–29), who was accidentally shot dead when a fight broke out among his audience at a performance. His "Pine Top's Boogie Woogie" (1928) was very widely imitated and gives a sense of how the music at a Chicago rent party must have sounded.

Meade "Lux" Lewis (1905–64), mentioned in the section on Albert

Ammons, had actually recorded his "Honky Tonk Train Blues" in 1927, well before Smith's first recording, but the Paramount company failed to issue it until later, although it became equally widely imitated with its representations of train sounds. Lewis wrote several other influential boogie woogie pieces and continued playing until late in his life. He experimented on other instruments, recording a series of sides with clarinetist Edmond Hall on which he played the celesta.

Jimmy Yancey (1900–51) was never a full-time pianist. From 1925 until his death he worked on the grounds at the home of the Chicago White Sox baseball team, Comiskey Park. Yet in his relatively few recordings he showed he was a boogie woogie player of great feeling, with a powerful blues ability. His playing has been widely analyzed because of the immense variety of the left-hand patterns in his compositions, which have names such as "State Street Special" and "Yancey Stomp."

Perhaps the person most associated with jazz piano around the world—who at first glance seems an unlikely figure—is the English-born **Marian McPartland** (born Marian Turner, in 1920). She was already an established pianist in Britain when she married cornetist Jimmy McPartland in 1945 and settled in the United States with him. She quickly became known as a major soloist on the New York scene, especially during a long residency at the Embers club with her trio. Subsequently she has become a tremendous ambassador for jazz, hosting a National Public Radio series *Piano Jazz,* which has been syndicated to many parts of the world since the 1970s. She has

Since the time this publicity shot was taken, pianist Marian McPartland has gone on to host a jazz radio program and to write several accomplished books about jazz.

interviewed and played with many of the world's major jazz pianists, among whom she herself is numbered, both as a composer and a performer, notably on her 1991 solo disc in a famous series from Maybeck Recital Hall in Berkeley, California.

The other jazz pianist who has made himself an equally significant ambassador for jazz through his playing, education work with the touring Jazzmobile concerts, and many years of radio and television broadcasting is **Dr. Billy Taylor** (born 1921). He worked on 52nd Street in New York in the transition from swing to bebop, and then became house pianist at the Birdland club as the modern jazz movement was at its height. At one time the bandleader on several series of television shows hosted by David Frost, he appears regularly on the CBS television program *Sunday Morning.* He has also written the standard history of jazz piano playing, *Jazz Piano: a Jazz History* (1982), and is adept at demonstrating all the styles he describes.

52nd Street in New York City between 6th and 7th Avenues where there were myriad jazz clubs during the 1940s was known as "the street that never slept."

4 Birth of Bebop— The Modern Jazz Revolution

At the end of the 1930s, just as the rumblings of World War II were beginning, the seeds were sown for a far-reaching revolution in jazz. The big bands of Count Basie, the Dorsey Brothers, Duke Ellington, Benny Goodman, Artie Shaw, and others were internationally popular, and the swing style of music that they played was the dance music of the day throughout the developed world. Indeed, the Swing Era was the last time in jazz history when jazz itself would be the prevailing type of popular music.

Yet popularity brought with it uniformity and orthodoxy, and musicians at every level began to chafe at the restrictions of the swing style. For a start, if a soloist had played a particularly popular solo on a record, the paying public wanted to hear that same solo every time the band played live. Instead of being able to improvise freely within the few measures of solo space allowed in most arrangements, instrumentalists found themselves hemmed in by their own past solos, or even more restrictively, by those of their predecessors. When veteran saxophonist Benny Waters replaced Willie Smith in the Jimmy Lunceford lineup, for example, he was not too thrilled to be packed off to learn all Smith's recorded solos by heart so that the band would still sound the same to its audiences.

Furthermore, the more successful a band was, the more it was constrained in what it could play. If it had a string of hits, then for most dances or concerts it would be expected to perform all of them, leaving limited room for new tunes. Consequently, very few evenings went by without, say, Count Basie's band having to play "One O'Clock Jump," "Jive at Five," Jumpin' at the Woodside," and all its other most popular numbers. The busiest bands of all avoided this. Cab Calloway, for example, with regular broadcasts and a monthly recording session, plowed through new arrangements and commissioned more songs about his stock characters Minnie the Moocher and Smoky Joe, shrewdly managing matters so that the subject matter remained familiar even when the songs were new. Even so, by the time his musicians had played four or five shows a day, they soon tired of even the most demanding new arrangements.

At the same time, small swing groups were playing in the smaller night-clubs of the big U.S. cities, or in after-hours bars that stayed open all night. These small groups encouraged the idea of the informal jam session where musicians got together to compete in improvising long solos over the melodies and

IN THIS PART

DIZZY GILLESPIE

CHARLIE PARKER

MILES DAVIS

BUD POWELL

THELONIOUS MONK

ART BLAKEY

CHARLES MINGUS

SARAH VAUGHAN

harmonies of well-known tunes. This was not unlike what had gone on in Kansas City (described in the Count Basie profile in section 2), but before the 1930s were over two things happened.

First, the practice of improvisation became international, and in doing so jazz moved irrevocably from using the melody of a tune to depending on its harmonic structure as the basis for improvisation. When visiting Americans like Fats Waller turned up in London, they were whisked off to after-hours venues such as the Bag O' Nails where they were encouraged to pit their wits against local players. Waller, Coleman Hawkins, Benny Carter, and members of the Duke Ellington, Cab Calloway and Teddy Hill bands all experienced this in Britain, as well as elsewhere in pre–World War II Europe. Hawkins, in particular, appeared as a soloist with local rhythm sections in Europe during a three-year stay in the 1930s. Because he was able to improvise lengthy solos on almost every tune he played, he moved forward the language of the saxophone in a way that would have been impossible if he had remained at home as a big-band sideman. When Hawkins and Carter, who also spent an extended period in Europe, returned to the United States they had a big impact on how soloists tackled improvisations. Hawkins cut his influential disc of "Body and Soul," in which his playing blatantly ignored the melody after a few bars, and wrought a new melodic line for the piece by using the underlying chords.

Second, within the United States big band players stifled by the lack of creativity in their regular careers (however well-paid and high-profile) started to use jam sessions to try out new musical ideas. In the band buses and rehearsal rooms of the swing era, a movement began which was to become known as the modern jazz revolution, and which was to acquire the trivial name of "bebop," taken from the title of a Dizzy Gillespie tune.

There were several characteristics of this revolutionary change. First, players tackled the underlying harmony of tunes, and substituted new chords with richer, less predictable combinations of notes. For example, the well-known ballad "I Can't Get Started," made famous by swing era trumpeter Bunny Berigan, received a completely new transition to its central theme, worked out by Dizzy Gillespie, Tadd Dameron, and Thelonious Monk, which made it sound immediately more modern and fresh. Many other famous tunes were similarly treated. Second, new harmonies were introduced to the melodies that players improvised. Stressing unusual intervals like the "flatted fifth"—lowering the fifth note of the scale by a half-tone to create a passing effect of dissonance—they played solos based on "extended" chords that used intervals of 9ths, 11ths, and 13ths. The resulting sound seemed "sour" to many 1940s listeners. Third they developed their techniques in order to play at dazzling speed. This was the hallmark of trumpeter Dizzy Gillespie, saxophonist Charlie Parker, and pianist Bud Powell. And fourth, they broke up the underlying rhythm so that the smooth four-beats-to-the-measure chug of a big swing band was replaced with jagged, broken punctuations from snare drum and bass drum, and the basic timekeeping moved to the cymbals.

Some commentators have viewed this period in jazz history as a moment of revolution. They believe that African-American jazz musicians developed a more complex style of playing to exclude white musicians—a form of protest against a music industry in which big bands like Goodman's or Shaw's were paid more and promoted better than their African-American equivalents. Such commentators view the after-hours clubs of New York, such as Minton's Playhouse and Clarke Monroe's Uptown House, as the hotbed of this revolution.

Like all such observations there is a grain of truth in this view, but the reality is far broader. The pressure for change was by no means restricted to New York or other big cities. Many of the new approaches to harmony and improvisation were worked out on the road within big bands and then tried out in late-night clubs wherever the band happened to be in its travels. Equally, the New York clubs encouraged swing stars with no revolutionary credentials to sit in and jam, whether black or white. And finally, among the most high-profile of the earliest bebop players were several white musicians, including trumpeter Johnny Carisi, pianists Al Haig and George Wallington, and drummer Stan Levey.

Underlying the bebop revolution was a far more fundamental issue than that of short-term protest, an issue that marked what the British critic Charles Fox called a "psychological shift" on the part of those who developed it. Jazz was no longer to be primarily music for social dance; it was to be music to *listen* to. No longer would commercial pressures be the main agent of change in jazz: From the 1940s on, change would come from the musicians themselves.

Finally, like any new style, bebop went hand-in-hand with a set of new fashions that included clothes, speech, and behavior. Both Dizzy Gillespie and Thelonious Monk sported goatee beards, horn-rimmed eyeglasses, and berets. Most players also adopted exaggerated pinstripe suits, and by the late 1940s, encouraged by marketing hype, Gillespie's audiences turned up wearing false beards, plus spectacles, and berets. Just as the music itself was higher, faster, and more complex than what had gone before, so was a new brand of scat singing that accompanied it.

Vocalists like Babs Gonzales, Joe "Bebop" Carroll, and Kenny Hagood specialized in numbers like "Oo-pap-a-da" or "Oop-Bop-Sh'Bam," in which they negotiated intricate melody lines while singing a stream of nonsense syllables that usually contained the words "bebop" and "rebop." This went together with behavior that challenged the establishment. At a superficial level, this meant fast-talking, hip slang, and hand-slapping greetings that were parodied in *Time* magazine with Benny Carter and Dizzy Gillespie demonstrating a "bebop greeting."

Before long several musicians, including Gillespie, Max Roach, and Charles Mingus, started their own record companies. Gillespie toured for the U.S. State Department, but insisted on ordinary people as well as diplomats and high society attending his concerts in the Middle East. On the whole, by freeing itself from some levels of commercial pressures the new music freed subsequent generations of jazz musicians to experience a healthy state of independence from the main currents in popular music.

Dizzy Gillespie

GROOVIN' HIGH

With his upswept horn, puffed-out cheeks, goatee, beret, and horn-rimmed spectacles, Dizzy Gillespie's extrovert persona typified the jazz revolution of the 1940s. His trumpet innovations made him the heir to Louis Armstrong and Roy Eldridge as the foremost trumpeter of his time, but he was also the first musician to write down, organize, and intellectualize the new developments in jazz that took place between 1939 and 1945. He went on to transfer these ideas to the big band format, helped popularize the bossa nova, and eventually became an elder statesman of jazz, continuing the ambassadorial role of Louis Armstrong.

Gillespie's birthplace, Cheraw, South Carolina, was a small southern settlement, in which segregation and poverty were facts of life for African Americans. His given name was John Birks Gillespie, and he was the youngest of nine children, two of whom died in infancy. His father James had an irascible temper, and he often savagely beat his children. In later life Gillespie attributed the rebellious streak in his own character to withstanding his father's brutal behavior.

Dizzy Gillespie in his New York apartment in 1946, wears bebop garb, including beret, glasses, and a pinstripe suit.

Ironically, James's hobby was music, and he ran a band in addition to his construction job. Several instruments were kept in the Gillespie home and sooner or later young John Birks tried his hand at them, helped along when the state donated more instruments to his school, where he took up trombone and then cornet.

James Gillespie died suddenly when John Birks was 10, leaving the family almost destitute, a situation made worse when the head of the local bank ran off with their savings. John Birks went wild for a time, but his teacher, Alice Wilson, recognized his talent, and encouraged his cornet playing. Like many other poor African-American children in the area, John took jobs in the cotton fields and on the road gangs around Cheraw during his vacations from school, but he vowed there had to be a better way to earn a living.

Fortunately, John Birks was accepted by the Laurinburg Institute in North Carolina. He got there on his musical and football abilities, although he soon abandoned sports to protect his teeth for playing the trumpet. He studied hard alongside his cousin, trombonist Norman Powe, and the two young men soon found that their work on brass and piano took them beyond the knowledge of the teachers at the institute.

In 1935, John Birks's mother and family left Cheraw for Philadelphia. Consequently, he dropped out of school, and traveled north to join them. His ambition was to join an established Philadelphia band, and he eventually played in one led by Frankie Fairfax, which had regular work around the city. The band's drummer took one look at John Birks fooling around on piano at a rehearsal and asked, "Who's that dizzy cat?" The name stuck, and for the rest of his life Gillespie was to be known as Dizzy.

With Fairfax, Gillespie developed his own style, based on Roy Eldridge's playing, helped along by section mates Carl "Bama" Warwick and Charlie Shavers. With similar young and adventurous musicians alongside him, Gillespie started to write and arrange, and was able to try out his ideas on the bandstand every night. Fairfax occasionally hired out his entire band to other leaders. It was with multi-instrumentalist Tiny Bradshaw that Gillespie got his first taste of life on the road, when Bradshaw "borrowed" Fairfax's orchestra in this way.

Bradshaw subsequently lured away Shavers and Warwick, who then joined Lucius "Lucky" Millinder's band. They persuaded Millinder to hire their friend Dizzy, but after Gillespie had moved to New York City in 1937, the job fell through. Fortunately, he sat in at the Savoy Ballroom with Chick Webb's band, which brought him to the attention of another regular there, Teddy Hill. Hill was about to set sail for Europe and needed a trumpeter. Gillespie accepted the job with alacrity. Within days he had made a set of discs with Hill's band, and they left New York for Paris, London, Manchester, and Dublin.

On their return to New York, Gillespie remained off and on with Hill for two years, also playing for Edgar Hayes. Hayes' drummer was a young man called Kenny Clarke, who was experimenting with new ideas about rhythm, transferring the beat to his cymbals and reserving his snare and bass drums for jagged, uneven punctuations that prodded the soloists and the band along. He and Gillespie struck up a friendship and on their nights off they went to Harlem's after-hours clubs like Monroe's Uptown House or Minton's Playhouse to sit in and try out new ideas.

In 1939 Gillespie joined Cab Calloway's Cotton Club Orchestra. The young trumpeter was quickly given a chance to display his solo talents and to contribute some of his arrangements

John Birks "Dizzy" Gillespie

BORN
October 21, 1917
Cheraw, South Carolina

DIED
January 6, 1993
Englewood Cliffs, New Jersey

EDUCATION
Robert Smalls School, Cheraw, South Carolina; music scholarship, Laurinburg Institute, North Carolina

MAJOR INTERESTS
Trumpet, bandleading, composing, arranging

ACCOMPLISHMENTS
A leading swing band trumpeter. Prime mover in establishing modern jazz (bebop) trumpet style; led pioneer bebop band on 52nd Street, 1943–44; co-led quintet with Charlie Parker; formed own big band, 1945. Founded own Dee Gee record label, early 1950s. Composed or co-wrote dozens of important pieces including "Algo Bueno," "A Night in Tunisia," "Cubana Be–Cubana Bop," "Groovin' High," "Manteca," "Ool-Ya-Koo," and "Salt Peanuts"

HONORS
Regular poll winner, including *Down Beat* critics' polls, 1971–75; honorary doctorate, Rutgers University, 1970; Handel Medal, New York, 1972; Commandant of the Ordre des lettres et arts, France; Smithsonian Institution medal, 1990; statue erected in Le Cannet, France, 1993

Gillespie began playing a trumpet with an upswept bell in the mid-1950s. He claimed that his instrument was accidentally bent during a party and he liked the sound. More probably, he had it specially made, in imitation of a British trumpeter he met in the 1930s.

to the band. Gillespie produced some spirited, forward-looking music for Calloway that already included many of the ideas he was to incorporate into bebop. There was the flatted fifth, audacious extended chords, and Gillespie's own rapidly developing trumpet technique that took him way into the upper register, coupled with a speed that many found uncanny and disorienting to listen to.

At after-hours clubs, Gillespie's movement toward a new trumpet style could be heard. He arrived at his new concept earlier than many others of his generation in New York, although there was a similar movement going on in places like Kansas City, where he bumped into saxophonist Charlie Parker and arranger Tad Dameron, when he was there on a Calloway tour during 1940.

Gillespie's personality got in the way of his relationship with Cab, and he was eased out of the limelight by Calloway's preferred soloist, Jonah Jones. Gillespie's temper was quickly roused, and he had an immature fondness for pranks. Eventually, when Jones flicked a spitball across the stage, Cab, ignorant of the culprit, blamed Gillespie. Gillespie flashed a knife. Cab was cut, and Gillespie was fired.

Gillespie left Calloway in late 1942. After a short spell with Ella Fitzgerald, he joined Benny Carter's small group for a four-month residency in New York City. This brought his innovative playing to the attention of critics, and within a few months of leaving Carter he made discs with Les Hite and Lucky Millinder. Gillespie's work on display on these recordings is that of a trendsetting individualist whose innovative playing stands apart from his more swing-oriented fellows. This was matched by a new direction and determination in Gillespie, fueled by some months he spent alongside Charlie Parker in Earl Hines' band in 1943, where both men had the chance to share the development of their ideas.

Parker did not stay with Gillespie after they both left Hines, and Dizzy had the honor of taking the first full-fledged bebop band into the heart of New York's clubland on 52nd Street in late 1943. Gillespie not only made headlines with his new music, he also accidentally gave it a name when journalists asking what he'd just played got the answer "Bebop!" He was giving the title of a tune, but the word stuck as the identification of the whole new genre.

When Gillespie and Parker reunited in 1945, first in Billy Eckstine's big band (an offshoot of Hines' group) and later in their own quintet on 52nd Street, bebop became firmly ensconced as a new and distinctive style. Many histories of jazz suggest that when Gillespie took his quintet with Parker to California in 1945–46 it was not a success, however the recordings and reputation they made were significant and the band was far more successful than such accounts would have us believe.

Back in New York City, Gillespie formed his first big band in 1945. It had a difficult tour of the South, but it marked the beginning of a successful sequence of orchestras in which he transferred the small-group ideas of bebop to a large ensemble. Gillespie's 1946–50 band took his new jazz to Europe in 1948, where they toured and made a string of remarkable recordings

"Our music is universal. It shares the rhythmic content of African music, music of the Western hemisphere and various lands of the East, and has merged this music with European harmonies, the soul of the slaves, the blues and spirituals to create jazz."

—Dizzy Gillespie in *To Be or Not to Bop* (1979)

that have seldom been surpassed for sheer energy and excitement. These included a dynamic fusion of jazz and Cuban music with a lineup that briefly included a brilliant Cuban percussionist, Chano Pozo, who was murdered at the height of his career.

Gillespie himself began to be featured as a soloist in Norman Granz's Jazz at the Philharmonic (JATP) concerts. In due course Granz took over Dizzy's recording career, teaming him up with Stan Getz, and later with Sonny Stitt and Sonny Rollins. Not all of Gillespie's own groups were as successful as these occasional recording projects or his JATP appearances. However, in 1956 he toured the Middle East and South America for the State Department with a new and remarkable big band that contained arrangers Quincy Jones and Melba Liston alongside an array of exceptional soloists. This band was one of the finest Gillespie led until the United Nation Orchestra of his final years, although his early 1960s collaborations with pianist and composer Lalo Schifrin produced some sparkling big band performances like the *Gillespiana Suite*.

With Schifrin he also recorded *bossa nova* tunes that helped launch the vogue for this Latin rhythm in the United States.

From the mid-1950s until the late 1980s, Gillespie usually worked with a quintet, often including saxophonist James Moody, continuing to play the kind of bebop with which he had made his name. Not every version of his band was up to his own highest standards, but by touring the festival and club circuit, Gillespie ensured that the worldwide public could continue to come face-to-face with him as a legendary innovator. He became seen as the father figure of jazz, appearing on everything from *The Muppet Show* to films about his triumphant visits to Cuba. His final United Nation Orchestra drew a lifetime of musical experience and his Baha'i spiritual beliefs about unity into a remarkably potent big band that eventually broke up with the onset of his final illness.

DISCOGRAPHY

Dizzy Gillespie 1945. Classics 888. [Cross section of Gillespie's 1945 sessions, including earliest discs with Charlie Parker.]

Dizzy Gillespie 1945–46. Classics 935. [Includes music recorded during Gillespie's 1945–46 West Coast tour.]

Complete RCA Victor Recordings. Bluebird 66528-2 (two- CD set). [Includes Gillespie's debut with Teddy Hill, and his own big bands from the late 1940s.]

Birks Works. Verve 527900 (two-CD set). [Gillespie's State Department tour big band.]

Dizzy's Diamonds: The Best of the Verve Years. Verve 513875-2 (three- CD set). [Highlights of Gillespie's collaborations

with Norman Granz, including exemplary quintets, big bands, and sessions with other Verve artists.]

Gillespiana/Carnegie Hall Concert. Verve 519809-2. [Extended compositions from 1960–61 by Lalo Schifrin for Gillespie and unconventional big band with only one reed and French horns added to the brass.]

Live at the Royal Festival Hall. Enja 6044. [1989 concert by United Nation Orchestra.]

Gillepie's recordings with Cab Calloway are listed in the Calloway discography in Part 2, and can be found on Classics 595, 614, and 625. See the Charlie Parker discography, in this section for other collaborations between Gillespie and Parker.

FURTHER READING

Gentry, Tony. *Dizzy Gillespie, Performer, Bandleader, and Composer*. New York: Chelsea House, 1991.

Gillespie, Dizzy, with Al Fraser. *Dizzy: To Be or Not to Bop*. New York: Doubleday, 1979.

Lees, Gene. *Waiting for Dizzy*. New York: Oxford University Press, 1991.

McRae, Barry. *Dizzy Gillespie: His Life and Times*. New York: Universe, 1988.

Shipton, Alyn. *Groovin' High: The Life of Dizzy Gillespie*. New York, Oxford University Press, 1999.

WEBSITE

http://www.geocities.com/BourbonStreet/8466/
Lengthy biography with many links.

Charlie Parker

BIRD LIVES

Whereas in the modern jazz revolution of the 1940s Dizzy Gillespie was the figure whose appearance, ideas, and compositions came to personify the style of bebop, Charlie Parker was the intuitive genius whose stylistic innovations and dazzling technical skill on the saxophone gave it heart and soul. He was among the first saxophonists to hear how the higher notes of a—the 9ths, 11ths, and 13ths that lie beyond the first octave—could be used as the basis for melody lines that, while firmly rooted in the underlying harmonies of a tune, sounded innovative and fresh.

Parker mastered the art of taking the structure of a familiar song or ballad and creating a new, modernistic tune over the same chords; examples include his complex melody "Koko," based on Ray Noble's "Cherokee," and "Anthropology," based on George Gershwin's "I Got Rhythm." Parker combined this melodic and harmonic awareness with a daring sense of rhythm. He played with immense fluidity and rapidity, often emphasizing the weaker beats in a measure,

The Charlie Parker quintet plays at Three Deuces on 52nd Street, New York, fall 1947. The players include, from left to right, Tommy Potter, Parker, Max Roach (almost obscured behind Parker), and Miles Davis. The quintet was completed by pianist Duke Jordan.

Charlie Parker reunited with Dizzy Gillespie on the stage of Carnegie Hall in September 1947. It was their first joint appearance since their 1945–46 tour to California.

in deliberate contrast to his accompanying piano, bass, and drums, which set up a dramatic tension between them.

It took great mental discipline for his accompanists to maintain their underlying pulse as Parker took his improvisations further and further away from it, before returning dramatically at the end of a phrase or chorus.

Parker's musical genius—and to many critics he was the most gifted of all improvisers in jazz history—went hand in hand with a wayward personality. He was casual about possessions, often pawning his saxophones or making do with borrowed or damaged instruments, and his enormous personal charm was at odds with his dependence on narcotics and his complicated family relationships.

Charles Parker Jr. was born on August 29, 1920, to Addie and Charles

Parker in Kansas City, Kansas. Across the Missouri River was the larger, flourishing town, also called Kansas City but in the state of Missouri. The family moved there in 1927. Like many others, including Count Basie, they took advantage of the regime of the Pendergasts, the dynasty who controlled the city, and through encouraging trade, gambling, and entertainment, managed to keep it alive as a commercial center during the Great Depression. Charles Sr., who had been a traveling musician, enjoyed the free and easy atmosphere of their new home, but within a year or two he had left the family for good.

For Charles Jr. living in Kansas City was an opportunity to hear jazz and blues at first hand, and to try playing saxophone himself. From all accounts, Parker's adolescence was an uneasy blend of brilliance and frustration. He often tried out new ideas before he had mastered the skills to play them properly, and it was not until 1939, during a visit to New York City, that he finally worked out how to play the new and exciting improvisations he had glimpsed in his imagination. He had dropped out of school early and forged his credentials to join the musicians' union at age 14, but he failed to land a mainstream job in music until he joined a big band led by pianist and singer Jay McShann in 1940, when he was 20.

McShann had sympathy for the young saxophonist. He himself had arrived in Kansas from Muskogee, Oklahoma, and was nicknamed "Hootie" by the local musicians after they managed to get him comprehensively drunk on local bootleg liquor on his first night in town. So he knew the frustrations of being picked on and criticized if you were a young player with something to prove. In his band, Parker flourished, becoming widely known as a new and rising star on the alto saxophone.

On June 24, 1940, Parker met the equally controversial trumpeter Dizzy Gillespie, who was at that time in Cab Calloway's band. They both realized that they had ideas in common, and their chance to try them out came when Earl Hines hired both Parker and Gillespie to join his touring big band in the early spring of 1943.

On the road, in hotel dressing rooms, in rehearsals, and on the bandstand, Parker and Gillespie thrashed out their ideas. Hines had little sympathy for them, believing that bebop, as it was eventually called, would not be popular dance music, which he was in business to provide. But the intense formal training ground of a band like

Hines', with constant new arrangements to learn, shows to back up, and a string of top-notch soloists to compete with, encouraged Parker and Gillespie's ideas. It was during this year that they worked out how to alter the whole basis of jazz improvisation. They created new melodies on the less familiar parts of a tune's harmonies and created long, rapid melodic lines that more often than not ignored the conventional pauses in a tune's structure and placed accents in unexpected and exciting positions.

Both men left Hines' band later in 1943 but were reunited in singer Billy Eckstine's big band in 1944 before forming a series of small groups to play their new music. They made their first discs together in 1945, including Parker's greatest improvisational triumph, "Koko." However, even by the time the two had met, Parker—nicknamed "Yardbird" or just "Bird"—was already a drug user and involved in a chaotic domestic situation with a teenage bride, Rebecca, and a young son, Leon. Gillespie appeared eccentric and outlandish on stage, but was in reality a shrewd organizer and businessman. Parker carried outlandishness into every area of his life.

When Parker, Gillespie, and their group set off for the West Coast in late 1945 to take their new music to California, Gillespie took vibraphone player Milt Jackson and saxophonist Lucky Thompson along as well, just in case the erratic Parker failed to make all their sessions. The few recorded pieces on which Parker appears are magnificent, but he failed to appear on several club and record dates, and when Gillespie returned to New York, Parker stayed in the West. His dependence on drugs with a less regular or familiar

Charles "Charlie" Parker Jr.

BORN

August 29, 1920
Kansas City, Kansas

DIED

March 12, 1955
New York, New York

EDUCATION

Crispus Attucks School and Lincoln High School, Kansas City, Missouri; played baritone horn in Lincoln High School band, learned saxophone informally at home from age 13

MAJOR INTEREST

Saxophone

ACCOMPLISHMENTS

Revolutionized jazz saxophone playing and influenced a school of saxophonists including Cannonball Adderley, Frank Morgan, Sonny Stitt, and Phil Woods. Created several tunes, of which many began as improvised solos, that became staples of the bebop repertoire, including "Anthropology," "Klaktoveedstedsteen," "Koko," "Moose the Mooche," Now's the Time," "Ornithology," and "Scrapple from the Apple." Helped make "difficult" modern jazz pieces popular with a wide audience

HONORS

Frequent winner of *Down Beat* and *Metronome* polls; statue erected at 18th and Vine streets in Kansas City, Missouri

> *"Bird contributed more and received less than anybody."*
>
> —Max Roach in *Bird: The Legend of Charlie Parker* (1988)

supply than he was used to in New York led to a breakdown, graphically, if inaccurately, portrayed in Clint Eastwood's 1988 film *Bird*, and Parker underwent a cure in a Camarillo, California, hospital.

When he returned to jazz, the last decade of Parker's short life was a series of peaks and troughs. His brilliance is captured in the series of recordings he made for the Savoy, Dial, and Verve labels. His fleetness of execution on his instrument and constant flow of ideas made him a hugely influential figure. Conversely, there are many stories of the degradation he imposed on himself through his drug habit, and there is no doubt that his fast-lane lifestyle contributed to his early death in March 1955. Before then, he had married again, twice, and produced further children. His second marriage, to Geraldine, lasted little longer than his first. Parker remained married to his third wife, Doris, until his death, but he also had a common-law wife, Chan, with whom he had two children. Of her three children, Parker's stepdaughter Kim and his son Baird, went on to become musicians.

He launched the career of Miles Davis through their recordings together in the late 1940s, and he controlled his habit sufficiently to tour Europe and to make recordings with strings and with all-star groups including Jazz at the Philharmonic and Stan Kenton's band.

The Birdland club was named for Parker in the 1950s, but, after playing at the New York City venue several times, his erratic lifestyle meant he was seldom booked there in his final years.

To all who knew him, Parker was a fascinating and compelling character whose sheer brilliance as a musician outshone all other aspects of his complex and problematic personality. He read widely and could converse on almost any subject under the sun. His main legacy is the music of a questing intelligence combined with an uncanny depth of feeling for the blues.

DISCOGRAPHY

Jay McShann: Blues from Kansas City. MCA GRD-614. [Parker's first commercial recordings, including "Swingmatism."]

The Charlie Parker Story. Savoy SV 0105. [Important November 1945 session marking Parker's debut under his own name, with a blistering version of "Koko." Miles Davis plays trumpet on several tracks.]

Charlie Parker on Dial: The Complete Sessions. Spotlite SPJ CD 4 4101 (four-CD set). [Covers 1946–47, spanning Parker's West Coast breakdown.]

Bird: The Complete Charlie Parker on Verve. Verve 837141 (10-CD set). [All of Parker's Verve recordings, 1946–54. Includes Parker with strings, reunited with Gillespie, in a series of his own quartets and quintets, and in Jazz at the Philharmonic concerts.]

The Quintet: Jazz at Massey Hall. Original Jazz Classics OJC 044. [1953 Canadian concert with Parker, Gillespie, Powell, Mingus, and Roach, often described as the most important bebop recording of all.]

See the Dizzy Gillespie discography, found earlier in this section, for additional quintet recordings.

FURTHER READING

Frankl, Ron. *Charlie Parker*. New York: Chelsea House, 1992.

Giddins, Gary. *Celebrating Bird: The Triumph of Charlie Parker*. 1986. Reprint, New York: Da Capo, 1999.

Koch, Lawrence O. *Yardbird Suite: A Compendium of the Music and Life of Charlie Parker*. Boston: Northeastern University Press, 1999.

Priestley, Brian. *Charlie Parker*. New York: Hippocrene, 1984.

Reisner, Robert George. *Bird: The Legend of Charlie Parker*. 1962. Reprint, New York: Da Capo, 1988.

Russell, Ross. *Bird Lives! The High Life and Hard Times of Charlie (Yardbird) Parker*. 1973. Reprint. New York: Da Capo, 1996.

Vail, Ken. *Bird's Diary: The Life of Charlie Parker 1945–55*. Chessington, Surrey, England: Castle, 1996.

Woideck, Carl. *Charlie Parker: His Music and Life*. Ann Arbor: University of Michigan Press, 1998.

——. *Charlie Parker Companion: Six Decades of Commentary*. New York: Simon & Schuster, 1998.

WEBSITE

http://www.charlieparker.com
A comprehensive site with biography, pictures, and sound files.

Miles Davis

PRINCE OF DARKNESS

B ecause Miles Davis followed in Dizzy Gillespie's footsteps as the frontline partner in Charlie Parker's quintet, and because he had been a member of Coleman Hawkins' transitional swing-to-bebop band, his earliest work clearly places him within the modern jazz revolution of the 1940s. From there he went on to be one of the most consistently inventive, trendsetting, and innovative musicians in jazz's later periods. Even though there were times when his career faltered from ill health, narcotics, or injury, he set the pace for jazz development over four decades, from the 1940s to the 1980s, and the breadth of his achievement is staggering. Unlike Gillespie, Davis was not a technical innovator on the trumpet. His playing lacked the rapidity, verve, range, and brilliance of the most consummate bebop trumpeters, who also included Fats Navarro, Howard McGhee, and Clifford Brown. Yet Davis created an immediately identifiable personal voice: a clear vibrato-free tone with a logic about

Miles Davis sits with his trademark muted trumpet at around the time he recorded his best-selling album *Kind of Blue* in 1959.

the placement of each note that stamped his authority on all his groups and dictated how those around him would approach his music.

With the guidance of arranger Gil Evans, Davis's nine-piece group launched the cool jazz movement of the late 1940s, and subsequent Evans–Davis collaborations included some of the most compelling jazz for soloist and large orchestra ever written, including *Sketches of Spain* and arrangements of *Porgy and Bess*. In the meantime, Davis's small groups moved during the 1950s from the bebop of his early bands to the exploration of modal jazz, which employs improvisations built around modal scales rather than conventional harmonic chord changes. This allowed complex solo improvisations over a relatively simple background and helped his music to remain accessible and popular. In the 1960s he experimented with freer approaches to rhythm before adding instrumentation more familiar in rock music to his lineup, and in the 1970s and 1980s he became a leading figure in jazz-rock fusion.

Miles Davis grew up in East St. Louis, Illinois, now one of the poorest cities in the United States, in dramatic contrast to its prosperous opposite neighbor, St. Louis, Missouri. But in the 1920s and 1930s when Davis was growing up there, it had been for a time a well-to-do black city.

Davis's father was a dentist, and in Miles's own words "one of the pillars of the black community." Davis senior was an educated, middle-class man, and he gave his son a fierce pride in being an African American, backed up by an old-fashioned sense of discipline, even when his rambunctious son rode a bicycle down the stairs in the house or set fire to the garage.

Davis took music lessons from his early teens, and encouraged by his school bandmaster Mr. Buchanan, he decided to become a musician. While he was still at school he became famous locally, working for local bandleader Eddie Randle. After a fortnight sitting in with Billy Eckstine's famous big band, which included Dizzy Gillespie and Charlie Parker, Davis went to New York City to attend the Juilliard School of Music.

Davis always said his real music lessons came from playing alongside the musicians who were inventing bebop at the after-hours sessions in New York's jazz clubs. Instead of finishing his studies at Juilliard, he sought out and became friends with Charlie Parker, but he also jammed with and learned from other trumpeters like Fats Navarro, Freddy Webster, and Dizzy Gillespie. In October 1945, Davis joined Parker's band for two weeks at the Three Deuces. It was the beginning of a long musical association in which Davis became as significant a partner for Parker as Dizzy Gillespie had been.

To have landed a job with the greatest saxophonist in modern jazz at the age of 19 was exceptional, but it was only the start of a career that went on to be truly extraordinary. Davis began leading his own groups in his early 20s, and he also got to know the arranger Gil Evans, who ran experimental workshops on jazz. Out of these, Davis and Evans developed a new sound in jazz, a nine-piece band that included the unusual tone colors of the French horn, tuba, and baritone sax as well as the more conventional small group instruments. They did not make a huge impression on the jazz world in their live appearances in New York, but their 1949–50 recordings had quite the opposite effect, influencing a whole new approach to jazz. With saxophonists Gerry Mulligan and Lee Konitz plus drummer Max Roach among the participants, and compositions by Evans, Mulligan, pianist John Lewis, and trumpeter Johnny Carisi, they recorded an album titled *Birth of the Cool*.

As other musicians, including the West Coast groups led by trumpeter Shorty Rogers, adopted Davis's new style, he himself moved on to something else—which he was to do many times in his career, leaving others to develop his innovations. Davis fought off heroin addiction during some dismal years in the early 1950s. His addictive personality later led him to use cocaine and overindulge in alcohol, but his will to perform and innovate and a high level of physical fitness helped by regular workouts and boxing bouts in the gym allowed him to master his drug problems. In the early 1950s he led his own groups on the road and on record, playing hard bop—a style that combined bebop solos with the rhythms and harmonies of gospel music—alongside pianist Horace Silver, trombonist J. J. Johnson, and saxophonists Jimmy Heath and Jackie McLean. His collaborations with Gil Evans continued for many years, however, and Davis's clear-toned trumpet added a poignant lyricism to their album *Sketches of Spain*.

Most critics feel that Davis's greatest period started in 1955 with a Newport Jazz Festival appearance that caused a sensation and led record producer George Avakian to sign Davis to Columbia, an association that lasted for virtually the rest of his life. He formed his own quintet, featuring first John Coltrane, then Sonny Rollins. His music, which began to explore ideas of modes instead of more conventional jazz harmony, became the dominant influence in the jazz of the 1960s. But as other groups copied the sounds of his 1959 *Kind of Blue* album, he was already moving on. First he moved toward free jazz—abandoning the normal harmonic and rhythmic structure of the music— in a quintet that included saxophonist Wayne Shorter and pianist Herbie Hancock. Then he tried jazz-rock fusion, his bands including Chick Corea, John McLaughlin, Jack DeJohnette, Keith Jarrett, and other rock-influenced players. The dark, brooding sounds and

Miles Dewey Davis III

BORN

May 26, 1926
Alton, Illinois

DIED

September 28, 1991
Santa Monica, California

EDUCATION

Trumpet lessons from Elwood Buchanan. Lincoln High School, East St. Louis, Illinois; Juilliard School of Music, New York City, for approximately one year from fall 1944

MAJOR INTERESTS

Trumpet, bandleading

ACCOMPLISHMENTS

Fronted *Birth of the Cool* recordings, 1949–50. Quintet that he led in 1950s pioneered the move from chordal to modal improvisation. Collaborated with Gil Evans on large-band projects including *Sketches of Spain*. In 1960s led influential quintet with Wayne Shorter, Herbie Hancock, Ron Carter, and Tony Williams. Progressively introduced jazz-rock instrumentation and rhythms into jazz; with his final bands, broke new ground by combining trenchant jazz soloing with a funk-rock background

HONORS

Frequent winner of *Down Beat* readers' and critics' polls; honorary doctorate from New England Conservatory of Music, 1986

Miles Davis on stage in 1986 wears the flamboyant clothes and luxuriant dark wig that added to his "Prince of Darkness" persona. His music at this time was full of rock and funk beats.

swirling, crowded backgrounds of albums from this period, like *Bitches Brew* and *Live–Evil* (which included imagery of a negative, diabolical side to the trumpeter's character), helped create a dark image of Davis that inspired his nickname "Prince of Darkness."

Davis's group appeared at rock and pop festivals from the 1970s onward, moving his music beyond category to something that generated a huge popular following, and his string of successful albums made him one of the biggest-selling jazz musicians in history. His final bands, which he led after recovering from a car crash and a stroke, were punchy rock-based outfits that included musicians like guitarists John Scofield and Mike Stern and saxophonists Branford Marsalis, Bill Evans, and Bob Berg. Davis did not like to look backward, and seldom returned to his earlier repertoire or

styles in his inexorable determination to innovate. One of his last big band projects was characteristically forward-looking, as he teamed up with a Danish all-star band to play Palle Mikkelborg's composition *Aura,* which playfully reused allusions to Davis's earlier work in a series of movements built around colors. Ironically, Davis's final recording at the Montreux Festival in July 1991 was an uncharacteristically retrospective concert, where for virtually the first time since the 1950s he played some of the music he and Gil Evans had pioneered, supported by a big band directed by Quincy Jones.

By the time of his death, Davis had become the best known musician in jazz, as popular in the second half of the 20th century as Louis Armstrong had been in the first, and like Armstrong, he was able to take his music to the broadest possible public.

DISCOGRAPHY

Birth of the Cool. Capitol CDP 792862.

Best of Miles Davis. Blue Note 7982872. [Cross section of Davis's 1950s work from *Birth of the Cool* to his sextet with Cannonball Adderley, 1958.]

Miles Davis and The Modern Jazz Giants. Original Jazz Classics OJC 347. [Mid-1950s Davis with Milt Jackson, Thelonious Monk, and John Coltrane.]

Miles Davis and Gil Evans: The Complete Columbia Studio Sessions. Columbia CXK 67397 (six-CD set). [All the 1957–68 large-group albums from *Miles Ahead*, through *Porgy and Bess* to *Sketches of Spain*, plus the originally unreleased suites *Time of the Barracudas* and *Falling Water*.]

Kind of Blue. Columbia CK 64935. [Modal jazz album with pianist Bill Evans and John Coltrane.]

Miles Davis Quintet: Complete Columbia Studio Recordings, 1965–68. C6K 67398 (six-CD set). [Davis's mid-1960s quintet with Wayne Shorter, Herbie Hancock, Ron Carter, and Tony Williams. Charts the experiments with freer rhythmic and compositional forms that took Davis to the brink of his free jazz and jazz-rock periods.]

In a Silent Way. Columbia 450982. [Another pioneering album using looped tapes of sections of music mixed into an abstract whole.]

Bitches Brew. Columbia 460602. [Free-form, abstract, and loud, with Davis on the cusp between his free jazz and rock-fusion periods.]

Live–Evil. Columbia C2K 65138 (two-CD set). [1970, the summit of Miles's free form period. Mixes live with studio tracks.]

You're Under Arrest. Columbia 468703. [1980s Davis, with surging funk rhythms and cover versions of "Time After Time" and Michael Jackson's "Human Nature"
marking a late stage of Davis's immersion in jazz-rock.]

Aura. Columbia 463351. [Danish big band project recorded in 1985.]

FURTHER READING

Carner, Gary. *The Miles Davis Companion: Four Decades of Commentary.* New York: Schirmer, 1996.

Carr, Ian. *Miles Davis. The Definitive Biography.* London: HarperCollins, 1998.

Chambers, Jack. *Milestones: The Music and Times of Miles Davis.* 1985. Reprint, New York: Da Capo, 1998.

Crisp, George R. *Miles Davis.* New York: Watts, 1997.

Davis, Miles, and Quincy Troupe. *Miles: The Autobiography.* New York: Simon & Schuster, 1989.

Frankl, Ron. *Miles Davis.* New York: Chelsea House, 1997.

Kirchner, Bill. *A Miles Davis Reader.* Washington: Smithsonian Institution Press, 1997.

Vail, Ken. *Miles's Diary.* Chessington, Surrey, England: Castle, 1996.

WEBSITE

http://www.miles-davis.com
Official website from Sony/Columbia.

Bud Powell

BUD'S BUBBLE

lthough Bud Powell was younger than his great friend Thelonious Monk, he made an impact on the jazz world much earlier. A child prodigy, he made his first records with Cootie Williams's big band in 1944, before he was out of his teens. Between them, Monk and Powell brought about the most far-reaching changes to the jazz piano tradition to arise out of the 1940s modern jazz movement. Powell's principal importance was as a player. He adapted the fleet right-hand melody lines of players like Teddy Wilson and Art Tatum and added a sparse accompaniment with his left hand that drew on the Swing Era technique of Billy Kyle, who was the pianist in big bands such as Lucky Millinder's and later in Louis Armstrong's small groups. In doing so, Powell became the first pianist to improvise on the keyboard with the same kind of linear imagination as a trumpeter or saxophonist, and his dazzlingly proficient runs matched the lightning-fast flow of ideas of Dizzy Gillespie or Charlie Parker. By contrast, Monk's impact on

This late portrait of a gaunt Bud Powell hints at some of the internal mental demons that dogged his short and tragic life.

jazz was more as a theorist and composer, his advanced harmonic ideas underpinning much of the entire bebop movement.

Bud Powell's revolutionary effect on jazz piano playing went hand in hand with a fragile existence marred by mental illness and addiction problems. Not only was his life cut short at the age of 41, but he also spent approximately two-thirds of his adult days in mental institutions or a sanitarium for tuberculosis instead of being able to play music. Although an extrovert in his piano playing, he had a withdrawn and introverted personality, and he acquired a reputation for "acting crazy" as a youth. Powell's real problems began when he received a savage beating at the hands of police in a racially motivated attack in Philadelphia in 1945. He was a member of Cootie Williams's orchestra at the time, and—according to drummer Max Roach—Powell had remained behind after the band left the city in order to hear his friend Thelonious Monk.

The attack left Powell with head wounds that caused him to return home to his mother's care and led to a long stay in the hospital and the onset of a schizophrenic condition. His subsequent career took place in periods of remission from his mental difficulties, or while he was taking medical treatments to suppress the symptoms. Moreover, he was drawn into the twilight drug world of 1940s New York City, and later into drinking alcohol excessively, in all likelihood to relieve the constant headaches he suffered.

Powell showed signs of talent from the moment he started piano at around age six. His father was a pianist in the stride style of Fats Waller and James P. Johnson, and his elder brother Bill was a trumpeter. His younger brother Richie, who was killed in a car crash in 1956, was also a pianist. Early in his teens Powell began to play in and around New York City, and combined

gigs with his elder brother and the female trumpeter Valaida Snow with sitting in at Minton's Playhouse in Harlem, the club where much of the experimentation that led to modern jazz took place. The musician who introduced the teenage Powell to Minton's was Thelonious Monk, and the two withdrawn, introverted pianists developed a close rapport, such that in later life Monk claimed to have written many of his compositions for Powell, and Powell reciprocated by continuing to perform Monk's tunes. In 1942, just as the American Federation of Musicians imposed its first ban on commercial recordings, Powell joined the big band of Duke Ellington's former trumpeter Cootie Williams, but only after Williams had agreed to become the underage pianist's official guardian.

This worked two ways for Powell. The upside was that he was in a top-flight big band, working at the highest musical level every night. We know from his recordings that his style was maturing into its final form by the time the band got into the studios in 1944, and we know from eyewitness accounts that Powell was even more impressive in live performance. Bassist Ray Brown told of seeing Powell steal the show while accompanying tap dancer Ralph Brown in a Pittsburgh variety bill where the Williams band was playing. "Hey, cool it! I'm the star!" shouted the dancer as Powell's dazzling piano playing drew the audience's attention away from the stage. The downside was that Williams was, until the police assault on Powell, very protective of his charge, so that when Dizzy Gillespie tried to get Powell to join his pioneering quintet on 52nd Street in 1943–44, Williams would not release the young pianist.

Powell did work with Gillespie and Charlie Parker in late 1945. He was the pianist in their quintet shortly before the band left for the West Coast at the end of that year. Al Haig made the trip

Earl "Bud" Powell

BORN

September 27, 1924
New York, New York

DIED

August 1, 1966
New York, New York

EDUCATION

De Witt Clinton High School, New York City

MAJOR INTERESTS

Jazz piano, composing

ACCOMPLISHMENTS

Developed the principal modern jazz piano style of performance, with linear right-hand melodies accompanied by occasional stabbing left hand chords. Played with pioneers of modern jazz, including Dizzy Gillespie and Charlie Parker. Recorded brilliant examples of his playing in solo, trio, and group contexts. Compositions include "Blues for Bouffemont," "Budo" ("Hallucinations"), "Bud's Bubble," "Buttercup," "Dance of the Infidels," "The Glass Enclosure," "Parisian Thoroughfare," "Tempus Fugit," "Un Poco Loco," and "Wail"

On many of Powell's discs he can be heard singing or grunting along with his piano playing. Here is an example of him doing just that in a Copenhagen jazz club in 1962.

West in Powell's place, because Powell's fragile health made it difficult for him to travel; in addition, he was beginning to be involved with narcotics. On the few occasions when Powell was reunited with Parker and Gillespie, he proved himself to be the natural pianist for their pioneering innovations. Sadly only a handful of recordings exist of the three of them together, including the famous Massey Hall concert in 1953, when they were brought together with Charles Mingus and Max Roach in Canada as the Quintet of the Year.

By 1953 Powell had endured several spells in institutions, at a time when the treatment for mental illness included ammoniac showers and electric shock therapy. In retrospect, it is surprising he survived as any kind of musician, but his talent was so strong and his will to play was sufficiently undimmed that he is reputed to have drawn a keyboard on the wall of his room and practiced on that. The recorded examples of his playing from the late 1940s and early 1950s include moments when he achieved seemingly impossible feats of dexterity and rapidity of thought. There are a few such moments on discs he made with

instrumentalists such as saxophonists Sonny Stitt and Dexter Gordon, or with trumpeters Fats Navarro and Kenny Dorham, but his most dramatic playing was in a trio setting.

In 1947, Powell's earliest trio recording shows the range of his playing from the rapid "Indiana" and "Bud's Bubble" to the hard-edged romanticism of ballads like "I Should Care" and "Everything Happens to Me." Powell's more up-tempo pieces required great rapport with a drummer, and Max Roach or Roy Haynes, who subsequently recorded with Powell's quintet and trio, provided him with ideal support, both flexible and propulsive, and able to keep pace with his rapid speeds.

For this work alone, Powell would be remembered as one of the most innovative of jazz pianists, but within a short period he also began to demonstrate a remarkable compositional ability. Either by using variations in form or unusual rhythmic backdrops, his pieces have an individuality that marks them out from most bebop pieces, many of which used Parker's principles of superimposing a new melody over old and familiar chords. Powell's "Un Poco Loco" uses Latin time—in other words South American rhythms instead of the usual four-four pulse of jazz. His "Parisian Thoroughfare" (a prophetic title given that he was later to live in the city) evokes the bustle of busy streets. *Glass Enclosure* is barely a jazz piece at all: the bowed bass—instead of the usual plucked or pizzicato style—together with the measured chording of the original recording makes it seem like a 20th-century classical composition.

In the 1950s Powell's health declined. His body rebelled against years of abuse; he developed a physical intolerance to alcohol that produced a rapid reaction and occasionally

> *"One of the most formidable creators of piano music in any time or idiom."*
>
> —Gary Giddins in *Visions of Jazz* (1998)

alarming symptoms if he so much as tasted a drink. His recordings suffered from a lack of consistency. Some are brilliant, but others show him struggling to retain command of the keyboard. This was partly due to his medication, which induced a trancelike state intended to keep his schizophrenic tendencies at bay. Powell developed a resistance to his medication and he often managed to perform having consumed a dosage that would have rendered most people unconscious. This came to light after Powell had resettled in Paris in the late 1950s, in an attempt to rebuild his life and career. His friend and subsequent biographer, Francis Paudras, moved Powell away from his common-law wife and manager, Buttercup (Altevia Edwards), and gradually weaned the pianist off medication and alcohol. The story of this unlikely friendship between an ailing jazz musician and a French photographer was not without its ups and downs, and it provided much of the source material for Bertrand Tavernier's film *Round Midnight*. Sadly, just as Powell's health appeared to be improving he was struck down with tuberculosis.

He recovered in France, and in the summer of 1964 made a few glorious recordings that suggest he was back to something approaching his early form. However, he was lured back to the United States to play some lucrative concerts in order to help pay off some of his medical bills. Away from Paudras, and back in New York's underworld, Powell gradually slipped from view, once more ill, unable to fend for himself, and succumbing again to the demons of drink and drugs that haunted him. He died in relative obscurity, leaving a legacy of outstanding recordings and influencing almost all the jazz pianists who followed with the strength of his keyboard innovations.

DISCOGRAPHY

The Complete Bud Powell on Verve. Verve 521669 (five-CD set). [1949–51 recordings.]

The Complete Blue Note and Roost Recordings. Blue Note CDP 830083 (four-CD set). [Powell's 1947–63 output.]

Complete Essen Jazz Festival Concert, Black Lion BLCD 760105. [1960 concert with Oscar Pettiford, Kenny Clarke, and Coleman Hawkins at a high point in Powell's European career.]

FURTHER READING

Giddins, Gary. "Bud Powell (Strictly Confidential)" in *Visions of Jazz*. New York: Oxford University Press, 1998.

Groves, Alan, and Alyn Shipton. *The Glass Enclosure: The Life of Bud Powell.* 2d ed. London and New York: Continuum, 2001.

Paudras, Francis. *Dance of the Infidels: A Portrait of Bud Powell.* Rubye Monet, Warren Bernhardt, translators. New York: Da Capo, 1998.

Smith, Carl. *Bouncing with Bud: All the Recordings of Bud Powell.* Brunswick, Maine: Biddle, 1997.

WEBSITE

http://www.cchr.org/art/eng/page28.htm
Psychological profile of Powell's tortured life.

Thelonious Monk

BLUE SPHERE

The contributions of various musicians to the development of jazz differ widely. For example, Bud Powell's most lasting effect on jazz history is in the area of piano technique, and only a few of his compositions became part of the standard repertoire, but exactly the reverse is true of Thelonious Monk. Only a few pianists, such as Kenny Barron or Monk's French biographer Laurent De Wilde, have managed to re-create the idiosyncratic nuances of Monk's piano style, but bands the world over regularly play his compositions, such as "Blue Monk" or "Straight, No Chaser," and have done so since the 1940s.

"Monk's contribution to the new music was mostly harmonic," recalled Dizzy Gillespie, who in the early1940s spent many hours at the piano with Monk, both at his own apartment and at the after-hours clubs in New York City, investigating the harmonic changes that underpinned bebop. Initially, Monk and Gillespie tried out chords that would alter the harmonies of existing well-known songs. For example, Gillespie often played the ballad "I Can't Get Started" as a trumpet feature, much as Swing Era players like Bunny Berigan had done in the 1930s. But Gillespie, using ideas he developed with Monk, began to change the harmonies beneath the tune, giving the piece a more modern sound, and in due course Monk adopted many of these harmonies into his own pieces, such as his ballad "Round Midnight." Before long a repertoire began to emerge that used the "new" chords that Monk had developed, notably by flatting the fifth note of the scale (referred to by bebop players as the "flatted fifth") and simultaneously playing the sixth note of the scale. To many older musicians this sounded like a jarring discord, but Monk was fascinated by the way certain notes, played together, worked both with and against each other, and he often built whole phrases round clusters of such "sweet and sour" juxtapositions.

Despite the modernistic character of his harmonic thinking and the short choppy phrases of some of his melodies, which suggest a radical departure from tradition, Thelonious Sphere Monk had quite a conventional start in jazz. Monk was born in North Carolina but was raised in New York City. His father left home when Monk was small and had no further contact with his family; Monk's unusual first and middle names and much of his approach to life came from the strong influence of his mother, Barbara Sphere Batts, whose singing he accompanied in church. As a teenager, Monk played piano in and around his neighborhood, close to what is now Lincoln Center on Manhattan's West Side, before taking to the road for a couple of years in

Thelonious Monk during his days as house pianist at Minton's in Harlem. Monk, at far left, stands with trumpeters Howard McGhee and Roy Eldridge and the club manager, Teddy Hill.

JAZZ MAKERS

Thelonious Sphere Monk

BORN
October 10, 1917
Rocky Mount, North Carolina

DIED
February 17, 1982
Weehawken, New Jersey

EDUCATION
Peter Stuyvesant High School, New York City; short period later at Juilliard School of Music, New York

MAJOR INTERESTS
Piano, composing, bandleading

ACCOMPLISHMENTS
A key innovator in the new harmonic thinking that underpinned 1940s modern jazz. Band and solo recordings from 1947 onward under his own name, becoming internationally famous pianist by late 1950s. Most important as a significant writer of modern jazz pieces; compositions include "Bemsha Swing", "Blue Monk," "Crepuscule with Nellie," "Criss Cross," "Eronel," "Evidence," "Hornin' In," "Jackie-ing," "Misterioso," "Round Midnight," "Ruby My Dear," "Skippy," "Straight, No Chaser," "Thelonious," and "Well You Needn't"

HONORS
Thelonious Monk Institute, founded in his memory, holds an annual jazz performance competition, initiated in 1988

the late 1930s singing gospel music with a touring evangelist.

By this time he was already an accomplished pianist, having learned to play the instrument and to read music alongside his older sister, Marion. Later, he had private tuition from her teacher, Mr. Wolff, and later still he took a course in harmony at the Julliard School of Music. His schooling at Peter Stuyvesant High School involved less music, but Monk—who was one of only a small number of African-American students there—was also gifted at math and sciences.

His piano playing absorbed the style of Harlem stride players like James P. Johnson and Fats Waller, along with the hymnlike harmonies of the African-American Christian church. By the end of the 1930s he could be heard around New York City, sitting in at the Savoy, playing in a quartet with drummer Keg Purnell, and freelancing with several other groups. As the 1940s began, while many other pioneers of bebop dropped in from time to time at Minton's Playhouse, the after-hours club on 118th Street where former bandleader Teddy Hill was the manager, Monk became the regular pianist in the club's house band.

Being the regular pianist meant that Monk not only accompanied the musicians who came to sit in—who ranged from swing veterans like Benny Goodman and Roy Eldridge to up-and-coming players like Charlie Parker and

Monk wears an example of his typically exotic headgear at London's Marquee club in 1965.

colleague Bud Powell to the club and encouraged him to play there, forging a friendship that lasted until Powell's early death.

Monk was something of an eccentric even in his early 20s. He had adopted the curious hats, ranging from derbys to furs, and straggly beard that he wore throughout his adult life, and he was erratic about turning up on time or keeping simple appointments. Yet beneath his outward appearance he was a man of shrewd intelligence, often far more aware of circumstances than he let on. He began to be noticed outside New York by recording with Coleman Hawkins, for whom he played from 1943 to 1945, although not everyone was convinced of his talent. One *Metronome* review complained that Hawkins's rhythm section was "hampered" by the pianist. Because he was busy working with Hawkins, he did little more than sit in with Gillespie's pioneering band on 52nd Street in 1943, and it was not until Hawkins joined Jazz at the Philharmonic in 1946 that Monk became a full-time member of Gillespie's big band. Unfortunately, his tendency to turn up late, or miss sets because he was writing music in the bandroom and lost track of time, lost him the job within a few weeks.

In 1947 the German expatriate Alfred Lion adopted Monk as a cause célèbre. Lion had founded his Blue Note record label in 1939, and guided by the tenor saxophonist Ike Quebec, he and his partner Francis Wolff started recording the musicians who were developing modern jazz. An aficionado of jazz piano, Lion had already supervised sessions by Albert Ammons and James P. Johnson, among others. In Monk's playing and writing he heard the spark of originality that marked what he later referred to as "a genius of

Dizzy Gillespie—but that he played regularly alongside the band's drummer Kenny Clarke, working out ways to put an appropriate rhythm to the new harmonic and melodic ideas of the beboppers. There could hardly have been a better place in which to establish a set of new principles for jazz. While Parker and Gillespie often worked at other clubs, or out of town on tour for much of the period up until mid-1942, and neither was a regular member of the Minton's house band, Monk was present throughout. He brought his young

> *"They somehow feel he's eccentric, but Monk knows exactly what he's doing. Precisely. Structurally and musically, he's very aware of every note he plays."*

—Bill Evans, pianist, 1966

DISCOGRAPHY

The Complete Blue Note Recordings. Blue Note CDP 830363 (four-CD set). [Includes Monk's first discs as leader and a live club session with John Coltrane.]

Monk Alone: The Complete Columbia Solo Recordings 1962–1968. Columbia 2K 65495 (two-CD set). [Collected piano solos.]

The Complete Riverside Recordings. Riverside 022 (15-CD set). [Monk's 1952–60 work.]

The London Collection, Vols. 1–3. Black Lion BLCD 760101, 760116, 760142 (three-CD set). [Monk's recording in London with Al McKibbon and Art Blakey, 1971, at the end of the all-star Giants of Jazz tour.]

FURTHER READING

Blake, Ran. "Thelonious Monk" in *The New Grove Dictionary of Jazz.* Barry Kernfeld, ed. London and New York: Macmillan, 1988.

Fitterling, Thomas. *Thelonious Monk: His Life and Music.* Robert Dobbin, trans. Berkeley, Calif.: Berkeley Hills, 1997.

Gourse, Leslie. *Straight, No Chaser: The Life and Genius of Thelonious Monk.* New York: Schirmer, 1997.

Isacoff, Stuart. *Thelonious Monk.* New York: Music Sales, 1997.

van der Bliek, Rob, ed. *The Thelonious Monk Reader.* New York: Oxford University Press, 2001.

modern music." Despite little commercial success with the newest music—his company made its money from discs like Sidney Bechet's recording of "Summertime"—Lion recorded several sessions by Monk in 1947 through 1952 that chart his emergence as one of the most original voices in modern jazz.

Then, after a brief time with the Prestige label, Monk found a similarly supportive producer in Orrin Keepnews of Riverside Records, who supervised most of his late 1950s discs. Whereas Alfred Lion encouraged Monk to record what he wanted and created sufficient rehearsal time and a supportive studio atmosphere to ensure it was done well, Keepnews was a more interventionist producer, which paid off. Monk had never made money for himself or Blue Note, but Keepnews' shrewd promotion brought him to a large audience. Following a period when Monk was prevented from working in New York City because his cabaret card had been withdrawn, on account of what turned out to be false imprisonment for drug offenses, Monk's career finally blossomed.

From his late 1950s quartet with John Coltrane, and later Johnny Griffin, and throughout the 1960s, Monk led a succession of distinguished small groups that played his own music and interpreted the music of other jazz composers in a unique fashion. He led an occasional big band and toured internationally in the early 1970s with an all-star bebop group, the Giants of Jazz, with Gillespie, Art Blakey, and saxophonist Sonny Stitt in the lineup. The recordings he made with Blakey and bassist Al McKibbon in 1971 are among his final appearances; by the mid-1970s he withdrew from public view. He eventually died at the home of his friend Baroness Pannonica de Koenigswater, across the river from New York City, in New Jersey.

Monk's legacy is of a collection of highly individual and challenging compositions, a new harmonic approach to the basis of jazz improvisation, and in his own playing a rich archive of recordings that unite his percussive, unorthodox piano style with his ability to interpret both his own music and that of other composers in a startling and unusual way. His son, the drummer T. S. Monk, played in some of his father's later groups and keeps the family's musical tradition alive, as well as supervising the charitable foundation named for his father that has educational courses and an annual competition for young jazz soloists.

WEBSITES

http://www.monkinstitute.com

The website of the Thelonious Monk Institute of Jazz, with information about program offerings and a brief biography of Monk.

http://www.pbs.org/jazz/biography/artist_id_monk_thelonious.htm

Website linked to Ken Burns's documentary *Jazz,* with biography and audio files.

Art Blakey

JAZZ MESSENGER

rt Blakey was one of the most significant drummers of the modern jazz movement, but even more important for jazz history, he was the preeminent talent scout of the post–World War II period. On his earliest discs recorded under his own name, he employed the brilliant but short-lived trumpeter Clifford Brown, and in his 1980s bands, he provided the first international platform for Wynton and Branford Marsalis. Later still, in his final 1990 lineups with pianist Geoff Keezer and saxophonist Javon Jackson, Blakey continued to show that after more than three decades after he retained his unerring instinct for spotting the most talented musicians in each generation. The names of those who worked in his bands read like a Who's Who of modern jazz. In addition to those musicians already mentioned, he employed (among others) trumpeters Kenny Dorham, Lee Morgan, Freddie Hubbard, and Woody Shaw; saxophonists Hank Mobley, Benny Golson, Wayne Shorter, and Johnny Griffin; and pianists Keith Jarrett, JoAnne Brackeen, and Benny Green.

Several drummers were equally as important as Blakey in redefining the role of the drums in a modern jazz ensemble. Kenny Clarke is credited with moving the basic rhythmic pulse from the bass and snare drum to the cymbals, allowing the drums to be used for punctuation and cross

Although Art Blakey recorded for many different labels, his longest and most prolific association was with Blue Note, for which he recorded from the 1940s to the 1980s.

rhythms rather than solely for basic time keeping. Max Roach took this further in Dizzy Gillespie's pioneering small group on 52nd Street in 1943, creating shifting flexible drum patterns behind Gillespie or in support of other leaders such as Charlie Parker and Bud Powell.

Art Blakey is remarkable for absorbing many of the innovations of Clarke and Roach and uniting them into a style that had its roots in the great swing bands. This style became the perfect accompaniment for the cross between bebop and gospel music that he and pianist Horace Silver pioneered, and which became known as "hard bop."

Blakey's parents split up before he was born, in Pittsburgh, Pennsylvania. They had married in a "shotgun" wedding, but his father left his pregnant bride and ran away to Chicago just minutes after the ceremony. Heartbroken, the new bride died not long after Blakey was born. He was brought up by distant family and friends, particularly one of his mother's friends whom he came to think of in time as being his mother. He had no fondness for Pittsburgh, which he called "a dirty, greasy town," but he got his start in music there, playing piano in a big band of fellow high school students at a club called the Ritz. When a traveling show came in from New York, bringing its own music for the band to play, Blakey's inability to read music fluently was exposed, and he transferred to drums, making way at the keyboard for a talented young pianist named Erroll Garner.

Around 1938, Blakey's band went out on the road, but the tour ended when they were stranded with no money. They returned to Pittsburgh, from where Blakey eventually moved to New York City. At about that time, Blakey met Chick Webb, who influenced the young drummer and helped him develop his distinctive press roll—

a snare drum roll played by rapidly alternating the hands in a "papamama" rhythm. Webb made the young drummer practice using a metronome to make the beats of each hand slow and precise, strengthening his technique for playing the roll at full speed. The swing drummer Sid Catlett gave Blakey similar advice, and whereas other modern jazz drummers evolved a technique that moved away from the rudiment-based drum style of early jazz, it remained a characteristic element of Blakey's playing throughout his life.

His early professional experience in New York reinforced Blakey's Swing Era credentials. He worked in Mary Lou Williams's band at Kelly's Stable in 1942, then went out on the road with veteran bandleader Fletcher Henderson, whom he left in 1943 after suffering a vicious racial beating while touring Georgia, which necessitated having a plate inserted in his skull. He settled in Boston to recuperate, and this led to his being recruited to play in the "bebop nursery" of Billy Eckstine's big band, alongside Charlie Parker and Dizzy Gillespie. This group, with several enthusiastic young musicians working out the elements of a new style and brimming with outsize musical personalities, was the perfect environment for Blakey. He always remarked on how many big bands were "fifteen musicians and a drummer," but that Eckstine's orchestra gave him a role equal to any of the other instrumentalists: "There were sixteen musicians, everybody got to play, and that made a difference," he said.

After Eckstine's band broke up, Blakey was reunited with some of its musicians, including Miles Davis and trumpeter Fats Navarro, in a 1947 band he called the 17 Jazz Messengers. This was the first recorded use of the name Messengers for one of Blakey's bands. Apart from an octet record date, the title did not reappear until 1954, when he formed a quintet with pianist

JAZZ MAKERS

Art Blakey

BORN
October 11, 1919
Pittsburgh, Pennsylvania

DIED
October 16, 1990
New York, New York

EDUCATION
Left high school in Pittsburgh early; no formal musical education, but had drum instruction from Chick Webb and Sid Catlett

MAJOR INTERESTS
Drums, bandleading

ACCOMPLISHMENTS
Worked with innovative modern jazz musicians including Thelonious Monk, Dizzy Gillespie, and Miles Davis. Founded Jazz Messengers, 1954; with Horace Silver, initiated "hard bop" movement of 1950s. Gained a reputation as jazz's leading talent scout, bringing gifted musicians from every generation into the personnel of the Messengers

Art Blakey as his many fans will remember him, photographed on tour in Europe two years before his death, still driving his band energetically from the drum set.

"Blues March," "Moanin'," "Ugetsu," and "Mosaic" defined the style.

Blakey's own role in the Messengers was revolutionary. He dictated the entire performance of the group from the drums, in the same way he had controlled the dynamics of a big band. Saxophonist Dexter Gordon recalled how he thought his first solo in Billy Eckstine's band was over and was about to walk away from the microphone when Blakey's drum roll hauled him back and compelled him to play until Blakey was ready to let him go. In the Messengers, Blakey refined the technique, and his live recordings from Birdland or the Café Bohemia in Greenwich Village are remarkable documents of how he controlled the texture of every performance. Virtually every musician who worked in the band also recalled how Blakey created an ideal playing environment, that his hard-swinging, positive drumming let them focus clearly on their own work.

Like many modern jazz musicians of the period, Blakey converted to Islam, taking the name Abdullah Ibn Buhaina for religious purposes, but retaining his original name professionally, although many friends and acquaintances called him Bu or Buhaina. His remarkable ability to find and employ up-and-coming talent meant that the Messengers constantly reflected something of the latest currents in jazz, yet without losing the overall hard bop feeling that was Blakey's own distinctive contribution to the band's sound. His own playing was immediately identifiable. His style was marked not only by the trademark rolls, but also by his insistent high-hat cymbal on the offbeats of every measure and his fondness for using the pressure of his hand or elbow to alter the tension of a drumhead and change the note of the drum as he played it.

Horace Silver to play at Birdland. By that time Blakey had traveled to Africa to investigate local drumming traditions, and also gained experience in Lucky Millinder's Orchestra, with Dizzy Gillespie's small group, and with clarinetist Buddy De Franco.

Silver reused the Messengers name for a regular quintet the following year, which functioned briefly as a cooperative until it eventually became Blakey's band—the group he led up until the time of his death. Blakey and Silver combined a danceable groove tempo with complex modern jazz harmonies but in which even the most convoluted melody line tended to be memorable and recognizable. "Hard bop," crossing over through its strong affinities with gospel into "soul jazz," was the genre they made their own. Blakey's recordings of pieces like "The Preacher,"

"[Working with Art Blakey] was like sitting on an atom bomb."

—Johnny Griffin, saxophonist, in a 1969 interview with Arthur Taylor

Despite a prolific recording career under his own name, Blakey made a significant contribution to the discs of many other musicians, notably Thelonious Monk, Miles Davis, Dizzy Gillespie, and the short-lived and highly innovative pianist Herbie Nichols. In these, as in his own groups, he thrived on risk taking and an explosive edge-of-the-seat sense of dynamic drama. Yet, he never lost sight of the principles he had learned at the hands of big band pioneers like Henderson, Webb, and Millinder about hard-driving swing and constant entertainment for the listener.

DISCOGRAPHY

A Night at Birdland, Vols. 1 and 2. Blue Note B21Y 46519-2 and 46520-2. [Prototype Jazz Messengers band with Horace Silver on piano and Clifford Brown on trumpet, recorded in early 1954.]

At the Café Bohemia, Vols. 1 and 2. Blue Note B21Y 46521-2 and 46522-2. [The Jazz Messengers with Kenny Dorham, trumpet, and Hank Mobley, tenor, live in Greenwich Village, 1955. Some of the best recorded collaborations between Blakey and Silver.]

Art Blakey's Jazz Messengers with Thelonious Monk. Rhino R2 75598. [1957 recordings originally made for Atlantic, re-released with new material for Atlantic's 50th birthday, 1998.]

The Best of Art Blakey and The Jazz Messengers. Blue Note CDP 793205-2.

[Anthology covering 1958–64 with lineups including Lee Morgan, Benny Golson, Freddie Hubbard, Cedar Walton.]

Child's Dance. Prestige PCD 24130-2. [Cross section of 1970s Messengers tracks].

Live at Montreux and North Sea. Timeless SJP 150. [1980 band with Wynton Marsalis paired with either his brother Branford or Bobby Watson.]

Art Collection. Concord CCD 4495 [Early 1980s bands anthology; musicians include Terence Blanchard, Jean Toussaint, Mulgrew Miller.]

Art of Jazz. In and Out 77028-2. [1989 special 70th birthday celebration for Blakey by Messengers past and present; includes an interview with Blakey.]

FURTHER READING

Enstice, Wayne, and Paul Rubin. "Art Blakey" in *Jazz Spoken Here: Conversations with Twenty-Two Jazz Musicians.* Baton Rouge: Louisiana State University Press, 1992.

Rosenthal, David H. *Hard Bop: Jazz and Black Music 1955–1965.* New York: Oxford University Press, 1992.

Taylor, Arthur. "Art Blakey" in *Notes and Tones: Musician-to-Musician Interviews.* 1977. Reprint, New York: Da Capo, 1993.

WEBSITE

http://www.jazzreview.com/artist2.html
Biography, discography, and links to other sites featuring Blakey.

Charles Mingus

"BETTER GIT IT IN YOUR SOUL"

Charles Mingus was an outsize personality, argumentative, prone to bragging, with occasionally outlandish ideas about his music, which perhaps explains why he was slow to receive the critical attention that he deserved. In the 21 years from his death in 1979 to the end of the 20th century, only a few books and articles were published that discuss his immense and rich contribution to jazz in any detail. Compared to the library shelves crammed with material about other jazz figures, this is puzzling, given his immense talents as an instrumentalist, both on double bass and piano, and also that he was—after Duke Ellington—the most prolific and versatile composer in jazz.

One clue as to why this is so is that Mingus saw himself as an outsider and often behaved as one. Although his frequently stated anti-establishment views, arguments with promoters, onstage comments, and occasionally shambling presentations tended to obscure the creative genius of his finest work, Mingus was justified in feeling like an outsider. His heritage included European, African, and Asian ancestors, and he was taunted in school by white children for being a "yellow nigger." He was unable to pass for white as his father, an ex-soldier, had done, nor was he made welcome as a child by his African-American contemporaries. Thus, he was effectively excluded from both of the predominant social groups in the area of Los Angeles in which he grew up—his family having moved from the Army post in Arizona, where he was born, when he was three months old. He recalled: "I just found myself with the Japanese, the Greeks, the Italians and Mexicans, and a few more guys like me."

This social isolation carried over into his education and his music. He had an unusually high IQ, but flunked most subjects in school, while as a trombonist and subsequently a cellist he was essentially self-taught, subconsciously holding back from learning to read music fluently by relying on his exceptional musical ear.

Those who recognized his musical gifts realized immediately that Mingus was outstandingly talented. Trombonist Britt Woodman and the reed player Buddy Collette were both childhood friends who encouraged him, even after he was humiliated for being unable to read music speedily enough to play cello in the local youth orchestra. It was Collette who started Mingus playing bass, and who then introduced him to Red Callender, a prominent bassist in Los Angeles who had worked with many high-profile musicians, including Louis Armstrong. Callender became a teacher and mentor for Mingus, who in due course ended up playing in Armstrong's big band himself.

Charles Mingus at Columbia's recording studios, with his producer, Teo Macero. Macero was a former alto saxophonist in Mingus's Jazz Workshop.

Charles Mingus

BORN
April 22, 1922
Nogales, Arizona

DIED
January 5, 1979
Cuernavaca, Mexico

EDUCATION
Jordan High School, Los Angeles; studied bass with Red Callender and Herman Rheinschagen from the New York Philharmonic Orchestra; studied composition with Lloyd Reese

MAJOR INTERESTS
Bass, piano, composing, bandleading

ACCOMPLISHMENTS
Technically one of the most accomplished bassists in jazz. Established Debut records with Max Roach, which issued many examples of his playing from the early 1950s. An imaginative composer with a prolific output of material for his own groups, including "Haitian Fight Song," "Love Chant" (1956); "Pithecanthropus Erectus" (1957); "Fables of Faubus," "Goodbye Pork Pie Hat" (1959); "Ecclusiastics" (1961); "The Black Saint and the Sinner Lady," "Orange Was the Color of Her Dress" (1963); "Three or Four Shades of Blues" (1977). Published autobiography, *Beneath the Underdog,* 1971

HONORS
Elected to *Down Beat* Hall of Fame; Guggenheim fellowship in composition, 1971

By this time, his personal confidence helped by intensive musical practice, plus self-defense training and weight lifting, Mingus decided to ally himself firmly with the Los Angeles African-American community, making what his biographer Brian Priestley describes as "a conscious choice to be an underdog rather than an outcast." This is an important clue to the way Mingus subsequently saw himself, and relates to the title of his own book, a strange mixture of fantasy and life story titled *Beneath the Underdog.*

The contradictions in Mingus's life carried over into his work. The world of African-American entertainment rubbed off on him from playing with Armstrong and other veterans like Kid Ory and Barney Bigard, but, like many musicians of his generation, he rejected the mugging stage persona of such older entertainers. Nevertheless, he simultaneously acquired a knowledge of and respect for the sounds they made; "our" music, as he called it. Much of his later work contains a dramatic balance between elements drawn directly from the vaudeville tradition (songs like

"Eat That Chicken," or his parody of a 1920s dance routine on "Cocktails for Two") with the dramatically modern improvisations of musicians like saxophonist Eric Dolphy. Similarly, he was to draw the sounds of gospel music and the church into his jazz vocabulary, just as he was to assimilate the compositional language of Duke Ellington, whose band made a huge impact on him in his youth. Initially, however, he became better known as a player than as a composer.

Until the start of the 1940s, the double bass had played a subordinate role in large and small jazz groups, its part often being restricted to playing simple fundamentals on the first and third beat of each measure, just as tubas had done on early recordings. In the late 1930s, this all began to change. Walter Page in Count Basie's band began to play smooth arpeggios (figures based on the first, third, and fifth of a chord) that blended forcefully with guitar and drums, and Israel Crosby in small groups with Roy Eldridge and Teddy Wilson began to play repeated patterns, or ostinatos, behind soloists.

Mingus on tour in 1970, some months after his return to playing. He produced some of his finest work in the years that followed, until the onset of Lou Gehrig's disease prevented him from playing the bass.

Milt Hinton in Cab Calloway's orchestra, who had trained as a violinist, played elegant bowed solos in pieces like "Ebony Silhouette," his improvised lines sounding more like those of a saxophone than most people's idea of a double bass. All these innovations came together in the short but bright career of Jimmy Blanton, who played briefly in Duke Ellington's orchestra before his early death from tuberculosis in 1942.

Blanton provided a way forward for bassists, an approach to the instrument as a full-fledged improvising member of a jazz group that underpinned many of the innovations of the modern jazz of the 1940s. Oscar Pettiford, one of the players to follow in Blanton's footsteps with Ellington, showed how mobile and flexible bass lines could combine with the more fluid drum style of players like Max Roach and Kenny Clarke. Ray Brown developed the style with

both Charlie Parker and Dizzy Gillespie. Mingus appeared on the scene just at the right moment to combine all these innovations with his own musical personality.

He was fortunate to become part of a group that was designed to show off the bass. Before 1950 he had mainly worked in big bands, including Lionel Hampton's, or on miscellaneous record sessions; but when he joined a trio with guitarist Tal Farlow and vibraphonist Red Norvo, their light, open sound was the perfect setting for his playing. He was with the group only until 1951, but in that short time they were well placed in jazz polls. They also recorded quite extensively, bringing to a wide public Mingus's virtuoso bass playing and some of his unorthodox ideas, including his high-note solos, while Farlow accompanied him with bass lines on the guitar.

After leaving Norvo, Mingus settled in New York City, where his reputation as an innovative and versatile bassist brought him work with several high-profile musicians, including Bud Powell, Billy Taylor and, briefly, Duke Ellington. Mingus and drummer Max Roach formed a record company together, called Debut, which preserved much of Mingus's work from this period, including his first attempts at a jazz workshop—a collective that explored composition and improvisation. This was to be his preferred method of evolving his compositions over the years that followed, and he liked to sing or dictate the parts each musician was to play so that they heard rather than read the music. In this way he turned one of his own early shortcomings, the inability to read music well, into a positive approach, even if his regular pianist, Jaki Byard, surreptitiously jotted down the parts so the band could remember them later. As he composed, Mingus increasingly used

"Imagine a circle surrounding each beat—each guy can play his notes anywhere in that circle, and it gives him the feeling he has more space . . . the pulse is inside you."

—Charles Mingus in *Beneath the Underdog* (1971)

the piano, and in due course incorporated playing piano into his live performances, interspersed with or instead of his bass playing.

At the core of the workshop approach to his music, Mingus established two constants: a set of related pieces that changed gradually from performance to performance, and a pool of players who specialized in interpreting his ideas. So, a composition like "Fables of Faubus," first written in 1959 and reworked in 1964, developed into "Original Faubus Fables" in 1960, and "New Fables" in 1964. The majority of his groups in the later 1950s into the 1960s used drummer Dannie Richmond, with whom Mingus developed a flexible rhythmic platform for his soloists. Bass and drums moved the beat around, made abrupt transitions into double or triple time, and sometimes dropped out altogether, leaving the brass and reeds to play with just handclaps or shouts for accompaniment.

Against this backdrop, in much the same way as Ellington had done, Mingus created music to exploit the musical personalities of his musicians: the jagged saxophone and bass clarinet of Eric Dolphy, the sparring saxes of John Handy and Booker Ervin, the gospel-tinged saxophones and flute of Roland Kirk, the rounded trombones of Jimmy Knepper and Britt Woodman, and the witty, eclectic piano of Jaki Byard.

As the 1960s began, Mingus entered his greatest period of creativity with a series of outstanding compositions. At the same time he took on the establishment by setting up rival concerts to the Newport Jazz Festival, launching a new independent record label, and organizing events that were an uncomfortable mix of rehearsal and performance. The 1962 New York Town Hall event—which is not to be confused with a highly successful event two years later—is generally regarded as a spectacularly disastrous example of these performances, where chaotic organization, a lack of rehearsal, and Mingus's highly charged personality prevented much music from being made. By the mid-1960s, as a consequence of his volatile behavior, clubs refused to employ him. Mingus was facing financial ruin, and he was also suffering from unstable mental health.

Mingus's career was put on hold until 1969, when he once more began to tour and perform. Soon afterward, he was awarded a Guggenheim fellowship, which gave him a degree of stability and public recognition. Until the onset of his final illness—amyotrophic lateral sclerosis (Lou Gehrig's disease), a form of muscular paralysis—he toured and recorded quite regularly with his quintet and collaborated with singer Joni Mitchell. He also established a big band, for which he reworked many of his earlier compositions. After his death, this group, managed by his widow Susan Graham Mingus, kept his musical legacy alive.

DISCOGRAPHY

The Complete Debut Recordings. Debut 12DCD 4402 (12-CD set). [Mingus's 1951–57 output for the label he co-owned with Max Roach.]

Pithecanthropus Erectus. Atlantic 81456.

Blues and Roots. Rhino R2 75205.

Mingus Ah Um. Columbia 450436.

Black Saint and the Sinner Lady. MCAD 5649.

Town Hall Concert 1964. Original Jazz Classics OJC 042. [Highlight of Mingus's work with saxophonist Eric Dolphy.]

Three or Four Shades of Blues. Atlantic 7567 81403. [Late examples of Mingus, 1977.]

FURTHER READING

Coleman, Janet, with Al Young. *Mingus/Mingus.* New York: Creative Arts, 1989.

Mingus, Charles. *Beneath the Underdog.* Nel King, ed. New York: Knopf, 1971.

Priestley, Brian. *Mingus: A Critical Biography.* London and New York: Quartet, 1982.

Santoro, Gene. *Myself When I Am Real: The Life and Music of Charles Mingus.* New York: Oxford University Press, 2000.

WEBSITE

http://www.mingusmingusmingus.com

The official Charles Mingus website with biography, discography, and news and tour information about the Mingus Big Band and the Mingus Orchestra.

Sarah Vaughan

THE DIVINE SARAH

arah Vaughan's two nicknames, "Sassy" and "The Divine One," represent the two extremes of both her character and her work. On the one hand, she was a consummate jazz singer, her vocals displaying the bold attitude of a carefree and fearless improviser. On the other, possessed of a remarkable voice with an exceptional range that stretched from the lowest contralto to the highest soprano pitch, she was the closest jazz has had to an operatic singer, and she frequently made discs in a grand manner, surrounded by orchestral strings and lush arrangements. Her most successful albums include several of the latter type, including a set of "songbooks" with items from famous stage shows, similar to those recorded by Ella Fitzgerald. Through these she had a great impact in introducing the sounds of jazz to the general public.

Yet despite the popularity of Vaughan in her "grand" or "divine" style, her lasting contribution to jazz itself comes from the way in which she extended the art of vocal improvisation. Because she started out playing piano as well as

Sarah Vaughan broadcasts live from the Café Society Downtown, in Greenwich Village, in 1946. While singing at Café Society Vaughan met the trumpet player George Treadwell, whom she married in 1947 and who became her manager.

singing, Vaughan's harmonic ear was unusually well developed. This equipped her to be the first significant vocalist within the bebop revolution, accurately incorporating the flatted fifths and other unusual intervals introduced by Charlie Parker, Dizzy Gillespie, and Thelonious Monk to the new song melodies she improvised.

To some extent this was due to the happy accident of being in the right place at the right time. At age 18 she won a talent contest at the Apollo Theater in Harlem, and soon afterward joined the big band of Earl Hines just at the point when it also contained Parker and Gillespie. However, Vaughan was no novice when she appeared on stage at the Apollo. From an early age she had sung in the choir of her local Mount Zion Baptist Church in Newark, New Jersey, and in 1936 she had been made organist. So, by the time she won the contest she had years of experience of playing and singing in public.

The 1943 Earl Hines band, which Vaughan had joined by April of that year, has been nicknamed the "bebop nursery." In the Charlie Parker profile earlier in this section there is an account of how Parker and Gillespie used their time together in the orchestra to crystallize their new style. They were part of an inner circle, a nucleus of musicians that included singer Billy Eckstine. These musicians reacted against the uniformity of swing big bands and wanted to break out and extend both the form and the musical content of what they played. For most of these players, the ideas that coalesced into bebop during about nine months in 1943 had already been tried out in whatever bands each had worked with previously, notably Gillespie with Cab Calloway and Parker with Jay McShann, but it was with Hines that everything came together.

To Vaughan, who became part of the circle, this was all new. "It was like going to school," she recalled. She learned avidly and incorporated what she heard into both her singing and her piano playing—she worked as a second pianist for Hines, playing with the band when he went in front to conduct. The following year she rejoined many of her former Hines colleagues in the new band set up by Eckstine, and by the time she made her first recordings she had clearly adopted the musical language of bebop. Vaughan took note of the obvious jazz influences of her Eckstine colleagues and of vocalists such as Ella Fitzgerald, who had been there to offer advice at her Apollo triumph. Yet, she also admired the work of singers outside the jazz tradition in mainstream popular music, notably Judy Garland. These dual interests remained a hallmark of her own work once she began to record.

Although she cut discs with Eckstine and in a small group with Gillespie for the entrepreneur Leonard Feather, it was her discs with the Parker–Gillespie quintet in 1945 that announced her arrival as a new and individual voice in jazz. In performances of "Lover Man" and "Mean to Me" she showed that she thought of her voice instrumentally, improvising new melodies, but also altering the tone or timbre of her sound. A growl at some points, crystalline clarity at others, were just as much part of her style as the actual notes or harmonies she used. In her later career, she tended to overuse the clear operatic high end of her range, which was at odds with her innate sense of jazz. But, from the mid-1940s until the late 1950s, she made plenty of discs that focused on her skills as a jazz singer, leaving her the maximum freedom to take her singing in any direction. In particular, her work for Mercury Records between 1954 and the end of the decade allowed her to separate the two extremes of her style. She sang on discs aimed at the commercial end of the market, such as her 1958 hit "Broken-Hearted

Sarah Lois Vaughan

BORN
March 27, 1924
Newark, New Jersey

DIED
April 3, 1990
Los Angeles, California

EDUCATION
Arts High for gifted students, Newark, New Jersey

MAJOR INTEREST
Singing

ACCOMPLISHMENTS
Won Apollo Theater talent contest as a singer. Recorded under her own name and with Dizzy Gillespie and Charlie Parker pioneering bebop vocal style; recorded for Columbia (until 1954), Mercury/EmArcy (to 1959) Roulette, Mainstream (1960s–70s), and Pablo (from 1978). Sings on film soundtracks of *Murder, Inc.* (1960); *Bob and Carol and Ted and Alice* (1969); *Cactus Flower* (1969); and *Sharky's Machine* (1981)

HONORS
A plaque in her honor was embedded in the sidewalk of New York's 52nd Street, 1980, and a star in Hollywood's Walk of the Stars, 1985; elected to Jazz Hall of Fame, 1988; winner of numerous polls, 1947 onward. Won Grammy for her album *Gershwin Live!*, 1982; received Grammy Lifetime Achievement Award, 1989

This 1946 advertisement for a concert close to the site of today's Lincoln Center in New York City announces Sarah Vaughan's appearance with many of the leading players in the new bebop jazz style of the period, including the misspelled Art Blakey.

"*Sarah Vaughan is the ageless voice of modern jazz—of giddy postwar virtuosity, biting wit and fearless caprice.*"

—Gary Giddins in *Visions of Jazz* (1998)

Melody," while also recording small-group jazz in the company of stars like Clifford Brown and Cannonball Adderley, or with her own trio.

From the point that she left Eckstine, Vaughan worked mainly as a soloist in her own right, although she did sing and record in the mid-1940s for bandleader John Kirby. There were periods such as the late 1960s when she did not record, but in general she made frequent discs for a succession of major labels and had a particularly successful run of albums after she moved to Norman Granz's Pablo label in 1978. Yet, even in her final years she continued to demonstrate both ends of her skills, appearing on a recording of the musical *South Pacific* but also continuing to make jazz discs and festival appearances.

One Sarah Vaughan number makes particularly clear the importance of her singing in the development of jazz: her own "Shulie A Bop," which appears on the album *Swingin' Easy*. The lyric fits into a new melodic line written to fit the same harmonies as George Gershwin's "Summertime." In addition to recasting the original just as Charlie Parker did with his interpretations of various well-known songs, Vaughan also sings nonsense scat syllables, which have a rhythmic freedom and melodic dexterity that make her every bit the equal of the instrumentalists who created bebop. This comparatively early session, singing with just a trio, encapsulates all the elements of her greatness.

Many, many audiences heard her sing with a trio over the years, yet she never got around to making a disc in this type of intimate setting of the song with which she traditionally closed her sets throughout her final years, Steven Sondheim's "Send in the Clowns" from *A Little Night Music*. What was so enchanting was that, familiar as the song was, her interpretation was full

of fleeting glimpses of different emotions, and consequently never the same twice. There, too, was the mark of her greatness. As she told British journalist Max Jones, "The way that I'm feeling is the way that I sing it."

DISCOGRAPHY

Sarah Vaughan 1944–46, Classics 958. [Anthology of Vaughan's earliest recorded work.]

The Divine Sarah: The Columbia Years 1949–1953. Columbia 465597 (two-CD set). [Several orchestral settings plus a 1950 small band with Miles Davis among others.]

Sarah Vaughan with Clifford Brown, EmArcy 814641.

Swingin' Easy. EmArcy 514072-2. [Vaughan's work with jazz trio, 1954–57.]

After Hours. Roulette 855468. [1961 small-group session.]

Send in the Clowns. Pablo 2312-137. [1980s session with members of Count Basie's band.]

Crazy and Mixed Up. Pablo 2313-137.

FURTHER READING

Brown, Denis. *Sarah Vaughan: A Discography*. Westport, Conn.: Greenwood, 1991.

Friedwald, Will. *Jazz Singing: America's Great Voices from Bessie Smith to Bebop and Beyond*. 1990. Reprint, New York: Da Capo, 1996.

Giddins, Gary. "Sarah Vaughan (Divine)" in *Visions of Jazz*. New York: Oxford University Press, 1998.

Gourse, Lesley. *Sassy: The Life of Sarah Vaughan*. New York: Scribners, 1993.

Jones, Max. "Sarah Vaughan" in *Talking Jazz*. New York: Norton, 1987.

Ruuth, Marianne. *Sarah Vaughan*. New York: Holloway/Melrose Square, 1994.

166 • JAZZ MAKERS

More Modern Jazz Pioneers to Remember

The development of bebop took several years, beginning around 1940 and ending in a mature form by 1945, when Dizzy Gillespie and Charlie Parker together recorded some of the cornerstone compositions in the style: "Groovin' High," "Dizzy Atmosphere," "Hot House," "Shaw 'Nuff," and "Salt Peanuts." At the end of 1945, Gillespie and Parker traveled to the West Coast, and this is often regarded as the moment when bebop left New York for the first time. In fact, because of the network of communication between big band musicians on the road, the ideas behind bebop had been traveling the country well before that. Many players had caught on to their message from hearing Parker and Gillespie with Earl Hines or Billy Eckstine long before they made their small-group records together.

One such player was trumpeter **Howard McGhee** (1918–87). After working with Lionel Hampton and Andy Kirk, for whom he played in a swing style close to that of Roy Eldridge, McGhee further developed his range and agility. Before long, through continued work in big bands and long after-hours practice in New York clubs like Minton's, he had paralleled many of the stylistic innovations of Dizzy Gillespie. Several months before Gillespie and Parker went to California, McGhee traveled there with Coleman Hawkins. Through his performances and discs with Hawkins, McGhee was just as influential in introducing bebop to the West Coast as the more famous names that followed. His career foundered in the 1950s, but from the 1960s on he was very active, especially at the head of his own big band.

Another very important trumpeter, **Fats Navarro** (1923–50), played alongside McGhee in Andy Kirk's band in 1943. (Charlie Parker also occasionally worked with Kirk at this point.) Navarro then replaced Gillespie in Billy Eckstine's band, and had he not died at 26 from tuberculosis, made worse by heroin addiction, he might well have continued to develop an approach to modern jazz trumpet that laid midway between the work of Parker and Gillespie. He left over 100 recordings during his short life which show that he had learned to transfer Parker's serpentine saxophone melodies to trumpet. Whereas Gillespie used dramatic ideas he brought from his experience as a trumpeter in swing bands, such as leaps of register or a sudden doubling of tempo, Navarro preferred the long phrases and subtle alterations of emphasis initiated by Parker, into which he introduced some of Gillespie's phrasing.

Equally short-lived but even more influential than Navarro was **Clifford Brown** (1930–56), who brought an

Alto saxophonist Sonny Stitt, musical heir to Charlie Parker, in London during the 1960s.

intense lyricism into bebop. He was technically comparable to Navarro and Gillespie, but he had an ability to improvise lengthy solos with an extraordinary logical construction, packed with memorable melodic twists and turns. He was killed in an automobile accident (in which Bud Powell's younger brother, the pianist Richie Powell, also died) at a time when his work in a quintet he co-led with Max Roach was at its most mature. He left a sufficient legacy of recordings to have become a major influence on the generation of trumpeters that followed him.

Just as Fats Navarro had carried forward Gillespie's role in the Billy Eckstine band, it fell to alto saxophonist **Sonny Stitt** (1924–82) to do the same for Parker. Stitt brilliantly absorbed Parker's style and emulated him on many discs with Gillespie's small group. His association with Gillespie continued on and off for many years, including in the Giants of Jazz in 1971–72, and he also worked with Miles Davis in 1960. Stitt never truly shed Parker's influence when playing alto sax, but when he moved to the larger tenor saxophone his own individual voice emerged and he made dozens of discs on the instrument, including a memorable quartet with Bud Powell.

Another alumnus of the Eckstine band who had a totally distinctive sound on tenor sax was **Dexter Gordon** (1923–90). He worked as a teenager with Lionel Hampton, but his importance as a bebop player began in Billy Eckstine's band, and he appeared in place of Charlie Parker on one of Gillespie's 1945 sessions that produced "Blue 'n' Boogie." The next year he led his own group on disc with Bud Powell, beginning his powerful influence on the generation of saxophonists that followed, including John Coltrane and Sonny Rollins. Gordon looked back, as Parker had done, to Lester Young's

playing for inspiration; but although he adopted aspects of Young's timing, he replaced the older man's delicate floating tone with a hard-edged, gritty timbre. Gordon was a particularly influential figure in Europe, where he lived from 1962 to 1977. Gordon was also an accomplished actor, winning an Oscar nomination for his role in *Round Midnight* (1986), in which he combined elements of the careers and characters of Bud Powell and Lester Young.

A number of pianists built on the groundwork of Bud Powell and Thelonious Monk. In particular, the various pianists who worked with Dizzy Gillespie were important. Gillespie himself had strong views on how chords should be played behind bebop soloists, and he coached **George Wallington** (1924–93) on the bandstand at New York's Onyx Club. He similarly encouraged another white musician, **Al Haig** (1924–82), who not only accompanied Parker and Gillespie to California, but went on to be a major voice in modern jazz piano through his work with Parker and Stan Getz.

John Lewis (1920–2001) was another of Gillespie's pianists, replacing Monk in his 1946 big band. Lewis was an instinctive teacher who went on to hold a number of distinguished university posts and was generous with his time toward Gillespie's band members, especially on a long sea voyage to Europe in 1948. He also wrote arrangements for the band, but his true vocation emerged when he and vibraphone player **Milt Jackson** (1923–99) fronted Gillespie's rhythm section in what soon became a separate band known as the Modern Jazz Quartet. This group, which lasted on and off until the death of drummer Connie Kay in 1994, popularized a cool approach to bebop into which Lewis introduced elements of classical counterpoint offset by Jackson's fiery individuality as a soloist.

The original bassist in this group was Gillespie's bass player **Ray Brown** (born 1926). Brown's importance was to combine the physical stamina needed to anchor a bebop rhythm section playing for long hours at high speed with an individual and creative solo voice. As the style of jazz drumming changed, the bassist became increasingly important to maintaining both the rhythm and underlying harmony of a band. Brown acquired an unerring harmonic sense that made him a valued accompanist to singers (notably Ella Fitzgerald, who was briefly his wife) and to touring concert packages like Jazz at the Philharmonic, in which he worked with Fitzgerald, and for many years in the Oscar Peterson Trio. Like Milt Jackson, with whom he often worked, including jointly leading a band, Brown's recent career involves international touring with his own groups.

The changes in jazz drumming that altered the role of the bassist were largely the work of two men, **Kenny Clarke** (1914–85) and **Max Roach** (born 1924). Clarke's background, like Gillespie's, was in swing bands, notably those of Edgar Hayes and Teddy Hill. In the late 1930s he had already started to abandon the four-beats-to-the-measure style of bass drum playing, preferring to keep the beat going with his cymbals and punctuate the band dramatically with the bass and snare drum. This led to unfair criticism: in Hill's band he was given the nickname Klook-a-Mop in imitation of his uneven drum patterns, and his sudden bass drum accents were known as "dropping a bomb." Yet Clarke pioneered the move away from the military or brass band concept of drumming that had been part jazz rhythm since the earliest days. He was equally adept at big band or small group drumming, and after moving to Europe in the late 1940s led a big band with pianist Francy Boland. He also cut many fine recordings in the Parisian trio led by Bud Powell.

Roach's importance to jazz drumming has every bit as much to do with his constant innovation and change during a long and distinguished career as with his impact on the jazz of the 1940s. Roach's drum patterns broke up the beat even further than Clarke's. This, and his innovations as a soloist and accompanist, paved the way for the styles of jazz drumming that followed, from the free playing of Billy Higgins to the thrashing energy of Elvin Jones. Roach has also had a long career as an educator.

Education, and in particular the passing on of its novel rhythmic and harmonic ideas, has become one of the most abiding characteristics of the bebop movement. In the late 1940s and 1950s, many musicians from Europe, including future stars like Ronnie Scott and John Dankworth, from Britain, obtained jobs on transatlantic liners to get frequent access to New York and its rapidly developing music. They sought out bebop innovators to teach and help them, in addition to packing the clubs of 52nd Street to hear what was going on.

Although many bebop musicians were generous with their time, it was the blind pianist **Lennie Tristano** (1919–78), who began teaching formally in 1951, who had most impact. His experiments included a prototype of free jazz—improvisation with no predetermined conditions—and exploring the role formal composition has to play in improvisation, but his main contribution was in developing the musical ear of his students, allowing them to improvise in almost all contexts. His students, notably including saxophonist **Lee Konitz** (born 1927), have made an impact on all areas of jazz since the 1950s.

Vibraphone player Milt Jackson playing with Dizzy Gillespie's orchestra in the late 1940s. Fellow band member Ray Brown is on bass.

BLUE TRAIN

john coltrane
blue note 1577

The most influential saxophonist of the 1960s, John Coltrane, signaled his move forward from hard bop into new territory with this allum.

5 Cool Jazz, Hard Bop, and Fusion

By the start of the 1950s jazz was no longer the mainstream popular music it had been in the three previous decades. Its place in the affections of the public was taken initially by rhythm and blues, then by rock and roll, and soul music. Yet each of these popular genres had a direct influence on the development of jazz, leading, for example, to the creation of hard bop, which fused the beat and gospel feel of soul music with the harmonies and melodic style of bebop, and to jazz-rock fusion. At the same time, the age of the three-and-a-half-minute, 78 rpm "single" disc as the standard length for most jazz pieces came to an end with the widespread adoption of magnetic tape for recording and the invention of the 33 rpm long-playing record. The way ahead in jazz was signaled by entire albums of material that initially were sequences of "single"-length pieces, but eventually involved far longer compositions and improvisations. A musician's career could now develop from album to album in a way that had never been possible during the age of the 78 rpm disc when each recording had been a snaphot, rather than a chance to preserve extended works.

The first new jazz style to emerge in the 1950s was "cool" jazz. This replaced the hot, energetic, and combative improvisation of 1940s bebop with something more contemplative. It began, as almost all the developments in this section did, with the work of Miles Davis. He and Gil Evans, with Gerry Mulligan, John Lewis, and Johnny Carisi, wrote the music for a nine-instrument group whose highly influential recordings became known as the "Birth of the Cool."

As Miles Davis moved on to explore other areas, Mulligan, trumpeter Chet Baker, and a group of West Coast musicians centered around trumpeter Shorty Rogers further explored the possibilities of cool jazz. Its hallmarks were unorthodox instrumentation, involving (initially) French horns and tubas, rather than the normal big band lineup, as well as vibrato-free solos that sought a purity of tone and thought. Such playing contrasted to the "hot" jazz styles of earlier players such as Louis Armstrong or Roy Eldridge who both used vibrato and growling "vocal" tones to impart heat, emotion, and energy to their playing.

Meanwhile, Miles Davis attacked a new area altogether, known as modal jazz. There had been some experiments in this direction before, notably with the late 1940s collaborations between Dizzy Gillespie and theoretician and composer George Russell, who used nonstandard scales known as modes as the basis of arrangements for numbers such as "Cubana Be–Cubana Bop." However, Miles Davis, on the disc *Kind of Blue* with saxophonist John Coltrane and pianist Bill Evans, showed in the late 1950s how a whole album of material could be built around modes and how tunes could be constructed over a simple alternation from one modal or scalar pattern to another, instead of the 12-, 16-, or 32-measure popular song sequences that had prevailed in jazz before then. Davis had recorded one or two modal pieces earlier, but by making modal jazz the style of the entire album *Kind of Blue* was as revolutionary a recording as *Birth of the Cool*.

After this, jazz went in two distinct directions. On the one hand, musicians like saxophonists Sonny Rollins and John Coltrane, who both left Davis to develop their own careers, explored extremes of saxophone technique. Rapidity of execution, the expression of extreme emotions, and new ways of improvising using tiny fragments of themes to build up solos were among the ideas they developed. On the other hand, Davis himself spent part of the 1960s investigating the concept of free improvisation, liberating himself and his band from the constraints of time signatures, keys, and formal compositions. These were ideas that coalesced in a movement begun in the late 1950s by saxophonist Ornette Coleman, and which was to combine with the ideas of European improvising musicians to create a major current in jazz history known as "free jazz." Yet at the very time when Coleman, trumpeter Don Cherry, bassist Charlie Haden, and drummer Billy Higgins were demonstrating the cohesive, challenging but often swinging jazz that could be created in an atmosphere of freedom, Miles Davis once again led the way in a different direction as he underpinned his own free-ranging improvisations with the hard-edged rhythms and instrumentation of rock music.

The Davis fusion bands of the 1960s and 1970s involved numerous significant figures in jazz-rock, among them, Herbie Hancock, Chick Corea, and the Englishman John McLaughlin, who went on to explore a different kind of fusion altogether, between jazz and ethnic "world" music.

The 1960s and 1970s were also a time when there was an increasingly politicized atmosphere in jazz. Collective organizations like the AACM (Association for the Advancement of Creative Musicians) in Chicago took a staunch position on promoting the cause of African-American musicians and reclaiming a heritage of jazz that they felt had been appropriated and exploited by the interests of commercialism and big business. The AACM was formed at a time when racial politics in the United States were tense and polarized. Just months prior to the assassination of President John F. Kennedy in 1963, Martin Luther King Jr. had delivered his "I have a dream" speech, hoping to usher in a new era of tolerance with the support of the Kennedy administration. However, King's call for tolerance was challenged by incidents of racially charged violence. For example, in Alabama, the integration of the university culminated in the firebombing of a local church, and the deaths of four innocent children. Musicians like Muhal Richard Abrams in Chicago, Julius Hemphill in St Louis, and Horace Tapscott in Los Angeles saw artistic endeavor as a way of unifying and dignifying African Americans, and above all restoring a sense of community that had been threatened by the political and social upheaval of the 1960s.

Anthony Braxton, one of the most prolific and diverse musicians to emerge from the AACM, is the representative of the movement in this section. Alongside him, trumpeter Lester Bowie, bassist Malachi Favors, saxophonists Joseph Jarman and Roscoe Mitchell, drummer Famadou Don Moye of the Art Ensemble of Chicago, Oliver Lake and Julius Hemphill of the World Saxophone Quartet, along with West Coast musicians like Arthur Blythe, have proved the movement's success. It has fostered a generation of musicians that developed from community roots and strong convictions to enrich jazz for the whole world.

John Coltrane

GIANT STEPS

The single most influential saxophonist of the period that followed bebop was John Coltrane. His frequent associate, Miles Davis, exerted a dominance over almost all spheres of jazz activity from the moment he emerged from the bebop movement to take center stage in most developments between the 1960s and the 1980s. By contrast, Coltrane's influence was concentrated into a much shorter period, from the recording of his album *Blue Train* in 1957 until his death 10 years later. In that time he made an impact on saxophone playing every bit as important as that of Charlie Parker in the 1940s and 1950s.

As a person, John Coltrane's peaceful character and strong religious convictions, which developed after a successful battle in the late 1950s against alcohol and drug addiction, were at odds with much of his emotional, passionate tenor playing, particularly his rapid flurries of notes that blurred together making up what critics came to call "sheets of sound." Yet the deeper qualities of his personality emerged in his contemplative soprano saxophone solos and in the more spiritually inspired compositions that followed his 1964 album *A Love Supreme*.

John Coltrane was the first musician since Sidney Bechet to popularize the soprano saxophone. *My Favorite Things* was the most popular recording on which he played this instrument, winning him a gold disc.

Coltrane's musical career began in High Point, North Carolina, not far from Hamlet, where he was born. His mother, Alice, was a trained musician and encouraged her son to attend concerts. At age 12 he began playing peckhorn, a rare type of alto horn, in the community band, later switching to clarinet. After he graduated from high school, Coltrane moved to Philadelphia, where he switched to saxophone. He had lessons at the Ornstein School of Music before he was drafted into a Navy band.

Like Miles Davis, Coltrane started playing during the bebop era, but much of his early professional work was with rhythm and blues bands, including those of Eddie "Cleanhead" Vinson and King Kolax. He was part of a thriving Philadelphia jazz scene and became a close associate of alto sax player Jimmy Heath, the two of them together learning Charlie Parker solos note for note. Along with Heath and several other players from Philadelphia, he joined Dizzy Gillespie's 1949 big band, with which he made his first discs, but when it broke up, he was the sole saxophonist to stay on, moving from the alto, which he had studied, to the tenor instrument.

Unfortunately this was at a time when Gillespie's own career was at a crossroads. Instead of getting the kind of public exposure that might have launched his career a little earlier, Coltrane was compelled to play rhythm and blues numbers—his first recorded solo is on a boogie woogie number with Gillespie—and to record for Gillespie's short-lived Dee Gee Records, which had poor distribution. Nevertheless, Coltrane had the chance to play on a handful of Gillespie's more significant discs from the period, like an early recording of "Tin Tin Deo." However,

Coltrane left the band because of his growing drug addiction problems.

These problems beset his career throughout the early 1950s, and they were still not under control when he played with alto saxophonist Johnny Hodges' band or when he first joined Miles Davis in 1955. Nevertheless, his playing in Davis's quintet between 1955 and 1957 brought him international acclaim, and he made vital contributions to numerous Davis albums, including *Relaxin'*, *Steamin'*, *Workin'*, and *Cookin'*, all made in a short space of time to complete Davis's contractual obligations to the Prestige record label before his long-term move to Columbia Records.

Coltrane left Davis in 1957 to return home to Philadelphia, where he finally kicked his drug and alcohol dependence. The musical results were readily apparent and he embarked on a prolific recording career under his own name for the Prestige label that Davis had recently quit. Yet there is a formulaic quality about these early discs. It took the extra rehearsal time and focused production offered by Alfred Lion and Francis Wolff at a competing company, Blue Note Records, to come up with Coltrane's first major success under his own name, the album *Blue Train*. He made only this single session for the label, owing to a handshake agreement with Lion that predated his Prestige contract, which Coltrane felt obliged to honor, demontrating his personal integrity.

Coltrane's solo on the title track "Blue Train" shows the way his playing was to develop for the next six years. Over the blues chord sequence, he asserts a strong, powerful tone, full of emotion yet with touches of vulnerability. He uses controlled flurries of notes played blisteringly fast, yet for almost the first time in his playing these are subservient to the emotional power of his solo. This was to be Coltrane's most influential contribution to jazz: to master a fearsome level of technical achievement in order to release his inner emotions as directly through his instrument as possible. Although this means that not all his discs make easy listening, there is never any doubt about the depth of his thought and feeling.

Coltrane continued to record for the rest of the 1950s under his own name while playing publicly with a variety of groups, including Thelonious Monk's quartet. Yet it was a return to Miles Davis and the album *Kind of Blue* that jolted Coltrane's career forward again. This disc uses modes (scale patterns) rather than the more normal sequences of chords as the underlying harmonies for improvising. As Davis's music began to move further forward to investigate fluid rhythms, which led in due course to his ideas of jazz-rock, Coltrane left the band again, and in his own playing continued rigorously to explore modal jazz. Once again his career was helped by the release of an inspired album, *Giant Steps*, which he cut in late 1959 and released in 1960. At this time Coltrane began to lead his own groups for good, rather than playing in someone else's band.

As Coltrane launched his own working band, *Giant Steps* and his next album, *My Favorite Things*, document his development. The title track of the first album is a gritty performance of one of the best of Coltrane's own compositions, but the disc also includes the tender ballad "Naima," which shows the contemplative side of Coltrane's work that was later to develop. My *Favorite Things* takes that very familiar song from *The Sound of Music* and develops it in unusual ways—from Coltrane's extended solo on the soprano saxophone, which he had recently taken up, to the piano playing of McCoy Tyner, who was to become Coltrane's regular pianist. Tyner juggles keeping sight of the theme with improvisation that moves some distance away from the original underlying chord structure by replacing it was a modal pattern.

Tyner was to be a key member of Coltrane's quartet in the years 1961–65, along with bassist Jimmy Garrison and drummer Elvin Jones, who was briefly replaced by Roy Haynes. According to Jones, the band's intensity onstage was matched by Coltrane's offstage, as he lived, breathed, and slept his music. Coltrane became capable of sustaining ever longer solos that balance anger and beauty, technical complexity and great simplicity. This reached its highest point in the 1964 disc *A Love Supreme*, on which Coltrane celebrates the spiritual liberation that accompanied his deliverance from drink and drugs. It is an extraordinary achievement, and it makes rich and complex music out of very little, the underlying themes being not much more than a four-note motif for "A Love Supreme" and the words of a prayer in the closing "Psalm." Again, from Jones' churning, restless drums to the passion of Coltrane's tenor saxophone, there are plenty of moments when the music is far from comfortable, but its emotional directness has made it one of the most popular jazz albums. Coltrane's playing influenced the entire generation of saxophonists who followed him.

The following year, although the quartet continued to work regularly,

John William Coltrane

BORN

September 23, 1926
Hamlet, North Carolina

DIED

July 17, 1967
New York, New York

EDUCATION

High school in High Point, North Carolina; Ornstein School of Music, Philadelphia, and Granoff Studios

MAJOR INTEREST

Tenor and soprano saxophone, bandleading, composition

ACCOMPLISHMENTS

In Thelonious Monk Quartet from 1957, he pioneered "sheets of sound" technique; with Miles Davis, 1958–60, developed modal jazz. His own quartet with McCoy Tyner (piano), Jimmy Garrison (bass) and Elvin Jones (drums) became the most innovative small group of the mid-1960s. Made several distinctive and innovative albums; composed a core of significant pieces, including "Blue Train" (1957); "Giant Steps," "Mr P. C.," "Naima" (1959); Equinox" (1960); "Impressions" (1961); and "A Love Supreme," "Psalm" (1964)

HONORS

Winner of many polls, including Jazz Musician of the Year in 1966 and *Down Beat* critics' and readers' polls

This ticket is for a New York City concert that Coltrane gave during the last year of his life. Jeanne Lee, an avant-garde vocalist who joined Coltrane for this performance, was among the younger generation of musicians encouraged by the great saxophonist.

Coltrane initiated several new directions in his music, most of which added a dimension of free improvisation to his modal and technical explorations. The first of these was a large collective group improvisation in 1965 on an album called *Ascension,* by turns dense, ugly, competitive, and for much of its length utterly fascinating. The second was to extend his own improvisations to greater and greater lengths. He had often played 15-minute solos on pieces from the early 1960s, but in 1965, documented in numerous concert recordings, he began to elaborate individual pieces into solos of over an hour.

This led to his third new direction, which arose from changes to the personnel of his quartet. His new, more drawn-out ideas required a different kind of accompaniment, so he brought in a new pianist, his wife Alice Coltrane (born Alice McLeod, 1937), and the drummer Rashied Ali, who between them brought an entirely different texture and feeling to the group. Essentially this came from a fragmentation of rhythm, an approach to time that has less to do with any concept of a beat than it has to using rhythm as an improvisational tool like pitch, harmony, and melody. At its peak, this approach was documented in a long duet between John Coltrane and Rashied Ali on the album *Interstellar Space* in 1967, among Coltrane's final recordings before his death from liver cancer.

Coltrane was immensely influential. In this 10-year period of recording, he encapsulated the main changes that were to happen in jazz for a far longer span of time. As a saxophonist he developed from the harmonic basis of bebop to the more fluid backdrop of modes, at the same time developing a speed and facility that have seldom been surpassed. He developed a way of building saxophone solos from stringing together tiny fractured motifs into long, logical, and endlessly fascinating constructions. He is largely responsible for once again making the soprano saxophone popular. His approach to the soprano was completely at odds with the robust power of older players like Sidney Bechet, and instead he stressed the contemplative character of the instrument.

Even more than that, he altered the way musicians play together in a group. The evolution of his quartet in the early 1960s shows a move from a bebop-based saxophone-plus-rhythm-section ensemble into something more completely interactive where every player balances an individual voice with a contribution to the collective whole. This approach was consolidated by his larger ensembles, which played freely with few of the usual constraints of arrangements, harmonies, or structures, and finally by the new, looser, concepts of time he explored with Rashied Ali. This list of achievements alone might be enough to mark Coltrane as a great jazz musician, but with it came Coltrane's emotional energy, his inner conflicts, and his spiritual humanity, all laid bare in his music in a way no jazz musician had managed so comprehensively before him.

For over 30 years after his death, generations of saxophonists were influenced by Coltrane and built on his legacy. The next generation includes Coltrane's son Ravi, who has developed a substantial international reputation in his own right on both tenor and soprano saxophone.

DISCOGRAPHY

The Ultimate Blue Train. Blue Note 53428. [CD ROM version of Coltrane's *Blue Train* album enhanced with alternative takes and visual material.]

Soultrane. Original Jazz Classics OJCCD 021. [Late 1950s quartet with Miles Davis's rhythm section.]

Giant Steps. Atlantic 781337.

My Favorite Things. Atlantic 782346.

Complete 1961 Village Vanguard Recordings. Impulse IMPCD 4232 (four-CD set). [Coltrane's long-lived quartet in a club setting.]

A Love Supreme. Impulse 11552.

The Major Works of John Coltrane. Impulse GRD 21132 (two-CD set). [Has "Ascension" and alternate takes of similar material.]

Live at the Village Vanguard Again! Impulse 12132. [The late quartet with Alice Coltrane, Rashied Ali, and percussionist Emmanuel Rahid.]

Interstellar Space. Impulse GRP 11102.

FURTHER READING

Cook, Richard, and Brian Morton. "John Coltrane," in *The Penguin Guide to Jazz on CD*. 5th ed. New York: Penguin, 2000.

Fujiyoka, Yasuhiro, Lewis Porter, and Yoh-Ichi Hamada. *John Coltrane: A Discographical and Musical Biography*. Metuchen, N.J.: Scarecrow, 1995.

Nisenson, Eric. *Ascension: John Coltrane and His Quest*. 1993. Reprint, New York: Da Capo, 1995.

Porter, Lewis. *John Coltrane, His Life and Music*. Ann Arbor: University of Michigan Press, 1998.

Priestley, Brian. *John Coltrane*. London: Apollo, 1987.

Selfridge, John W. *John Coltrane: A Sound Supreme*. New York: Franklin Watts, 1999.

Simkins, C. O. *Coltrane: A Biography*. New York: Herndon, 1975.

Thomas, J. C. *Chasin' the Trane: The Music and Mystique of John Coltrane*. Garden City, N.Y.: Doubleday, 1975.

Woideck, Carl. *A John Coltrane Companion: Four Decades of Commentary*. New York: Schirmer, 1998.

WEBSITE

http://www.downbeat.com/sections/artists/text/bio.asp?from=fans&id1=3648

Down Beat magazine's official website, including brief biography and links to classic articles and discography with audio clips.

Sonny Rollins

SAXOPHONE
COLOSSUS

T he most abiding image of tenor saxophonist Sonny Rollins comes from the time between 1959 and 1961 when he withdrew from playing publicly but spent long hours practicing in the open air on New York City's Williamsburg Bridge. This time of personal rediscovery and internal musical exploration, later commemorated in the album *The Bridge*, epitomizes several aspects of Rollins' music. A man of striking appearance, whether exotically hatted, shaven-headed, bearded, or with swept-back messianic locks, he has always played every bit as much for himself as for his public, following those lines of musical enquiry most necessary for his own questing imagination. He has never been afraid to withdraw from professional music, such as when he traveled to India in 1968 and took another period out in 1969–71. Yet the supreme irony about his years practicing on the bridge is that he chose such a public place to withdraw. He remained both approachable and isolated at the same time, and it is this mixture that remains present in much of his music. He is the man who wrote the enduring

Sonny Rollins and pianist Mark Soskin (left), who was a regular member of Rollins' band from 1978 until the mid-1990s, work together during a studio session.

and hummable calypso theme "St. Thomas," but he is also the man with a uniquely spartan tone, and who has the ability to deconstruct even the best-known ballad into myriad hard-edged musical fragments.

Stylistically, Rollins' influence on the development of jazz saxophone is comparable to John Coltrane's, spanning the period from bebop to the end of the 20th century. Technically his mastery of the tenor saxophone is on a par with Coltrane's, but where Coltrane expressed a range of emotion from rage to spiritual awakening, Rollins's equivalent emotional range explores everything from his joyous Caribbean-inspired pieces to more somber feelings of bleakness and restlessness. He is also capable of witty and humorous content in his solos, sometimes inserting quotations from other songs to add a musical commentary on his work—only Charlie Parker has come close to Rollins' encyclopedic command of quotes.

Even when he is backed by the most sympathetic rhythm sections, Rollins is almost always self-sufficient, often giving the impression that he is working out his own line of thought, unbending, whatever his surroundings. As if to underline the point, his concerts from the 1960s onward often included a section in which he played completely unaccompanied, a skill demonstrated on the 1985 recording *The Solo Album*. Such solos are so intense that sometimes he can lose track of time, and there are stories of audiences being kept waiting in line outside while he continued playing a long improvisation for an earlier house.

The main reason that Rollins exerted an influence on contemporary saxophonists as great as that of John Coltrane is that he showed a logical route forward from Charlie Parker's work by vastly extending the type, length, speed, rhythm, and structure of the phrases he used to build into solos.

Rollins grew up in a section of New York City where there was plenty of musical activity; his brother was a trained violinist who later played with the Pittsburgh Symphony Orchestra, and his sister played piano. At Benjamin Franklin High School, he was in the center of a group that included many future modern jazz stars, including alto saxophonist Jackie McLean and drummer Art Taylor. McLean recalled the outstanding saxophonist of their schooldays as being Andy Kirk Jr. (son of the swing bandleader with whom Mary Lou Williams played). Then Rollins went away for a few months in his late teens, and on his return to New York had practiced hard enough to develop a truly remarkable technique that outshone Kirk. At 19, Rollins was playing club dates with Miles Davis and had already worked closely with Thelonious Monk and Bud Powell, with whom he recorded in 1949.

In the late 1940s Rollins shared the enthusiasm for bebop with most of the jazz musicians of his generation, and his earliest recordings with Bud Powell or Miles Davis reveal a debt to Charlie Parker. Briefly in the early 1950s, Rollins was drawn into the world of narcotics, but by 1955 he kicked the habit, as did Jackie McLean, who had played alongside him for a year or two in Miles Davis's band. At that point, McLean's style was also directly derived from that of Charlie Parker. However, the differences between his playing and that of Rollins emphasized the fact that as early as 1952 Rollins had moved far beyond Parker and developed his own individual voice. Before he left Davis in 1954, Rollins recorded a number of his own compositions with the band, including "Airegin" and "Oleo."

By the time Rollins rejoined Davis briefly in 1957, during the period when John Coltrane was out of the lineup, he had established himself as one of the

Theodore Walter "Sonny" Rollins

BORN
September 9, 1930
New York, New York

EDUCATION
Benjamin Franklin High School,
New York City

MAJOR INTERESTS
Tenor saxophone, bandleading

ACCOMPLISHMENTS
Numerous recordings as a freelancer, 1949–54; a member of Miles Davis's band for much of this period. With Max Roach 1955–57, as part of Clifford Brown–Max Roach Quintet to mid-1956; also recording as freelancer; with Davis again, 1957. In 1960s led own bands, recorded extensively. Wrote score for movie *Alfie* (1965); subject of film *Sonny Rollins Live* (1973). Led own bands continuously through 1990s; maintained focus on tenor saxophone, but used soprano and lyricon in 1970s. Compositions include "Airegin," "Blue 7," "Don't Stop the Carnival," "Doxy," "Oleo," and "St. Thomas"

HONORS
Numerous awards as saxophonist and recording artist; Elected to *Down Beat* Hall of Fame, 1973

which Coltrane makes a guest appearance), and *Tour De Force*.

When Rollins left Davis for the second time, and before his first period of retreat from public performance, he kept up his prolific flow of discs, several of them reflecting his live concert or club appearances, often with just bass and drums. These included his famous Village Vanguard recordings and his *Freedom Suite*, produced in the studio with a similar bass and drums lineup.

By the time Rollins was ready to perform in public again in 1961, the jazz world had moved on. Coltrane and Davis had begun their exploration of modes, while Ornette Coleman's first discs had introduced concepts of free jazz to a wide public. Rollins' instincts allied him with the free jazz players for a while; he cut discs with musicians who had worked with Coleman, including trumpeter Don Cherry and drummer Billy Higgins. These were not particularly successful but underlined Rollins' basic individuality and his independence from fashionable currents in jazz. As a consequence, one major outcome of the 1960s was his growing tendency to play unaccompanied, which remained a major aspect of his work for the next three decades.

This is at the heart of why Rollins has continued to be so influential on other saxophonists. Fashions have come and gone around him, but he has continued his own development within a worldwide touring career that has brought his playing to several generations of international audiences. He has surrounded himself with musical associates such as trombonist Clifton Anderson, pianist Mark Soskin, and bassist Bob Cranshaw who are sympathetic to supporting him effectively, and above all to creating space for his

Rollins wears one of his unusual hats in a concert at London's Royal Festival Hall in 1980.

leading saxophonists at the cutting edge of jazz development, if not the foremost. He achieved this both through his membership of the Clifford Brown–Max Roach Quintet and his subsequent work with Roach after Brown's accidental death, and through a series of quite exceptional recordings under his own name, made in 13 months from December 1955, which included the albums *Saxophone Colossus*, *Tenor Madness* (on

> *"I'm playing and thinking about trying to get the music across and nothing else. Time doesn't matter."*
>
> —Sonny Rollins in a 1971 interview with Arthur Taylor

dramatic and lengthy solos. While many younger saxophonists have looked to the technical command of John Coltrane and his emotional intensity as a role model, Rollins' wealth of ideas, and the entertaining way in which he combines these with recognizable ballad or calypso themes have made him an equally potent force.

DISCOGRAPHY

The Complete Prestige Recordings. Prestige 4407 7 (seven-CD set). [Nine original albums, including the widely praised *Saxophone Colossus.*]

Newk's Time. Blue Note B21Y-84001-2.

A Night at the Village Vanguard, Vols. 1 and 2. Blue Note B21Y-746517-2 and 746518-2. [Rollins playing live at the club with just bass and drums in support.]

Complete RCA Victor Recordings. RCA 09026 68675-2 (six-CD set). [Rollins' major discs from 1962 onward, including several famous albums, notably *The Bridge* and *What's New?*]

Sunny Days, Starry Nights. Milestone 9122. [1984 sessions by Rollins' regular band of the time.]

The Solo Album. Original Jazz Classics OJC 956. [1985 unaccompanied recital.]

Falling in Love with Jazz. Milestone 9179. [1989 studio dates with Branford Marsalis as guest.]

Silver City. Milestone 2501 (two-CD set). [Cross section of material, 1972–95, plus an interview.]

FURTHER READING

Hultin. Randi. *Born Under the Sign of Jazz.* London: Sanctuary, 1998. [Preface by Sonny Rollins.]

Nisenson, Eric, and Sonny Rollins. *Open Sky: Sonny Rollins and his Words of Improvisation.* New York: St. Martin's, 2000.

Taylor, Art. "Sonny Rollins," in *Notes and Tones: Musician to Musician Interviews.* 1982. Reprint, New York: Da Capo, 1993.

Wilson, Peter Niklas. *Sonny Rollins: The Definitive Musical Guide.* Berkeley, Calif.: Berkeley Hills Books, 2001.

WEBSITE

http://www.pbs.org/jazz/biography/artist_id_rollins_sonny.htm

Biography and audio links from Ken Burns' documentary *Jazz.*

Gerry Mulligan

BIRTH OF THE COOL

S imply by specializing on the relatively cumbersome and unfashionable baritone saxophone, and imparting to it the grace, lightness, and airy beauty achieved by tenor saxophonists like Lester Young or Stan Getz, Gerry Mulligan would have secured his permanent place in jazz history. In addition, however, he was an arranger of rare originality and a bandleader who managed to be innovative whether in a quartet setting—in which he is generally regarded as the pioneer of the "pianoless" lineup with two melody instruments plus bass and drums—or in larger ensembles. Furthermore, although as an arranger he employed new and experimental voicings amid unusual chord structures, in both his playing and writing he managed to retain the basic characteristics of melody and of simple, direct communication to his listeners.

Communicating to listeners was the earliest concern of Mulligan's professional career in music. He grew up in the Philadelphia area, where he learned piano as well as saxophone, and he sold his first arrangements to a local radio

The young Gerry Mulligan, around the time he launched his pianoless quartet with Chet Baker in 1952, presents a clean-cut image.

band led by Johnny Warrington. He was still in his teens at the time, and he had not yet turned 20 when he went on to join the high-profile swing orchestra of drummer Gene Krupa as an arranger. In those early days Mulligan occasionally played alto saxophone in big bands, but his important work was as a writer, not a player. This continued to be the case as he wrote for the orchestras of Claude Thornhill and Elliott Lawrence, but in 1948 he met arranger Gil Evans, who also wrote for Thornhill.

Evans lived in Manhattan, where he held an almost permanent open house for fellow musicians, who made their way to his small apartment to share ideas about music and write and play together. The Miles Davis profile in Part 4 discusses the album *Birth of the Cool,* which grew out of a nonet (nine-piece group) that Davis fronted at the Royal Roost, and that played arrangements in a new style worked out by Evans and Davis. Mulligan was a key ingredient in the creative process that produced *Birth of the Cool.* He was one of the regular visitors to Evans' home, he wrote arrangements for the band to play, and he joined the nonet lineup on baritone saxophone. He had not long since transferred from the alto, and it was on the baritone that he quickly developed his very individual solo voice. He played on the 1949 and 1950 recording sessions by this group.

Mulligan's contribution to the beginning of cool jazz is important in another, more long-lasting way. As Davis and Evans moved on to new areas of music, which they worked on individually and together, Mulligan stayed with many of the ideas behind the Davis nonet to develop them further. He liked the tonal possibilities offered by the unusual instrumentation of tuba, French horns, and saxophones. He was intrigued by the flexibility of a group that could muster much of the power of a big band, yet retain the intimate dynamics and collective feel of a smaller ensemble. He was also sympathetic as a soloist to the kind of relaxed and unrushed backdrop the group created for improvising. Furthermore, he knew that he could develop his writing in the direction begun with Davis and Evans. So in 1951 he formed his own "tentet," a ten-piece band, and made numerous returns to this size and type of group throughout his career, notably in the 1950s and 1970s, culminating in a disc that re-recorded the original *Birth of the Cool* repertoire in 1992. Sadly, this recording was without Miles Davis, who had indicated his willingness to participate as he had in 1991 reunions with numerous other former associates, but who died a few months before the session.

In later life, Mulligan wrote mainly for his own bands or solo projects, but at the outset of his career, and for a period in the 1960s, he was still writing for other leaders. In the early 1950s he contributed scores to the library of Stan Kenton's band. At that time he settled in Los Angeles, and it was there in 1952 that he put together the lineup of his first pianoless quartet with trumpeter Chet Baker as his front-line partner. Baker's cool, vibrato-free tone echoed the sound of Miles Davis, and to some extent the group sounded like a scaled down version of the "Birth of the Cool" nonet. Baker was also a singer, with a casual throwaway vocal style and an understated melodic approach to songs that he carried over into his trumpet playing. His lean, lyrical trumpet lines merged gracefully with Mulligan's baritone, and the absence of a piano threw their interplay into sharp relief. Although it was rumored that the band omitted a piano because the club where they played did not have one, Mulligan had reached a point in his writing where he wanted to try out such a lineup. He had already recorded some trio tunes with just bass and drums when he secured the

Gerald Joseph "Gerry" Mulligan

BORN
April 6, 1927
New York, New York

DIED
January 19, 1996
Darien, Connecticut

EDUCATION
Clarinet lessons in Reading, Pennsylvania, with Sammy Correnti; West Philadelphia Catholic High School for Boys

MAJOR INTERESTS
Composing, arranging, bandleading; baritone and soprano saxophone

ACCOMPLISHMENTS
Arranged pieces recorded by Gene Krupa, 1947, and Claude Thornhill, 1948; played baritone sax and arranged for *Birth of the Cool* sessions, 1949–50. Formed first "pianoless" quartet from 1952; led Concert Jazz Band, 1960–63. Recorded own *Age of Steam* compositions, 1971; other compositions include "Disc Jockey Jump" (1947); "Jeru," "Venus de Milo" (1949); "Bark for Barksdale," "Line for Lyons" (1952); "Rocker," "Walkin' Shoes" (1953); "Grand Tour" (1971); "Flying Scotsman" (1988)

HONORS
Frequent winner of musician polls, consistently topping *Down Beat* baritone sax category in 1960s and 1970s

In later life, Mulligan's clean shave and crew cut gave way to his trademark long gray hair and beard.

quartet was one of a handful of groups that came to symbolize "West Coast Cool," namely the predominately California-based coterie of white musicians who, like Mulligan, developed ideas from Mile Davis's 1949–50 nonet. In photographs, the two front-line partners projected a clean-cut image with crew cuts and tee shirts. This image came to be at odds with the musicians' lifestyles, as both dabbled in narcotics, Mulligan briefly, Baker for longer and ultimately fatally.

When Mulligan was briefly imprisoned for a drug-related offense in 1953, Baker went his own way, becoming for a while a pin-up idol and romantic vocalist while continuing to record his relaxed trumpet features. Mulligan's quartet resurfaced with Jon Eardley on trumpet, then Bob Brookmeyer on valve trombone, and finally Art Farmer on trumpet, each bringing a distinctive and recognizable character to the band while not losing sight of the pianoless concept. A different, more ethereal sound came into the group on a 1957 recording when Mulligan replaced his brass playing counterparts with alto saxophonist Paul Desmond. Desmond had made his name with pianist Dave Brubeck, with whom Mulligan was later to work in 1968–72.

In 1960, after winning a succession of music critics' polls for his baritone playing, Mulligan formed his Concert Jazz Band, a 13-piece group that shifted the focus from his playing to his writing and arranging. In 1971 he took this side of his work a stage further in an album called *Age of Steam*, in which a group of similar size played a series of first-rate Mulligan compositions inspired by steam railroads. Many jazz musicians, from Meade Lux Lewis and Duke Ellington onward, have written music around train themes, but Mulligan's,

quartet's first job at the tiny Haig Club on Wilshire Boulevard in Los Angeles, where the piano had simply been moved out of the room to create extra space for paying customers.

As well as reinterpreting standards such as "My Funny Valentine," the quartet was also successful in establishing Mulligan's original compositions such as "Line for Lyons," named for Jimmy Lyons, the record producer and later organizer of the Monterey Festival, and "Bark for Barksdale." The

> *"Certainly he was one of the greatest composers in the history of jazz as well as its primary baritone soloist."*
>
> —Gene Lees in *Arranging the Score* (2000)

written at a time when railroad companies around the world finally abandoned the thunderous power of steam locomotives, combined romantic images of a fading era with the hard-edged sound of rock drumming and guitar playing. He was to return to this source of inspiration again in the 1980s with a commission for Scotland's Glasgow Festival about the famous record-breaking train *Flying Scotsman*.

For a time in the 1970s, Mulligan lived in Europe, touring from his base in Italy with a quartet. Back in the United States in the 1980s, he divided his time between composing for sporadic large band projects or the occasional orchestral suite, and performing as a soloist in a series of hard-blowing small groups, including his quartet with pianist Ted Rosenthal, bassist Dean Johnson, and drummer Ron Vincent. He played on a jazz cruise, just weeks before his death from cancer.

Mulligan was a widely accomplished musician across many styles and areas of jazz, but his seminal importance was in extending the ideas of cool jazz first worked out in the late 1940s and applying them to both large and small ensembles. At the same time, he developed into one of the most distinctive solo voices in jazz, on one of its most unforgiving instruments.

DISCOGRAPHY

Miles Davis: Birth of the Cool. Capitol CDP 792862.

The Best of the Gerry Mulligan Quartet with Chet Baker. Pacific Jazz CDP 7 95481-2.

Pleyel Concerts 54, Vols. 1 and 2. Vogue 113411 and 113412. [1954 quartet with Bob Brookmeyer in concert in Paris.]

Gerry Mulligan–Paul Desmond Quartet, Verve 519850. [1957 recordings; pianoless quartet with two-saxophone front line.]

What Is There to Say?. Columbia 475699. [1958–59 quartet with Art Farmer as Mulligan's front-line partner.]

Verve Jazz Masters 36. Verve 523342. [Early 1960s anthology representing the Concert Jazz Band.]

The Age of Steam. A and M 396996-2. [1971 large band album.]

Soft Lights and Sweet Music. Concord CCD 4300. [1986 session with Scott Hamilton on tenor sax.]

Re-Birth of the Cool. GRP GRD 9679. [1992 remake of 1949 arrangements with Wallace Roney cast as Miles Davis.]

Dream a Little Dream. Telarc 83364. [Quartet session by Mulligan's regular early 1990s group.]

FURTHER READING

Horricks, Raymond. *Gerry Mulligan's Ark*. London: Apollo, 1986.

Klinkowitz, Jerome. *Listen: Gerry Mulligan–An Aural Narrative in Jazz*. New York: Schirmer, 1991. [Includes discography.]

Lees, Gene. *Arranging the Score: Portraits of the Great Arrangers*. London and New York: Cassell, 2000.

WEBSITE

http://www.loc.gov/loc/lcib/9906/gerry.html

Library of Congress's website page describing the Gerry Mulligan collection with biography and images.

Stan Getz

MY LIFE IS MUSIC

It is seldom long before any description of Stan Getz arrives at the subject of his individual tone on the tenor saxophone. He took the light, airy sound of Lester Young and burnished it into a feathery, translucent perfection unequalled by any other saxophonist in jazz. In addition to his tonal control, Getz transported the immediacy and melodic basis of Young's approach into the more sophisticated harmonies and dazzling tempos of the post-bebop period. Whether he was wringing every ounce of emotion from a ballad, or floating effortlessly over chorus after chorus of inventive variations on an up-tempo song, his sound was remarkably consistent. Through his many recordings of ballads and bossa novas Getz went beyond a dedicated jazz audience to become a truly important figure in the world of international popular music.

For much of his career Getz wrestled with drug problems; in addition, he had an abrasive personality completely at odds with the serene beauty of his playing. His contrary character had its origins in a tough childhood in Philadelphia and subsequently New York City, where his professional playing career began when he was 15. There seems to have been little question about Getz's early talent. However, although he played in and occasionally recorded with the bands of Jack Teagarden, Stan Kenton, Jimmy Dorsey, and Benny Goodman, it was not until he joined Woody Herman's band in 1947 that he emerged as a significant jazz voice in his own right. Not only was this the time he began to record under his own name, but he made several critically acclaimed discs as a member of the Herman saxophone section, in which he was one of the "Four Brothers," along with fellow tenorists Zoot Sims and Herbie Steward and baritone saxophonist Serge Chaloff.

The most important of Getz's Herman recordings was his solo on a piece by the band's arranger Ralph Burns called "Early Autumn." It was not the only solo on the disc, but Getz's tone, and the clarity and beauty of his improvisations, seemed three-dimensional in comparison to the rest of the playing. These were the characteristics he developed when he left Herman in 1949 to begin his own solo career. From that point on he was a star soloist, leading his own groups or touring on his own, and even when he worked with somebody else's band, as he did with Stan Kenton in 1953–54, he did so as a featured guest artist.

In 1952, Getz moved from the poorly distributed but artistically successful Roost record label to Norman Granz's Verve stable. This brought his work to a wider audience. Despite a period of imprisonment for drug-related reasons in 1954 that temporarily halted his career, Getz seized the

Stanley "Stan" Getz

Stan Getz at the height of the 1960s bossa nova craze with Brazilian guitarist Joao Gilberto. Getz's first bossa nova hit, "Desafinado" recorded with guitarist Charlie Byrd, went to number two on the rock and roll charts.

BORN
February 2, 1927
Philadelphia, Pennsylvania

DIED
June 6, 1991
Malibu, California

EDUCATION
James Monroe High School, Bronx, New York, where he had lessons from Albert Becker on bassoon and other reed instruments

MAJOR INTERESTS
Tenor saxophone, bandleading

ACCOMPLISHMENTS
Perfected an unusually light and pure-toned approach to playing tenor saxophone. Worked with Jack Teagarden (1943), Stan Kenton (1944–45), Jimmy Dorsey (1945), Benny Goodman (1945–46); made his reputation with Woody Herman (1947–49), by which time he was recording under his own name. Joined Jazz at the Philharmonic (1957–58). Recorded influential bossa nova albums in 1962–64. Artist in residence, Stanford University, 1980s

HONORS
Frequent *Down Beat* poll winner (1960s and early 1970s); Grammy awards for *Desafinado* (1963), *Getz/Gilberto* and *The Girl from Ipanema* (1965), *I Remember You* (1991); honorary doctorate, Mercy College, Dobbs Ferry, New York, 1980; *Down Beat* Hall of Fame, 1986

opportunity presented by Granz to record prolifically, to join forces in the studio with other Verve artists like Dizzy Gillespie and Oscar Peterson, and in due course to tour with Granz's Jazz at the Philharmonic concert packages.

In the 1950s, Getz's most consistent, inventive, and polished playing took place on a series of discs made for Verve on the West Coast in his small group with pianist Lou Levy. Little of the repertoire was new, most of it consisting of the standard tunes Getz played on his live concerts, but however familiar and well-worn these were, he invested them with such freshness that the discs remain unparalleled interpretations of what British critic Stanley Dance christened the "mainstream" repertoire.

Despite the continued high quality of his playing, Getz life involved further narcotics and domestic problems. In 1958–61 he lived in Scandinavia, for the most part in Copenhagen, Denmark, where he worked with a variety of local musicians and fellow American expatriates. Not long after his return to the United States he embarked on the second wildly successful period of his time working for Verve records, by becoming a major part of a new craze for jazz based on Latin American rhythms—particularly the bossa nova, a type of Brazilian music related to samba, which has a soft understated feel, and simple melodies backed by sophisticated harmonies.

Getz was not the first, or the only American musician to catch on to this movement. For example, the ever-prescient Dizzy Gillespie preceded Getz by some months when he returned from a tour to Brazil to record compositions by songwriter, pianist, and guitarist Antonio Carlos Jobim. But good as Gillespie's discs were, they failed to ignite public demand in the same way as Getz's 1962 collaboration with guitarist Charlie Byrd on an album called *Jazz Samba*. Byrd's subtle guitar playing was a perfect complement to Getz's feathery tone, and their breezy playing on the gently swinging "Desafinado"

Stan Getz plays the saxophone that is now displayed in his memory at Berklee College of Music in Boston, Massachusetts.

ushered in a new movement in jazz. This was swiftly followed up by Getz working directly with Latin musicians, including guitarists Joao Gilberto and Jobim, and arranging for them to perform in New York City and to accompany him on recordings.

The highpoint of this collaboration was a disc on which the untutored voice of Astrud Gilberto, Joao Gilberto's wife at the time, haltingly picked its way through the lyrics of the song "The Girl from Ipanema." Its success was undoubtedly due to the extraordinary way in which Getz's urbane and sophisticated saxophone solo counterbalanced Gilberto's naive vocal performance.

The dominance of rock music in the mid-1960s eventually killed off the bossa nova craze. Getz, who had all along led a series of first-rate touring jazz groups while making his bossa records, returned to his life on the road, employing several talented young players including vibraphonist Gary Burton, bassist Steve Swallow, and pianist Chick Corea. Yet as these musicians

moved on to encompass new movements such as jazz-rock, Getz found himself becoming isolated from prevailing fashion. He returned to Europe, where he was able to pick and choose his work more readily and to continue to play in the style he had made his own.

Once again, he returned to the United States, this time in 1972, to record regularly and tour internationally from a base on the West Coast. In the same way as he had picked out emerging talents in the 1960s, he was to go on discovering interesting new players in the 1970s and 1980s, mingling them in his backing groups with more seasoned hands. His own playing remained incomparable; even when he became terminally ill, he resisted the onslaught of cancer and continued to tour and play at a remarkably high level. In his latter years, he alternated periods of semiretirement with regular playing, and he also undertook some teaching while artist in residence at Stanford University in the mid-1980s.

"On the tenor the tone is completely individual for each man, once he can play."

—Stan Getz in a 1971 interview with Max Jones

DISCOGRAPHY

Woody Herman: Keeper of the Flame. Capitol 984532-2. [Recordings by Herman's "Second Herd," including Getz's solo on "Early Autumn."]

Early Stan. Original Jazz Classics OJC 654. [Getz's first sessions under his own name.]

The Complete Roost Recordings. Roost 859622-2 (three-CD set). [Getz's early 1950s discs for the Royal Roost club label. Important colleagues include pianists Al Haig and Horace Silver, and drummer Roy Haynes.]

At the Shrine. Verve 513753-2. [1954 concert from Los Angeles' Shrine Auditorium with Bob Brookmeyer on trombone alongside Getz.]

The West Coast Sessions. Verve 531935-2 (three-CD set). [Exceptional recordings from California, 1955–57.]

In Sweden 1958–60. Dragon DRCD 263 (two-CD set). [Work from Getz's European years.]

The Girl from Ipanema. Verve 823611-2 (four-CD set). [All of Getz's best 1960s bossa nova work with Charlie Byrd, Joao and Astrud Gilberto, and Antonio Carlos Jobim.]

The Lyrical Stan Getz. Columbia 471512-2. [Anthology of Getz's 1970s recordings.]

Pure Getz. Concord CCD 4188. [1982 set showing Getz at the peak of his 1980s form.]

Yours and Mine. Concord CCD 4740. [1989 concert recording from Glasgow, Scotland, that shows Getz playing impressively for a festival crowd.]

FURTHER READING

Gitler, Ira. *Jazz Masters of the Forties.* New York: Macmillan, 1966.

Jones, Max. "Stan Getz" in *Talking Jazz.* New York: Norton, 1987.

Maggin, Donald S. *Stan Getz: A Life in Jazz.* New York: Morrow, 1996.

Palmer, Richard. *Stan Getz.* London: Apollo, 1988.

WEBSITE

http://www.duke.edu/~lmw4/
Unofficial Getz homepage with biography, selective discography, and links.

Ornette Coleman

FREE JAZZ

Since his 20s when, in 1959, he moved from Los Angeles to New York City, Ornette Coleman has been an elemental force in jazz, a revolutionary figure as significant as Miles Davis or John Coltrane, and for much of his career a questing, restless innovator. Although the term "free jazz"—meaning improvisation freed from the usual constraints of pitch, meter, and structure—had been used before, it was Coleman who brought it into the everyday language of jazz. His first important quartet included trumpeter Don Cherry, bassist Charlie Haden, and drummer Billy Higgins. In the fall of 1959, they opened at the Five Spot Club in New York City, then followed up this engagement—in which their uncompromising rejection of many aspects of jazz of the time caused a great critical controversy—with a series of discs for the Atlantic label. With this group, Coleman took jazz several leaps further than anyone else had so far managed.

At the heart of Coleman's music was a different way of thinking about improvisation. To some extent this had to

Ornette Coleman demonstrates his unorthodox style of violin playing—holding the instrument on his chest like a fiddler. He also designs his own clothes, which add to his dramatic stage appearance.

do with his own playing, which mixed his instinctive sense of melody with unorthodox pitching and harmonic intervals, but it was even more strongly a result of the way the group improvised and interacted together. There were clear recognizable melodies, there were solos by different instruments in the group; but the players did not improvise around chords or a harmonic structure as they might have done in the contemporary groups of John Coltrane or Sonny Rollins. Nevertheless, there was generally a sense of key, and also of jazz timing. Haden and Higgins often played a more straightforward jazz rhythm than could be found in the fragmented accompaniments of John Coltrane's quartet.

In Coleman's group, sometimes the bass or drums took the lead while his own alto sax or Cherry's trumpet would take on a supporting role to the rhythm players, phrasing in such a way as to complement the work of the others and throw it into sharp relief. When Coleman emerged from the ensemble to take a solo, his playing, like that of Charlie Parker, had a strong blues feeling about it.

Such a radical departure from what had gone before was not arrived at suddenly or by accident, although Coleman has given varying accounts of how he got there. These accounts have added a sense of mystique to his early career, and particularly the events that precipitated his move back from tenor saxophone to alto, the instrument on which his future career was to be based. He had played tenor in his teens, but alto was the instrument he first learned in high school, where he played alongside such future associates as saxophonist Dewey Redman and drummer Charles Moffett.

It seems that he started out, like many Texas musicians, by playing the blues. Relying on an ability to copy the sounds of other musicians, his professional life began as a tenor saxophonist

in several rhythm and blues bands, working throughout his native Texas and as far afield as New Orleans and the West Coast. He returned to playing alto in New Orleans when he was taken in by the family of trumpeter Melvin Lastie after being beaten up while playing tenor for bluesman Clarence Samuels. Coleman's open-ended accounts of this incident leave it open to interpretation if the attack was motivated by racism, by Coleman's long hair and vegetarianism, or by the wild solos he inserted into routine blues pieces.

Coleman spent most of his 20s in Los Angeles, working as an elevator operator and only playing sporadically with a few like-minded individuals. All this time he was working out his own theories and absorbing many of the books written about harmony and music theory. He had always had a mental image of the kind of music he wanted to play. In the 1950s his theoretical ideas began to coalesce, especially after he began playing with the musicians who were eventually to form his quartet as well as with trumpeter Bobby Bradford and drummer Ed Blackwell. In due course, Coleman named his theories "harmolodics," specifically referring to the way in which a tune behaves in respect to harmony, movement, and melody when it is played simultaneously in different registers, pitches, or tonalities. By the late 1950s his emergent form of new music was heard by players like the bassist Red Mitchell and pianist John Lewis (of the Modern Jazz Quartet), who encouraged Coleman to record, and then to move east.

The success of his early quartet was swift and dramatic, and Coleman soon became one of the highest profile jazz musicians in the United States. Yet in the midst of this early success with an established group, Coleman made two experimental recordings that were pointers to his later career. One was

Ornette Coleman

BORN

March 9, 1930
Fort Worth, Texas

EDUCATION

I. M. Terrell High School,
Fort Worth, Texas; subsequently
self-taught

MAJOR INTERESTS

Alto saxophone, trumpet, violin;
bandleading, composing

ACCOMPLISHMENTS

Formed electric band Prime Time, 1975; active performing and recording career, with his extant groups, new duos, and his quartet Sound Museum. Compositions include "Congeniality," "Free," "Lonely Woman," "Ramblin'" (1959); "A Dedication to Poets and Writers" (1962); "Skies of America" (orchestra, 1972); "Sex Spy" (1977); "Time Design" (1983); "Sacred Mind of Johnny Dolphin" (chamber ensemble, 1984); "Notes Talkin'," "Trinity" (1986); "The Country that Gave the Freedom Symbol to America" (1989); "Story Writing" (1996). Appeared in the film *Ornette, Made in America* (1986), and on the soundtrack of *Naked Lunch* (1991)

HONORS

Down Beat Hall of Fame, 1969; *Down Beat* Musician of the Year, 1987. Retrospective festival of his compositions at Cité de la Musique, Paris, 1997, followed by celebratory Coleman season at Lincoln Center, New York City

Once Coleman played an unusual plastic saxophone, but more recently he has used a metal alto, which is lacquered to appear similar to the plastic instrument. This picture was taken during a 2001 performance of the music he and Howard Shore wrote for the movie *Naked Lunch,* in which his group and the BBC Concert Orchestra played live as the film was projected behind them.

"*If you take an instrument and you happen to feel it in a way you can express yourself, it becomes its own law.*"

—Ornette Coleman

a disc by an octet (actually a double quartet with two trumpets, two reed instruments, two basses, and two sets of drums) of completely spontaneous improvisation that he titled *Free Jazz,* and which used some of the same personnel as Coltrane's *Ascension,* although with an even greater sense of liberation. The second recording mixed his plaintive alto saxophone with a string quartet, two basses, a guitar, and percussion in a series of composed works called *Jazz Abstractions,* written in part by theorist, composer, and author Gunther Schuller, an early enthusiast of Coleman's work.

Coleman's freer improvisational concepts were followed up in his mid-1960s groups, after he took over two years out to learn trumpet and violin, instruments on which he could try out his musical ideas with no preconceptions about how they should be played. His violin playing was unusual. He held the instrument in the position of a country fiddler, on the chest rather than under the chin, and he wove themes and ideas from hoedowns and other traditional forms of music into his playing. Composer George Russell wrote his symphonic piece *Dialogue with Ornette* to recapture the sounds he heard when Coleman first played violin. Coleman's own more formal interests led him from *Jazz Abstractions* to composing and playing his own pieces for wind quintet, and eventually to his *Skies of America* for full orchestra.

In the mid-1960s he toured first with a quartet that included saxophonist Dewey Redman, and then in a trio that had just bass and drums in support of his own instruments. He also recorded with John Coltrane's former rhythm section. But in the 1970s, just as his career seemed to be becoming static, he confounded his critics by forming the electric band Prime Time, which mixed rock and funk elements with his own improvisations and with ideas drawn from Moroccan music.

By the 1990s, Coleman had successfully revived almost all aspects of his musical career. With composer Howard Shore he rekindled his interest in orchestral music in the soundtrack for the movie *Naked Lunch*. Until Don Cherry's death in 1995, his original quartet occasionally reassembled. Prime Time continued to tour, and his other chamber and symphonic works were performed. Coleman also formed a new acoustic quartet with pianist Geri Allen, bassist Chamett Moffet, and his son Denardo on drums. As a duo, he and German pianist Joachim Kuhn presented a series of acclaimed concerts. This latter context put Coleman in a particularly exposed position. There was no strutting electric rhythm section, no fallback on his earlier quartet routines; he had to rely on lightning responses and keen interaction with one of Europe's consummate improvisers. Coleman triumphed both with an inspired sequence of new compositions and by showing that in his late 60s he remained one of the most resourceful and original soloists in jazz.

DISCOGRAPHY

Something Else! OJCCD 163. [Early examples of Coleman on the West Coast, 1958.]

Tomorrow Is the Question. OJCCD 342. [Coleman's first important disc.]

The Shape of Jazz to Come. Atlantic 781339.

Change of the Century. Atlantic 781341.

Free Jazz. Atlantic 781347. [1960 double quartet with obvious affinities to Coltrane's *Ascension* project; personnel include Freddie Hubbard, Don Cherry, and Eric Dolphy.]

Ornette on Tenor. Atlantic 781394.

Art of the Improvisers. Atlantic 781572

At the Golden Circle, Stockholm, Vols. 1 and 2. Blue Note 84224 and 84225.

New York Is Now. Blue Note 84287.

Skies of America. Columbia KC 31562. [Large-scale orchestral project from 1972.]

Body Meta. Verve/Harmolodic 531 916. [Rock-influenced music from 1975, the year Coleman founded his band Prime Time.]

Soapsuds, Soapsuds. Verve/Harmolodic 531 917. [1977 duo with bassist Charlie Haden.]

In All Languages. Verve/Harmolodic 531915. [1987 reunion of Coleman's 1960 quartet, plus Prime Time.]

Virgin Beauty. Columbia RK 44301. [Celebrated album with guitarist Jerry Garcia of the Grateful Dead.]

Tone Dialing. Verve/Harmolodic 527483. [1995 Prime Time lineup.]

Sound Museum, Three Women. Verve/Harmolodic 531 657. [Intriguing mid-1990s group with pianist Geri Allen.]

Colors. Verve/Harmolodic 537 789. [Duo with German pianist Joachim Kuhn.]

FURTHER READING

Balliett, Whitney. "Ornette" in *Jelly Roll, Jabbo, and Fats.* New York: Oxford University Press, 1983.

Litweiler, John. *Ornette Coleman: The Harmolodic Life.* London: Quartet, 1992.

Shipton, Alyn. "Ornette Coleman" in Dave Gelly, *Masters of the Jazz Saxophone: The Story of the Players and Their Music.* London: Balaphon, 2000.

Spellman, A. B. *Four Lives in the Bebop Business.* New York: Limelight, 1985.

Taylor, Art. "Ornette Coleman" in *Notes and Tones: Musician to Musician Interviews.* 1982. Reprint, New York: Da Capo, 1993.

Williams, Martin. "Ornette Coleman" in *Jazz Changes.* New York: Oxford University Press, 1992.

Wilson, Peter Niklas. *Ornette Coleman: His Life and Music.* Berkeley, Calif.: Berkeley Hills, 1999.

WEBSITE

http://www.harmolodic.com

Coleman's official website with his history and current plans.

Bill Evans

CONVERSATIONS WITH MYSELF

There is a perception of Bill Evans as an introspective, lyrical pianist who specialized in slow ballads that he explored with a deep sense of emotion and feeling. Such a perception was heightened by his appearance, which for much of his career was gaunt, bespectacled, and slightly academic, with swept-back hair and a stooped posture in which he crouched over the piano, his head hanging low above the keys.

This is only part of the story. He was capable of dazzling speed and extraordinary dexterity, and he always acknowledged the fleet-fingered Bud Powell as a major influence, but what he brought to jazz was a complete harnessing of his formidable technique to serve the expression of his emotional ideas. In this he was the most influential jazz pianist of the 1960s, every bit as important as his one-time associates Miles Davis and John Coltrane were on their instruments. He chose unusual voicings for his chords, varied his touch minutely to create rippling effects of light and shade, and had an extraordinarily well-developed sense of form that allowed him to create extended solos using long, flowing melodic lines. He also took a novel approach to the art of playing in a piano, bass, and drums trio, creating a delicate balance between the instruments in which each played a full and equal part, often experimenting with the flow of time just as much as with the melodic and harmonic elements of their playing. All these elements in Evans' music combined into a talent for conveying feeling and meaning through his work and establishing a uniquely personal level of contact with his listeners.

Evans was a gifted pianist from childhood, although he hated formal practice, preferring to spend hours each day sight reading endless albums of piano music and mastering tricky fingerings and chord positions in context, rather than through scales or exercises. In high school he also studied violin and flute, playing the latter instrument during his brief army service in the early 1950s. But before entering the military, he had moved away from home to study at Southeastern Louisiana University on a music scholarship. Those who heard him there say that his impressive technique and individual piano style were already well on the way to being formed. By the time he served in the army, he had already met and worked with various other musicians in New Jersey, including bassist Red Mitchell and guitarist Mundell Lowe, and when he began playing with clarinetist Tony Scott in the late 1950s he was already identifiable as a new keyboard talent.

William John "Bill" Evans

Bill Evans's playing posture, bent low over the keyboard, reinforced his image of introspection and sensitivity.

BORN
August 16, 1929
Plainfield, New Jersey

DIED
September 15, 1980
New York, New York

EDUCATION
Southeastern Louisiana University; majored in music and music education

MAJOR INTEREST
Piano, leading own trio

ACCOMPLISHMENTS
Studied with and recorded for George Russell; went on to work with Charlie Mingus and Miles Davis, with whom he recorded *Kind of Blue*. His 1960 trio marked a high point in the art of trio playing, as did several subsequent lineups following the death of bassist Scott La Faro in 1961. Compositions include "Comrade Conrad," "One for Helen," "Peace Piece," "Peri's Scope," "Re: Person I Knew," "Show-type Tune," "Two Lonely People," "Very Early," "Waltz for Debby"

HONORS
Several Grammy awards, including for *Conversations with Myself* (1963), *Live at Montreux* (1968), *Alone* (1970), *Bill Evans Album* (1971); regular winner of *Down Beat* and *Playboy* polls

Not long after arriving in New York City in 1955, Evans met and learned from the composer and theorist George Russell, whose exploration of modes influenced him. Indeed, Evans played on recordings of some of Russell's key compositions with his jazz workshop in 1956–59. This gave him the reputation of being a swift learner and adaptable ensemble pianist and he played for other bands, including Charles Mingus and the Art Farmer–Benny Golson Jazztet. In 1959, as a member of the Miles Davis band, which at the time also contained John Coltrane, Evans appeared on all tracks but one of the *Kind of Blue* album, in which Davis introduced modal jazz to a mass audience. Evans had officially left Davis when the album was recorded, exhausted by eight months on the road with the sextet, but he returned to make this disc, which consolidated many of the ideas about new approaches to harmony that had evolved during his time with Davis.

There is little doubt that the unique tonality of Evans's piano chording, which introduced many listeners to the idea of open-ended shifts from one scalar pattern to another and back again, did much to establish the way in which modes would be used within a jazz rhythm section. However, by this time Evans had already recorded his own trio album *Everybody Digs Bill Evans*, which showed he also had new things to say both at rapid bebop tempos and in slow, haunting ballads. After he left Davis in 1959, he went on to form in the following year what became, for many listeners, his greatest trio, with bassist Scott La Faro and drummer Paul Motian—both of whom had been members of Tony Scott's groups, alongside Evans.

Bill Evans at a studio session in the 1960s. The bassist is Eddie Gomez, one of the line of distinguished players who followed Scott La Faro as a member of Evans's trio.

La Faro's speed and accuracy in the upper register, and the uncanny way his melody lines intertwined with Evans' own made him an ideal partner for the pianist. Motian's ability to sense minute variations in tempo—from hesitations and spaces to slight accelerations or skips and jumps— without losing an overall sense of swing and momentum, completed the exceptional lineup. At the moment they achieved their highest level of cooperation, La Faro was tragically killed in an accident, a few days after recording two outstanding albums of material at the Village Vanguard in New York City. Evans was devastated, and did not play for some months. "When you have

evolved a concept of playing which depends on the specific personalities of outstanding players, how do you start again when they are gone?" he asked in one interview. He was already addicted to heroin, and the emotional shock of his bassist's death did little to help him overcome his use of the drug—something he did not manage to do for some years. Even then his life was a constant battle against returning to his addiction, and he suffered other emotional upheavals, including the suicide of his first wife, who had also fought drug addiction.

Evans's first albums did not sell well, but by the time his trio with La Faro and Motian reached its zenith, he

> *"For me, technique is the ability to translate your ideas into sound through your instrument."*
>
> —Bill Evans in a 1976 interview with Len Lyons

was beginning to find a bigger public. After his return to playing, he swiftly became recognized as a major talent, in due course moving from the independent Riverside label to major companies like Verve, Columbia, and eventually the West Coast Fantasy label. The intellectual and thoughtful content of his music reflected a man who carried his ideas over into titles. Many of his best-known themes are titled with clever anagrams or plays on words; for example, "Re: Person I Knew" is a re-arrangement of the name of his long-term producer Orrin Keepnews.

In his trio work Evans formed partnerships with three more bassists, first Chuck Israels, then (briefly) Gary Peacock, and later Eddie Gomez, all of whom developed aspects of La Faro's technique, focusing on mobility and high-register playing. Drummers changed more often, but he had a long-term trio in which Marty Morell played drums alongside Gomez. Eventually, he settled on a final lineup with bassist Marc Johnson and drummer Joe LaBarbera. In each trio, Evans' own playing continued to develop, burnishing his sensitivity of touch, and moving toward ever greater freedom of time and phrasing. His final trio even moved beyond the achievements of his early group with La Faro and Motian in terms of group interplay, and at the time of his death from drug-related problems,

Evans was still exploring fresh ground as a pianist.

As an unaccompanied soloist, he was even more exploratory than with his trios, creating dense personal interpretations of his own compositions like "Peace Piece" and "Epilogue." Then for producer Creed Taylor at Verve, he created the album *Conversations with Myself*, on which he overdubbed additional piano parts. In his portrait of Evans, Gene Lees tells how even when suffering from the sweats and shakes of heroin withdrawal, Evans managed the dazzling intellectual and physical challenge of creating the multiple piano parts for the love theme from the 1960 film *Spartacus* that appears on this album. He subsequently made a follow-up album of similar overdubs, but despite critical acclaim he felt these did not reach to his own high standards.

In his final years, Evans's appearance altered. He grew his hair and beard, and during the parts of the late 1960s and 1970s when he managed to conquer his addiction, he looked fitter and healthier than at any previous time in his career. His powers of invention continued to the very end of his life, many critics marveling at the degree to which there was constant movement and development in his work, but ultimately the demons inside led him back to addiction and a shockingly early death.

DISCOGRAPHY

Sunday at the Village Vanguard. OJC 140. [First of two final 1961 albums by the trio with La Faro and Motian.]

Waltz for Debby. OJC 210 [Second album from the Village Vanguard, 1961.]

How My Heart Sings! OJC 369.

Undercurrent. Blue Note 790538-2. [1962 duos with Jim Hall.]

Conversations with Myself. Verve 521409-2. [Groundbreaking solo album with overdubbed second and third piano parts]

Best of Bill Evans on Verve. Verve 527906-2. [Cross section of Evans' work, 1963–69.]

Complete Fantasy Recordings. Fantasy 1012. (nine-CD set). [1973–79 work.]

Turn Out the Stars. Warner Bros. 45925-2 (six-CD set). [Evans' final great trio, with bassist Marc Johnson and drummer Joe LaBarbera.]

FURTHER READING

Lees, Gene. "Bill Evans: The Poet" in *Meet Me at Jim and Andy's: Jazz Musicians and Their World.* New York: Oxford University Press, 1988.

Lyons, Len. "Bill Evans" in *The Great Jazz Pianists: Speaking of Their Lives and Work.* New York: William Morrow, 1983.

McPartland, Marian. "Bill Evans, Genius" in *All in Good Time.* New York: Oxford University Press, 1987.

Pettinger, Peter. *Bill Evans: How My Heart Sings.* New Haven: Yale University Press, 1998.

WEBSITE

http://www.njmetronet.com/billevans/index1.html

Biography, albums listed, reviews, other articles, awards, and links

Herbie Hancock

THE CHAMELEON

N ot even Miles Davis spanned so many different styles of music with the effortless authority that Herbie Hancock has managed throughout his career. Starting as a child prodigy who played the classics, Hancock played hard bop with trumpeter Donald Byrd, avant garde with saxophonist Eric Dolphy, free jazz and jazz-rock with Miles Davis, and then mastered the art of jazz funk with his own Head Hunters band. Coinciding with his return to playing straight-ahead jazz in duo with Chick Corea, or with his acoustic quintet VSOP (for "very special one-time-only performance"), he entered the Top Ten chart listings with "Rockit," a funk-disco crossover. He won an Oscar for his score for the 1986 movie *Round Midnight,* and he went into the 1990s with a delicate balancing act between all the different strands in his music, typified by his New Standard band, which gave jazz treatments to rock tunes he felt had become the new "standards" of the era, by such composers as Prince and Kurt Cobain.

Herbie Hancock demonstrates his command of keyboards and electronics with his Head Hunters band in the 1970s.

> *"We still keep calling those old songs the standards . . .*
> *so we're going to go another 40 years and still call the same*
> *things standards? Or are we going to start looking around*
> *for some new ones?"*

—Herbie Hancock in an interview with Mark Gilbert,
Jazz Journal International (August 1996)

More than any other keyboard player in jazz, Hancock is the link between the 1960s era of acoustic jazz dominated by Miles Davis and the eclectic state of the music at the dawn of the 21st century. In every aspect of his work he has astutely balanced his own keyboard artistry with compositional flair. Even when he has relied on other arrangers such as Bob Belden, who wrote parts of the New Standard album, or bassist Bill Laswell to create a context for his playing, his powerful musical personality swiftly endows everything he touches with a recognizable individuality.

Yet when he first emerged on the jazz scene, Hancock was clearly deeply influenced by Bill Evans. Many of his early records show traces of Evans' long clear lines and unusual chord voicings, but there are also examples of the innovations pioneered by other pianists: Horace Silver's gospel-tinged rhythms and comping, Wynton Kelly's lyricism, and the melodic invention of McCoy Tyner. Hancock's ability to combine all these elements into his own identifiable style was exceptional, and owed something to his early Chicago influences. As a teenager he listened with equal interest to doo-wop and soul influenced groups like the Hi-Los, to the orchestral writing of Robert Farnon, and to a local pianist with unconventional harmonic ideas named Chris Anderson, who only began to record on an international level in the 1990s. Hancock absorbed aspects of all these sounds into his musical subconscious and called on them at later stages in his career.

He was only 11 when he made his first appearance, playing part of a Mozart concerto with the Chicago Symphony Orchestra, having started on piano four years earlier. His first teacher, Mrs. Whalen, was based at the local Baptist church, but his playing improved when, at age 10, he moved to a new teacher, Mrs. Jordan, who helped him develop his touch. Later, Hancock taught himself jazz by transcribing recorded solos by Oscar Peterson, as well as music by local bands such as the Hi-Los.

A decade after his performance with the Chicago Symphony Orchestra, Hancock made another precocious debut at age 21 when he joined Donald Byrd's band. Byrd hired Hancock after he substituted for Byrd's regular pianist Duke Pearson, who failed to arrive one night during a blizzard. At that stage, Byrd was the preeminent hard bop trumpeter, having continued the type of playing pioneered by Clifford Brown. His band exposed Hancock to the full glare of the media spotlight, starting with a disc backing up the band's saxophone player Pepper Adams for the Warwick label. This was followed by Byrd's own recordings for Blue Note, which was not only a major-league jazz label but which paired Hancock for the first time with saxophonist Wayne Shorter.

Herbie Hancock onstage during his international tour with his New Standard band. The band created jazz interpretations of contemporary music by Prince, Sade, and Kurt Cobain, as well as earlier rock hits by Simon and Garfunkel and the Beatles.

This recording led to Hancock's first album for the label in 1962, *Takin' Off*, with Freddie Hubbard on trumpet and Dexter Gordon on tenor. Critics everywhere recognized this as a remarkably assured performance for so young a musician. The album secured its place in history because it contained Hancock's first hit, "Watermelon Man," a tune made famous by Mongo Santamaria. Based around the sounds of a watermelon seller in the backstreets of Chicago and the rhythms of his horse and cart, it has been recorded hundreds of times since.

In 1963 Hancock joined Miles Davis, becoming part of the trumpeter's innovative quintet with Shorter (preceded for a while by tenorist George Coleman), bassist Ron Carter, and drummer Tony Williams. In the six years he stayed with this group, Hancock was an integral part of Davis's explorations of freer rhythms, his fragmentation of standard tunes like "My Funny Valentine" and "Stella by Starlight," and new music written by members of the quintet, like Shorter's "Nefertiti" and "ESP," Davis's own "Circle" and "Country Son," and Hancock's "Madness." By the end of

the decade, Hancock was playing electric piano or keyboards with Davis and had made a similar move in his own series of influential discs for Blue Note.

From the very start of his work for Blue Note's producers Alfred Lion and Frank Wolff, Hancock concentrated on his own compositions. He firmly established several of these as core parts of the 1960s jazz repertoire, including "Canteloupe Island," "Maiden Voyage," and "Dolphin Dance." He also cut a full jazz version of his theme music for Michelangelo Antonioni's 1966 movie *Blowup*. This film score was just one of many varied musical projects with which he became involved; his ready ability to find a melody and set it quickly and efficiently to a contemporary accompaniment put him in great demand as a composer.

Some of his most enduring jazz came from re-recording themes he had put together for advertising jingles. For example, the tune "He Who Lives in Fear" was originally written for a cigarette commercial. In the midst of this, he experimented with rhythm and blues, and made a gradual but sure transition to producing rock-influenced themes of his own. By the time he left

Blue Note to sign with Warner Brothers, Hancock had also appeared as a freelancer on recordings by a Who's Who of the 1960s jazz scene, from saxophonists Sonny Rollins, Stan Getz, Phil Woods, and Joe Henderson, to bassist Ron Carter, not to mention crossover artists like guitarist George Benson, or avant garde saxophonist Eric Dolphy.

In much of Hancock's late 1960s work there was a strong political focus; pieces like "I Have a Dream" and "The Prisoner" have clear references to the civil rights movement. As the 1970s dawned, Hancock turned his attention to Africa, as did many politically minded African Americans. He briefly adopted the Swahili name Mwandishi (composer), which became the title of one of his most African-influenced discs and the term by which his band was known at the time. In three short years on the Warner label, Hancock migrated from being a jazz musician to a position as a key figure in funk and soul, culminating in his 1973 move to Columbia Records and his powerful and influential Head Hunters band.

Utilizing his early experience of electronics—Hancock had studied electrical engineering at Grinnell College in Iowa—he became adept at playing a whole range of electronic keyboard instruments. He explained his move to critic Leonard Feather by suggesting that he did not feel he was a genius like Miles Davis or John Coltrane, that he would forget about becoming a legend and instead "create some music to make people happy." But, through his sheer mastery of a wide range of music, Hancock showed that he was as much a genius as Davis or Coltrane, and his pervasive influence continues to be felt in many areas of jazz and beyond at the start of the 21st century.

To some of those who found much to admire in Hancock's brilliant jazz piano playing in the 1960s, there was little to get excited about in the long-drawn-out funk performances of the Head Hunters. Even when the band revisited his earlier pieces like "Watermelon Man," the solid bass line and occasional solo emerging from the funk backdrop seemed a long way from the effortless movement, light, and shade of his acoustic jazz works. The public thought otherwise, and Hancock entered a period of great commercial success.

His more jazz-oriented listeners were delighted when Hancock suddenly changed direction in the 1980s. In addition to his jazz-rock activities, he appeared playing piano duos with Chick Corea and then fronted his own acoustic jazz band VSOP, which reunited the 1960s Davis rhythm section of himself, Ron Carter, and Tony Williams backing Freddie Hubbard. Set up to play a few times and then disband, the group became too popular for that to happen, and they continued to play sporadically into the 1990s first with Hubbard and subsequently Wynton Marsalis or Wallace Roney, with Wayne Shorter joining the lineup from time to time.

This aspect of Hancock's work received one of its highest awards in 1986 when his soundtrack for the French director Bertrand Tavernier's film *Round Midnight* won an Oscar. In addition to his VSOP associates, Hancock's fellow musicians on the soundtrack included the film's star, Dexter Gordon, vibes player Bobby Hutcherson, guitarist John McLaughlin, and veteran French bassist Pierre Michelot. Hancock, like virtually all these musicians, was encouraged to take a speaking role in the film, in which Tavernier broke down the barriers between musicians and actors more successfully than in any other jazz movie.

Herbert "Herbie" Hancock

BORN
April 12, 1940
Chicago, Illinois

EDUCATION
Hyde Park High School, Chicago; Grinnell College, Iowa; studied electrical engineering before focusing on music; postgraduate study at Manhattan School of Music

MAJOR INTEREST
Keyboards, bandleading, writing, arranging

ACCOMPLISHMENTS
With Miles Davis' band, 1963–69; made own discs for Blue Note, pioneered jazz rock fusion with Head Hunters band in 1970s; returned to acoustic jazz with Chick Corea, late 1970s, and in own VSOP band into 1990s. International tours with Wayne Shorter and New Standard band, from 1990s. Movie scores include *Blowup, Death Wish, Round Midnight*. Compositions include "Canteloupe Island," "Chameleon," "Dolphin Dance," "Madness," "Maiden Voyage," "The Sorceror," "Speak Like a Child," "Riot," "Watermelon Man"

HONORS
Frequent *Down Beat* poll winner; *Cash Box* R&B awards; Best Original Score Oscar for *Round Midnight* (1986); Grammies include *Gershwin's World* (1999)

Although Hancock continued to write and perform funk and soul, achieving chart success, *Round Midnight* was a cathartic moment in his career and that of Wayne Shorter, who had been similarly immersed in jazz-rock through playing in the band Weather Report. Both men told the author that the experience of working on the film, with its veneration of the art of jazz, changed their lives. In its aftermath they once again became close associates in the 1990s, often touring together to play acoustic jazz, and cutting an informal duo album, *1+1*. In the same year as that duet, 1996, Hancock recorded his *New Standard* album followed by an international tour with its participants, Michael Brecker, John Scofield, bassist Dave Holland, drummer Jack De Johnette, and percussionist Don Alias. This group bridged the generations between Miles Davis's 1960s alumni—Hancock, Holland, and De Johnette—and younger musicians who had taken jazz into new areas in the 1980s and 1990s.

Hancock rounded off his 20th-century output with a centenary tribute to George Gershwin involving a similarly mixed cast list of experienced voices and newer ideas. Taking his inspiration from a figure as old as jazz itself, he returned to standard songs a generation or two older than the rock music he created with New Standard. At the start of the 21st century, with his earlier albums such as *Sextant* being raided by dub and turntable artists, Hancock has enjoyed a new level of popularity. His *Future 2 Future* project, begun in 2001, incorporates dub and sampling techniques into his musical language, in a collaboration with bassist and producer Bill Laswell, who had previously worked with Hancock in his chart-topping "Rockit."

DISCOGRAPHY

Donald Byrd, Free Form. Blue Note B21Y 84118. [Examples of Hancock's work in 1961 with the band that launched his career.]

Takin' Off. Blue Note 746506. [Hancock's 1962 debut album under his own name.]

Maiden Voyage. Blue Note 746339. [Recorded in 1964 with most of Miles Davis's band; Hancock's masterpiece from his Blue Note period.]

Empyrean Isles. Blue Note 784175. [Sister album to the above.]

Miles Davis, Highlights from the Plugged Nickel. Columbia 481434. [Best moments from Hancock's most celebrated live session with Davis, 1965.]

The Complete Sixties Blue Note Sessions. Blue Note 95569 (six-CD set). [Charts Hancock's progress from hard bop with Byrd to funk.]

Mwandishi: The Complete Warner Bros. Recordings. Warner 245732 (two-CD set). [Hancock's final transitional phase from jazz to funk, 1969–72.]

Head Hunters. Columbia 471239. [Hancock's funk masterpiece.]

An Evening with Herbie Hancock and Chick Corea. Columbia 477296. [1978 set of piano duos.]

Quartet. Columbia 465626. [1982 touring band with Wynton Marsalis on trumpet.]

Future Shock. Columbia 471237. [1983 album, with chart-topping "Rockit."]

Dexter Gordon, The Other Side of Round Midnight. Blue Note 46397. [Outtakes from the film music impeccably performed by the bands assembled to play Hancock's score.]

A Tribute to Miles. Qwest/Reprise 45059. [VSOP in 1992, with Wallace Roney recreating some of Davis's best-known mid-1960s repertoire.]

The New Standard. Verve 527715. [1996 all-star album with Michael Brecker and John Scofield, giving jazz treatment to songs by Kurt Cobain, Peter Gabriel, Prince, and Sade.]

Gershwin's World. Verve 314 557 797. [1998 treatment of predominantly Gershwin material in the composer's centenary year.]

Future 2 Future. Transparent CD 001. [Hancock's 2001 reunion with "Rockit" producer Bill Laswell, which uses sampling and digital editing techniques to move Hancock's music into the 21st century.]

FURTHER READING

Belden, Bob. "The Life and Times: Reflections on a Jazz Legend" liner note booklet to *Herbie Hancock: The Complete Sixties Blue Note Sessions*, Blue Note 95569.

Gridley, Mark C. "Bill Evans, Herbie Hancock, Chick Corea and Keith Jarrett" in *Jazz Styles, History and Analysis*. Englewood Cliffs, N.J.: Prentice-Hall, 1985.

Lyons, Len. "Herbie Hancock" in *The Great Jazz Pianists: Speaking of Their Lives and Work*. New York: Morrow, 1983.

Walser, Robert, ed. "Soul, Craft and Cultural Hierarchy" in *Keeping Time: Readings in Jazz History*. New York: Oxford University Press, 1999.

WEBSITE

http://www.herbie-hancock.com
Biography, discography, photos, forum, and links.

Chick Corea

ECLECTIC, ELECTRIC, AND ACOUSTIC

Armando "Chick" Corea, like Herbie Hancock, started out as a precocious classical talent and swiftly discovered an aptitude and liking for jazz. In 1968–70 Corea succeeded Hancock in the Miles Davis band, although because Hancock sporadically returned to the lineup, the two men appeared together on a number of Davis's discs including *Live–Evil* (see the profile of Davis in Part 4). In 1978 he and Hancock recorded and toured as a piano duo, by which time both of them had made different but significant marks on the fields of both free jazz and jazz-rock. What distinguishes Corea is his continuing sympathy for classical music—he has written and recorded a piano concerto—and his fascination with Latin rhythms and meter.

Corea's childhood was full of music. His father, a trumpeter and bandleader in New England, taught the young Armando music, encouraging him to play piano, and he was

Chick Corea, with microphone, and arranger Quincy Jones take the stage at a New York City concert hosted by *Down Beat* magazine.

Chick Corea plays piano in London in the fall of 1999, when he was beginning one of the most versatile times of his eclectic career. Since 1999, he has played club dates with his band Origin, performed classical compositions by Mozart and himself at major concert halls, and recorded two solo albums.

soon copying what he heard on records while simultaneously developing a very accomplished keyboard technique and a highly sensitive ear. Corea also learned to play drums, which underpinned the strong rhythmic element in all his work as a pianist and bandleader. One early keyboard influence was Horace Silver, whose discs Corea learned by heart, and another was Bud Powell, to whom Corea recorded an affectionate and knowledgeable tribute in the 1990s. He also absorbed the work of several other significant pianists, including Art Tatum, Thelonious Monk, and Bill Evans, drawing

together elements of their work. From Silver he absorbed the rhythmic patterns that combined gospel and bebop; from Powell and Tatum he learned how to manipulate his fingers through rapid runs across the whole range of the keyboard; and from Evans, as well as from John Coltrane's pianist McCoy Tyner, he adopted chords built on intervals of a fourth, rather than the thirds of conventional harmonies. Whereas simply mixing these ingredients would have produced a competent but derivative pianist, Corea added his own lyrical sense that found expression both in his formal compositions and in his ability to improvise freely and coherently at the keyboard.

Despite this focus on the work of the pianists who had created modern jazz, Corea's own first professional jobs were with Latin-oriented musicians such as Mongo Santamaria and Willie Bobo, with whom he worked in his very early 20s. This may explain Corea's fondness for Latin rhythms and harmonies, and why he subsequently included players like Airto Moreira and singer Flora Purim, both from Brazil, in his bands of the 1970s and 1980s. It is certainly the case that Corea developed an innate sense of Latin rhythm, in which basic pulses of three and two coexist simultaneously in his playing. This applies to his writing as well; his composition *Litha* alternates between a meter of six beats to the measure and one with four.

Soon after his early period in various Latin groups, Corea joined the band led by trumpeter Blue Mitchell in 1964 Mitchell gave Corea public exposure and recording experience with the Blue Note label. During this period in the early 1960s, a number of Corea's own compositions were first recorded with Mitchell's band for the company.

As a freelancer, Corea also recorded as a pianist with the flute player Herbie Mann. He then joined Stan Getz, in whose band he played alongside his own long-term associate, drummer Roy Haynes. At this point the influences of other pianists on his playing were still obvious, but he was beginning to develop his own voice, which he demonstrated in his first trio albums cut in 1966 and 1968.

During the period of just over two years Corea spent with Miles Davis in 1968–70, his interests changed. Although Corea began with Davis's standard quintet, with Wayne Shorter, Ron Carter, and Tony Williams, he joined just as Davis was going through a period in which he was simultaneously exploring rock backgrounds and free-form abstraction, and both areas had a profound effect on Corea's subsequent music. "They had the tunes so facile and abstracted that even a musician's ear couldn't tell what chord changes were going by," Corea recalled. Corea reacted to Davis's experimental music and enlarged band by adopting electronic keyboards and electric piano. Corea and the English bassist Dave Holland quit Davis's group, and together created a free-form trio with drummer Barry Altschul, later joined by saxophonist Anthony Braxton.

Called Circle, this band created some stormy and exhilarating free improvisations, which contrasted with Corea's more contemplative approach to his unaccompanied playing, documented on a series of solo albums. Circle was, recalled Corea, "based on the game of pure improvisation, meaning that we would improvise on the structure of what we played as well as the content." Despite the deep thinking that went into what the band was doing, and the close relationship

between the players, it reached a level of abstraction that many listeners found hard to follow.

In 1971, ever sensitive to his audience but particularly because he found it hard to explain his music to his own family, Corea changed direction, telling interviewers that he felt the subtlety and complexity of the free music he was playing was beyond the comprehension of many audiences. The group he formed next was considerably more accessible. Called Return to Forever, the band played his own lyrical and highly structured compositions, many of them consisting of several interrelating parts, with forceful Latin rhythms from Airto Moreira on percussion, a pulsing bass line from Stanley Clarke, and the charismatic singing of Flora Purim. Modest beginnings in and around New York led to international tours, and in due course, concerts to audiences of thousands. Throughout the 1970s, Corea led various versions of the band, each lineup altering the group's character, from the hard-driving, heavily rock-influenced sound of the mid-1970s to the acoustic character of the final version, which incorporated strings and brass. It was also during this period that he first became involved in the study of Scientology, which influenced his views about mental and physical well-being and encouraged his desire to communicate easily to his audience.

Although Return to Forever regrouped for a tour in 1983, by this time Corea's musical ideas had moved on. He formed a number of duos in which he mixed the playing of standards and new compositions with the opportunity to improvise on a one-to-one basis with other gifted jazz musicians. His duo with Herbie Hancock was often scintillating, both

Armando Anthony "Chick" Corea

BORN
June 12, 1941
Chelsea, Massachusetts

EDUCATION
Studied piano as a teenager with Salvatore Suolo in Boston; briefly attended Columbia University, New York, and Juilliard School of Music

MAJOR INTERESTS
Piano, bandleading, composing

ACCOMPLISHMENTS
Pioneered free jazz in Circle and fusion in Return to Forever, 1972–80. Led several bands, and played in duos with Herbie Hancock and Gary Burton. Compositions include "Crystal Silence," "La Fiesta," "Litha," "Piano Concerto No. 1," "Return to Forever," "Spain," "Spanish Song," "Tones for Joan's Bones," "What Games Shall We Play Today?" and "Windows"

HONORS
Winner of many *Down Beat* and other polls, including first award for electric piano, 1975; Jazz Instrumental Grammy for his duo "Rhumbata" with Gary Burton on *Native Sense*, 1999

players challenging one another to more audacious keyboard efforts. His more reflective duo with vibraphonist Gary Burton was longer lasting, with occasional tours continuing through the late 1990s, following their exemplary recording of Corea's *Crystal Silence* in 1979, and with the two men usually fitting in a reunion once a year.

In the 1980s, Corea's work mixed playing with various all-star jazz lineups and duos with writing and performing compositions in a classical context, from his 1982 *Lyric Suite for Sextet* to his piano concerto. He also formed his own record label, Stretch, to issue his archive recordings and to present his own new work and that of his colleagues and contemporaries. Typical examples include a Montreux concert with veteran Blue Note tenor saxophonist Joe Henderson and a 1981 studio set with tenor saxophonist Michael Brecker in his relatively early years.

All the while, Corea continued to perform and record as an unaccompanied soloist as well as with a trio of bassist John Patitucci and drummer Dave Weckl, most often known as the Akoustic Band, but which, when Corea adopted electronic keyboards and added more intruments, became his Elektric Band.

Never one to stand still, in 1998 Corea joined forces with the New York band led by Israeli-born bassist Avishai Cohen to create a new group called Origin. With a front line of two saxophones and trombone, and a rhythm section in which Corea plays marimba as well as piano, the band is redolent of the acoustic sound of the 1960s Blue Note era. However, Cohen's unorthodox bass playing and Jeff Ballard's rock-inflected drumming introduce a contemporary flavor to the band, and to the rhythm section, which tours independently as Corea's "new" trio. At the close of the 20th century, Corea was combining work with this band with a renewed interest in his classical pieces, culminating in a recording and worldwide concerts of his piano concerto that cemented his position as a major keyboard soloist, but above all as a creative and consistently exploratory composer.

DISCOGRAPHY

Now He Sings, Now He Sobs. Blue Note 90055. [1968 trio.]

Song of Singing. Blue Note CDP 746401-2. [1970 trio with Holland and Altschul.]

A.R.C. ECM 1009. [Slightly later trio with Holland and Altschul.]

Return to Forever. ECM 1022. [The 1972 album that first carried this title with Flora Purim and Airto Moreira along with flutist/saxophonist Joe Farrell and bassist Stanley Clarke.]

Return to Forever, Return to the Seventh Galaxy. Verve 533108 (two-CD set). [The best 1972–75 material by Corea's bands carrying the name forward from 1972.]

Crystal Silence. ECM 1024. [Duets with Corea and Gary Burton, 1979.]

Akoustic Band. GRP 95822. [Trio with bassist John Patitucci and drummer Dave Weckl.]

Expressions. GRP 900732. [1993 piano solos.]

Remembering Bud Powell. Stretch SCD 9012. [1996 all-star band.]

Music Forever and Beyond: Selected Works of Chick Corea 1964–1996. GRP GRD 5 9819 (five-CD set). [Includes fragments of Corea's earliest recordings from childhood and a broad cross section of his 1990s recordings.]

Corea Concerto. Sony Classical SK 61799. [1999 recording with London Philharmonic of Corea's "Piano Concerto No 1," and "Spain," arranged for sextet and orchestra.]

FURTHER READING

Gridley, Mark C. "Bill Evans, Herbie Hancock, Chick Corea, and Keith Jarrett," in *Jazz Styles, History and Analysis.* Englewood Cliffs, N.J.: Prentice-Hall, 1985.

Lyons, Len. "Chick Corea," in *The Great Jazz Pianists: Speaking of Their Lives and Work.* New York: Morrow, 1983.

Owens, Thomas. "Forms" in *The New Grove Dictionary of Jazz*, Barry Kernfield, ed. London and New York: Macmillan, 1988.

WEBSITE

http://www.chickcorea.com

Includes scrapbook, awards, discography, and personal writings.

John McLaughlin

MAHAVISHNU

I n the first half of the 20th century, despite the worldwide acceptance of and enthusiasm for jazz, there was a widespread view that apart from odd exceptions like the French gypsy guitarist Django Reinhardt, the music was an entirely American art form that only a very few Europeans managed to master. In the years following World War II this became an increasingly inaccurate view. Many Americans settled in Europe, notably African Americans seeking the liberal political climate of France or Scandinavia. At the same time, many Europeans began working on equal terms with their transatlantic counterparts on both sides of the ocean. In the 1950s the French saxophonist Barney Wilen and his Belgian contemporary Bobby Jaspar made discs with American jazz musicians, while Englishmen like multi-instrumentalists Vic Lewis and Victor Feldman worked with groups in the

The young John McLaughlin with one of the unusual guitars in which he has specialized. Other unusual instruments he has used include guitars with two necks, one with twelve and one with six strings.

John McLaughlin enjoys a moment on stage in 1995. "I love India, its music and its spirituality," he says. "The spirituality is in the music—you can't separate the two like you can in Western music."

Hendrix, fused distortion and high-wattage amplification with the gritty sound of urban blues. The self-taught McLaughlin adopted many of the same ideas, but also played various styles of jazz. He added a dazzling technique and harmonic knowledge to the mix, which allowed him to play high-energy solos at blistering speed while incorporating all the technical innovations used by 1960s rock musicians.

Although, McLaughlin had few formal lessons, he came from a musical family. His mother played violin, and his brothers and sisters also played instruments. McLaughlin himself had piano lessons, but learned guitar by playing along with blues records. This gave him the basis of his style by the time he moved from his native Yorkshire to London. McLaughlin made his first mark on the late 1960s British free jazz scene with saxophonist John Surman and drummer Tony Oxley. He arrived in this style of music after playing traditional jazz in the late 1950s and then working with a series of bands that combined bebop with elements of blues and rock. Those bands notably included Georgie Fame's Blue Flames, a chart-topping group that epitomized the "mod" movement in British pop culture; Alexis Korner's Blues Incorporated; the Graham Bond Organization; and Trinity, led by organist Brian Auger.

With Surman, Oxley, and bassist Brian Odges, McLaughlin recorded *Extrapolation*, an album of music that was markedly different from anything going on in the United States at the same time. It adopted unorthodox time signatures (such as 13/8) along with the kinds of recognizable folk melody that Surman knew from his upbringing in the west of England and from his choral training. These were mixed with a powerful blend of rock rhythms from

United States. In the following decade, prompted particularly by Miles Davis, many other European musicians found themselves on the world stage.

In Miles Davis's band, two British musicians stood out. One was the bassist Dave Holland, and the other guitarist John McLaughlin. Whereas Holland brilliantly absorbed the nuances of American jazz, McLaughlin brought into the music the raw uncompromising edge of 1960s British rock. In a decade when, from the Beatles to the Rolling Stones, English musicians were making significant appearances on the world rock scene, the innovations of guitarists like Jeff Beck and Eric Clapton, as well as British-based Jimi

Oxley, dissolving abstract phrases from Surman and McLaughlin, and the high-wattage energy of McLaughlin's recent blues band experience.

It was McLaughlin's success in this quartet that led Dave Holland to recommend him to his Miles Davis band colleague Tony Williams. A drum prodigy who had been playing professionally since his mid-teens, Williams was leaving Davis to form a group of his own called Lifetime. In 1969 he added McLaughlin to a lineup that included organist Larry Young and bassist Jack Bruce, a veteran of the British rock group Cream, but also an accomplished jazz musician. While he was in the United States with Williams, McLaughlin contributed his distinctive guitar sound to Miles Davis's albums *In a Silent Way* and *Bitches Brew* (see the Davis profile in Part 4).

Lifetime was a pioneering group in many ways. Musically, in its integration of intricate arrangements and long improvisations, it was ahead of its time. But it was held back by a combination of bad luck, poor management, and a record contract that was not as high-profile as that of Miles Davis. McLaughlin left the group in 1970. After working again with Miles Davis on the albums *Jack Johnson* and *Live–Evil*, he formed his own band, the Mahavishnu Orchestra, the following year. This band, in tune with the times, mixed heady rock-based playing with tenets of Eastern thinking and living.

McLaughlin had been interested in Indian philosophy and religion since the British bandleader Graham Bond kindled his desire to discover more about Eastern thought. Under the guidance of a guru, Sri Chinmoy, McLaughlin himself adopted the name Mahavishnu, which means "divine compassion, power, justice." Dressed in white, his hair cropped short, and

publicly disassociating himself from drugs and alcohol, McLaughlin advocated clean living and the power of meditation. During his time off the road he also devoted himself to studying Indian music; this had an increasingly noticeable effect on the sound of his groups in the 1970s.

The Mahavishnu Orchestra captured the mood of the "flower power" generation and became immensely popular on the world festival circuit. Bandleader Ian Carr described it as "the greatest jazz-rock band." At around this time McLaughlin also started playing an unorthodox guitar with two necks, one with 12 strings and one with 6, which allowed him to alternate immediately between different types of instrumental effects. Supported by drummer Billy Cobham's complex rhythms and the power of keyboard player Jan Hammer, the band also featured a violinist, Jerry Goodman. A slightly later lineup, from 1974—after the original group became a victim of its own success and broke up when underlying tensions between its members surfaced—featured French violinist Jean-Luc Ponty.

By this time, as an antidote to the huge power and volume of the Mahavishnu Orchestra, McLaughlin had formed an acoustic group that included Indian violinist L. Shankar and Zakir Hussein, who played the tabla, Indian hand drums. Called Shakti, this became an extremely popular crossover band, pioneering the fusion of jazz and Indian music, and building on earlier experiments in Europe by John Mayer's Indo-Jazz Fusion and Manfred Schoof with the Swiss pianist Irene Schweizer. Shakti Revisited, with almost the same lineup, was touring widely in 1999, proving the durability and popularity of the formula.

After recording the album *Electric Guitarist* in 1978, McLaughlin seemed

John McLaughlin

BORN
January 4, 1942
Kirk Sandall, Yorkshire, England

EDUCATION
Piano lessons from age 9, self-taught guitar from age 11; studied Ethnomusicology, specializing in Karnatic music and Vina, Wesleyan University, Middletown, Connecticut, 1970–71

MAIN INTERESTS
Guitar, bandleading

ACCOMPLISHMENTS
Worked with Tony Williams and Miles Davis; formed various incarnations of Mahavishnu Orchestra 1971–73, 1974–75, 1988–86; played in acoustic group Shakti, 1970s and 1990s; played in guitar trio in 1980s; formed trio with Kai Eckhardt and Trilok Gurtu, late 1980s, and organ trio with Joey DeFrancesco, early 1990s. Appeared in film *Round Midnight* (1986). Composed *Guitar Concerto*, 1985; wrote *Mediterranean Concerto* for guitar and orchestra, 1990, which premiered in Glasgow, Scotland, that year

to lose some of the clear direction that had made his career such a success to that point. He had settled in France, where he believed jazz was treated with the respect due to a major art form, and he tried various short-lived lineups while working on his technique and stylistic range. One enduring outcome of this period was that McLaughlin set up various acoustic guitar trios, the most successful involving Paco De Lucia and Al DiMeola. Another was his composition *Guitar Concerto*, which he performed with the Los Angeles Philharmonic in 1985.

In 1984 McLaughlin once again played for Miles Davis on the album *You're Under Arrest*, and he contributed to Davis's 1985 *Aura* disc as well. Shortly after this he appeared in the 1986 film *Round Midnight*. This seemed, as it did for Herbie Hancock and Wayne Shorter, to have a galvanizing effect on his career, as he launched himself into a series of new musical projects. After a short-lived "new" Mahavishnu Orchestra, he toured with a trio including bassist Kai Eckhardt and percussionist Trilok Gurtu. Then he formed his enduring organ trio with Joey DeFrancesco on organ and Dennis Chambers (replaced on one disc by Elvin Jones) on drums. The trio, which worked consistently in the 1990s, coincided with a revival of interest in this type of lineup, which was pioneered in the 1950s by Jimmy Smith.

As the 20th century reached its end, McLaughlin had consolidated his position as one of the most versatile and accomplished guitarists in jazz on both the electric and acoustic instruments—the leading pioneer of jazz-rock fusion and of integrating jazz with elements of world music.

"Mahavishnu's exotic sound is among the finest to arise from the musical experimentation of the past decade."

—Jim Schaffer in *Down Beat* (April 26, 1973)

DISCOGRAPHY

Extrapolation. Polydor 841598. [A critically acclaimed 1969 album made with a quartet including saxophonist John Surman and drummer Tony Oxley.]

Mahavishnu Orchestra, Inner Mounting Flame. Columbia CK 31067. [1970 debut of this powerful fusion band.]

Shakti. Columbia 467905-2. [Deeply textured acoustic music with tabla and traditional Indian percussion, 1975.]

Johnny McLaughlin: Electric Guitarist. Columbia 467093. [1978 cross section of McLaughlin from a re-formed Mahavishnu Orchestra to his colleagues in Tony Williams' band Lifetime.]

Live at the Royal Festival Hall. JMT 834436 [Trio with bassist Kai Eckhardt and percussionist Trilok Gurtu, recorded in McLaughlin's home country.]

After the Rain. Verve 527 467-2. [1994 organ/drums trio with Joey DeFrancesco and Elvin Jones.]

The Promise. Verve 529 828-2. [A 1995 attempt to do something similar to the *Electric Guitarist* album of almost 20 years earlier, with a cross section of McLaughlin's 1990s colleagues.]

The Guitar Trio. Verve 533215. [1996 trio with fellow guitarists Paco De Lucia and Al Di Meola.]

The Heart of Things. Verve 539153. [1997 all-star band with overtones of the early Mahavishnu Orchestra.]

FURTHER READING

Carr, Ian. "John McLaughlin" in Ian Carr, Digby Fairweather, and Brian Priestley, *Jazz: The Rough Guide.* 2nd ed. London and New York: Rough Guides, 2000.

Gridley, Mark C. "Twenty Years of Jazz, Rock and American Popular Music 1960s–1980s" in *Jazz Styles, History and Analysis.* Englewood Cliffs, N.J.: Prentice-Hall, 1985.

Nicholson, Stuart. *Jazz Rock—A History.* Edinburgh: Canongate, 1998.

WEBSITE

http://www.cs.cf.ac.uk/Dave/mclaughlin/home.html

Articles, interviews, pictures, music files, sound bytes, and more.

Anthony Braxton

TRI-VIBRATIONAL
DYNAMICS

With his slightly ruffled appearance, round steel-rimmed spectacles, and a spoken vocabulary that draws on a vast range of intellectual sources, the first impression of Anthony Braxton is that he is some kind of college professor, which in fact he is, having taught at Mills College, Oakland, California, and then Wesleyan University in Middletown, Connecticut, for a considerable part of his career. Yet Braxton is far more than that. He is one of the supreme multi-instrumentalists in jazz, with a fearsome command of almost all the reed instruments, as well as piano and drums. He is a prolific recording artist and an indefatigable composer who, in the manner of classical musicians, allots opus numbers to his

Anthony Braxton plays his contrabass saxophone, the deepest-sounding member of the saxophone family.

> *"It's partly because of my respect for what I call the tri-vibrational dynamics that I try to function in bebop and demonstrate some musics from the traditional continuum. I think that's important. It's just that we have to teach people to deal with the future too."*
>
> —Anthony Braxton in *Forces in Motion* (1988)

work. He has played in almost every area of jazz, from the performance of standards to completely free improvisation, and in every size of ensemble from unaccompanied soloist to the largest big bands and orchestras. He is also a student of philosophy and an expert chess player, and he has published articles and papers on a staggering range of topics from Shakespeare and his contemporary British playwright Christopher Marlowe to the art of musical composition.

Braxton's ceaseless curiosity, mixed with his quirky humor and analytic intelligence have led to accusations of his music being "cold" and "emotionless" from within the jazz movement, and too "random" or "improvisationbased" from the classical camp. To Braxton, it is all music, and he views much criticism of him as representing a mentality he abhors, one that categorizes music stylistically or even worse racially. "There are still black charts and a mind-set that prevents meaningful communication between the African-American aesthetic and the European tradition," he has said. "I count Schoenberg and Webern as my daddies, too." Braxton has done more than most musicians to break down such artificial barriers, since the days when his first significant work came out of a movement of the 1960s that

was determined to alter the status of African-American musicians for good.

This was the AACM (Association for the Advancement of Creative Musicians), formed in Braxton's hometown of Chicago in 1965 by pianist and composer Muhal Richard Abrams. The organization was a collective designed to foster the work of young predominantly African-American musicians and composers, with a heavy emphasis on older more experienced musicians training their younger counterparts. Braxton, who later performed often with Abrams, was particularly influenced by Abrams' interests in the jazz tradition and European concert music. However, he was equally affected by hearing recordings of the saxophone playing of Warne Marsh, a Californian tenor saxophonist who combined melodic lines of intricate complexity with a profoundly beautiful tone. As Braxton developed as a musician, he perfected a technique on alto and later on other saxophones that combined Marsh's total control of the instrument with the ideas of freedom and cooperation advanced by the AACM.

The AACM was one of a number of community-based organizations that sprang up in 1960s urban America to harness the positive creativity within the African-American community. Others included the Pan-Afrikan People's Arkestra in Los Angeles and the Black Artists' Group (BAG) in St. Louis. Through the AACM, Braxton teamed up with violinist Leroy Jenkins and trumpeter Leo Smith. They formed a band called Creative Construction Company, which also included the drummer Steve McCall.

Like other AACM members, they thought deeply about the differences between improvised and composed music, a distinction which Leo Smith described in a 1971 liner note to

Braxton's collected recordings of the period as being between *composition*, "conceived by one or more individuals as abstracted symbols . . . that remain inactive until brought alive by interpretation," and *improvisation*, in which "the four primary elements, sound, rhythm, silence, space, are organized and delivered instantaneously as they are conceived." In other words, between music that is interpreted from the written word, as opposed to music in which all its component parts are improvised. Both composition and improvisation were present in the group's performances, which some audiences of the time loved, and others thought were simply weird.

When Braxton's group moved to Paris in 1969 with other AACM members, European audiences—who were looking for the fire and heat they were used to hearing from the earlier generation of African-American bebop musicians who settled in Europe—dismissed Braxton's contemplative performances, which were full of suspense, space, and moments of silence, as "cold." Whereas other members of the group of AACM Chicago émigrés went on to found the highly successful and long-lived Art Ensemble of Chicago, Braxton was compelled to break up his band and return to New York City, where he temporarily abandoned music and established himself as a chess player.

Before going to Europe, he had already started to record. His discs included *For Alto*, cut in 1968, which was an extended alto saxophone solo, one of the first solo saxophone improvisations ever recorded at full album length. This became something of a cult disc when it was released following Braxton's return to the United States, and was at its most popular not long after Braxton had returned to music and was playing in Chick Corea's group

Circle. After Circle, Braxton spent much of the next few years alternating between playing in his own quartet, which included Dave Holland and Barry Altschul (the other former members of Circle) plus either Canadian trumpeter Kenny Wheeler or fellow Chicagoan trombonist George Lewis, and giving unaccompanied concerts that recreated the style of music from his album. He recorded a number of follow-up solo discs including *Saxophone Improvisations Series F* in 1972.

In the 1970s Braxton took a major part in the workshops held at the Creative Music Studios in Woodstock, New York. He also spent a considerable amount of time in Europe, where he worked with a range of figures on the cutting edge of free and improvised music, such as London-based guitarist Derek Bailey, as well as within the European art music tradition. His collaborations with the Italian group Musica Elettronica Viva, notably with the group's synthesizer player, Richard Teitelbaum, are particularly fascinating. These European musicians were discovering improvisation from a background of playing avant garde classical music by such composers as Karlheinz Stockhausen and the Viennese serial composers Alban Berg and Anton Webern. Meanwhile, Braxton in many ways was traveling in the opposite direction, having begun as a jazz improviser, but becoming increasingly interested in contemporary classical composition. His fascination with classical music and also with large-scale compositions led him to produce work as varied as his *For Two Pianos* (which has overtones of Stockhausen and the American minimalist composer John Cage) and his *For Four Orchestras*. He has also led occasional jazz big bands, including the ensemble that recorded *Creative Orchestra Music, 1976*.

Anthony Braxton

BORN

June 4, 1945
Chicago, Illinois

EDUCATION

Music lessons with Jack Gell, Chicago School of Music to 1964; studied music at Wilson Junior College, later at Chicago Musical College; studied philosophy at Roosevelt University, Chicago

MAIN INTERESTS

All saxophones, especially alto; clarinets, flutes, piano; composing, bandleading, recording

ACCOMPLISHMENTS

Recorded solo alto album, 1968; took trio (occasionally quartet) to Europe, 1969–70. Joined Chick Corea (1970), continued to alternate quartet and solo appearances. From mid-1970s composed prolifically for all ensemble styles and sizes. Led big bands, quartets, and duos in concert and on disc into the 1990s; experimented with ghost trance music, operatic form, and with integrating actors and video material. Teaches at Wesleyan University; runs own record label; author of many publications. Compositions include the vast *For Four Orchestras* and the opera *Trillium R*

HONORS

Many awards, including MacArthur Foundation Fellowship "genius grant"; Rockefeller Foundation grant for his opera *Trillium R*

Onstage, Braxton is surrounded by a cross-section of the instruments he might use in the course of a performance, including several different flutes, saxophones, and clarinets.

widely between free playing, his own highly structured compositions and—most intriguing—explorations of the jazz standard repertoire, including a particularly effective collection of Thelonious Monk tunes. More recently his excursions into standards have included discs on which he plays piano, and a series of duets with multi-instrumentalist Stewart Gillmor called *14 Compositions (Traditional)* in 1996, which interpret music by Louis Armstrong, Hoagy Carmichael, Duke Ellington, Earl Hines, and Fats Waller.

In his writing, Braxton has tended to group his music according to overall themes or concepts. Much of his 1990s composition was concerned with "ghost trance" music, material that sought through repetition of tiny motifs, or endless improvisation within a fairly limited range, to capture some of the heightened consciousness found in trance-inducing music of the Native Americans or in the Middle Eastern traditions. Some of this is performed by a quartet, other pieces have a larger ensemble and longer running times, and some, like *Composition 192* with singer Lauren Newton, are determined by the turn of a wheel of fortune or the throw of a die. A different section of the piece is played according to which number comes up, and at the end of each section, the wheel is turned or dice thrown again, to determine the next part to be played.

Braxton is fascinated with the immediacy of the electronic gadgets that fill early 21st-century lives: multi-channel television, video games, the Internet. So he has constructed pieces that have a built-in ability to change with the rapidity and startling juxtaposition of content that we find by flipping the channels on television or playing video games. He achieves this random element by turning a number

In addition to this breadth of activity, plus a teaching career that began in the early 1980s, for most of the time from the 1970s until the 1990s Braxton continued to lead a quartet in which he played alto saxophone and other reed instruments, with piano, bass, and drums accompaniment. Notable among his personnel have been pianist Marilyn Crispell, drummer Gerry Hemingway, and bassist Mark Dresser. His recordings in this configuration range

wheel or using a pack of cards in the same way as in *Composition 192*. Many of his pieces also incorporate random loops of video tape and recorded sound effects that interact with live performers, and his *Composition 102* involves interaction between the music and a puppet show.

In the late 1990s Braxton became Artistic Director of his Tri-Centric Foundation, a loose-knit repertory ensemble of musicians, actors, and video graphics specialists created to perform his works. This coincided with completion of a version of his epic opera *Trillium R*, and theater pieces such as *Composition 173* for actors, improvisers, and ensemble groups. His foundation takes its name from Braxton's study of numbers, which gives him the belief that many things naturally group in triplicate, so his performances are most often planned over three days, with three levels of activity: main events, splinter groups, and lectures, or as Braxton calls them "informances."

Because his music has integrated with so many other areas of late 20th-century thought, performance, improvisation, and composition, Braxton has had a more far-reaching effect than many of his contemporaries in the AACM. He has broken new ground in "trans-African" (jazz-related) and "trans-European"(European–American-related) music within North America. He has simultaneously embodied many of the principles of jazz musicians like Warne Marsh, John Coltrane, and Ornette Coleman; of interdisciplinary specialists like his AACM colleagues; and of composers such as Charles Ives and John Cage. While the experimental nature of some of his music makes it hard to understand or approach, Braxton remains one of the most provocative and original figures in jazz history.

DISCOGRAPHY

Three Compositions of New Jazz. Delmark DS 423. [1968 debut of Braxton's trio plus Muhal Richard Abrams.]

Silence/Time Zones. Black Lion BLCD 760221. [Paris performance, plus early duos with Richard Teitelbaum.]

Creative Orchestra (Köln) 1978. Hat Art CD 61711/2 (two-CD set). [European–American big band with many of Braxton's associates, including Kenny Wheeler, Leo Smith, Marilyn Crispell.]

Quartet (Coventry) 1985., Leo CD LR 204/5 (2-CD set). [From a series of concerts, most also issued by Leo, from Braxton's United Kingdom tour with Crispell, Hemingway, and Dresser.]

Six Monk's Compositions (1987). Black Saint 120 116. [A good starting point to understanding Braxton's impressive strengths as an improviser, playing Monk tunes with a quartet including veteran bebop pianist Mal Waldron.]

Eugene (1989). Black Saint 120 137. [Large band organized by Braxton's Wesleyan colleague and biographer Mike Heffley, in concert, playing a cross section of Braxton's 1975–89 work.]

Seven Compositions (Trio) 1989. Hat Art CD 6025. [Braxton on various saxophones with Adelhard Roidinger, bass, and Tony Oxley, drums.]

Knitting Factory (Piano/Quartet): Vol. 1. Leo CD LR 222/3. [1994 group in which Braxton plays piano with Marty Ehrlich playing reeds.]

Sextet (Istanbul) 1995., Braxton House No 1 (two-CD set). ["Ghost trance" music recorded in concert at a major Turkish jazz festival.]

Solo Piano (Standards) 1995. No More Records No. 2 (two-CD set). [Braxton's assured and stylistically varied piano playing.]

Composition 192. Leo CD LR 251. [Smaller scale trance music with singer Lauren Newton.]

14 Compositions (Traditional) 1996. Leo CD LR 259. [Duo with Stewart Gillmor.]

FURTHER READING

Braxton, Anthony. *Tri-Axium Writings 1–3*. Lebanon, N.H.: Frog Peak Music, 1985.

———.*Composition Notes A–E*. Lebanon, N.H.: Frog Peak Music, 1988.

Heffley, Mike. *The Music of Anthony Braxton*. Westport, Conn.: Greenwood, 1996.

Lock, Graham. *Forces in Motion: The Music and Thoughts of Anthony Braxton*. 1988. Reprint, New York: Da Capo, 1988.

Radano, Ronald M. *New Musical Figurations: Anthony Braxton's Cultural Critique*. Chicago: University of Chicago Press, 1993.

WEBSITE

http://www.wnur.org/jazz/artists/braxton.anthony

Offers links to biography, interviews, photos, sound samples, and a complete discography.

More Cool, Hard Bop, and Fusion Players to Remember

Just as Miles Davis is the musician who has had most direct influence on the majority of musicians in this section, his collaborator from the 1940s–1970s, **Gil Evans** (1912–88) was a behind-the-scenes influence on many of them as well. Evans' background in his native Canada and in California, where he had his own first bands in the 1930s, is relatively obscure. What is in no doubt is that by the mid-1940s, with Claude Thornhill's band he had found an original and influential voice as an arranger. His arrangements have been described by Gunther Schuller as "orchestral improvisations," and his use of tuba, French horn, and baritone saxophone was a key ingredient of the sound of "cool" jazz. Having first collaborated with Miles Davis on *Birth of the Cool* in 1949–50, Evans collaborated with Davis again in the late 1950s, the results including *Porgy and Bess* (1959) and *Sketches of Spain* (1960). In later life he led a big band in New York that played weekly and acted as an immediate sounding board for his constant flow of new compositions and arrangements. Like Davis, he brought electronics into his bands, adding to his existing mastery of tonal effects.

Of the musicians who emerged in the cool jazz movement pioneered by Evans, Davis, and Gerry Mulligan, the key players were trumpeters **Chet Baker** (1929–88) and **Shorty Rogers** (1924–94). Although Baker's career was blighted by problems associated with drug addiction, he established his musical credentials playing with Charlie Parker before joining Gerry Mulligan's quartet. He achieved his greatest fame as a singer and trumpeter, fronting his own groups in the mid-1950s. His trumpet style echoed that of Davis, with a restricted range of pitch that concentrated in the middle register, along with a mellow tone achieved by avoiding extremes of volume. His last years were documented in the film *Let's Get Lost* (1989), which took its ironic title from one of Baker's early hit songs.

Shorty Rogers, by contrast was a musician who was almost lost to playing jazz through his skills as a film composer and arranger. Following his scoring of *The Man with the Golden Arm* (1955), he spent 25 years in the studios writing soundtrack music for everything from episodes of the television series *Batman* to major movies. Fortunately, prior to this, and after returning to regular performance in the 1980s, he produced many important jazz recordings. With quirky titles like "Cool and Crazy," "Martians Go Home," and "The Sweetheart of Sigmund Freud," his pieces for small group or large band retained a basic lightness of touch entirely in keeping with Gil Evans's vision of cool jazz. Rogers combined voicings that echoed those of the Davis

nonet (nine-piece group) with a driving swing rhythm influenced by Count Basie's Kansas City small groups. He first made his mark as a trumpeter and arranger in the big bands of Woody Herman and Stan Kenton, and in his last years toured widely with the Lighthouse All Stars, the alumni of a famous Los Angeles club that had been a center of West Coast cool in the 1950s.

Pianist **Horace Silver** (born 1928) is generally regarded as the father of hard bop. He made his reputation with Stan Getz at the beginning of the 1950s, and worked as a freelancer in New York City before beginning a long association with Blue Note records in 1952. He and Art Blakey both played in the Jazz Messengers until Blakey took the band over, leaving Silver to lead his own influential quintets. In the opinion of many critics, Silver refined the quintet format to a level only surpassed by Miles Davis's 1960s band, and in doing so established the core approach of hard bop. This involved Silver and his rhythm section setting up blues or gospel-based accompaniments to the punchy bebop solos played by trumpeters such as Art Farmer, Blue Mitchell, and Woody Shaw, and saxophonists Benny Golson, Joe Henderson, and Junior Cook. Silver's many compositions include "The Preacher," "Sister Sadie," and "Song for My Father."

With the advent of John Coltrane's quartet in 1960, the aggressive power and forward momentum of hard bop was combined with some of the modal ideas Coltrane had explored with Miles Davis. His drummer, **Elvin Jones** (born 1927), was a significant contributor to Elvin Jones was not only a brilliant drummer, but the youngest of three brothers who all made their mark on jazz. Pianist Hank Jones, the eldest brother, had an accomplished career and trumpeter Thad Jones played with the Count Basie Orchestra, Charles Minugs's Workshops, and led his own band with drummer Mel Lewis.

this by developing the rhythmic aspects of the style. Whereas bebop drummers like Art Blakey, Max Roach, and Kenny Clarke varied the accents they played within an overall four-to-the-measure pulse, Jones was able to play several rhythms in different meters at the same time. This allowed him to use rhythm as an improvisational tool on equal terms with the melodic instruments in the group. His use of cross-rhythms was exceptional, and his placing of accents was not always determined by the underlying pulse but often by a secondary rhythm that he had added on top of it. This created dense rhythmic textures that were influential both on the work of all post-bop drummers from the 1960s onward, and also on many free jazz players who developed Jones's ideas of texture and abandoned the practice of maintaining an underlying pulse.

Another musician who began playing hard bop and then explored elements of free jazz was saxophonist **Wayne Shorter** (born 1933), who in his work with Miles Davis and later, also became a pioneer of jazz-rock. Shorter's career began with Horace Silver in 1956, then from 1959 he was music director of Art Blakey's Jazz Messengers. He next was the reed player in Miles Davis's quintet in 1964–70, during the time Davis experimented with a freer approach to time, with greater abstraction in improvisation, and with the beginnings of jazz-rock. Shorter continued to make his own discs during this period, often with Herbie Hancock on piano or keyboards., Shorter worked regularly with Hancock in the 1980s and 1990s.

After leaving Davis in 1970, he founded the hugely influential jazz-rock band Weather Report, with Austrian keyboard player and composer **Joe Zawinul** (born 1932). Both Shorter and Zawinul, who was also briefly in Miles Davis's band, were significant composers, Shorter writing pieces like "E.S.P." and "Nefertiti" for Davis, while Zawinul's "In a Silent Way" became a Davis album title track, although the gospel-influenced "Mercy, Mercy, Mercy" and disco hit "Birdland" were his most successful pieces. Their most illustrious colleague in Weather Report was the short-lived bass guitarist **Jaco Pastorius** (1951–87), who did much to transform what had been merely an accompanying instrument in rock into a full-fledged jazz solo instrument.

Although **Keith Jarrett** (born 1945) joined Miles Davis for two years in 1969, at a time the trumpeter was exploring many aspects of rock music, his main interests lay in the direction of the abstract ideas Davis was exploring. This followed from his playing in the pioneering quartet of saxophonist **Charles Lloyd** (born 1938), which played a lyrical variety of free jazz and which had been among the first jazz groups successfully to appear on the rock festival circuit. After leaving Davis, in his own trio recordings Jarrett successfully linked the lyrical, reflective qualities of Bill Evans with the improvisational openness of Ornette Coleman. He went on to be a pioneer of playing solo improvised concerts in which pieces and ideas run seamlessly on from one to another, drawing effectively on his knowledge of the classical keyboard repertoire and on folk music.

Whereas Jarrett has enjoyed great commercial success, for much of his career **Cecil Taylor** (born 1929), the most influential of free jazz pianists, alternated between what one biographer summed up as "high critical acclaim and little or no work." Taylor's intense keyboard style can involve hitting groups of notes with his forearms or flat palms, skittering runs, enormous variation in volume and speed, and many of the devices found in European avant garde composition. Virtually all his music has to do with establishing a mood or series of moods. Whether playing alone or in partnership with a sympathetic partner, such as South African **Louis Moholo** (born 1940), Taylor does this with total commitment. His early lack of success was in due course transformed, both through his teaching activities and through his lionization by a generation who realized the importance of his contribution to free jazz, and who pack the world's concert halls on his occasional tours to hear him.

In the early 1960s, Taylor led a quartet that, like Ornette Coleman's, was resident at the Five Spot in New York City. Its tenor saxophonist was **Archie Shepp** (born 1937). Shepp's music combined many of the ingredients of Coleman's—collective free improvisation, atonal passages, jagged snatches of melody—with a strong political conviction. In many ways his music links the overtly political work of the Association for the Advancement of Creative Musicians and similar organizations with the musical innovations of Coleman. However, whereas Coleman's later work explored rock through his band Prime Time, Shepp looked back at earlier stages in African-American music to explore ballads, the blues, and marches. Much of his work involved linking music with elements of poetry and drama. Since the 1970s, he has combined an active touring career with his work as a professor at the University of Massachusetts–Amherst. His successor in Taylor's band, **Albert Ayler** (1936–70), took free improvisation much further than Shepp. Amid similar devices—jagged themes, dense collective playing, and noises like honks and squeals—he presaged the work of 1990s players like John Zorn and Peter Brotzmann. Ayler's 1964 recording *Ghosts* is a remarkable exercise in progressive deconstruction of a recognizable melody.

One member of the free jazz community whose influence stretched far beyond his early work with Ornette Coleman, Archie Shepp, and Keith Jarrett is bassist **Charlie Haden** (born 1937). Particularly important is Haden's Liberation Music Orchestra, which performed various songs of revolution in a big band setting from the 1960s to the 1980s. In his work, and that of his colleague, composer and pianist **Carla Bley** (born 1938), many of Gil Evans' ideas came full circle, as concepts that grew up during the 1960s and 1970s from free jazz to jazz-rock were absorbed back into the big band tradition. In their music, and that of their contemporary Chinese-born Japanese big band composer **Toshiko Akiyoshi** (born 1929), the balance between innovation and tradition that was to be the main feature of the 1990s and beyond was established.

6 A Century of Jazz

By the 1980s, jazz could no longer be described simply in terms of American music; it had become international. Also, following the death of John Coltrane in 1967 it was no longer easy to see a simple line of historical development that could be traced from the work of one great player to another. Jazz became many different types of music, all existing together and competing with one another for the listener's attention.

Many jazz historians have attempted to find a simple, single story to describe what was happening, but as can be seen in the music of Herbie Hancock, Chick Corea, John McLaughlin, and Anthony Braxton, between the 1960s and 1980s too much was going on for a simple story to emerge. However, these musicians and almost all the others profiled in Part 5 were in one way or another influenced by the all-pervasive presence of Miles Davis.

Davis himself had an instinctive gift for capturing fleeting movements in jazz and popular music and making something individual and innovative from them. With his death in 1991, there remained no comparable overarching presence. Nevertheless, in the years leading up to the 21st century several strong movements did emerge that guaranteed jazz a healthy future, yet one that would still include controversy, debate, and unexpected development.

In many respects, this diversity can be traced back to the 1970s, when something happened across the whole of society to change the old-style continuity of development forever: the emergence of new technology. At a stroke most of the history of the music became available in recorded form—allowing musicians to access almost any aspect of jazz as the basis for further development. Not only musicians but visual artists, novelists, poets, and playwrights faced the same dilemma of absorbing tradition and simultaneously participating in, and even creating, the very newest growth and inspiration.

From the 1970s onward, any jazz musician seeking to make a mark on the world now has to take a different route from his or her predecessors. Instead of absorbing the lessons of the recent past, learning a style from a relatively small number of key influences, and mainly competing with musicians of the same generation, it is now necessary to compete with the entire history of recorded jazz. As the compact disc era has dawned, reissues from every period of jazz have crowded the record stores along with a flood of new recordings by every up-and-coming artist.

NEWPORT JAZZ FESTIVAL/NEW YORK
1954-1978/25 SUMMERS OF JAZZ
JUNE 23-JULY 2

International jazz festivals, such as the annual Newport event, have had a huge influence by providing a platform for performers from all over the world. After originally being staged at Newport, Rhode Island, the festival moved during the 1980s to New York City, where it has been staged as "Newport in New York" for many years since.

Under the influence of Wynton Marsalis, musicians have looked back to earlier periods of jazz and sought to take from them elements of instrumental technique and musical approach that will enrich the playing tradition of the future. Marsalis has become an eloquent spokesman for jazz, and a motivating teacher and bandleader. Yet his conservative, traditional approach to the music contrasts strongly with other musicians who continue to search for the new and the unexpected.

David Murray and Jan Garbarek have found this in the synthesis of music from other cultures, while Geri Allen has given prominence to the voice of women in jazz, for too long a minority restricted to vocalists and a handful of instrumentalists. Michael Brecker, by contrast, has explored every aspect of technical perfection in his saxophone playing, showing that there are still new things to be discovered in this stalwart instrument. He has also demonstrated how a new instrument, the EWI (Electronic Wind Instrument—a breath-operated synthesizer), can bring the wind-player's skills into the field of synthesizers and electronics.

And finally, Joshua Redman, like Wynton, Branford, and Jason Marsalis, has shown that a new generation of musicians born into the jazz heritage can take the music into the 21st century with the joy of performance intact. This new generation proves that a new audience can be built for the music as these players come to extend its boundaries still further.

David Murray

POSTMODERN
SAXOPHONIST

In the late 1980s, a consensus emerged among the critics of literature, the visual arts, and architecture that whereas what was called "modern" had once been daring and adventurous, it had now become something stale and conventional. Such critics including Ihad Hassab, Charles Jencks, and Jean-François Lyotard, promoted the idea that to recapture a sense of daring and adventure, a new "postmodern" approach was needed that would emerge as a consequence of blending ideas from the past and present.

The same became true in jazz, where the bebop revolution that produced "modern" jazz had become the orthodox approach to jazz for most players from the 1940s onward. If a new style or approach to jazz was to emerge, it, too, would involve a synthesis of new ideas with material drawn from the past. Far from being daunted by the mass of material available on disc, on the Internet, and on the world concert circuit, the saxophonist David Murray sees it as a challenge: "By the time I die, I would like to be able to play with any musician on the planet and know something about what they do as well as they know something about what I do."

From the moment he arrived in New York City in 1975 from his native California, Murray chose to meet that challenge head on. It took him, he believes, another seven or eight years to arrive fully at his own style, which involves a mastery of techniques drawn from the entire history of the tenor saxophone. In particular, he has a command of all the registers of the instrument, leaping from its depths to the highest, squeaky harmonics it can produce, with a warm tone that goes back to that of older players like Paul Gonsalves, Coleman Hawkins, and Ben Webster. He also plays bass clarinet with a fierce energy that has helped bring this once-forgotten instrument back into the limelight.

Watching him play, he seems to go into a trance, closing his eyes as his pupils roll upward and furrowing his brow in concentration. "Swinging can get to the point where it's almost like spirit possession," he has said. By swinging he means arriving at the highest level of creativity possible: "If you can get to that high point every moment while you're playing, then I would say you're swinging."

Murray grew up in Berkeley, California, in a family that started him early on playing music. His father had been a circus acrobat and played guitar in a family band; his mother played gospel piano. Murray got his own start playing rhythm and blues with a band called Notations of Soul. At Pomona College in Claremont, California, he studied with drummer and social historian Stanley Crouch. By the time he arrived in the East, at the same time as Crouch, he was

David Murray, left, plays with fellow tenor saxophonist Ravi Coltrane, son of John Coltrane, who has an international career as a soloist in his own right.

David Murray

BORN
February 15, 1955
Berkeley, California

EDUCATION
Pomona College, California

MAIN INTERESTS
Bass clarinet, tenor saxophone, bandleading, composing

ACCOMPLISHMENTS
Played free jazz in New York from 1975; founding member of World Saxophone Quartet, 1976. Led own bands, from duos to a full big band, but guested widely on other leaders' albums. Has combined touring with workshops and teaching in many of the world's major music colleges. Has worked with traditional musicians in many countries of the world including Turkey, the Antilles, and Senegal. Theater projects have included 1970s collaborations with Ntozake Shange, and *Music for a Private World* with the African-American poet and writer Amiri Baraka (1984); film appearances include *Speaking in Tongues* (1986), *David Murray Live at the Village Vanguard* (1987), *Say Brother* (1993)

HONORS
Frequent winner of *Down Beat* and other polls; Grammy for *Blues for Coltrane*, 1988; Guggenheim Fellowship, 1989; *Village Voice* Musician of the Decade (1980s); Danish Jazzpar Prize (the "jazz Oscar"), 1991; New York *Newsday* Musician of the Year, 1992

ready to immerse himself in the free jazz of New York's 1970s loft scene of semiformal concerts given in the areas of Manhattan where former factories and warehouses were being converted into living and performance spaces.

The loft scene was a semiunderground movement, involving some significant pioneers of free jazz such as Ornette Coleman but also creating a forum for young, talented improvisers like Murray to mingle with like-minded musicians and a cross section of New York's radical intellectuals. Some of Murray's earliest recordings date from this period. Even if he felt his own voice was not yet fully developed, his work with trumpeter Lester Bowie and bassist Fred Hopkins from one prominent venue in the loft scene, the Lower Manhattan Ocean Club, in 1977 shows the genesis of many of the ideas that were to recur in his later work. On his disc of live recordings from the club, a swing-flavored tribute to Sidney Bechet

sits alongside much more uncompromising free improvisation.

The dual influences at work in those early loft sessions—pieces that nod in the direction of the jazz tradition on the one hand, and those that are new and spontaneous on the other—were to crystallize into different strands of Murray's own working life in 1977 with the formation of the World Saxophone Quartet. This band also included three radical members of the St. Louis Black Artists' Group, alto saxophonists Oliver Lake and Julius Hemphill, plus baritone saxophone player Hamiett Bluiett. It had no rhythm section, and used the dynamic interplay between the four saxophones to create all the elements of jazz: rhythm, harmony, accompaniment, solos, and so on. The quartet was able to reinterpret traditional material in a fresh and novel way, and so Murray found himself exploring a repertoire, including new pieces by the band's

Murray has done much to bring the bass clarinet back to the foreground as a solo instrument.

over such pieces, not only mastering the underlying structure but creating solos that show a remarkable command of detail, and a clarity that makes his playing easy to follow and understand however complex the setting.

As Murray's reputation grew, he began to be invited to make guest appearances in live concerts and on discs with all manner of other musicians. These appearances opened the doors to a remarkably diverse career in which he has played on hundreds of recording sessions from the Grateful Dead to the Senegalese group Fo Deuk Revue. He tried electric funk with guitarist James "Blood" Ulmer and bassist Jamaaladeen Tacuma; he played post-bop with Jack De Johnette's Special Edition; and by the start of the 1990s he settled into leading a small number of different lineups of his own, each of which approached jazz from a slightly different standpoint. These lineups included a free jazz trio with bassist Fred Hopkins and drummer Andrew Cyrille, a quartet called Shakill's Warriors built round the powerful Hammond organ playing of Don Pullen, a post-bop group known as the "Power" quartet with pianist John Hicks, and above all Murray's own octet and big band.

The octet included several soloists who were also key members of his big band, notably trumpeters Hugh Ragin and Rasul Siddik, trombonist Craig Harris, and saxophonist James Spaulding. For a time, the big band worked regularly at New York City's Knitting Factory club, a bastion for avant-garde forms of jazz, where it was conducted by Butch Morris. Morris pioneered a novel style of free improvisation called "conduction" in which gesture was used to direct an otherwise completely spontaneous performance. On leaving the Knitting Factory in 1996, Murray and Morris went their separate ways, and

members, that involved conventional harmonies and structures, but in a very unconventional setting. Their 1986 album of Duke Ellington material perfectly demonstrates the originality of its approach.

Simultaneously, in his other work Murray was tackling far less conventional music in free-form ensembles that varied in size from duos to his own nascent quintet, which later burgeoned into a big band, and in which cornetist Lawrence "Butch" Morris played and wrote much of the material. One typical example of a Morris composition, "Fling," has a complex construction with an unusual harmonic basis and a rhythm with seven beats to the measure. Murray confidently improvises

> *"His development from the twenty-year-old college dropout cautiously finding his technique in New York lofts to a forty-something expatriate commanding musical armies with implacable authority is minutely traceable."*
>
> —Gary Giddins in *Visions of Jazz* (1998)

Murray worked on putting together a version of his big band that played more conventionally in the jazz tradition to tackle "The Obscure Works of Ellington and Strayhorn" for Ellington's centenary in 1999. On some concerts the competition for solo space from his all-star lineup worked against him, but the sure touch of his own playing, and the new twist given to Strayhorn's music by flutist James Newton was as rewarding as any music in Murray's career.

The tour of that all-American big band was unusual. In the preceding years, as Murray's work became more and more in demand, he traveled the world to play his big band arrangements with the members of his octet and then recruited the rest of the big band on location. For example, in Britain he formed his "UK Posse," local musicians who came together to form a big band in which the octet players were key soloists. In 1994, Murray met the Senegalese drummer Doudou N'Daiye Rose and a new strand of collaboration emerged. As he moved into the 21st century, Murray brought his vital, forward-looking improvisation and the many areas of jazz he has managed to master in the preceding 25 years to a world music context. In doing so, he acknowledges one influence above all others. He told the author: "I think it's important to develop leadership qualities like Duke Ellington, my hero. He had the ability to lead like a great general, or like a great president or prime minister, to gather people behind him and motivate them. That's what I like—to motivate people, to clap together, sing together, and play together."

DISCOGRAPHY

Live at the Lower Manhattan Ocean Club. India Navigation IN 1032. [Free jazz quartet from 1977.]

Interboogiology. Black Saint 120018. [1978 quartet with Butch Morris.]

World Saxophone Quartet: Steppin'. Black Saint 120027. [Early album (1978) by this important band.]

Ming. Black Saint 120045. [1980 Octet album with the earliest version of many core Murray pieces, including "The Hill."]

The Hill. Black Saint 120110. [Murray in a trio setting with bass and drums. Combines standards like "Chelsea Bridge" with Murray originals and includes some of his best work on bass clarinet.]

World Saxophone Quartet Plays Duke Ellington. Elektra Musician 979137. [1986. High point in the music of the quartet, performing music by Murray's hero.]

Ballads. DIW 840. [One of a series of quartet albums from the late 1980s that achieved great popularity for Murray.]

Shakill's Warrior. DIW 850. [Organ quartet with Don Pullen in masterly form alongside Murray looking back at his rhythm and blues origins.]

Ballads for Bass Clarinet. DIW 880. [An exceptional disc devoted to Murray's "other" horn.]

South of the Border. DIW 897. [Murray's New York big band from 1992 in top form.]

Picasso. DIW 879. [An octet disc based around a reinterpretation of Coleman Hawkins' "Picasso," commissioned by the Lila Wallace Foundation in 1992.]

Dark Star. Astor Place TCD 4002. [Album inspired by Grateful Dead material.]

Fo Deuk Revue, Justin Time. JUST 94. [Murray's 1996 summit meeting with Senegalese traditional musicians.]

FURTHER READING

Davis, Francis. "The Tenor of These Times (David Murray)" in *In the Moment: Jazz in the 1980s*. New York: Oxford University Press, 1986.

Giddins, Gary. *Rhythm-a-ning: Jazz Tradition and Innovation in the '80s*. New York: Oxford University Press, 1985.

———. "David Murray (Profuse)" in *Visions of Jazz*. New York: Oxford University Press, 1998.

Milkowski, Bill. "David Murray: So Much Music, So Little Time." *Down Beat*, January 1993, p. 24.

WEBSITE

http://members.tripod.com/go54321/dm/davidmurray.html

David Murray homepage, featuring news, discography, links, and more.

Michael Brecker

HEAVY METAL BEBOP

For many years Michael Brecker's career was inextricably linked to that of his trumpet-playing brother, Randy, who was born four years before Michael, in 1945. Together they led one of the most successful jazz-rock fusion bands of all, the Brecker Brothers, and they appeared on countless recording sessions as freelance musicians, bringing their high standards of technical excellence to music in almost all spheres, from the pop discs of Paul Simon to straight-ahead jazz. Since 1987, when Michael launched the first of many albums under his own name, he has become the most influential contemporary saxophonist in jazz. Thousands of students in jazz courses around the world regard him as the model player and aspire to come close to his daunting proficiency on the tenor saxophone.

Whereas David Murray has dug deep into the tradition of saxophone playing and absorbed influences that range from rhythm and blues via Duke Ellington's soloists to avant-garde players like Albert Ayler and Archie Shepp, Brecker's style can be seen as a continuous line of development from

Michael Brecker (left), onstage with his brother Randy, says: "We came on the scene at a time when we were influenced by the Beatles, and were listening to rock as well and were fascinated by it. We found a new power by taking some sensibilities from pop and R&B and infusing it with jazz harmony."

that of John Coltrane, whom he heard as a teenager in 1960s Philadelphia. He is capable of reproducing Coltrane's dazzlingly fast runs, and he has an apparently inexhaustible fund of ideas to create endless improvised variations on either a modal or a conventional harmonic basis. Like Coltrane, he is able to convey a convincing emotional range in his playing. But whereas Coltrane's career ended at a time when his accompanying bands were increasingly abstract, Brecker's long experience in rock fusion and his close working friendship with guitarist Pat Metheny have given him a sure touch in creating settings for his playing that are approachable and undaunting for his listeners. Brecker has also adopted a completely new instrument, the EWI (electronic wind instrument), which is played like a saxophone but is a form of synthesizer. It allows him to harness his formidable technique to create sounds more usually produced from a keyboard, but with the authentic timing and phrasing of a wind player.

There seemed little doubt that Michael Brecker would become a musician, from the time he first played as a child in a family band with his brother and sister. Their father was an attorney who played jazz piano for fun. As a boy Brecker was exposed to a wide range of jazz on disc, and only a brief period when he thought he might become a basketball player distracted him from music. He learned solos from records when he was as young as nine, and with his father on piano and his brother Randy on trumpet, the family would jam together most evenings after dinner, giving him a chance to play what he had learned. His admiration for Coltrane grew as a consequence of his teenage friendship with a classmate named Eric Gravatt, who later became the drummer in the band Weather Report. Together they explored Coltrane's conception of music and played as a duo, perhaps fostering

Brecker's ability to be entirely self-reliant regarding harmonic accompaniment. Also, from that stage onward Brecker formed a clear concept of the importance of rhythm in his playing, saying later, "Rhythm has always been the essential thing for me, notes are more for decoration."

Despite this interest in jazz, and in Coltrane in particular, Brecker's first experiences were in playing rhythm and blues, rock, and soul. These were what he played during his short-lived career at the University of Indiana and when he first followed his brother to New York City in 1969. By this time Randy Brecker had already made his mark playing in the rock band Blood, Sweat, and Tears, as well as with jazz musicians like Horace Silver. After working in a band called Birdsong, which mixed elements of jazz harmonies with funk and rock rhythms, Michael teamed up with his older brother, pianist Don Grolnick, guitarist John Abercrombie, and drummer Billy Cobham to form a band called Dreams. The band recorded a couple of successful albums and was very much a prototype for their own group, the Brecker Brothers' Band, formed in 1975.

Before coleading their own group, the brothers played together in Horace Silver's 1973 quintet, proving that they had equally strong talents as conventional hard-bop jazz players as they had as jazz-rock musicians. The brothers' first album, *Sneakin' Up Behind You*, successfully crossed over into the pop world, and a single from their follow-up album, called *East River*, made it into the pop charts. The key to the band's sound was the tight-knit jazz front line of the two brothers and alto saxophonist David Sanborn, backed up by a rhythm section that captured the funk and rock rhythms that were becoming the basis of disco music in the late 1970s. The concept had jelled during informal jam sessions at Don Grolnick's house. The majority of the band's

Michael Brecker

BORN

March 29, 1949
Philadelphia, Pennsylvania

EDUCATION

As a teenager studied with Vince Trombetta and Joe Allard; University of Indiana for one year (studied fine art rather than music)

MAIN INTERESTS

Saxophone, bandleading

ACCOMPLISHMENTS

Played in Dreams; played jazz-rock with Billy Cobham, hard bop with Horace Silver, rock with James Taylor. Formed Brecker Brothers Band with Randy Brecker on trumpet, mid-1970s; became hugely influential figure in jazz-rock. Participated in hundreds of freelance studio sessions. Played EWI and saxophone with Steps (later Steps Ahead), 1979–87. Since 1987 has pursued a solo career, becoming one of the most influential saxophonists in jazz. Compositions include "African Skies," "Escher Sketch," "Slings and Arrows," and "The Nightwalker"

HONORS

Winner of numerous polls as tenor saxophonist; several Grammies, notably for *Don't Try This at Home*, and two for *Tales from the Hudson*

Michael Brecker warms up for a concert backstage. He constantly explores new ideas, saying: "Finding ways to play that are new for me is a challenge."

winning a Grammy for the 1994 album *Out of the Loop*. After it first broke up, Michael Brecker, with drummer Steve Gadd and pianist Don Grolnick from the Brecker Brothers Band, joined vibraphonist Mike Maineiri in a new band called Steps, later renamed Steps Ahead. As this group progressed, it gradually added the resources of digital technology to its sound, Maineiri using his vibes to trigger a synthesizer and Brecker adopting the EWI. The band's initial acoustic lineup, with Bill Evans' former bassist Eddie Gomez, was progressively replaced with a more electronically oriented one featuring guitarist Mike Stern and Miles Davis's bassist Darryl Jones, who later went on to join the Rolling Stones. The group offered Michael Brecker plenty of opportunity to solo, and he was officially coleader by the mid-1980s, but following the release of his own first album in 1987, he left the band.

Steps Ahead had been incredibly popular, especially in Japan, where its first three albums were recorded, so it might have seemed a risky strategy for Brecker to go it alone. But in fact it was the push he needed to play at an even higher level. In the 1990s he became a superstar of the saxophone, with a string of distinguished albums and invitations to take part in recordings with the cream of jazz and rock musicians. In 1991 he joined Paul Simon's international Rhythm of the Saints tour, working alongside African and Brazilian musicians and playing to vast audiences of 10,000 or more. Typically, Brecker reacted without being fazed by his new audience. Instead, he learned from the African and Latin musicians on the tour and adapted their kinds of traditional meter in which two pulses in six and four coexist. He said that this had affected

numbers were written by Randy Brecker, who had a flair for neat, memorable themes that lent themselves to the crossover treatment they received. As if touring and recording prolifically were not enough to occupy them, at this point the Breckers opened a club in New York City called Seventh Avenue South, which became a popular venue at which to hear many of the musicians in their immediate circle.

When the brothers' record contract with RCA ended in 1979, the band split up, although it re-formed to tour in the early 1980s and early 1990s,

> "Brecker's blustering eloquence and technical command receive near universal respect, his sound shaping a generation of saxophonists the way Coltrane did in the 1960s."

—Chris Parker in *The Times*, London (July 1996)

the way he heard rhythms inside his own head, leading him to write complex pieces like "Escher Sketch," which has a polyrhythmic texture, inspired by the lithographs of the artist M. C. Escher.

At the start of the 21st century, Brecker had consolidated his position as a hugely influential saxophonist, dividing his time between touring and recording with his own high-energy acoustic quartet. He also occasionally reunites with his brother (including a 2001 acoustic version of the band) and takes part in the occasional rock-based project, such as Herbie Hancock's New Standard all-star band.

DISCOGRAPHY

Brecker Brothers Collection, Vols. 1 and 2. RCA Novus 90442 and 83076 (two-CD set). [The best of the brothers' fusion band, 1975–81.]

Steps Ahead Steps Ahead. Elektra Musician 60168. [Representative example of Brecker's work with this fusion band, 1983.]

Michael Brecker. MCA 01132. [Brecker's 1987 debut as leader.]

Don't Try This at Home. Impulse 42229-2. [All-star supporting cast includes Herbie Hancock, guitarist Mike Stern, bassist Charlie Haden.]

Brecker Brothers: Return of the Brecker Brothers. GRP 96842. [1992 reunion album, with an updated version of the 1970s band and an appealing blend of electric and acoustic instruments.]

Out of the Loop. GRP 97842. [Brecker Brothers 1994 Grammy-winning album.]

Tales from the Hudson. Impulse 11912. [1996 example of the kind of music Brecker plays on tour with his acoustic quartet, including an acoustic reworking of the fusion number "African Skies," originally recorded by the Brecker Brothers.]

Two Blocks from the Edge. Impulse 12612. [Brecker's regular working band of the late 1990s with pianist Joey Calderazzo.]

FURTHER READING

Brecker, Michael. *Artist Transcriptions: Michael Brecker.* New York: Hal Leonard, 1995. [Notated examples of Brecker's solos, transcribed from his best-known discs.]

Carr, Ian. "Michael Brecker" in Ian Carr, Digby Fairweather, and Brian Priestley, *Jazz: The Rough Guide.* 2nd ed. London and New York: Rough Guides, 2000.

Herrington, Tony: "Heavy Metal Bebop Brother" in *The Wire*, No. 89, July 1991, p. 34.

Nicholson, Stuart. *Jazz Rock: A History.* New York: Schirmer, 1998.

WEBSITE

http://www.michaelbrecker.com

Offers discography and concert information.

Jan Garbarek

SCANDINAVIAN
SAXOPHONIST

I f Michael Brecker is the principal person who developed the technical element of John Coltrane's playing then by contrast the Norwegian saxophonist Jan Garbarek has done more than any other musician to extend the spiritual, contemplative side of Coltrane's work and the preoccupations with folk and non-Western music that went hand in hand with it. Garbarek's beautiful tenor and soprano saxophone tone, often imbued with a lyrical, singing sense of melody, nevertheless retains some characteristics of the chilly Northern atmosphere of his home country. However, he has integrated his sound with all kinds of creative and innovative settings, from improvising jazz groups of varying size to collections of ethnic Indian and Middle Eastern instrumentalists to the polyphonic singing of early music specialists in the Hilliard Ensemble.

Garbarek demonstrates the point that by the end of the first century of jazz, players from outside the United States were making as significant and forward-moving a contribution to the overall development of the music as were Americans themselves. Yet it was specifically the playing of John Coltrane that first inspired Garbarek to take up the saxophone when he was 14 years old. Before he heard Coltrane's recording of "Countdown" on the radio one day in 1961, Garbarek had had no particular interest in music. He had grown up in and around Oslo, having been born in a camp for people displaced by World War II, to a father who had been expelled from Poland by the Nazis and a Norwegian mother. He had certainly heard the marching bands that played traditional music of Norway during the country's annual independence celebrations each May, and he had no doubt heard a wide range of folk, pop, and classical music on the radio, but it was not until he encountered the passionate sound of Coltrane that Garbarek discovered the force inside himself that would make him a musician.

Even before his parents bought him a tenor saxophone, Garbarek had acquired an instruction manual and worked out for himself how to place his fingers on the keypads. "When I got the saxophone, I was really prepared for it. I was very, very eager," he recalled. For a couple of semesters he attended lessons at the Oslo Conservatory, but quit in favor of studying on his own and with a growing collection of like-minded contemporaries and friends who congregated at the Gamlebyen Jazz Club in Oslo. Within a year of quitting the conservatory, Garbarek had won his first competition as a player. He rapidly became known as a talented young musician, who even though he was in his teens, began to play in a Coltrane-inspired style with many of the established local players.

Jan Garbarek in a pensive moment during a recording session for the Munich-based ECM label, for which he has recorded his entire career.

Jan Garbarek

BORN
March 4, 1947
Mysen, Norway

EDUCATION
Briefly attended Oslo Music Conservatory, 1961–62; thereafter self-taught

MAJOR INTERESTS
Tenor and soprano saxophone, bandleading

ACCOMPLISHMENTS
In late 1960s worked in quartet with Terje Rypdal, then led own quartet and trio; toured and recorded with Keith Jarrett; led own bands (generally including bassist Eberhard Weber) since 1982. Many and varied recording projects, including elements of world music and partnerships with other ECM artists. In late 1990s began successful partnership with Hilliard Ensemble, who sing arrangements of early music combined with Garbarek's saxophone

HONORS
Norwegian Amateur Jazz Championship, 1962; impressive record of awards and prizes including Paul Robeson Prize, 1992, and Order of St. Olav, 1998

Scandinavia in the 1960s was a particularly fertile place for jazz. Many American musicians, including the saxophonists Ben Webster and Dexter Gordon and pianist Kenny Drew, either settled in the region or spent large amounts of time there, playing the main clubs in Oslo, Stockholm, and Copenhagen and appearing at the growing number of festival events. Such players worked alongside, taught, and encouraged a generation of local musicians, who soon developed the confidence, knowledge, and originality to work on equal terms with their American counterparts. Garbarek heard most of the American visitors to Oslo, including a concert by Coltrane's quartet in 1963. He also studied the recordings of his American idols, who included Pharoah Sanders and Archie Shepp as well as Coltrane, in detail. It was, however, the direct influence of two American musicians who became short-term Scandinavian residents that shaped his very individual approach to jazz in the mid-1960s: theorist, pianist, and composer George Russell, and Ornette Coleman's former trumpeter Don Cherry.

By the time he got to know Russell, Garbarek was playing regularly in the group led by singer Karin Krog, who was herself expanding the horizons of vocal jazz. Krog's open-minded approach to singing spilled over to the attitudes of her accompanists, so Garbarek was well prepared to absorb Russell's theoretical ideas about modal jazz and about improvising "inside" (based on conventional tonality) and "outside" (based on freer melodic and harmonic concepts). Russell had moved on from his work in the 1940s when he had been Dizzy Gillespie's arranger for pieces like "Cubana Be–Cubana Bop." After being the leading light in a jazz workshop for much of the 1950s, he

Garbarek (left) with two fellow musicians who have also done much to bring world music influences into jazz, Brazilian multi-instrumentalist Egberto Gismonti (center) and American bassist Charlie Haden.

had left New York for Europe, where he focused on creating a repertoire based on the principles of his own highly complex theory, Lydian Chromatic Concept of Tonal Organization.

In Russell's groups, Garbarek was encouraged to find his own distinctive solo voice within a framework that also made space for electronics, tape loops, and the hard-edged distortions of Terje Rypdal's electric guitar. He went on to work with several of the musicians who were involved in Russell's projects, including Rypdal, bassist Arild Andersen, and drummer Jon Christensen, with all of whom he cut his debut album for the ECM record label in 1970. What Garbarek took from the experience of working with Russell was the ability to combine his improvisations with the unconventional settings in which Russell specialized. The development of his tone was helped along by the influence of the Swedish tenor saxophonist Bernt Rosengren, who was

already established as one of Europe's leading solo voices and who played alongside Garbarek in Russell's lineups.

While Russell's bands provided Garbarek with a number of long-term musical associates and new ways of thinking about improvisation, tone colors, and structural settings, it was trumpeter Don Cherry who opened his ears to the rich oral tradition of Norwegian music and the ways in which thematic and atmospheric elements of it could be combined with jazz.

"It was Don who first got us interested in our own folk music, who made us realize how much there was to check out in our own back yard," wrote Garbarek. He recalled a moment in the late 1960s when he was working with Cherry on a broadcast; Cherry, who had settled in Sweden, suggested they base their playing on a Norwegian folk tune. In keeping with his own mixed Native American and African-American ancestry, Cherry put

> *"The roots we have can be combined with expressions within a form of music which originated in very different surroundings."*
>
> —Karin Krog in liner notes to *Til Vigdis*, Garbarek's first LP (1967)

together groups that combined musicians and ideas from many parts of the globe. His interest in the movement that became known as "world music" spilled over into Garbarek's consciousness. While in the late 1960s this movement was restricted to the use of the occasional exotic instrument, such as a wooden flute, it later became a cornerstone of Garbarek's explorations of the heritage of Scandinavian melody and form, and of his experiments in mixing the sound of his saxophone with that of musicians from all corners of the world.

In 1969 Garbarek began an association with a man just as significant in terms of his career as either Russell or Cherry. This was Munich-based record producer Manfred Eicher, who was establishing a new company called ECM (Edition of Contemporary Music). Eicher's vision for his label amounted to a comprehensive set of aesthetic ideas that embraced everything from the cover artwork and graphic design of each disc to the minimalism of his liner notes and the clear unfettered acoustics he achieved in his studio sessions. Eicher developed a roster of musicians who shifted the emphasis of the jazz discs he produced away from the United States and toward Europe, although he forged

long and productive associations with several U.S. stars, from Keith Jarrett to Chick Corea. Garbarek's unusual sound, his distinctive tone, and his increasingly independent repertoire made him an ideal recruit for the label; he has remained an ECM artist since his first disc for the firm in 1970.

Garbarek's first ECM recordings were made at a time when electronic effects were beginning to be part of the jazz musician's available resources. Particularly through his work with Rypdal, who incorporated into his playing the distortions and high volume of Jimi Hendrix or Eric Clapton, Garbarek initially employed echoplex effects and other electronics. He used these along with the kinds of free improvisation pioneered by Ornette Coleman and the AACM in America, as well as German musicians such as the trombonist Albert Mangelsdorff. Garbarek's own playing came closest to that of such free-improvising musicians in his album *Tryptikon*, with Finnish drummer Edward Vesala and bassist Arild Andersen, which also included some of his earliest attempts to use Norwegian folk songs as source material.

After recording with Keith Jarrett and in his own popular quartet with pianist Bobo Stenson, Garbarek signaled his future direction with the album *Dis,* cut with guitarist Ralph Towner. It was an exercise in paring away excess notes and instruments to a simple, unadorned duo. The poetic and uncluttered aspects of this disc struck a chord with the public, and Garbarek has continued to make recordings that emphasize this side of his work in settings that range from Middle Eastern strings and percussion to the sung polyphony of early church music.

His own groups have often discarded ingredients that tend to be thought of as vital elements of jazz, such as the usual set of drums. Garbarek has just as often worked with Brazilian percussionist Nana Vasconcelos or his Danish counterpart Marilyn Mazur as he has with a conventional jazz drummer such as Billy Hart or Michael DiPasqua. He often plays with German bassist Eberhard Weber, a player who has designed his own unusual-looking instrument, which he combines with a sophisticated range of electronics.

At the start of the 21st century, Garbarek divides his time among three pursuits: concerts and recordings with the Hilliard Ensemble, in which his saxophone moves like a free contrapuntal voice amid the singers; touring and recording in his own group; and special projects for ECM that team him with musicians from many parts of the world, from Georgia to the Balkans and from Latin America to the Far East. The common ground among these activities, he feels, is the heartfelt emotion he found in that first broadcast he heard by John Coltrane. He believes that in today's world it is no longer necessary to look purely at the African-American heritage to find it. He says, "Instead of searching for roots in Mississippi, I was looking in the Norwegian valleys. What I found was purely Norwegian, yet for that matter, it does share some common ground with Mississippi."

DISCOGRAPHY

Afric Pepperbird. ECM 1007. [1970 debut album.]

Triptykon. ECM 1029. [1972 trio which includes drummer Edward Vesala.]

Witchi-Tai-To. ECM 1041. [1973 quartet with pianist Bobo Stenson, built round the title track by Native American saxophonist Jim Pepper.]

Dis. ECM 1093. [1976 disc with various settings involving guitarist Ralph Towner.]

It's OK to Listen to the Gray Voice. ECM 1294. [1984. Garbarek teamed with bassist Eberhard Weber and drummer Michael DiPasqua.]

I Took Up the Runes. ECM 1419. [1990 band in one of a series of discs exploring Nordic themes.]

Ragas and Sagas. ECM 1442. [Pioneering example, 1990, of Garbarek's world music ideas with Indian singers, tabla, and sarangi.]

Twelve Moons. ECM 1500. [1993 release by Garbarek's regular working band of the time.]

Officium. ECM New Series 1525. [First of Garbarek's discs with the Hilliard Ensemble, 1993 incorporating elements of early music.]

Mnemosyne. ECM New Series 1700. [1999 sequel to *Officium.*]

FURTHER READING

Hultin, Randi. *Born Under the Sign of Jazz.* Tim Challman, trans. London: Sanctuary, 1998.

Tucker, Michael. *Jan Garbarek: Deep Song.* Kingston-Upon-Hull: University of Hull Press, 1998.

WEBSITE

http://www.ecmrecords.com/ecm/artists/68.html
Biography and discography.

Wynton Marsalis

SWEET SWING BLUES

To millions of people round the world, Wynton Marsalis is jazz. He is its spokesperson, its advocate, its ambassador and protector, and he is also one the finest trumpeters in the entire history of the music. He has played with many of the great names of jazz, led his own groups, and is director of the Lincoln Center Jazz Orchestra, which is dedicated to keeping alive the music of Duke Ellington. He is also an accomplished classical musician who has won awards for his sparkling interpretations of the classical trumpet repertoire. He is a cultured, often impassioned, thoughtful writer, and a brilliant communicator and educator. His family is a musical dynasty that has dominated several areas of jazz for many years. His father, Ellis Marsalis, is a respected pianist and teacher in the family's hometown of New Orleans, and three of his brothers are also professional musicians at the highest level.

The oldest brother, Branford, is a soprano and tenor saxophonist who initially worked alongside Wynton, including a period with Art Blakey, who has also crossed over into the worlds of rock (with Sting), rap and hip-hop with his

Wynton Marsalis with his neatly suited, dapper stage presence is known to audiences of millions round the world.

Marsalis's passion for education and the involvement of young musicians in jazz has led him to organize workshops and master classes in most of the major cities of the world.

group Buckshot LeFonque, and hard bop, which he plays in his own quartet. After leading the band on television's *Tonight Show*, Branford became artistic consultant to the jazz division of Sony Records. The next brother, Delfeayo, is a trombonist and composer who has become a successful record producer, while the youngest, Jason, is an accomplished drummer who has toured the world with pianist Marcus Roberts.

Right from the outset, Wynton Marsalis seemed to have something to prove. In his early days he was immediately successful in proving that it was possible to excel at playing both classical music and jazz. As a child he was given a trumpet by traditional New Orleans trumpeter Al Hirt. He began studying in earnest as he hit his teens, taking part in the rich musical diet that New Orleans had to offer. While he was trying his hand in everything from funk to old-style street parade music, he also became a fixture in the New

Orleans Civic Orchestra. At 14 he appeared with the local Philharmonic Orchestra playing the Haydn trumpet concerto, then went on to the famous music summer school at Tanglewood in Massachusetts's Berkshire Mountains.

He surprised many people, when, with the impeccable classical credentials that had brought him to the Juilliard School in New York City, he swiftly became a member of Art Blakey's Jazz Messengers, proving that he was a remarkably assured hard bop player. From there it was a short step to making his own first disc, produced by Herbie Hancock, and becoming one of the most talked-about musicians on the New York scene. This was reinforced by his superlative classical recordings of concerti by Franz Joseph Haydn, Johann Hummel, and Leopold Mozart (Wolfgang Amadeus Mozart's father).

Yet, as the 1980s went on, he began to assume a more philosophical position about the music he played, and to make strong and frequently outspoken comments about the state of jazz. He was critical of his brother Branford for leaving the jazz quintet in which they both worked to join the touring rock band led by Sting, although they were later reunited on a record, despite Branford's frequent forays into rock and pop styles. He was equally tough on jazz-rock fusion, notably as played by his one-time hero Miles Davis, which led to a famous confrontation between the two men in 1986 in Vancouver, when Miles stopped his band as Wynton appeared on stage to sit in with them.

Beneath the exaggerated press reports of this confrontation, Marsalis was deadly serious about what he saw as threats to the music he loved, and the history that he was increasingly getting to know. He started to question many of the assumptions that had lain behind the attitudes of both musicians and critics: that jazz was constantly evolving from one movement to the next, reflecting the culture of the day.

"Jazz music has many elements and aspects," he said in an interview with British writer Justin Quick. "Group interaction—What about not soloing all night? That's a concept in jazz. What about the fact that jazz has a fundamental and functional African component which means the music has to reinforce fundamental mythological things about the people it comes out of? That means you don't need to have a new movement every five years."

His discs, his playing, his public pronouncements, and the notes about his work written by critic Stanley Crouch eventually led Marsalis to a movement of his own. He spearheaded a reevaluation and consolidation of the jazz tradition, with disciplined and subtle collective interaction between musicians, and an exploration of the core repertoire, in particular of Duke Ellington, whom he came to see as "the greatest sustained development in jazz history." With the founding of his own septet in 1992, and his appointment the same year as artistic director of New York's Jazz at Lincoln Center program, he was soon able to extend the Ellington legacy as he saw it. He wrote new material in a style that was obviously indebted to Ellington and paternally encouraged a tight-knit group of fellow musicians to find and develop their individual voices within his bands, just as Ellington had done. As he traveled the United States giving workshops and educational concerts, he sought out and encouraged young musicians, many of whom ended up coming to New York City and taking their places alongside him in the Lincoln Center Jazz Orchestra.

At the heart of Marsalis's philosophy is the contention that jazz is of itself always modern. That the very act of collectively improvising music of the kind that jazz is, working out what he calls "a collective resolution," is a modern idea, and it underlies his method of writing, bandleading, and soloing. His own septet and the Lincoln Center Jazz Orchestra that he directs are models of ensemble discipline. They are testament to the values of Ellington's generation, which were handed down to Marsalis by his own father, who had worked with many of the great names in jazz.

In the late 1990s, he went further than any musician since Ellington in attempting to realize his vision of jazz. His opera Blood on the Fields was an epic, stretching over three CDs. It revealed a passionate and sensitive feeling for African-American history and a sure hand in creating a vibrant musical setting to express deep-seated emotion going back to the era of slavery. In 1999, Ellington's centenary year, the Lincoln Center Jazz Orchestra's concerts featured only the music of Ellington, in a public awareness campaign highlighted by a school band competition, workshops, and broadcasts to make the great man's music better known and to keep it alive. Nevertheless, in the studio, as the Lincoln Center band approached the millennium, it produced a series of discs exploring the great themes in jazz and popular music, none better than Marsalis's own set of compositions inspirited by the heyday of the American railroad.

Added to Marsalis's television appearances, his writing, and his

Wynton Marsalis

BORN
October 18, 1961
New Orleans, Louisiana

EDUCATION
Studied trumpet with John Longo; Berkshire Music Center, Tanglewood; Juilliard School of Music

MAJOR INTERESTS
Trumpet, composing, bandleading, teaching, broadcasting, writing

ACCOMPLISHMENTS
Many jazz and classical recordings. Artistic Director of Jazz at Lincoln Center. Compositions include In this House, On this Morning (1993), Blood on the Fields (opera, 1994, recorded 1997), Octoroon Balls (string quartet, 1995), Jump Start and Jazz (ballet, 1997), Marciac Suite (1997), Ghost Story (1998), Fiddler's Tale (orchestral, 1998), Big Train (1999)

HONORS
Harvey Shapiro Award for Brass, Tanglewood, as a teenager; frequent poll winner; won two simultaneous Grammy awards, for classical and jazz solo performance (1984); Grammy for Standard Time Vol. 5: The Midnight Blues (1998); Peabody Award for National Public Radio series Making the Music (1996); Essence Award (1997); Pulitzer Prize for Blood on the Fields (1997); Young Audience Children of the Arts Medal (1998). Several honorary degrees. Foreign awards include Grand Prix du Disque (France), Edison Prize (Netherlands)

educational work, his musical achievements are just one aspect of the herculean task he has set himself to keep jazz at the center stage in American culture, and for which he was awarded the Pulitzer Prize that somehow never was awarded to Duke Ellington himself. One particularly high-profile example of his efforts to keep jazz in the forefront of the public imagination was his appearance in the multi-part television series *Jazz*, by the filmmaker Ken Burns, in which Marsalis was one of the principal speakers, as well as recording examples of the music for the soundtrack.

DISCOGRAPHY

Wynton Marsalis. Columbia 468708. [1981 debut album for a major label, with all-star cast including Herbie Hancock, Ron Carter, Tony Williams.]

Art Blakey: Keystone 3. Concord CCD 4196. [Branford and Wynton Marsalis in the Messengers' 1982 lineup.]

Hothouse Flowers. Columbia 468710. [1984 disc with Branford and Wynton, Kenny Kirkland on piano, Jeff Tain Watts on drums.]

J Mood. Columbia 468712. [1985 quartet that shows how much Marsalis's solo voice had matured since his debut.]

Marsalis Standard Time, Vol. 1. Columbia 468713. [The beginning of Marsalis's conscious attempts to dig further back into the tradition, with a collection of well-worn tunes, including "Cherokee."]

Live at Blues Alley. Columbia 461109 (two-CD set). [Marsalis as an untrammeled modern jazz player in the Jazz Messengers tradition.]

The Majesty of the Blues. Columbia 465129. [New Orleans traditionalists join Marsalis's regular group to explore early jazz styles.]

Blue Interlude. Columbia 471635 [1992 debut for Marsalis's septet, allowing him to arrange for a typical Ellingtonian small group format.]

Blood on the Fields. Columbia CXK 57694 (three-CD set). [Marsalis's magnum opus, a jazz opera exploring themes connected with slavery and oppression.]

Lincoln Center Jazz Orchestra: Live in Swing City. Columbia CK 69898. [1999 centenary tribute to Duke Ellington.]

Lincoln Center Jazz Orchestra: Big Train. Columbia/Sony Classical CK 69860. [1999 suite of compositions by Marsalis celebrating the railroad train as it has been portrayed in jazz.]

FURTHER READING

Cook, Richard, and Brian Morton. "Wynton Marsalis" in *The Penguin Guide to Jazz on CD*, 5th ed. New York: Penguin, 2000.

Gourse, Leslie. *Wynton Marsalis: Skain's Domain—A Biography.* New York: Schirmer, 1999.

Marsalis, Wynton. *Marsalis on Music.* New York: Norton, 1995.

———. *Sweet Swing Blues on the Road.* New York: Norton, 1994.

Walser, Robert, ed. "Soul, Craft and Cultural Hierarchy" in *Keeping Time: Readings in Jazz History.* New York: Oxford University Press, 1999.

WEBSITE

http://www.wyntonmarsalis.net
Features news, biography, tour, and message board.

Geri Allen

THE PRINTMAKER

One of Geri Allen's earliest recordings was called "Open on All Sides," which would be a suitably apt description of her own approach to music. She has played with some of the great names in free jazz, from Ornette Coleman to members of the Art Ensemble of Chicago; she has been a sensitive accompanist for the standard repertoire and new songs of the singer Betty Carter; and she was a founding member of the M-Base collective of young New York-based musicians who brought the sounds of hip-hop and rap rhythms into modern jazz. In her recent career she has established herself as one of the most original composers and keyboard artists in jazz.

The earliest sound Allen recalls was the Motown soul music of Detroit, where she grew up. As time went on, she heard the way in which the city's jazz players adapted their bebop style to play backing tracks on soul records, something she later did herself with Mary Wilson and with the

Geri Allen demonstrates the intense concentration she brings to her work in many styles of jazz.

> "We can put different influences in the music like funk, hip-hop, calypso and reggae without being self-conscious."

> —Geri Allen in "Moving the Music" (1991)

Supremes. Her schoolteacher father was a jazz fan, so as a child she heard his Duke Ellington and Charlie Parker discs playing alongside the soul music listened to by her own generation. Her parents made sure she also attended theater and ballet as a child, and they bought her a piano when she asked for one while still very young. Before she left her hometown, she had begun to connect with the strong local tradition of jazz piano playing, which stretched back to famous players who accompanied Ella Fitzgerald, like Hank Jones and Tommy Flanagan. Through other local musicians, such as trumpeter Marcus Belgrave—the artist in residence at her high school and who was later to appear on some of her own discs—she became part of the local jazz scene herself before leaving for Howard University in Washington, D.C. "There was this strong sense of tradition in Detroit's music and I carried on that tradition in a traditional way in that you learn from your elders," she says.

At Howard, she explored the connections between the African traditions in the United States, Cuba, and Latin America. That sparked an interest in ethnomusicology, which she went on to study at the University of Pittsburgh, in the program run by jazz saxophonist Nathan Davis. She also played at Howard with trumpeter

Wallace Roney, who later became her husband.

It was a school friend, Dwight Andrews, who introduced her to saxophonist Oliver Lake, one of the World Saxophone Quartet, and also a former member of the Black Artists' Group in St. Louis. Not long after her arrival in New York City in 1992, she began playing in Lake's quintet, with whom she recorded a number of albums. Lake combined a formidable technique as a saxophonist with a wide-ranging interest in theater, poetry, and many forms of music, from classical forms to reggae (he led the successful reggae band Jump Up as a lead vocalist, in addition to his jazz playing). His breadth of interests matched Allen's own. He and fellow reed player James Newton, who became a regular member of David Murray's big band, encouraged Allen to find her own distinctive jazz voice. What emerged was a very hard-edged approach to bebop and a free jazz and compositional style that had a noticeable delicacy and femininity about it. Some critics have even regarded this as a "soft-centered" quality in her work. She sees this delicacy as integral to the development of her own sound, which has been conditioned by the elements that went into her childhood and upbringing, as well as the whole jazz tradition. "There's been a lot of strong voices from women musicians throughout the history of this music that have made it possible for me to do what I'm doing," she says.

In the mid-1980s, as well as launching her own solo recording career Allen became part of a collective of musicians called M-Base. The group experimented with mixing a range of contemporary African-American urban styles of music with jazz, drawing in the culture of funk, rap, and hip-hop to redefine the role of the rhythm section and the background against which soloists were to improvise. She worked closely with saxophonists Greg Osby and Steve Coleman, playing keyboards, synthesizer, and piano in a variety of settings. She also became one of a coterie of high-profile female musicians who were part of the collective, including singer Cassandra Wilson, pianists Renee Rosnes andMichele Rosewoman, and drummer Teri Lyne Carrington.

In M-Base, Allen's work mixed her sensitive introspective style on pieces like Greg Osby's "Silent Attitude," from his disc *Mindgames*, with humor, such as a church organ parody on Steve Coleman's *To Perpetuate the Funk* (from *World Expansion)*, as well as her direct jazz playing.

After two or three years of working regularly with various M-Base members, Allen moved on to play in a much broader context. She established her current position as a musician who moves comfortably between many styles and areas of jazz, from free to funk, and from mainstream to avant garde, without ever sacrificing her own voice. The strength of her inner sound became obvious from the unorthodox music on her own discs, such as *Twylight*, where her distinctive piano work was combined with the kind of playing she had perfected on keyboards with M-Base in a dreamy landscape of percussion accompaniments, as well as in appearances of the internationally touring trio she joined with bassist Charlie Haden and drummer Paul Motian, veterans respectively of Ornette Coleman's quartet and Bill Evans' trio.

By the start of the 1990s Allen was a well-known and widely respected pianist, and she began an association with the Blue Note record label for her own discs. She simultaneously formed a close working relationship with Betty Carter, one of the most distinctive singers of the 1980s and 1990s, who inherited the role of the world's leading female jazz vocalist with the deaths of Ella Fitzgerald and Carmen McRae. Carter took dramatic liberties with pitch, speed, and melody, coaxing even the best-known songs into new shapes, and finding fresh meanings in even the most well-worn lyrics. Allen was her ideal accompanist, one who shadowed Carter's every mood, a daunting task for any pianist. Carter had a reputation for hiring the most talented up-and-coming players; her endorsement of Allen was yet more evidence of the young pianist's brilliance and individuality.

This was further confirmed when Ornette Coleman, famous for leading bands that had no piano at all, hired Allen as pianist in his Sound Museum acoustic quartet, the first time he had regularly employed a pianist for over 30 years. Coleman told the author that he did not ask Allen to join him because she was a pianist, but because she was a musician he wanted to work with who happened to play piano.

With a string of first-rate albums to her name, including a trio in the daunting company of bassist Ron

Geri Allen

BORN

June 12, 1957
Pontiac, Michigan

EDUCATION

Played in Detroit's Jazz Development Workshop, after studying at Cass Technical School, with support from trumpeter Marcus Belgrave; graduated in jazz studies, Howard University, Washington, D.C., 1979; studied piano with Kenny Barron; master's degree in ethnomusicology, University of Pittsburgh, 1982

MAJOR INTERESTS

Piano, bandleading

ACCOMPLISHMENTS

Played with avant-garde musicians associated with BAG and Association for the Advancement of Creative Musicians; mid-1980s, worked with Steve Coleman and M-Base collective. Wrote her own music and formed trio with bassist Charlie Haden and drummer Paul Motian, both of which explored free improvisation and conventional mainstream jazz. Toured and recorded with singer Betty Carter, early 1990s; composed prolifically; recorded with Ornette Coleman's acoustic quartet

HONORS

Distinguished alumnus award, Howard University; SESAE Special Achievement Award; Eubie Blake Award from Cultural Crossroads; *Down Beat* poll winner, 1993, 1994; Danish Jazzpar Award for work as composer and leader, 1996

Carter and drummer Tony Williams—former colleagues of Miles Davis and Herbie Hancock—Allen's international reputation as one of the world's top jazz musicians was assured by the mid-1990s, when she won the Danish Jazzpar prize. Her resultant album, *Some Aspects of Water,* is a characteristically individual piece of work, enhanced by the presence of a brilliant former associate of Charles Mingus, trumpeter Johnny Coles, in one of the last discs he made before his death.

As she has moved into the 21st century, Allen has begun to reexplore some of the styles of music she first tackled in M-Base. Her album *The Gathering* mixes acoustic jazz with material that reexamines rock rhythms and synthesized settings, but above all it demonstrates her openness to music of all kinds as fuel for her own very personal musical voice.

DISCOGRAPHY

Printmakers. Minor Music 8001. [Allen's 1984 debut under her own name.]

Home Grown. Minor Music 8004. [1985 solo piano disc.]

Steve Coleman: Motherland Pulse. JMT 834401-2. [1987 disc featuring most of the M-Base collective, including Cassandra Wilson.]

Charlie Haden/Paul Motian: Etudes. Soul Note 121 162-2. [1988 recording debut of trio that went on to make several further discs.]

Twylight. Verve 841 152-2. [An unusual 1989 album entirely of Allen compositions on which her piano and synthesizer are accompanied by assorted percussion.]

The Nurturer. Blue Note CDP 7 95139 2. [1991 sextet with Allen's mentor Marcus Belgrave on trumpet.]

Twenty-One. Blue Note 830028. [1994 trio with bassist Ron Carter and drummer Tony Williams.]

Betty Carter: Feed the Fire. Verve 314523600-2. [1994 London concert in which Allen, Dave Holland, and Jack DeJohnette accompany the great singer.]

Ornette Coleman: Sound Museum. Harmolodic/Verve 531 914-2.

Some Aspects of Water. Storyville 4212. [Allen's Jazzpar-winning compositions played by international U.S.–Danish band.]

The Gathering. Verve 567 614-2. [1999 all-star session under Allen's leadership.]

FURTHER READING

Giddins, Gary. "Jackie Terrasson/Geri Allen" in *Visions of Jazz.* New York: Oxford University Press, 1998.

Gourse, Leslie. *Madame Jazz: Contemporary Women Instrumentalists.* New York: Oxford University Press, 1995.

Mandel, Howard. *Future Jazz.* New York: Oxford University Press, 1999.

WEBSITE

http://kzsu.stanford.edu/~cathya/geriallen.html
Biography, discography, news, links, and more.

Joshua Redman

FATHERS AND SONS

T he Marsalis family is one significant example of the way that jazz is being carried forward across generations. No less important is saxophonist Joshua Redman, whose father, Dewey, made his name as a free jazz player and close colleague of Ornette Coleman. However, Redman's parents separated around the time he was born in California (his mother was the dancer Renee Schedroff, of Russian Jewish background). Joshua grew up on a different side of the continent from his father, who had returned to New York City, and they saw one another only occasionally. What Redman learned of his father's jazz playing, he did by listening to records. They did not get to play together until he was 21, when he appeared alongside his father at the Village Vanguard.

By that time it was clear that music would play a big part in the younger Redman's life, although this was not always the case. With plans to be a doctor or lawyer, Joshua

Joshua Redman plays alto saxophone at a recent performance. His playing moves forward from the tradition of earlier masters of the instrument, John Coltrane and Sonny Rollins.

Joshua Redman joins a group of musicians that combine experience from across the generations, including his young contemporaries bassist Christian McBride, Redman himself, trumpeter Wallace Roney, saxophonist Kenny Garrett, plus veteran bebop drummer Roy Haynes and pianist Chick Corea.

did not take his saxophone playing too seriously in high school. Although he had received a number of scholarships to help his playing along, after he graduated from Harvard he had already been accepted at Yale to study law. Before going to law school, he took a year off during which he tried his hand at music. For the most part, his playing had been shaped by listening to John Coltrane and Sonny Rollins as much as to his father's discs. Alongside this, like most people growing up in the 1970s and 1980s, Redman listened to pop

music, from the Beatles and the Rolling Stones to James Brown and Prince. He arrived at a style of his own that was firmly rooted in the tradition of jazz tenor playing consolidated by Coltrane and Rollins, but with plenty of pop overtones and allusions. Yet, with the kind of intuitive understanding of recorded jazz that is acquired by long and careful listening, Redman also absorbed ideas from further back in jazz: the playing of Swing Era players like Coleman Hawkins and Don Byas. In particular, he arrived at a strong and individual tone on the saxophone that was warm, robust, and immediately identifiable as his own voice.

There are two defining characteristics of Redman's playing. It is intensely energetic and totally absorbing; it also gives the impression of being conversational—the music talking directly to the listener, and sometimes even involving conversations with itself, such as in his habit of playing a phrase and then echoing the same phrase in a different register of the instrument. He is an instinctive communicator, careful to balance his appearances before sizable festival and theater audiences with plenty of club sessions in which he can exploit the proximity between band and audience and, as he puts it, retain his "acoustic subtlety and shading."

Even so, he might well have pursued legal studies if he had not developed remarkably rapidly into a mature player, recording alongside his father on the album *Choices* and almost by accident winning the 1991 Thelonious Monk competition. "I was getting gigs without really looking for them," he said. "Then I entered the Monk competition just for experience and ended up winning."

The gigs he had been doing were a mixture of studio sessions in which he turned up to sight-read his way through almost anything put in front of him, and jazz club gigs on which he was a sideman. The contractors who booked him were impressed with what they heard, and despite Redman's modesty, so were the competition judges. "Redman had a sound," wrote the master of ceremonies of the Monk contest, Gary Giddins. "It might not be the sound he would have the next year or the year after that, but it pealed with

personality and utterly subsumed his ample technique."

Lionized by the critics, securing a major label record deal, and immediately setting off on the route to leading his own group with all its implications of a regular payroll, a road manager, and constant traveling—everyone seemed sure about Redman's talent except, when he had time to think about it, himself. "One summer I'm jamming with peers from college, and next winter I'm on stage with Elvin Jones, Pat Metheny and Jack DeJohnette," he said shortly afterward. "I just wasn't confident that I could deliver the goods." Despite his buoyant good humor and confidence on stage, he frequently thought about quitting, until a series of successful albums and consistently favorable audiences convinced him to stay in music for the long haul.

Despite periods of frenetic activity, when Redman and his band have undertaken punishing tours and concert dates, he has managed to pace his career and find time to compose and develop new ideas. In particular, his choice of fellow musicians has colored his work: the introspective piano of Brad Mehldau contrasting with the more extroverted styles of Kevin Hays or Peter Martin. He was quick to spot the potential for dancing rhythms and funk beats offered by a New Orleans–born rhythm team, centered on the drumming of Brian Blade, and he also drafted in a frontline partner, guitarist Peter Bernstein, to extend the "conversational" aspects of his band's work. His own compositions catch many of the moods recalled from his teenage listening to everything from rock to hip hop. In an album such as *Timeless Tales* he reflects a similarly broad spread of

Joshua Redman

BORN

February 1, 1969
Berkeley, California

EDUCATION

Graduated summa cum laude from Harvard with a B.A. in social studies, 1991

MAJOR INTERESTS

Tenor and soprano saxophone

ACCOMPLISHMENTS

Won Thelonious Monk award, 1991, and embarked on high-profile international career; guested on albums by many jazz greats, including his father, fellow saxophonist Joe Lovano, and bassist Ray Brown; began a distinguished recording series for Warner Brothers; artistic director of the spring season of the San Francisco Jazz Festival (from 2000)

HONORS

Two Leonard Bernstein Music Scholarships; Joseph L. Merrill Scholarship; won many polls and awards for his playing and albums

"My goal is to be as creative, open and genuine as possible, and not to enter a situation with preconceived notions which limit experience."

—Joshua Redman in "Simply Redman" (1993)

repertoire. Asked why he had chosen to record tunes by Bob Dylan and the Beatles, he said "I grew up with rock and soul, so these songs are my life."

Redman has had to mature rapidly in the commercial world of major label deals, international festivals, and high-profile albums. Refreshingly, when the author asked him about his underlying philosophy, he replied: "It's not that I think of jazz intellectually, and I don't have a set of theories about it. It's more that I try to come up with an approach to the music. I want a way of arriving at an emotional sense of what I want to communicate through jazz. So it's an emotional, active, spiritual philosophy I have, rather than a theoretical one."

As he moves into the 21st century, expression and communication continue to be high on his agenda. His audiences, about which he cares passionately, are generally young and wildly enthusiastic. As jazz begins its second hundred years, it is in good hands with Redman's generation of musicians, who as well as keeping the music alive instrumentally, are committed to keeping it alive in terms of building a new and continuing audience to hear it.

DISCOGRAPHY

Joshua Redman. Warner Bros. 945242-2. [1992 debut disc, mainly with trio of Kevin Hays, Christian McBride, and Gregory Hutchinson.]

Wish, Warner Bros. 945365-2. [1993 follow-up, with Pat Metheny on guitar.]

Mood Swing. Warner Bros. 9362 45643-2. [1994 quartet with Brad Mehldau on piano.]

Spirit of the Moment. Warner Bros. 945923-2. [1995 live session from the Village Vanguard with New Orleans-based rhythm section of Peter Martin, Christopher Thomas, and Brian Blade.]

Freedom in the Groove. Warner Bros. 46330-2. [1996 disc with similar quartet to *Spirit of the Moment*, plus guitarist Peter Bernstein.]

Timeless Tales for Changing Times. Warner Bros. CDW 47052-2.

FURTHER READING

Giddins, Gary. "Joshua Redman (Tenor of the Times)" in *Visions of Jazz*. New York: Oxford University Press, 1998

Kynaston, Trent. *The Music of Joshua Redman*. New York: Warner Brothers, 1998. [Transcriptions of Redman's recorded solos.]

WEBSITE

www.joshuaredman.com
The official Joshua Redman website featuring a biography, photos, merchandise, discography, and links.

More Contemporary Jazz Players to Remember

In the 1990s one saxophonist above all others proved that it was possible to play effectively in almost all the styles of jazz from swing to free jazz, and from bebop to fusion. His name is **Joe Lovano** (born 1952). The son of a musician, he learned his music from an early age by listening to his father's records. Lovano studied at the Berklee College of Music in Boston, and served an apprenticeship in the bands of Woody Herman and Lonnie Liston Smith, but he reached a wide public in the 1970s when he worked with drummer **Paul Motian** (born 1931). Motian had gone on from his work with Bill Evans to become as formidable a talent spotter as Art Blakey had been, and Lovano is proof of his astute choice of musicians. In a long series of discs for the Blue Note label, Lovano has worked in a variety of formats and genres, from duos with Cuban pianist **Gonzalo Rubalcaba** (born 1963) to a trio with bass and drums, as well as in conventional quintets with a full rhythm section. In 2001 he became the Gary Brubon Professor of Jazz Performance at Berklee, passing on his broad range of skills to new generations of players.

The tradition of the after-hours jam session reemerged in the closing years of the 20th century as New York clubs like Small's in Greenwich Village opened their doors. Trumpeter **Roy Hargrove** (born 1969) made his reputation as a player who would take on all comers in cutting contests. His prodigious trumpet technique has been heard on many albums with his own small group, as well as a Cuban fusion band he calls *Crisol*. He also leads a big band that has played to great acclaim but which had not recorded at the start of the 21st century.

Saxophonist **Steve Coleman** (born 1956) grew up in the musical melting pot of Chicago, and went on to become part of the M-Base collective in New York City. Whereas Hargrove explored the music of the Caribbean, Coleman's projects with his band Five Elements look at music of the Old World. He has worked extensively with African musicians, and he has explored the Indian and Southeast Asian rhythmic heritage fully in his "Mystic Rhythm Society."

A generation of musicians continued to preserve the influential legacy of Miles Davis in the 1990s, none more notably than saxophonist **Kenny Garrett** (born 1960). He worked briefly with Davis in the mid-1980s and has continued to extend his virtuoso saxophone technique while keeping an open, exploratory mind consistent with Davis's final years of covering many different genres. Other former Davis sidemen who have gone on to be influential players include guitarists **John Scofield** (born 1951) and Mike Stern (born 1953), and saxophonist **Bill Evans** (born 1958).

Courtney Pine, whose educational workshops and concerts explore the interface between computers, turntables, and improvising jazz musicians, combines the best of the jazz tradition with the sounds familiar to a young contemporary audience.

In many ways the side of Miles Davis that was fascinated by the music of Prince and which was at the heart of Davis's own experiments in fusing jazz with a funk beat has been captured in the music of saxophonist **Greg Osby** (born 1961). Although Osby is a formidable player in the bebop and post-bop style, he has been an outspoken critic of some aspects of the conservatism of Wynton Marsalis. To make his point, his Blue Note recordings contain jazz music built around rap and hip-hop, which captures the urban mood of the times, much as the London-born tenor saxophonist **Courtney Pine** (born 1964) has done. Pine is part of a vital generation of British players of Caribbean origin who have done much to revivify jazz in Europe, His touring bands have often included rappers and turntable players as well as conventional instrumentalists.

Singer **Cassandra Wilson** (born 1955) was, like Coleman and Osby, involved in the group M-Base. She has proved in common with other jazz vocalists like **Dianne Reeves** (born 1956) that it is possible to draw elements of pop singing into jazz vocals, and yet remain true to the essential qualities of jazz—improvisation, collective discovery, and above all, the sound of surprise.

Glossary

accent—To emphasize a note; also the name of the note that is emphasized.

accompaniment—The background played for a singer or solo instrumentalist. It can be played by a single musician (such as a pianist) or by an ensemble.

arrangement—The organization of a performance. In jazz this ranges from informal "head" arrangements in which musicians agree loosely how to allocate a theme or accompanying riffs between them, to a full score or "chart," which has composed parts for each instrument.

Austin High School Gang—Informal collection of Chicago musicians of the 1920s, largely consisting of alumni of Austin High.

ballad—A form of song originally based on long stanzas (or verses) in which little or none of the melody is repeated during each one. The sense is broadened in U.S. popular music to encompass most types of sentimental song. In jazz the term defines slow melodies which often form the basis of rhapsodic solo improvisations.

battle of bands—A type of contest current in the 1920s and 1930s at theaters or dance halls in which two bands played alternately and competed for the favor of the audience.

bebop—The name given to the type of modern jazz pioneered in the early 1940s by such players as Dizzy Gillespie, Thelonious Monk, and Charlie Parker.

big band—A large jazz ensemble consisting of the following sections: three to five trumpets, two to four trombones, four to five saxophones, guitar, piano, bass, and drums.

blues—A type of African-American popular music with similar origins to those of jazz. Its principal form is a song consisting of 12 measures in a consistent harmonic structure, the supporting lyrics grouped in stanzas of three lines. The first line of these words is often sung twice.

boogie woogie—A style of piano playing that developed in and around 1920s Chicago, distinguished by its repetitive left-hand patterns. Many boogie woogie compositions create musical images, one common example being a railroad train.

book—A collection of arrangements or "charts" belonging to a band.

break—A moment in a jazz piece when the rhythm section stops playing for a measure or two, leaving one or more solo instruments to play through the resulting space in the accompaniment.

chart—Musicians' slang for an arrangement.

Chicago jazz—A kind of traditional jazz played by white musicians in 1920s Chicago based on the collectively improvised Dixieland first brought to the city from New Orleans. Its principal exponents were the Austin High School Gang and the circle of musicians who played with guitarist Eddie Condon.

chord—A collection of notes sounded together. A "chord sequence" is the name given to the underlying harmony in a jazz piece.

chorus—In popular songs, the refrain sung at the end of each verse or stanza. In jazz it has a similar meaning, referring to each repetition of the chord sequence of a tune over which either the melody is played or soloists improvise.

counterpoint—A term used in classical music to describe the simultaneous playing of two lines of melody.

Creole—A person or group of people generally from the Caribbean area who have mixed ancestry, generally combining two or all three of African, Hispanic, and French backgrounds. In jazz, the most significant Creole population is that of New Orleans.

concerto—A piece of classical music for one or more soloists accompanied by an orchestra. The genre has been adopted in jazz by such musicians as Duke Ellington (who wrote "concertos" for his major soloists such as Cootie Williams and Barney Bigard), Artie Shaw, and Woody Herman (for whom Stravinsky composed his *Ebony Concerto*).

cool—A style of modern jazz developed by Miles Davis and Gil Evans that included the unusual tone colors of the French horn, tuba, and baritone sax as well as the more conventional small-group instruments, and which encouraged soloists to play in a clear, logical style with minimal vibrato. It often gives an impression of detachment, as indicated by the name of the genre.

cutting contest—A type of jam session at which soloists vie to outplay one another.

dance band—A group with comparable instrumentation to a jazz big band, and which plays arrangements that are not exclusively jazz-related.

discographer—A person who studies and catalogs sound recordings.

Dixieland—A style of traditional jazz dating from the earliest days of the music that relies on collective improvisation by a front line of trumpet, trombone, and clarinet, accompanied by a rhythm section.

drumhead—The skin or vellum part of a drum that is hit by sticks or beaters to produce the sound.

drum roll—The effect made by rapidly alternating drum sticks to produce a continuous rolling tone.

dynamics—The control of volume in playing an instrument.

ensemble—A group of instrumentalists or passages that are played by instrumentalists together.

floor show—A revue or dance performance on the stage or dance floor of a club, for patrons to watch rather than participate in.

free jazz—Jazz improvised without the conventional structures of harmony, melody, and rhythm, often created entirely spontaneously by one or more instrumentalists.

front—To be a nonplaying bandleader. Some leaders who fronted a band were accomplished musicians themselves, such as singer Cab Calloway, or drummer and dancer Tiny Bradshaw, whereas others, like Lucky Millinder, played no instrument and did not sing, but specialized in directing the band's performances.

front line—The melody instruments in a jazz group that are not part of the rhythm section.

fusion—A mixture of different styles of music, generally used to describe the joining together of jazz and rock.

gospel music—A type of religious song. The term is generally used in jazz to refer specifically to the context of African-American church music.

harmony—The combination of notes into chords, and the compilation of these into successions or sequences that become the underlying structure of most jazz pieces.

head—The opening melody or first chorus of a piece.

head arrangement—An informal arrangement between musicians as to how a piece should be played that is not written down or notated.

horn—Jazz slang for any wind or brass instrument.

hot—A sense of intensity produced by an instrumentalist using a combination of factors: "dirty" or "vocal" tone, exaggerated syncopation, and driving rhythm. It is generally applied to jazz of the early and swing eras.

house pianist—The resident pianist at a performance venue or record company.

impresario—The organizer, producer, or manager of entertainment events; also, a powerful band manager or booker.

improvisation—The art of spontaneous composition while playing.

interval—The distance in pitch between two notes. This is generally measured in tones of the scale; for example, two notes sounded three tones apart represent an interval of a third.

jam session—An informal event in which jazz musicians congregate to improvise together.

Jazz Age—The 1920s, when jazz came to be a widespread form of popular music.

jazz band—Any jazz ensemble, but particularly a group using the traditional or Dixieland configuration of trumpet, trombone, clarinet, piano (and/or guitar), bass or tuba, and drums.

keyboard—Any keyboard instrument; in jazz, generally used to mean an electronic keyboard or synthesizer.

Latin time—South American rhythm as opposed to the usual four-four pulse of jazz.

lineup—The instrumentation of an ensemble.

lyrics—The words of a song.

mainstream—A term coined by critic Stanley Dance to denote a tuneful, harmonically straightforward style of post–Swing Era jazz that did not encompass all the harmonic and rhythmic complexity of modern jazz.

melody—A series of notes arranged in a sequence that forms a recognizable pattern or tune.

modal jazz—Music built on a system of scales or "modes" that take the place of chordal harmony in the underlying musical structure.

modern jazz—The term used to describe the revolutionary (or as Dizzy Gillespie put it, evolutionary) jazz of the 1940s that followed swing by introducing more complex harmonies, fragmenting the underlying drumbeat or pulse, and adopting rapid and convoluted melody lines that were often played fast and high.

musicologist—A person who engages in the scholarly study of music.

octave—An eight-note interval made up of five whole tones and two semitones, in which both the top and bottom tones carry the same name; e.g., from "middle C" on the piano keyboard to the "C" above it is one octave.

orchestra—In jazz, generally a big band, although smaller recording groups of the 1930s and early 1940s often carried the name (e.g., John Kirby and His Orchestra was a sextet). In classical music the term generally refers to a symphony orchestra.

ornament—A musical decoration, such as a trill, added to a melodic line to enrich it.

ostinato—A regularly repeated pattern of notes that continues throughout

a piece, generally played in the bass register.

passing chord—An additional chord introduced by an improviser in place of or between the usual chords of a harmonic sequence.

pianola—A kind of player piano.

pick-up band—A group of musicians that is assembled on a one-time or spontaneous basis, often for a recording session or a single engagement.

pitch—The degree to which an individual note or sound corresponds to a note of a specified scale. A sound that corresponds to a precise note of the scale is said to be in or have "definite" pitch; a note or sound with less exact of no correspondence is of, or has, "indefinite" pitch.

player piano—A kind of piano equipped with a perforated paper roll through which compressed air is pumped to operate the notes. These rolls were often made by skilled pianists whose performances could be reproduced on the player or "reproducing" piano, although the mechanism could not retain every nuance of their live playing. The instruments were widely used as an early form of sound recording.

producer—In jazz, usually a record producer, who organizes recording sessions on behalf of record companies. The most skillful producers have had a huge influence on the presentation of individual artists and on the way we listen to jazz. Examples of those who developed the careers of individual musicians include Milt Gabler, who

produced sessions by Ella Fitzgerald and Louis Armstrong, and Norman Granz, who also recorded Fitzgerald, along with many other musicians in this book such as Dizzy Gillespie, Charlie Parker, Oscar Peterson, and Art Tatum. Those who have influenced the ways we hear music include Alfred Lion and Frank Wolff at Blue Note, who with recording engineer Rudy Van Gelder sought a new level of technical excellence from the 1940s to the 1960s, and Orrin Keepnews, who developed ways to present the difficult music of Thelonious Monk.

Prohibition—The period from 1920 to 1933 when the 18th Amendment to the U.S. Constitution prevented the manufacture, sale, or transportation of intoxicating liquor in the country. Repealed by the 21st Amendment in 1933.

ragtime—The style of syncopated piano music popular from the 1890s to the 1920s that was in part a precursor of jazz.

rent party—An event in a private apartment at which admission was charged or contributions were solicited in exchange for musical entertainment and food to raise money to pay the rent.

revue—A loose-knit collection of sketches and musical acts which together form a cabaret or stage presentation.

rhythm and blues—The form of urban blues that developed in the 1940s by combining elements of sung country blues with electric guitars and basses, a drum backbeat, and a saxophone or brass section modeled on swing small groups of the preceding decade.

rhythm section—The part of a band that supplies its underlying harmony and rhythm, generally consisting of a permutation of piano, guitar, bass, and drums.

ring shout—An element of worship from the collective music-making of African Americans dating from the period of slavery which survived into some aspects of ragtime, blues, and jazz. In it, worshippers formed a circle or ring, and moved around in a shuffle, to the accompaniment of sung spirituals. The word "shout" decribes the movement, which was a kind of dance that avoided the secular elements of dancing.

scale—An ascending or descending sequence of notes, heard most commonly in jazz based on the pentatonic scale of the piano keyboard.

scat—Jazz singing in which nonsense syllables are improvised in the manner of an instrumentalist.

section—A group of instruments of the same type within a larger musical group. In a jazz big band, the sections are usually brass (trumpets and trombones), reeds (clarinets, flutes, saxophones), and rhythm (see above).

sideman—A rank-and-file or ensemble member of a big band.

soloist—A musician who plays alone in front of a rhythm section or similar accompaniment as a featured performer, or one who carries the major line of development during some part of a piece.

spasm band—An informal group of musicians generally playing homemade instruments, such as a broom-handle bass, a washboard, and a kazoo, who rendered pieces in a jazzy style. In New Orleans at the beginning of the 20th century, many jazz musicians began their careers in children's spasm bands.

speakeasy—A club or illicit premises selling alcohol during the period of Prohibition.

spiritual—A kind of African-American religious folksong, dating from the 19th century.

straightahead jazz—Acoustic jazz varying in style from mainstream to post-bop, but retaining the 4/4 pulse of swing and not involving rock rhythms nor instrumentation.

stride—A style of jazz piano named for its left-hand "walking" or "striding" patterns, which alternate individual bass notes with chords.

string band—A group of instrumentalists playing predominantly stringed instruments, often consisting of violin or mandolin to play the melody, banjo and guitars for accompaniment, plus a double bass and simple percussion.

swing—Both the predominant jazz style of the 1930s big band era, and the action of injecting rhythmic passion into a performance so that it "swings."

syncopation—A heavily accented rhythm achieved by playing a note fractionally before or after the precise beat on which it would normally fall.

territory band—A touring big band working mainly in the Midwest, Southwest, and South (known as the "territories") during the 1920s and 1930s.

Tin Pan Alley—Not a specific location, but the nickname given to the popular music publishing industry in New York from the dawn of the 20th century.

vaudeville—The name given to theatrical programs composed of several acts of popular entertainment, especially on touring circuits.

virtuoso—A particularly skilled instrumentalist.

workshop—A forum organized for collective improvisation and also to explore the boundaries between composition and improvisation. Notable exponents include George Russell and Charles Mingus.

Essential Listening

The CDs listed below provide a general introduction to the main artists and periods in jazz history. The list includes several discs selected from those listed at the end of each individual profile, but it also covers several wider-ranging anthologies that put each artist and period in context. The majority were currently available at the time this book went to press, but those that are temporarily out-of-catalog are worth seeking out from libraries or specialist dealers both for their breadth of coverage and for the quality of remastered older recordings.

General Collections

Jazz: The Definitive Performances. Sony Jazz J2K 65807 (two-CD set). [33-track anthology released in 1999 covering the entire history of jazz from the ODJB to Wynton and Branford Marsalis.]

Visions of Jazz, Blue Note 7087 6 10180-2-8. (two-CD set). [38-track anthology to accompany Gary Giddins' personal view of the first century of jazz, as described in his book of the same name.]

The Pioneers

The Complete Rags of Scott Joplin. Musicmasters 7061-2 C (two-CD set). [All Joplin's rags, played by William Albright.]

The Complete Jelly Roll Morton 1926–1939. RCA Bluebird ND 82361 (five-CD set).

King Oliver, Volume One, 1923–1929. CDS RPCD 607.

King Oliver, Volume Two, 1927–1930. CDS RPCD 608.

Louis Armstrong: Highlights from His American Decca Years. GRP 26382 (two-CD set).

Sidney Bechet 1932–43: The Bluebird Sessions. Bluebird ND 90317 (four-CD set).

Bix Lives! Bluebird ND 86845.

Bessie Smith: Empress of the Blues, The Complete Recordings, Vols. I–IV, Columbia 47091, 47431, 47474, 52838 (each a two-CD set).

Swing Bands and Soloists

Early Ellington: The Complete Brunswick and Vocalion Recordings of Duke Ellington, 1926–1931. MCA GRP 36402 (three-CD set).

The Bluebird Sampler, 1990. Bluebird ND 82192. [Cross section of those who recorded for this Victor label, including most of the musicians profiled in sections 1–4.]

Memorable Recordings. Topaz TPZ 1035. [Excellent cross section of early jazz to swing.]

Top Soloists. Topaz TPZ 1032. [Good examples of all soloists in this section.]

The Great Bands. Topaz TPZ 1031. [23 tracks from pioneers like Morton and Armstrong to the birth of bebop with Jay McShann and Charlie Parker.]

The Great Vocalists, Topaz TPZ 1033. [Anthology of Swing Era jazz singing.]

The Piano Giants

Barrelhouse and Boogie. RCA Bluebird ND 88334. [Various artists.]

Turn on the Heat: The Fats Waller Piano Solos. RCA Bluebird ND 82482-2 (two-CD set).

Blue Boogie. Blue Note CDP 799099-2, [Anthology of jazz piano from Albert Ammons to Earl Hines and Art Tatum.]

The Ultimate Oscar Peterson. Verve 539786.

Atlantic Jazz Keyboards. Rhino 8122-71596-2. [Anthology of modern jazz piano from Monk to Keith Jarratt and Chick Corea.]

Birth of Bebop—the Modern Jazz Revolution

The Bebop Boys. Indigo 1GO CD 2071. [Anthology of pioneering bebop tracks from 1946.]

Dizzy Gillespie/Charlie Parker: Bird Meets Diz. Charly Le Jazz CD 21.

Best of Blue Note. Blue Note 0 7243 829964-2. [Anthology of pioneer bebop musicians, including Blakey, Monk, Parker, and Powell.]

Best of Miles Davis. Blue Note 7982872.

The Divine Sarah: The Columbia Years, 1949–1953. Columbia 465597.

Cool Jazz, Hard Bop, and Fusion

Coltrane: Complete 1961 Village Vanguard Recordings. Impulse IMPCD 4232.

Sonny Rollins: Complete RCA Victor Recordings. RCA 09026 68675-2.

Miles Davis: Birth of the Cool. Capitol CDP 792862.

The Best of the Gerry Mulligan Quartet with Chet Baker. Pacific Jazz CDP 7 95481-2.

Stan Getz: The West Coast Sessions. Verve 531935-2.

Ornette Coleman: The Shape of Jazz to Come. Atlantic 781339.

Best of Bill Evans on Verve. Verve 527906-2.

Herbie Hancock: The Complete Sixties Blue Note Sessions. Blue Note 95569.

Anthony Braxton: Quartet (Coventry) 1985. Leo CD LR 204/5.

A Century of Jazz

Blue Note Critics' Choice. Blue Note 7 99790-2-4. [12 tracks by current acclaimed musicians, including Geri Allen.]

Future Jazz. Knitting Factory Records KFR 249. [14 tracks by contemporary musicians looking forward from the 1990s.]

World Saxophone Quartet Plays Duke Ellington. Elektra Musician 979137.

Brecker Brothers Collection, Vols. 1 and 2. RCA Novus 90442 and 83076.

Jan Garbarek: Twelve Moons. ECM 1500.

Wynton Marsalis. Columbia 468708.

Geri Allen/Charlie Haden Paul Motian: Etudes. Soul Note 121 162-2.

Joshua Redman: Freedom in the Groove. Warner Bros. 46330-2.

Further Reading

Dictionaries and Encyclopedias

Carr, Ian, Digby Fairweather, and Brian Priestley. *Jazz: The Rough Guide*. 2nd ed. London and New York: Rough Guides, 2000.

Kernfeld, Barry, ed. *The New Grove Dictionary of Jazz*. 2nd ed. London and New York: Macmillan, 2001.

Larkin, Colin, ed. *The Virgin Encyclopedia of Jazz*. London: Virgin, 1999.

General Histories

Collier, James Lincoln. *The Making of Jazz*. London: Macmillan, 1978.

Gioia, Ted. *The History of Jazz*. New York: Oxford University Press, 1997.

Shipton, Alyn. *A New History of Jazz*. New York: Continuum, 2001.

Histories of Jazz and Related Styles

Berlin, Edward A. *Ragtime, A Musical and Cultural History*. Berkeley: University of California Press, 1980.

Davis, Francis. *In the Moment: Jazz in the 1980s*. New York: Oxford University Press, 1986.

Deffaa, Chip. *Voices of the Jazz Age*. Oxford, Miss.: Bayou Press, 1989.

Feather, Leonard. *Encyclopedia of Jazz in the Sixties*. 1966. Reprint, New York: Da Capo, 1984.

Friedwald, Will. *Jazz Singing: America's Great Voices from Bessie Smith to Bebop and Beyond*. 1990. Reprint, New York: Da Capo, 1996.

Giddins, Gary. *Rhythm-a-ning: Jazz Tradition and Innovation in the '80s*. New York: Oxford University Press, 1985.

———. *Visions of Jazz*. New York: Oxford University Press, 1998.

Goodman, Benny, with Irving Kolodin. *The Kingdom of Swing*. New York: Stackpole, 1939.

Gourse, Leslie. *Madame Jazz: Contemporary Women Instrumentalists*. New York: Oxford University Press, 1995.

———. *Swingers and Crooners: The Art of Jazz Singing*. New York: Franklin Watts, 1997.

Gridley, Mark C. *Jazz Styles, History and Analysis*. Englewood Cliffs, N.J.: Prentice-Hall, 1985.

Hadlock, Richard. *Jazz Masters of the Twenties*. New York: Macmillan, 1965.

Jones, Max. *Talking Jazz*. London, Macmillan: 1987.

Lyons, Len. *The Great Jazz Pianists*. New York: Morrow, 1983.

Mandel, Howard. *Future Jazz*. New York: Oxford University Press, 1999.

McCarthy, Albert. *Big Band Jazz*. New York: G. P. Putnam, 1974.

Nicholson, Stuart. *Jazz Rock: A History*. New York: Schirmer, 1998.

Oliver, Paul. *The Story of the Blues*. 1969. Reprint, Radnor, Pa.: Chilton, 1982.

Rosenthal, David H. *Hard Bop: Jazz and Black Music 1955–1965*. New York: Oxford University Press, 1992.

Schuller, Gunther. *Early Jazz: Its Roots and Musical Development*. New York: Oxford University Press, 1968.

———. *The Swing Era*. New York: Oxford University Press, 1989.

Silvester, Peter. *A Left Hand Like God: A Study of Boogie Woogie*. London: Quartet, 1988.

Simon, George T. *The Big Bands*. 4th ed. New York: Schirmer, 1981.

Taylor, Billy. *Jazz Piano: A Jazz History*. Dubuque, Iowa: Brown, 1982.

Williams, Martin. *Jazz Changes*. New York: Oxford University Press, 1992.

Biographies and Personal Histories

Kaminsky, Max. *My Life in Jazz*. London: Deutsch; New York: Harper & Row, 1963.

Lomax, Alan. *Mister Jelly Roll*. New York: Pantheon, 1993.

Stewart, Rex. *Boy Meets Horn*. Claire P. Gordon, ed. Oxford, Miss.: Bayou Press, 1991.

Wilber, Bob, with Derek Webster. *Music Was Not Enough*. New York: Oxford University Press, 1987.

Wilson, Teddy. *Teddy Wilson Talks Jazz*. Arie Ligthart and Humphrey Van Loo, eds. London and Washington: Cassell, 1997.

Record Guides

Cook, Richard, and Brian Morton. *The Penguin Guide to Jazz on CD*, 5th ed. New York: Penguin, 2000.

Cowley, John, and Paul Oliver, eds. *The New Blackwell Guide to Recorded Blues*. Oxford and Cambridge, Mass.: Blackwell, 1996.

Kernfeld, Barry. *The Blackwell Guide to Recorded Jazz*, 2nd ed. Oxford and Cambridge, Mass.: Blackwell, 1995.

Additional Sources

Blesh, Rudi. *Combo USA*. Philadelphia: Chilton, 1971.

Crow, Bill. *Jazz Anecdotes*. New York: Oxford University Press, 1990.

Freeman Bud. *Crazeology*, Oxford, Miss.: Bayou Press, 1989.

Lees, Gene. *Arranging the Score: Portraits of the Great Arrangers*. New York and London: Cassell/Continuum, 2000.

Websites

http://www.allaboutjazz.com

This website features reviews of CDs, concerts, books, and videos; a calendar of events and festival schedules; and ample reader forums. It also includes biographies, interviews, quotes, and multimedia.

http://www.bbc.co.uk/music/jazz/

The BBC online groups jazz and blues together, and includes news, information on gigs, TV and radio listings, reviews, and artist profiles.

http://www.redhotjazz.com

Features lists of bands and musicians—with their respective biographies and discographies—films, essays, and its own condensed history of jazz.

http://www.jazzcorner.com

This site contains photos, interviews, reviews, links to individual musicians' websites, and a calendar of upcoming performances, all on a nicely animated page.

http://www.wnur.org/jazz/

Listings of artists (with biographies, discographies, and reviews), performances (festivals, venues, reviews, and regional jazz information), and links to various jazz media are presented on this page. Also, there is jazz art (visual, literary, essay) and a map that traces the history of jazz.

http://www.52ndstreet.com

52nd Street Jazz has many recent reviews, as well as an extensive archive of reviews, which are categorized as new mainstream, vintage mainstream, singing, latin, contemporary instrumental, or miscellaneous. There are also three reader forums.

http://www.gallery41.com

Features interviews, sound clips, and photos of current and past jazz figures.

http://www.nprjazz.org

This is the jazz website for National Public Radio. It has reviews, events, links to NPR jazz stations, a listening library, and more.

http://www.town.hall.org/Archives/radio/Kennedy/Taylor/

Dr. Billy Taylor, noted jazz pianist, historian, and educator, shares glimpses of his knowledge of jazz music from its roots in the African-American slavery experience, through the early days of ragtime, and onward through swing, bop, and progressive jazz.

http://www.jazzreview.com

A large site that features reviews, interviews, articles, and photography.

http://www.pbs.org/jazz

The website is based on the Ken Burns' PBS documentary, *Jazz*. It includes biographies of prominent jazz musicians, as well as the basics in the musical and historical aspects of jazz music.

http://www.eyeneer.com/Jazz/index.html

Information and a small number of photographs about players from the more contemporary jazz scene.

http://www.jazzhouse.org/

Although this is the site of the Jazz Journalists' Association, its members include some of the best and most interesting writers in jazz, and there is plenty for those with a non-professional interest. Its news, discussion forums, photos, and obituaries are among the best on the web.

http://www.jazzservices.org.uk

One of the leading international websites about jazz that also hosts the electronic edition of the monthly journal *Jazz UK*.

http://www.jazzwest.com/

One of the most informative regional jazz websites in the United States, this is a reminder of the importance of the West Coast, and particularly the Bay Area, in the history and current state of jazz.

Museums and Places to Visit

United States

Chicago Jazz Archive

Regenstein Library
University of Chicago
1100 East 57th Street
Chicago, IL 60637-1596
773-702-3721
http://www.lib.uchicago.edu/e/su/cja/

Houses many special collections covering the story of jazz in Chicago, and offers help to researchers from high school students to scholars. Presents occasional concerts and events.

DuSable Museum of African-American History

740 East 56th Place
Chicago, IL 60637
773-947-0600
http://www.dusablemuseum.org

Sets the story of Chicago blues and jazz in the context of African-American history from the time of slavery to the present.

Kansas City Museum

3218 Gladstone Boulevard
Kansas City, MO 64123
816-483-8300
http://www.kcmuseum.com

Presents materials relating to the rich jazz history of the city, including photographs and interview documents from Nathan W. Pearson's oral history project Goin' To Kansas City.

The American Jazz Museum

1616 East 18th Street
Kansas City, MO 64108
816-474-8463
http://www.americanjazzmuseum.com/

Opened in fall of 1997, it is the only museum in the United States devoted exclusively to jazz. The museum complex includes major interactive exhibits celebrating the memory of the legends Louis Armstrong, Duke Ellington, Ella Fitzgerald, and Charlie Parker.

Institute of Jazz Studies

Cotton Dana Library
Rutgers/State University of New Jersey
185 University Avenue
Newark, NJ 07102
973-353-5595
http://www.libraries.rutgers.edu/rulib/abtlib/danlib/jazz.htm

Not a museum, but the world's leading collection of jazz research materials including the Jazz Oral History Project, and many thousands of books, magazines, and journals. Also, has a voluminous collection of sound recordings.

Old U.S. Mint

Louisiana State Museum
400 Esplanade Avenue
New Orleans, LA 70116
504-568-6968
http://lsm.crt.state.la.us/

The new home of the New Orleans Jazz Museum, this has a show devoted to the story of jazz, and exhibits including Sidney Bechet's saxophone and Louis Armstrong's first cornet.

William Ransome Hogan Jazz Archive

Joseph Merrick Jones Hall
Tulane University
Freret Street
New Orleans, LA 70118
504-865-5688
http://www.tulane.edu/~lmiller/JazzHome.html

The archive displays a small exhibition of materials, but also offers access to a vast range of sound recordings and photographs.

Schomburg Center for Research in Black Culture

515 Malcolm X Boulevard at 135th Street
New York, NY 10037
http://www.nypl.org

One of New York City's public research libraries, the Schomburg Center has a large collection of materials relating to jazz and blues. Not a lot of this is on public view, but permanently displayed alongside Aaron Douglas's mural paintings from the Harlem Renaissance are cases with letters and artifacts from "the father of the blues," W. C. Handy, and Louis Armstrong.

Louis Armstrong Archive

Queens College
65-30 Kissena Boulevard
Flushing, NY 11367
718-997-3670

Contains Armstrong's vast personal collection of photographs, papers, scrapbooks, recordings, memorabilia, and musical instruments, housed in a state-of-the-art archival center in the Benjamin S. Rosenthal Library on the campus of Queens College.

Scott Joplin's House

2658 Delmar Boulevard
St. Louis, MO 63103
314-340-5970
http://www.mostateparks.com/scottjoplin.htm

Property of the Missouri State Parks system, this house was where Joplin lived from 1900 until his move to New York. Rescued from dereliction in 1984, the house has many Joplin artifacts and furniture from the Ragtime Age.

National Museum of American History

Smithsonian Institution
14th Street and Constitution Avenue, N.W.
Washington, DC 20560
202-357-2700
http://americanhistory.si.edu/

Covers big band jazz, gospel and African-American sacred and folk music. Includes the Duke Ellington Collection, spanning his entire life and career and the Sam DeVincent Collection of Illustrated American Sheet Music containing images, music, and lyrics of American life and culture between 1790 and the 1980s.

Belgium

La Maison du Jazz

11 rue sur les Foulons
B-4000 Liège
32 4 221-1011
http://www.liege.be/visitelg/musees/noncommu/jazz.htm

Belgian jazz archives, with a collection of print and recorded material relating to jazz in the Low Countries.

Canada

Concordia University Archives

Hall Building
1455 de Maisonneuve Boulevard West
Montréal
Québec H3G 1M8
514-848-7775
http://archives3.concordia.ca/Jazz.html

Houses a number of collections of jazz-related materials, including photographs, early recordings, published sheet music, published and original arrangements, original scores, annotated books on jazz, periodicals, record catalogues, recorded interviews with jazz musicians.

France

La Maison du Jazz

BP. 434-16
F-75769 Paris Cedex 16
33 1 48 59 03 96
http://www.maisondujazz.org

A recently formed organization, and as well as building up a collection of French jazz materials, it holds regular afternoon seminars on jazz research topics.

Germany

Jazz-Institut Darmstadt

Bessunger Strasse 88d
63285 Darmstadt,
49 6151 963700
http://www.darmstadt.de/kultur/musik/jazz/

Europe's largest public jazz archive and a unique source of information about all aspects of jazz history and present.

Holland

Nederlands Jazz Archief

Prins Hendrikkade 142
NL-1011 AT Amsterdam
31 20 627-1708
http://www.jazzarchief.nl/

Publishes the *Nederlands Jazz Archief Bulletin*, a quarterly newsletter covering historical, discographical, and musicological aspects of the Dutch jazz scene.

Switzerland

swissjazzorama

Asylstrasse 10
CH-8610 Uster
41 1 940-1982
http://www.jazzorama.ch/index2.html

Swiss national jazz archive and jazz museum.

United Kingdom

National Jazz Foundation Archive

Loughton Central Library
Trapps Hill
Loughton
Essex
1G10 1HD
44 208 502 0181
http://www.essexcc.gov.uk/libraries/whatsinside/jazz.htm

Just outside London, and linked to the city by a nearby station on the London Underground railway, it contains a vast amount of magazine and periodical literature, sound recordings, displays of posters, instruments, and other artifacts relating to British jazz.

Index

Acknowledgments

My first debt of gratitude is to my family, who have put up with jazz CDs all over the house, not to mention far too many books about music, and a manuscript that has accompanied us on several holidays. They have also been firm and attentive critics, giving me plenty of advice, whether or not it was asked for.

I would also like to thank my producers at the BBC, Felix Carey, Terry Carter, Derek Drescher, and Oliver Jones, for whom I have had the opportunity to make programs about several of the figures in this book, as well as to interview some of the musicians themselves. Derek Drescher has also usually had his camera handy on such occasions, and I am delighted that some of his photographs have been included. I would also like to thank Peter Symes for his help in supplying or researching many more of the illustrations and Marty Baldessari, who researched pictures at the Library of Congress.

I am grateful to Tony Russell and Jenny Mulherin—who are respectively the editor and publisher of the Marhsall Cavendish Jazz Greats series—for giving me the opportunity to compile CDs of the music by several of the subjects of chapters in the book. This gave me the chance to listen to many out-of-the-way recordings, as well as to get to know the music a little better, while I wrote listening notes for that series. As always, there were plenty of questions to be answered, and I would like to thank Howard Rye and John Chilton for their advice, as well as the librarians and staff of the music reading room in the Bodleian Library, Oxford University.

Thanks are also due to Julie Allison at Universal Jazz, Sharon Kelly at Sony Jazz, and Grianne Devine at BMG / RCA for their help in finding many of the recordings listed in the discographies.

Finally, I am indebted to my publisher at Oxford, Nancy Toff, for turning from poacher to gamekeeper, and to Brigit Dermott, my project editor, for all her hard work toward the final appearance of this book.

Picture Credits

Aram Avakar / Institute of Jazz Studies, Rutgers University, 143; Author's collection, 12, 14; Courtesy of Blue Note Records, 156, 170; Danny Barker Estate, 54; Capitol Records / National Archives, 123; Concord / Stretch Records / Institute of Jazz Studies, Rutgers University, 244; Derek Drescher, 228; Frank Driggs Collection, 34, 42, 46, 71, 116, 134, 148, 187; ECM Records / Institute of Jazz Studies, Rutgers University, 231, 232; Sulaiman Ellison / Institute of Jazz Studies, Rutgers University, 214; William P. Gottleib, 80, 82, 88, 118, 121, 130, 139, 140, 153, 164, 169; Jerome Harris / Institute of Jazz Studies, Rutgers University, 178; Randi Hultin Collection, 127; Institute of Jazz Studies, Rutgers University, 8, 36, 97, 207; Sy Johnson, 161, 198; Library of Congress, 44, 56, 59, 64, 67, 70, 94, 101, 104, 114, 129, 182, 221; New York Public Library, Performing Arts Collection, Lincoln Center, 75, 203; Jan Persson, 150, 158, 162, 173, 188, 195, 196, 211; Charles Peterson, courtesy of Don Peterson, 27, 48, 51, 63, 76, 78. 86, 91, 93, 98, 105; Frank Stewart / Jazz At Lincoln Center, 236; Red Baron / Institute of Jazz Studies, Rutgers University, 223; Raymond Ross, 190; Duncan P. Scheidt, 17, 18, 22, 25, 32, 37, 38, 60, 72, 84, 109, 166; Rex Stewart Estate / Claire P. Gordon, 30; Peter Symes, 146, 180, 184, 192, 200, 204, 208, 224, 226, 235, 239, 243, 248; Symil Library 29, 52, 106, 124, 136, 154, 168, 217; Mary Lou Williams Collection, 2, 112.

Alyn Shipton presents radio programs for the BBC and is also a jazz critic for *The Times* in London. His biography of Dizzy Gillespie, *Groovin' High*, published by Oxford University Press in 1999, was voted book of the year by *Jazz Times* and won the prestigious Association of Recorded Sound Collections award. His other books include biographies of Fats Waller (1988) and Bud Powell (1993) and *A New History of Jazz* (2001). In addition, he edited the memoirs of Danny Barker and Doc Cheatham and wrote a multi-volume introduction to musical instruments for children. In a long publishing career, he was Consultant Editor of *The New Grove Dictionary of Jazz*, and saw into print the life stories of such jazz musicians as Buck Clayton, Bud Freeman, Andy Kirk, Rex Stewart and Teddy Wilson. As a double bassist, he has played with a huge variety of traditional and mainstream jazz groups, most famously with Ken Colyer's Jazzmen in the 1970s and early 1980s. In addition to touring with such legendary figures as Bud Freeman, Herbie Hall, Louis Nelson, Sammy Price and Kid Thomas Valentine, he played in the London Ragtime Orchestra and the big band Vile Bodies. At home in England, he currently plays with the Anglo-French band Chansons.